**advanced
history
core texts**

THE SCHOOLS HISTORY PROJECT

·S·H·P·

OFFICIAL TEXT

FASCIST ITALY

advanced
history
core texts

advanced
history
core texts

FASCIST ITALY

John Hite

Chris Hinton

Series Editor: Ian Dawson

JOHN MURRAY

In the same series

Britain 1790–1851　　　　　　　　　　　　　　ISBN 0 7195 7482 X
Communist Russia Under Lenin and Stalin　　ISBN 0 7195 7488 9
The Early Tudors: England 1485–1558　　　　ISBN 0 7195 7484 6
The Reign of Elizabeth: England 1558–1603　ISBN 0 7195 7486 2
Weimar and Nazi Germany　　　　　　　　　ISBN 0 7195 7343 2

The Schools History Project

This project was set up by the Schools Council in 1972. Its main aim was to suggest suitable objectives for history teachers, and to promote the use of appropriate materials and teaching methods for their realisation. This involved a reconsideration of the nature of history and its relevance in secondary schools, the design of a syllabus framework which shows the uses of history in the education of adolescents, and the setting up of appropriate examinations.

Since 1978 the project has been based at Trinity and All Saints' College, Leeds. It is now self-funding and with the advent of the National Curriculum it has expanded its publications to provide courses for Key Stage 3, and for a range of GCSE and A level syllabuses. The project provides INSET for all aspects of National Curriculum, GCSE and A level history.

Dedication
For Claire and David; Cathy, Ciara, Thomas and Patrick, who gave their support and 'their' time to this book.

Acknowledgement
The authors would like to thank John Whittam for his helpful advice on this book.

© John Hite, Chris Hinton 1998

First published in 1998
by John Murray (Publishers) Ltd, a member of the Hodder Headline Group
338 Euston Road
London NW1 3BH

Reprinted 2000, 2001, 2002, 2003

Layouts by Jenny Fleet
Artwork by Art Construction
Typeset in 10/12pt Walbaum Book Regular by Wearset, Boldon, Tyne and Wear
Printed in Great Britain by J. W. Arrowsmith Ltd, Bristol

A catalogue entry for this title is available from the British Library

ISBN 0 7195 7341 6

Contents

Acknowledgements

The authors and publishers would like to thank John Whittam and Sandra Raban for their advice and suggestions.

Copyright photographs are reproduced by courtesy of the following:

Cover *background* Weidenfeld & Nicolson Archives, *inset* Civici Raccolte d'Arte, Milan; **p.2** *l & r* Hulton Getty, *c* Edizione Scolastiche Bruno Mondadori; **p.6** *tl* Edizione Scolastiche Bruno Mondadori, *bl* Hulton Getty, *br* Farabolafoto, Milan; **p.7** *t & b* Edizione Scolastiche Bruno Mondadori; **p.16** *l* Hulton Getty, *r* Moro Roma ©; **p.17** Collezione Riccardo e Magda Jucker, Milan/ Bridgeman Art Library, London; **p.22** Weidenfeld & Nicolson Archives; **p.24** *l* Hulton Getty, *r* Edizione Scolastiche Bruno Mondadori; **p.25** Farabolafoto, Milan; **p.27** Hulton Getty; **p.33** *l* Moro Roma, *r* © Archivio Storico Il Dagherrotipo, Rome; **p.37** Hulton Getty; **p.38** *l* Hulton Getty, *r* Edizione Scolastiche Bruno Mondadori; **p.40** *t* Edizione Scolastiche Bruno Mondadori, *b* Hulton Getty; **p.42** Hulton Getty; **p.52** Moro Roma; **p.53** Moro Roma; **p.56** Hulton Getty; **p.59** Hulton Getty; **p.60** *from top* Edizione Scolastiche Bruno Mondadori; © Archivio Storico Il Dagherrotipo, Rome; Hulton Getty; © Archivio Storico Il Dagherrotipo, Rome; © Archivio Storico Il Dagherrotipo, Rome; **p.67** © Wide World/Associated Press (photo: Hulton Getty); **p.68** Hulton Getty; **p.69** Hulton Getty; **p.70** *t* Moro Roma, *cl* Moro Roma ©, *cr* © Archvio Storico Il Dagherrotipo, Rome, *bl* Popperfoto, *br* Edizione Scolastiche Bruno Mondadori; **p.75** Ashmolean Museum, Oxford; **p.76** *l* © Archvio Storico Il Dagherrotipo, Rome, *r* Edizione Scolastiche Bruno Mondadori; **p.80** Edizione Scolastiche Bruno Mondadori; **p.81** *t* Edizione Scolastiche Bruno Mondadori, *b* Punch; **p.85** *l & r* Hulton Getty, *c* Peter Newark's Military Pictures; **p.86** *t* Hulton Getty, *b* Popperfoto; **p.87** Hulton Getty; **p.88** *l* Hulton Getty, *r* Edizione Scolastiche Bruno Mondadori; **p.89** *tl* Hulton Getty, *tc* Farabolafoto, Milan, *tr* Farabolafoto, Milan, *cl* © Wide World/Associated Press (photo: Hulton Getty), *c* © Archivio Storico Il Dagherrotipo, Rome, *cr* Hulton Getty, *bl* Edizione Scolastiche Bruno Mondadori, *br* Farabolafoto, Milan; **p.90** Hulton Getty; **p.94** Peter Newark's Military Pictures; **p.96** Farabolafoto, Milan; **p.97** Edizione Scolastiche Bruno Mondadori; **p.102** *l* Moro Roma, *r* Academie der Künste, Berlin, © DACS 1998 (photo: Roman März); **p.109** *t & b* Edizione Scolastiche Bruno Mondadori; **p.110** *t* Farabolafoto, Milan, *b* Moro Roma ©; **p.111** *t* Hulton Getty, *b* Farabolafoto, Milan; **p.112** *t* Civici Raccolte D'Arte, Milan, *bl* Edizione Scolastiche Bruno Mondadori, *br* © Archivio Storico Il Dagherrotipo, Rome; **p.113** *t* Banca Populare di Cremona, *c* Edizione Scolastiche Bruno Mondadori, *bl* Moro Roma ©, *br* Civico Museo Revoltella, Trieste; **p.114** *tl* Museo d'Arte Contemporanea di Villa Croce, Genoa, *tr* Galleria Nazionale d'Arte Moderna, Rome (photo: Giuseppe Schiavinotto, Rome), *b* Scala; **p.116** *l* Associated Press, *r* Edizione Scolastiche Bruno Mondadori; **p.117** *tl & tr* Edizione Scolastiche Bruno Mondadori, *bl & br* Farabolafoto, Milan; **p.118** Moro Roma ©; **p.119** *t & b* Moro Roma ©; **p.128** Moro Roma; **p.129** *t* Edizione Scolastiche Bruno Mondadori, *b* Farabolafoto, Milan; **p.132** Farabolafoto, Milan; **p.133** Farabolafoto, Milan; **p.139** *t* Moro Roma ©, *b* Galleria Arco Farnese, Rome; **p.144** Farabolafoto, Milan; **p.150** *t* Moro Roma ©, *b* Topham Picturepoint **p.153** Peter Newark's Military Pictures; **p.155** Hulton Getty; **p.157** Moro Roma; **p.158** Edizione Scolastiche Bruno Mondadori; **p.159** Moro Roma ©; **p.164** Edizione Scolastiche Bruno Mondadori; **p.165** *l* Farabolafoto, Milan, *r* Moro Roma ©; **p.168** *t & b* Farabolafoto, Milan, *c* Edizione Scolastiche Bruno Mondadori; **p.170** Edizione Scolastiche Bruno Mondadori; **p.176** Edizione Scolastiche Bruno Mondadori; **p.177** Süddeutscher Verlag Bilderdienst; **p.181** *t & br* Hulton Getty, *bl* Popperfoto; **p.183** *l* © Archivio Storico Il Dagherrotipo, Rome, *r* Moro Roma; **p.185** © Archivio Storico Il Dagherrotipo, Rome; **p.190** Hulton Getty; **p.193** *br* Farabolafoto, Milan; **p.205** *t* Farabolafoto, Milan, *bl* Edizione Scolastiche Bruno Mondadori; **p.206** *tl & tr* Peter Newark's Military Pictures, *c* London Evening Standard/Solo, *b* Edizione Scolastiche Bruno Mondadori; **p.216** *l & r* London Evening Standard/Solo; **p.217** *tl & tr* Punch, *cr* London Evening Standard/Solo, *bl* Moro Roma ©; **p.218** *l* Moro Roma, *r* Farabolafoto, Milan; **p.221** Farbabolafoto, Milan; **p.223** Farabolafoto, Milan; **p.224** *l & r* National Archives; **p.227** Ullstein; **p.229** *br* Peter Newark's Military Pictures; **p.230** *l & r* Punch; **p.232** Hulton Getty; **p.233** Hulton Getty; **p.236** *l* The Washington Post, *r* Süddeutscher Verlag Bilderdienst; **p.250** *l* Moro Roma, *r* Edizione Scolastiche Bruno Mondadori

b = bottom, *c* = centre, *l* = left, *r* = right, *t* = top

Visual sources
Every effort has been made to provide as much information as possible about the visual sources used, which include some photographs not previously published in Britain. However, there are occasions when not all the details that a historian really needs were available from the photographic libraries. We will be pleased to rectify any mistakes at the earliest opportunity.

Secondary sources
Many secondary sources are cited in this book. Full details of the source are given the first time it is quoted. Later use of the same title is accompanied by only a brief reference. Full bibliographic details for all works cited are gathered in the Bibliography on page 270.

The authors and publisher would like to thank the following for permission to reproduce text extracts:

Addison Wesley Longman Ltd: P.Bell, *The Origins of the Second World War in Europe;* M. Clark, *Modern Italy 1871–1982*
Cambridge University Press: C. Maier, *In Search of Stability*
Chatto & Windus: R. Eatwell, *A History of Fascism*
Hodder & Stoughton: M. Robson, *Liberalism and Fascism 1870–1945;* D. Williamson, *Mussolini, from Socialist to Fascist*
Macmillan Press Ltd: P. Morgan, *Italian Fascism 1919–45*
Manchester University Press: D. Thompson, *State Control in Fascist Italy*
R. Overy with A. Wheatcroft, *The Road to War,* reprinted by permission of the author, c/o Rogers, Coleridge & White Ltd, 20 Powis Mews, London W11 1JN
UCL Press: S. Payne, *History of Fascism 1914–45*
Wayland Publishers: C. Leeds, *Italy under Mussolini*

While every effort has been made to trace copyright holders, the publishers apologise for any inadvertent omissions and will be pleased to make any further acknowledgements.

Using this book

This book is different from many others which are available for Advanced Level history. Like others it provides the content you need for exam success; unlike others it also provides a wide range of activities and features which help you analyse and understand that content as you read.

In-depth study

This is an in-depth study of Fascist Italy. Look at the contents list and you will see that it provides comprehensive analysis of the rise and fall of Fascism.

We have deliberately aimed to study themes, issues, people and events that other books have left alone because we believe they are interesting and worthwhile in their own right but also because we believe they will deepen understanding of other central issues.

There can be a price to be paid for depth however – it is easy to get overwhelmed by the amount of content to be covered. So remember you do not need everything in this book. You might, for example, only need to skim read the summaries for some of the chapters. Likewise you do not need to use all the tasks and all the features. They are there to help you think about and analyse the period. Use those that help. Ignore those that do not.

Independent learning

Many of the features – the focus route activities, for example, or the learning trouble spots – are designed particularly for independent learning when you are working through this material on your own.

Class-based learning

Other features assume you are learning with others. Many of the activities work best in a group where you can compare your ideas with others. The talking points are aimed at stimulating discussion among students.

These are the features built into this book and how they aim to help you:

■ **Sections**   The four main sections have introductions which use sources, timelines and tasks to highlight the main themes of the section. At the end of each section is a review activity.

■ **Chapters**   Each chapter begins with a Chapter overview which lists the main enquiries pursued in the chapter. There is also a review at the end of each chapter including key points – a boxed five- or ten-point summary of the content of the chapter.

■ **Focus route**   Throughout the book, on every topic, this feature guides you to produce the notes essential for understanding and later revising your work.

■ **Charts**   These provide a large amount of important information about the topic in compact diagrammatic form.

■ **Learning trouble spots**   Teaching and examining experience shows that some topics cause problems for students time and again. This feature identifies these topics and suggests how to avoid the common misunderstandings.

■ **Glossary**   The Glossary on page 268 gives definitions of the key terms needed for answering questions about Fascist Italy. These are printed in SMALL CAPITALS when they first appear in a chapter.

■ **Activities**   These offer a range of exercises to enhance your understanding. They vary in style from individual essays to collaborative exercises; from interpretation of contemporary sources to analysis of historians' viewpoints.

They also include exercises which ask you to think about events from the standpoint of people at the time and not from the point of view of an objective historian today. This is not a diversion from 'real learning' or from exam success – such activities will improve your essays as you gain deeper understanding of the motives and other factors influencing individuals' actions.

■ **Talking points**   These are asides which do not fit the normal pattern of written exercises. They are designed to provoke discussion which will
- illuminate understanding of the period
- make links between the present and the past
- highlight aspects of the process of studying history.

Introduction

Ambition!

SOURCE 1   Mussolini in around 1905

SOURCE 2   Mussolini speaking to his mother

One day I shall astonish the world.

Glory!

SOURCE 3   The Duce Mussolini addressing a crowd in Venice in the 1930s

SOURCE 4   From an article written by Mussolini, published in the *Daily Express* in December 1935, and reprinted in July 1943

The crowd will always love strong men: in that respect the mob is like a woman . . .
  I am immortal.

Humiliation!

SOURCE 5   Mussolini's body, displayed in Milan 1945

SOURCE 6   King Victor Emmanuel addressing Mussolini, July 1943

Italy has gone to bits. You are the most hated man in Italy.

In May 1936 the lion roared in front of an ecstatic crowd of adoring Italians. Benito Mussolini, the DUCE, was addressing his people. Italy had just conquered Abyssinia, and a new Italian EMPIRE was proclaimed. The country appeared to be united and powerful, and Mussolini was the most popular leader Italy had ever seen. His doctrine, Fascism, was declared to be **the idea** of the twentieth century. Yet within ten years those same Italians had killed their leader, desecrated his body, and Italian Fascism had, as Hitler bitterly remarked, 'melted like snow in the sun'.

This book will explore the path of Mussolini's extraordinary career from SOCIALIST revolutionary to Fascist DICTATOR, and consider whether he really was a skilled politician, or a mere loudmouth and buffoon. It will also examine the nature of the Fascist state he created, and the impact it made on Italy.

What is Fascism?

Before we can look at the growth of Fascism, we need to understand what the term Fascism means.

You will come across many political IDEOLOGIES during your course, and some may be new to you. Fascism is the central ideology in our study of Italy, and an understanding of its broad ideas will help you identify the reasons why Mussolini, the Fascist leader, became Prime Minister of Italy in 1922.

A good place to start looking at a political belief is in its name. For example, LIBERALISM describes the belief in individual liberty. Modern Britain, France, and the USA would be termed 'liberal' states. By this we mean a state which has:

- an elected assembly (Parliament) that makes laws
- a CONSTITUTION laying down and restricting the powers of the government, with clear rules for governing the country
- a variety of political parties competing for support
- formal protection for key individual rights or liberties, such as free speech, freedom of the press, free practice of religion, and equality before the law.

Mussolini once described Fascism as 'action and mood, not doctrine'. It had no founding father who laid down its fundamental principles, as Karl Marx did for COMMUNISM. Fascism took different forms in different countries. It gained support both for what it offered, but also, significantly, for what it opposed. The word Fascism seems rather meaningless, and indeed the term does not originate from an idea about how to run society. Read the Fascio explanation on page 4, which tells us the origins of the word and gives us our first clues about the nature of Fascism.

Fascism **favoured** the following:

- NATIONALISM (see page 10)
- A powerful leader or dictator
- One-party government
- National unity
- PARAMILITARY organisations
- War

Initially though, it defined itself mainly by what it was **opposed** to:

- INTERNATIONALISM
- Liberal DEMOCRACY
- MARXIST Socialism/Communism
- Class conflict
- PACIFISM

Activity

Using just the word itself, what can you deduce about the following ideologies? It may help you to look up the stem (or beginning) of the word in a dictionary.

Liberalism – favouring individual liberty
Communism –
Capitalism –
Conservatism –
National Socialism –
Imperialism –
Democracy –
Anarchism –

CHART A What is Fascism?

The first Fascist movement was founded by Mussolini in Italy, but similar movements developed elsewhere. Fascism has been seen as a response to the political and economic tensions in much of Europe after the First World War, but it has also arisen in other countries at times of strain.

Fascism is normally viewed as a RIGHT-WING movement, but it initially had some aspects in common with LEFT-WING ideologies, as there were some anti-CAPITALIST elements within it. It began as a protest movement seeking change, but where Fascists gained power, as in Italy, the regime was in some respects conservative, protecting the social STATUS QUO.

Fascio

When Mussolini founded his first Fascist squads in March 1919, they were called fascio di combattimento. Their badge was the rods and axe, symbols of authority in ancient Rome. The term fascio had no precise meaning in 1919. It had been used by radicals in the late nineteenth century, and by various political groups in World War I. The literal meaning is 'bunch' or 'group', and once in power Mussolini linked it to the bound sticks or fasces which the Roman lictor (a magistrate) had used as a symbol of office. It is thought Mussolini wanted his fighting groups bound by ties as close as those that secured the sticks of the Roman lictors.

■ **Activity**

Divide into pairs.

1 In your own words describe to your partner what Fascism favoured, and to what it was opposed.
2 In what circumstances do you think people might support a Fascist movement?

■ **Talking point**

Why do you think Britain has never had a strong Fascist movement?

CHART B   Key features of Italian Fascism

Blackshirts

- The uniform of the Fascist movement, worn by the Fascist squads who attacked opponents
- Copied from the uniform of the Arditi, the Italian shock troops in the First World War
- Used by d'Annunzio in Fiume (see page 27)

Fascist salute

- Copied from the straight-arm salute used by the ancient Romans
- Used by d'Annunzio

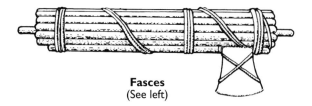

Fasces
(See left)

Why study Mussolini and Fascist Italy?

If you are one of the lucky ones for whom history is simply the most interesting subject you have studied (and if it is, you probably can't explain why – it just is!) you don't need any justification for studying Mussolini and Fascist Italy. For the rest of you – whose basic justification may be that it's on the syllabus – this page may persuade you that studying this topic is about even more than the very important business of getting a good grade.

The greatest justification for studying the past is that it helps us to understand and live in the present. Here are three ways in which your responses to today's issues may be sharpened by your increased knowledge of and understanding of this particular topic.

A Are historical parallels with today's events accurate?

The interwar period saw the rise of several dictators and political decisions today may be affected by ideas about what happened in the 1930s. Politicians may feel they must 'stand up to' contemporary dictators because appeasement did not stop war in 1939. But is that an accurate representation of the events of the 1930s? If it isn't, are today's decisions affected by an oversimplification of past events? Once you know more about this period you will be likely to make fewer glib comparisons with the past and hence be better positioned to appraise politicians' use of the past to justify current policies.

B Are they all the same?

Mussolini, Stalin, Hitler, Franco – dictators all, but were they all the same? Studies of this period should stop us generalising about people and events. The more sophisticated our understanding of the similarities and differences amongst the dictators of the 1930s, the better equipped we are to avoid sweeping generalisations about political leaders who seem similar today. The fewer generalisations we make, the better our judgements are today.

C It couldn't happen here?

It is easy to look back at TOTALITARIAN regimes and feel secure within our political system. Only other people fall victims to extremist governments – or so we may think. Detailed study of the rise of a dictator like Mussolini makes us more aware of how easy it is for such a development to take place. His power was not solely the product of a dominating personality and cunning propaganda but was at least as much the result of other people's failure to stop him when they had the opportunity. This period shows how tempting it is to avoid involvement, to wait, to go along with the mood of the majority – or with what the mood of the majority appears to be. It couldn't happen here – only so long as people take action to stop such a development.

Why did Mussolini come to power in 1922?

Activity

Study the timeline and Sources 1–6.
Find evidence of the following
preconditions:

a) The strength of Italian NATIONALISM
b) The success (or failure) of Italy's
   foreign policy
c) Discontent within the Italian state
   and government reaction to it
d) The impact of the First World War
e) The nature of Fascism

Introduction

In 1922 Mussolini became the first-ever Fascist leader to form a government. The theme of Section 1 is 'Why did Fascism gain power in Italy?'

To answer this question, we need to look at the longer-term background to the growth of Fascism. Historians have identified five main factors which were the PRECONDITIONS for the Fascist rise to power (see Activity).

CHART A   SECTION OVERVIEW

Section 1 Why did Mussolini come to power in 1922?

1 How secure was Liberal Italy in 1914? (pp. 8–21)

2 How great a challenge did the First World War and Socialism pose to the Liberal state? (pp. 22–35)

3 Why was Mussolini, the Fascist leader, appointed Prime Minister of Italy in 1922? (pp. 36–62)

Review: Why did Mussolini come to power in 1922? (pp. 63–66)

SOURCE 1   The Italian nationalist
Garibaldi leading his expedition to Sicily,
1860. Although he gained mass support for
his campaign, his peasant followers were
hoping for social reforms rather than for a
united Italy

SOURCE 2   Pope Pius IX (1846–78). He
and his successors condemned the new
Italian LIBERAL state

SOURCE 3   Painting of the defeat of the Italians at Adowa, Abyssinia, 1896

SOURCE 4 An Italian cartoon. 'Guerra' means 'war'

SOURCE 5 Fascist Blackshirt stamping on a Socialist flag

SOURCE 6 Mussolini speaking about Fascism in September 1922

Our programme is simple: we wish to govern Italy ... The state does not represent a party, it represents the nation as a whole.

CHART B Timeline of Italy 1861–1922

UNIFICATION

Till 1861	Italy is divided into eight main states, some ruled by Austria
1859	Armies of the North Italian state Piedmont and France defeat Austria and expel it from most of northern Italy
1860	Garibaldi's expedition conquers southern Italy and hands it over to the King of Piedmont, Victor Emmanuel II
1861	New united Kingdom of Italy proclaimed. New Parliament elected by two per cent of the population
1860s	Wave of peasant unrest in the South
1866	Prussia beats Austria; Italy gains Venetia
1870	Prussia beats France; Italy gains Rome
	Pope condemns the new Italian state

LIBERAL ITALY

1881	Italy fails to gain Tunisia
1882	Italy joins Germany and Austria–Hungary in the Triple Alliance
1880s	Italy gains some lands in Eastern Africa
1892–94	Major peasant unrest in the South
1892	Italian SOCIALIST Party created
1896	Italy beaten by Abyssinians at battle of Adowa
1898	Major industrial unrest in the North met by fierce repression
1900	King Umberto assassinated
1900–14	Rapid industrialisation in the North
1903–14	Giolitti is Prime Minister for much of this time. Series of reforms to try to win over the masses
1911	Italy defeats Turkey and gains Libya
1912	Mussolini emerges as major leader of RADICAL Socialists
	Vote given to most men
1914	Wave of unrest; Red Week

FIRST WORLD WAR

1914	Aug	Italy stays neutral when First World War breaks out
	Nov	Mussolini expelled from Socialist Party for advocating that Italy should join the war. Founds his own newspaper, *Il Popolo d'Italia*
1915	Apr	Treaty of London with Allies promises Italy major gains if it joins the war
	May	Italy joins Allies against Austria–Hungary and Germany
1917	Oct	Italy defeated at battle of Caporetto
1918	Oct	Italy wins battle of Vittorio Veneto

POST-WAR TURMOIL: SOCIALISM AND FASCISM

1919	Mar	Mussolini founds a radical Fascist movement; gains some support from bitter ex-soldiers
	Jun	Italy fails to make major gains in Versailles Settlement
	Sept	Nationalist d'Annunzio seizes the port of Fiume
	Nov	Election. Socialist Party and new Catholic Party gain over half of all votes but fail to form a government
1919–20		Two years of Socialist unrest (Biennio Rosso)
1920	Sept	Workers seize control of many northern factories
		Fascism gains support from frightened conservative groups and moves to the Right
1920–22		Wave of Fascist violence against opponents
1921	May	Election. Fascists linked to the government gain seven per cent of the vote. Mussolini and 34 Fascist MPs elected
	Nov	Fascist Party established
1922	Oct	Fascists seize control of many northern cities
		Fascists plan a march on Rome to gain power
		Mussolini appointed Prime Minister

How secure was Liberal Italy in 1914?

The Risorgimento

The Risorgimento is the name given to the period during which Italy became one united state. In 1859 the Italian people were divided and ruled by foreigners. Most states had absolute rulers, with no elected Parliament. Yet within two years, there had been a mass uprising; Austria had been defeated; most of Italy had been united and this new state was ruled by a CONSTITUTIONAL MONARCH, with an elected Parliament. Italy's heroic leaders, Cavour and Garibaldi, had triumphed. A remarkable rebirth, or Risorgimento, indeed!

This sounds like a triumph for NATIONALISM and suggests that the new Italy would be a strongly united country. However, let's look at these events from a different angle.

- Cavour had not been trying to create a united Italy, but only an enlarged state in the North.
- Most of the initial fighting to expel the Austrians was done by French troops; in 1866 it was Prussian, not Italian, troops who were victorious against the Austrians.
- Most of those who participated in the popular uprising in Sicily in 1860 did not know what the word 'Italy' meant.
- More Italians were to die rebelling against 'their' new government in the 1860s than died fighting for it in 1859–60.
- Garibaldi, Mazzini and other nationalists were disappointed with the new Italy, as it did little to improve the lives of the mass of Italians.
- A new Italian state had been created; but the economic and social structure was kept largely intact.
- At first only two per cent of the people had the vote.
- Austria ruled North-East Italy until 1866. The Pope ruled Rome until 1870.
- Austria kept Trentino and the South Tyrol in North Italy.

The aim of this chapter is to help you understand the nature of the Italian state between 1870 and 1914. To do this we need briefly to look at the way the new united state was created in the Italian RISORGIMENTO (see left). This will help you to understand why the Fascists came to power in 1922.

A How was a united Italian state created?

The story of how Italy became unified between 1859 and 1870 is a stirring one, involving dramatic battles and political intrigue. There is a summary of the key features in Chart 1B. Our main concern is to show how the way Italy was unified helps to explain some of the weaknesses in Liberal Italy between 1870 and 1914. In addition, you can see the reasons why some historians argue there is a connection between the Risorgimento and the later coming to power of the Fascists.

Italian unification also illustrates how the same event can be seen in two very different ways. Italian nationalists saw the Risorgimento as a great triumph for popular Italian national feeling. Its critics saw it as a product of diplomatic manoeuvres, led by politicians, Italian and French, who were distrustful of the mass of the people. In this view, right from the beginning the new Italy was a seriously flawed state.

The issue of the relationship between the Italian people and the state is to be an important theme throughout this book.

■ Activity

Summarise the criticisms of the Risorgimento made below by Antonio Gramsci, an Italian MARXIST imprisoned by the Fascists.

The leaders of the Risorgimento said they were aiming at the creation of a modern state in Italy, and in fact they produced a bastard. They aimed at stimulating the formation of an extensive and energetic ruling class and they did not succeed; they aimed at integrating the people into the framework of the new state, and they did not succeed. The paltry political life from 1870 to 1900, the fundamental rebelliousness of the Italian popular classes, the narrow existence of a cowardly ruling stratum, they are all consequences of that failure.

CHART 1B The key features of Italian unification

In the nineteenth century the Italian people were neither unified nor did they rule themselves.
In 1848–49 there was a series of revolts throughout Italy. Piedmont led a war for independence against Austria, but was defeated.

1. Cavour does a deal with Napoleon III to get French help to expel Austria. He wants to create an independent Italian state in the North and Centre, but not to include the backward South.

2. French and Piedmontese troops defeat the Austrians at Magenta and Solferino. Piedmont takes over Lombardy and the Central Duchies, but not Venetia which Austria retains.

3. Garibaldi organises a nationalist expedition to unify Italy, and march on Rome. He joins a peasant revolt in Sicily, and conquers Sicily and Naples.

4. Piedmontese troops occupy much of the Papal States to link up with Garibaldi and ensure he hands over his conquests to King Victor Emmanuel.

5. 1861 New Kingdom of Italy proclaimed in Turin.

6. Prussia and Italy fight Austria. Italy loses, but Prussia wins. Austria hands Venetia to Italy.

7. 1862, 1867 Garibaldi leads two failed expeditions attempting to march to Rome to gain control of the capital.

8. 1870 Prussia defeats France who withdraws its troops (protecting the Pope) from Rome. Italian troops move in. Rome becomes the capital of a fully united Italian state.

Cavour. Prime Minister of Piedmont 1852–61. Moderate Liberal, aiming to create a Liberal independent state in the northern half of Italy. Realised Piedmont would need French help to defeat Austria. Worried about radical nationalists. He eventually outmanoeuvred them to create a Liberal Italian state as an extended form of Piedmont.

King Victor Emmanuel II of Piedmont. Head of House of Savoy. He became first king of Italy.

Piedmont. Important northern state; not ruled by foreigners. Since 1848 it was a constitutional monarchy, with an assembly elected by about two per cent of the population. Its rulers were eager to expand its territory.

Papal States. Ruled by the Pope as a TEMPORAL ruler

Kingdom of Naples. The Neapolitan State covered Naples and Sicily, and was ruled by Spanish Bourbon kings

Emperor Napoleon III of France. Nephew of Napoleon I. He sent 100,000 troops to help expel Austria in exchange for gaining Nice and Savoy for France.

Garibaldi. Radical nationalist guerrilla leader. Popular with masses. Aimed to liberate the masses, but trusted Victor Emmanuel. In 1860, 1862 and 1867 he tried to march on Rome to gain it for Italy.

0   100   200   300 km

Austrian-ruled territory

Mazzini. Radical republican nationalist Failed to inspire mass revolts. He became fierce critic of the 'conservative revolution' nature of unification.

Is there a connection between the Risorgimento and Fascism? Many historians would answer yes. As a direct result of the way Italy was created but not fully unified, the new Italian state suffered from a variety of weaknesses, which you will soon be examining. The new Liberal Italian state was unable or unwilling to tackle these. This made Italy susceptible to, or likely to be affected by, the appeal of Fascism.

CHART 1C   From the Risorgimento to Fascism

Domestic issues
- The lack of popular involvement in making Italy meant that the mass of the people did not identify with the new Italian state. They were not given the vote in the new state.
- The unification process was dominated by the ELITE (the wealthy and educated), who were not committed to major social reforms.
- The Pope was hostile to the new Liberal state.
- The makers of Italy had not intended to include the backward South in a united Italy, and they neglected its problems.
- Debts incurred in the wars of unification meant the new government imposed high taxes and restricted spending on social reforms.

Foreign policy
- The reliance on foreign armies to unify Italy contributed to a national inferiority complex, and a desire to show that Italy was a great power.
- Italy's failure to defeat Austria in 1866 left Austria holding Italian land.

Overall
- The creation of a new state raised expectations of social reform and national greatness which were not fulfilled by Liberal Italy, and which Fascism offered to deliver.

■ **Talking point**

Discuss whether you think the nation state has had its day.

FOCUS ROUTE

Look at pages 8–10.
1 Study Chart 1C. List five ways in which the way Italy was unified left problems for the new Liberal united kingdom.
2 What contributes to a people's national identity?
3 Why did nationalism increase during the nineteenth century?

What exactly is nationalism?
Do you want the British entry in the Eurovision song contest to win? Do you want British tennis players to win major tournaments? Most of us would say yes, and thus we might be called nationalistic.

Do you think Britain is the best country in the world? The answer to this question is more troublesome. Many Britons might well say no, but still claim to be nationalistic.

Why is this? Perhaps it is because they are aware of how support for one's own nation can easily degenerate into hostility to others. This is broadly what happened to many nationalist movements from the nineteenth century to the twentieth.

Nationalism means a sense of belonging to a nation. So what defines a nation? This question is not as easy to answer as it might seem. People of a nation usually have some of the following in common: language, culture, religion, geographical area, tradition/history, racial type. Not all of these always apply; many nations are divided by religion, and many historians would argue all nations are divided by class. What is often crucial is whether people feel they are a nation.

Why did nationalism grow in the nineteenth century?
To be a nationalist you have to identify with other people in your nation and your state. Nationalism therefore tends to increase with improved communications and education. For example, in 1860s Sicily, few of the population would have had any contact with Italians from the North; and they might not have been able to understand them if they had. However, the advance of education, railways and, in the 1920s, radio brought potential means to link Italians more closely together.

In the nineteenth century not all European states were nation states. There were several multi-national, MONARCHICAL EMPIRES, such as the Austrian, Russian and Ottoman (Turkish) Empires. As nationalist sentiment grew, these regimes were challenged by various nationalist movements. Most nationalists wanted to replace monarchical empires with more liberal nation states. They argued that just as national boundaries should be drawn on the basis of a common people, so states should reflect the wishes of those people, as represented in elected assemblies. LIBERALISM and nationalism were closely linked.

By the twentieth century nationalism had changed considerably. It was now also used by established regimes as a means to gain the support of their peoples, and also sometimes to justify foreign expansion in the interests of making their nation great. This extreme form of nationalism denied the national rights of these conquered peoples. Fascism represented such an extreme form of nationalism.

Is nationalism declining?
Today, many people argue that in the age of global communications and economies, nation states are becoming redundant, and the future lies with continent-wide organisations like the European Union. Parallel with this, in some of the established nation states, there are groups who want to divide the state into smaller units, or new nations as they see them. For example, there is a movement for the North of Italy to break away from the rest of the country. Such groups look to a Europe of regions within a loose FEDERAL organisation.

■ Activity

Study Charts 1D and 1E.

1 Mark the following key features on an outline map of Italy.
  a) Three major industrial cities
  b) One major administrative city
  c) The most important southern city
  d) Italy's most important river

2 Around the outline map, make a list of evidence showing:
  a) Italy's backwardness
  b) signs of modernisation
  c) regional differences
  d) Italy's comparative military might.

3 a) What evidence is there to suggest why so many people emigrated?
  b) How might emigration actually help the stability of the state? Refer to:

  • emigration's influence on unemployment
  • its influence on wages
  • the impact of remittances (money sent back from abroad) from emigrants
  • the idea of emigration as a safety valve.

B Had Liberal governments created a more united nation by 1900?

'We have made Italy. Now we must make Italians.' D'Azeglio, a government minister, made this statement after Italy had been formally unified. Much needed to be done by the Liberal governments that ruled Italy after 1861 to overcome the problems they inherited. The newly unified Italian people needed to see success in both domestic and foreign policy if they were to be won over to the new state. You are now going to try and assess the problems facing the governments and how far they had overcome the divisions and backwardness by the turn of the twentieth century.

The problems facing Italian governments

CHART 1D   Italy in c. 1900

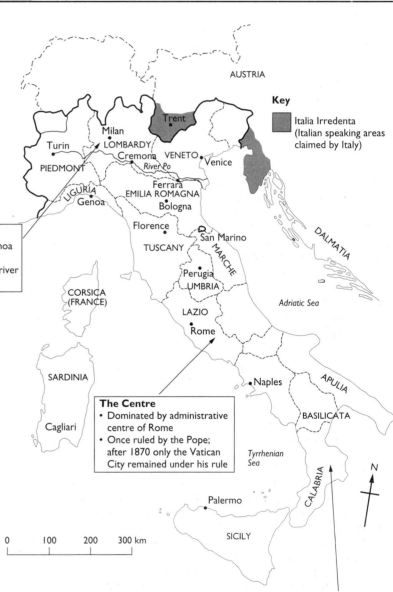

Key

▨ Italia Irredenta (Italian speaking areas claimed by Italy)

The North
• Industrial, especially engineering centres of Milan, Turin, Genoa
• 1880s widescale migration to growing towns
• Po Valley: area of advanced agriculture based around major river
• Medium-sized farms, commercial farming

The Centre
• Dominated by administrative centre of Rome
• Once ruled by the Pope; after 1870 only the Vatican City remained under his rule

The South (called in Italy the Mezzogiorno)
• Little industry
• Once the 'grain basket' of Europe; by twentieth century soil exhausted
• Large, inefficient noble-owned estates (latifundia)
• 1914 0.01% of the population owned 50% of the land
• Frequent social unrest
• Powerful clans and Mafia

Regional variations in 1861				
Area	Agric.	Rail km	Road km	Illiteracy %	Education
North	170	1370	38,000	68	80
Centre	120	360	38,000	78	34
South	80	100	13,800	87	18

Agric.: value of agricultural production, lire per hectare (10,000 m²)
Educ.: % primary school attendance

Examples of dialect variations		
	'Thursday'	**'boy/child'**
Italian	Giovedi	Bambino
Lombardy	Giuedi	Bagai
Tuscany	Zovedi	Bimbo
Lazio	Giovedi	Regazzino
Sicily	Ioviri	Picciottu

Agriculture
• Majority of population was rural: 1913 57% (Britain 15%).
• There were a few enterprising, large landowners (AGRARI); but most were small agricultural labourers (braccianti). There were also tenant farmers, SHARECROPPERS (mezzadri)

CHART IE How great a power was Italy? Economic and military statistics

Economy

- Steel production (million tonnes)

	1890	1910
Italy	0.1	0.7
Britain	3.6	6.5
Germany	2.2	13.7
France	0.7	3.4

- Value of foreign trade (in $ billion)

	1860	1913
Italy	0.3	1.8
Britain	2.0	7.5
Germany	0.8	4.3
France	0.5	2.2

- Railways (km)

	1880	1913
Italy	9,290	18,873
Britain	28,846	38,114
Germany	33,838	63,378
France	23,089	40,770

Emigration, mainly to USA

1870s	168,000
1880s	992,000
1890s	1,580,000
1900s	3,615,000

Agriculture

- Yields (mid-nineteenth century) low, e.g.
  - Italy average 9 hectolitres (= 100 litres) of wheat per hectare
  - France   19
  - Britain   25

Communications

- Most railways were confined to coastal areas.
- Few navigable rivers
- In the 1890s 90% of the South had no roads.

Industry & trade

- Silk and engineering were the major industries.
- Virtually no coal; little iron or other minerals; no oil discovered (until 1950s); 1890s increasing use of hydro-electric power in Alps

Social conditions

- Wealth: per capita GDP (gross domestic product) 1860–96
  - Italy increased by 4%
  - France, Germany, Britain increased by 40–50%
- Deaths per 1000 (1880s)

North	South	Britain
26	29	19

KEY PROBLEMS

Opposition of Church
- The Pope told Catholics not to participate in the new state
- Priests helped to stir up unrest amongst peasantry

Economic problems
- Government debt
- High taxes on poor
- The North–South divide was increased by northern industrialisation
- Frequent unrest, especially in Sicily; 1860s, 1893–94 major revolts

Political problems
- Limited SUFFRAGE meant most Italians were uninvolved in the new state, apart from paying taxes and being conscripted into the army
- Politicians were seen as corrupt; frequent changes of government

Foreign policy
- Italia Irredenta (see page 15): areas populated by Italians kept by Austria 1866
- Government had inferiority complex
- Defeat at Adowa in 1896 (see page 15)

Military might in 1914

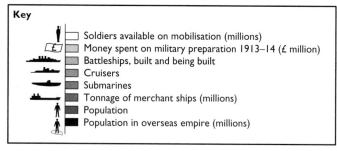

Key
- Soldiers available on mobilisation (millions)
- Money spent on military preparation 1913–14 (£ million)
- Battleships, built and being built
- Cruisers
- Submarines
- Tonnage of merchant ships (millions)
- Population
- Population in overseas empire (millions)

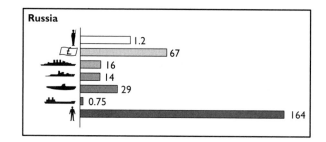

Russia
- 1.2
- 67
- 16
- 14
- 29
- 0.75
- 164

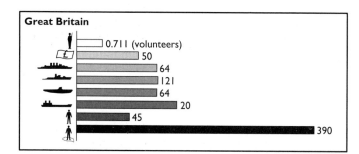

Great Britain
- 0.711 (volunteers)
- 50
- 64
- 121
- 64
- 20
- 45
- 390

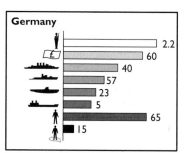

Germany
- 2.2
- 60
- 40
- 57
- 23
- 5
- 65
- 15

Italy
- 0.75
- 10
- 14
- 22
- 12
- 1.75
- 35
- 2

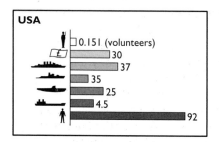

USA
- 0.151 (volunteers)
- 30
- 37
- 35
- 25
- 4.5
- 92

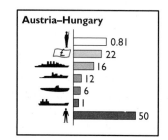

Austria–Hungary
- 0.81
- 22
- 16
- 12
- 6
- 1
- 50

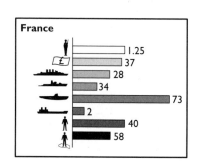

France
- 1.25
- 37
- 28
- 34
- 73
- 2
- 40
- 58

Did governments really try to unite Italy?

We need to examine how far the various Liberal governments pursued policies which would create a fully united Italy. As you read the following account of Liberal Italy, consider those aspects which might help explain why later on the Fascist movement gained support.

Let us first consider the operation of the political system, which in some respects was like our own.

CHART 1F   The political system in Liberal Italy

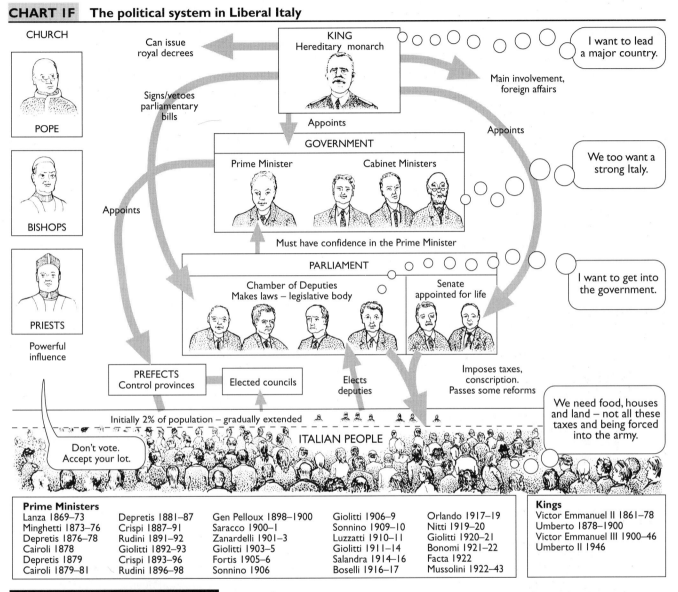

Prime Ministers

Lanza 1869–73	Depretis 1881–87	Gen Pelloux 1898–1900	Giolitti 1906–9	Orlando 1917–19
Minghetti 1873–76	Crispi 1887–91	Saracco 1900–1	Sonnino 1909–10	Nitti 1919–20
Depretis 1876–78	Rudini 1891–92	Zanardelli 1901–3	Luzzatti 1910–11	Giolitti 1920–21
Cairoli 1878	Giolitti 1892–93	Giolitti 1903–5	Giolitti 1911–14	Bonomi 1921–22
Depretis 1879	Crispi 1893–96	Fortis 1905–6	Salandra 1914–16	Facta 1922
Cairoli 1879–81	Rudini 1896–98	Sonnino 1906	Boselli 1916–17	Mussolini 1922–43

Kings
Victor Emmanuel II 1861–78
Umberto 1878–1900
Victor Emmanuel III 1900–46
Umberto II 1946

FOCUS ROUTE

Using pages 11–15, make notes explaining how successful Liberal governments were by 1900 in the following areas, all crucial for reducing internal divisions:

- Political reforms
- Economic and social change
- The Catholic Church
- National boundaries and foreign policy.

You might like to do this either by completing an assessment grid, with successes and failures, or by looking at the issue from the point of view of Italians at the time, and writing a report to a government minister.

The political system

You might think that the most effective way of creating a truly united state would be to involve the Italian people in its affairs. Give the people – the men, and even the women! – a say. Well, this did not happen. The Liberal politicians who controlled the unification process did not think ordinary people had the ability to participate in government. They believed in having a Parliament, but one which was chosen by the wealthy and educated elite, not the masses. Their time would come later, as wealth and education spread. Most politicians, however, did not consider spreading wealth to be a priority. Balancing the budget and building up Italy's military might were far more important.

The constitution laid down the powers of the monarch and guaranteed basic individual rights like free speech and religious freedom. Initially very few people had the vote (although this was raised to 25 per cent of adult males in 1882 and to most males in 1912). This meant that political parties did not really reflect popular wishes. Instead, groups of politicians did deals amongst

How liberal was Liberal Italy?

a) **How liberal was the political structure?**

The new Italian kingdom created in 1861 is known as Liberal Italy. This is because it had a written constitution, giving legislative (law-making) powers to an elected assembly, and guaranteeing basic individual freedoms. However, it was not truly democratic since only a small minority of men had the vote.

b) **How liberal were the politicians?**

The various politicians who ruled Italy between 1861 and 1922 are normally called Liberals, as they supported the fundamentals of the Liberal system. However, do not confuse them with your image of Liberals in Britain. In Italy at this time it was the general name given to the vast majority of Deputies. Many of these could also be called conservative as they wanted to maintain the existing structure; others were more reforming and would be more like what we understand as Liberals.

■ Talking points

1 What are basic liberal freedoms?

2 What are the main similarities and differences between Liberal Italy and our political system?

3 How might Italy's lack of key economic resources like coal and iron affect Mussolini when he later attempted to obtain glory for Italy?

4 What are the advantages and disadvantages of education being used to develop a sense of nationalism?

■ Activity

Explain what is meant by the gulf between legal and real Italy. How great a potential weakness was this for the regime?

themselves to form governments. An ambitious politician could try and win enough support from other Deputies to form a government. This might mean winning over his former opponents, by offering them certain jobs, other favours, or services for their constituencies. The politician Crispi described the situation in the Assembly in the 1890s thus: 'Utter pandemonium, especially when an important vote comes along. Government agents run through rooms and down corridors, collecting votes and promising subsidies, decorations, canals and bridges.' This political manoeuvring was known as TRASFORMISMO. It created the impression that politics was all about deals. This increased the sense of alienation the masses felt from the system.

Corruption was also prevalent in local government. The central government appointed PREFECTS, who virtually ran the provinces, and made sure that government-supported candidates won elections. Bribery and inefficiency were widespread within the administration. This served to discredit further the Liberal system in the eyes of many Italians.

There thus existed a gulf between 'legal Italy' (the Italy of Parliament and the political class who ran the country) and 'real Italy' (the ordinary Italians with their day-to-day concerns). The majority knew little of what went on beyond their villages. For them, Italy was not their country, it was just the power that forced them to pay taxes and do military service.

Economic and social development

Although in the decade after 1900 industry was to develop considerably in the North, Italy's industrial development was always going to be limited by its lack of key resources such as iron and coal.

The new Italian government united Italy economically by abolishing internal TARIFFS and establishing a single Italian market (internal free trade). This, however, harmed what little industry existed in the South, which could not compete with the more advanced North. The rapid growth of industry in the North after the turn of the century reinforced the economic divide between North and South, a still unresolved Italian problem.

Most Italian governments put a high priority on balancing the budget (trying to make their revenue match their expenditure). The new state inherited large debts caused by the wars of unification, and raised taxes to pay off these debts. Taxes fell mainly on the poor, and by 1900 Italians were estimated to be the most highly taxed people in Europe. When workers tried to strike for higher wages, the government supported employers rejecting such demands.

Most governments did, however, consider education an important issue, not least to try and create a greater sense of nationalism. In northern Italy the percentage of the adult population who were illiterate fell from 42 per cent in 1871 to 11 per cent in 1911; in the South the fall was from 88 to 65 per cent.

The Catholic Church

In order to understand what Italy was like at this time you have to realise the great influence of the Catholic Church, which was far more powerful than churches today. The Pope, as well as being spiritual head of the Catholic Church, had been the ruler of the Papal States covering much of central Italy. However, between 1861 and 1870 when the Kingdom of Italy was created, most of this land was taken from him. He was left with the area around St Peter's Church in Rome, the Vatican City. The Pope denounced the new Italian state which had taken his land. Furthermore, he considered Liberalism a sin as it allowed religious freedom. The Pope believed that Catholicism was the only true religion.

This rift between Church and state was a major problem facing the new kingdom. In 1874 the Pope instructed Catholics not to participate in the new state, for example by not voting. Bishops and priests reinforced this message to Italians. For many, the parish priest was their main source of information.

By the early twentieth century there was some reduction in Church–state hostility. The Pope became worried at the advance of SOCIALISM. The Marxist Socialists not only criticised the power of the Church, but also rejected religion itself. In 1904 the Pope authorised bishops to advise Catholics to vote in elections if it helped defeat Socialists.

Italia Irredenta
This was the name for the lands on Italy's north-east border (see Chart 1D) where a majority of the population spoke Italian. They had been retained by Austria in 1866, and consisted of the South Tyrol (or Alto-Adige), Trentino and Istria.

The Battle of Adowa 1896
This was a major defeat of Italian forces by the Abyssinians. Italy suffered 15,000 casualties, and many Italian prisoners were castrated. This was a humiliating defeat at the hands of an African country.

■ Talking point

How might Liberal Italy's international failure later help Mussolini gain support?

Did foreign policy help create a greater sense of nationalism?

An aggressive foreign policy can often be used by politicians to try and build up support. Some Italian Liberals favoured this tactic, but Bismarck (the German Chancellor 1871–90) appropriately described Italy as having a 'large appetite but little teeth'. Italians felt dissatisfied because they had never gained all the land they claimed on their north-east borders. Italian governments resented not possessing these 'unredeemed lands' (Italia Irredenta), but realised Italy was not strong enough by itself to take on Austria. However, the state's ambition was made clear in a school song which spoke of how children, when adults, would 'rise up, as warrior cohorts ... and die, fair Italy, for thee'.

Successful foreign policy might serve to make more Italians identify with their country. On the other hand, the cost of war might increase discontent.

Italy wanted to rival the Great Powers of Europe; this meant gaining colonies. It hoped to take control of Tunisia where there were already many Italian emigrants, but in 1881 France took it. The next year, Italy joined the anti-French Triple Alliance with Austria–Hungary and Germany. It also built up its influence in the Horn of Africa. In 1896 Italy attempted to take over Abyssinia (now Ethiopia), but was humiliatingly defeated at Adowa.

SOURCE 1.1 Italy's colonies

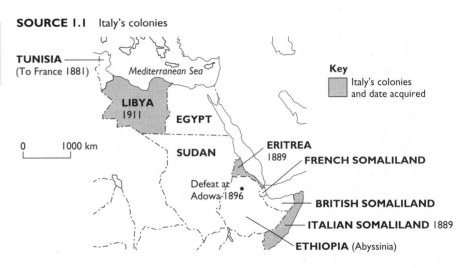

The 1890s: a decade of crises for the Liberal state

In the 1890s the Liberal state faced major challenges both from the Left and Right (see Chart 1G). Mass unrest was met by repression, and there was an attempt to set up a more AUTHORITARIAN government, relying on royal decrees. This has been seen as a precursor (forerunner) to Fascism. However, a resurgence of support for Liberal candidates in the 1900 election helped re-establish the dominance of Parliament.

The Liberal state had survived, but some politicians realised it could not rely on repression alone and that fundamental changes were necessary to reduce the gap between real and legal Italy.

CHART 1G   The crises of the 1890s

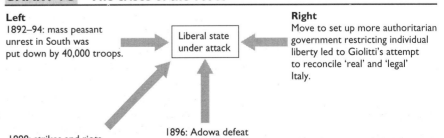

Left
1892–94: mass peasant unrest in South was put down by 40,000 troops.

Right
Move to set up more authoritarian government restricting individual liberty led to Giolitti's attempt to reconcile 'real' and 'legal' Italy.

1898: strikes and riots in northern cities. 100 demonstrators shot
1900: anarchists assassinated King Umberto.

1896: Adowa defeat

■ Activity

In 1903 Giovanni Giolitti became Prime Minister. As his chief adviser list the three most important problems that need to be tackled to create a more united Italy.

Carefully read the account of the Giolitti era (pages 16–18). Under the heading Optimistic Points, list the points suggesting Giolitti was making Liberal Italy a more secure state.

Under the heading Pessimistic Points, list the evidence that his policies were inadequate to solve Italy's problems, and that various groups were becoming more discontented.

■ **Activity**

Look at the cartoon (Source 1.2) and Giolitti's comments (Source 1.3).

1 What seems to be new about his approach to the working class?
2 What criticism is the cartoon making?

Giovanni Giolitti, 1842–1928

■ University-educated
■ Elected to Parliament 1882
■ Quickly became a minister. Was briefly Prime Minister 1892–93, but resigned over banking scandal
■ From 1903–14 dominated Italian politics, either as Prime Minister, or from behind the scenes. Master politician; skilful at winning majorities in the assembly, and using the prefect system to enhance his power. The period 1903–14 is known as the 'Giolitti era', when a series of reforms were passed.
■ Later he returned as Prime Minister June 1920–July 1921, and played a role in helping Mussolini to power.

 # How far did Giolitti succeed in bringing Italians together by 1914?

In the decade before the First World War, economic growth and the leadership of Giovanni Giolitti from 1903–14 seemed to offer a new chance for the Liberal state to establish itself. Some historians argue that Liberal Italy was by 1914 well on the way to security; others argue that, despite Giolitti's reforms, the regime was still far from secure.

The key issues that confronted Giolitti in his efforts to make the regime more secure were:

- Could he gain the support of the masses yet keep that of the traditional elites?
- Could he reconcile Catholicism and the newly developing forces of Socialism and assertive nationalism into the state?

SOURCE 1.2 An Italian cartoon

SOURCE 1.3 Comments by Giolitti to Parliament, 1900

The country is sick politically and morally, but the principal cause of its sickness is that the classes in power have been spending enormous sums on themselves and their own interests, and have obtained the money almost entirely from the poorer sections of society.

It is irrational to think low wages help industry. Low wages mean a poor diet; an underfed worker is both physically and intellectually weak.

To the chiefs of police, 1906

I remind all state officials that in this period of profound transformation, government action must be inspired both by absolute neutrality in the struggle between capital and labour, and by an affectionate concern for the legitimate aspirations of the working classes.

New enemies!

Socialists

We have already seen how the Italian state since 1861 had faced opposition from the powerful Catholic Church. Giolitti had to face up to a new challenge: the growth of Socialism. This was a development which frightened many of the existing elites, particularly the Catholic Church.

The development of industry in the North in the 1880s and 1890s was paralleled by the founding of trade unions and co-operative organisations. Many of these became linked together in the Socialist-controlled General Confederation of Labour (CGL). By 1900 there was an organised Socialist party, the PSI (Italian Socialist Party), which began winning seats in Parliament. By 1913 the PSI was winning over 20 per cent of the total vote.

Within both the political (PSI) and industrial (CGL) wings of the labour movement, there were splits between moderates and revolutionaries. The moderates or Minimalists argued that peaceful pressure could gain reforms, and they should aim for a minimum programme of measures to help workers improve their living standards. The RADICALS or Maximalists argued that the PSI should strive to achieve its full programme of a Socialist state. There were also those who argued that unions should organise strikes to overthrow the system, and set up a new society based on union organisation. These were known as SYNDICALISTS. Some of their ideas would later contribute to Fascism.

Control of the PSI fluctuated, but in 1912 the Maximalists gained control. One of their leaders was Benito Mussolini.

CHART 1H   Types of Socialists

Wing	Organisation	Moderates	Extremists
Political	PSI	Minimalists	Maximalists
Industrial	CGL	Reformers	SYNDICALISTS

Italian nationalists

In the early twentieth century the Liberal system was challenged from a new quarter. In 1911 the Italian National Association was set up. It drew support from a mixture of business interests, journalists, poets and painters. They were disillusioned by what they saw as the feeble foreign and domestic policies of Liberal governments. They wanted a vigorous authoritarian government to inspire the masses, extinguish class warfare, and lead the nation forward to greatness. On their banners was the slogan 'Our country is nothing without conquest'. Fascism was later to express many of the same feelings.

SOURCE 1.4 A Futurist painting: *The Charge of the Lancers* by Boccioni (1915)

Futurists

Futurism was a cultural movement which was part of the early twentieth-century mood of revolt against the existing boring, staid world. The Futurists rejected the Liberal view that the supreme aim of life was a comfortable BOURGEOIS existence. Instead, they glorified speed, action, conflict and violence. They were strong supporters of nationalism and IMPERIALISM. Fascinated by the industrial age and modern technology, the Futurists glorified the beauty of 'a roaring motor-car, which runs like a machine gun'. The most famous Futurist was Marinetti, who was a writer and an early supporter of Fascism, and later gave prestige to the movement.

■ **Activity**

1 Explain what
   a) Socialists and
   b) nationalists
   criticised in Liberal Italy.

2 Debate the proposition that 'Giolitti was making good progress towards uniting Italy'. Use your notes to argue one side of the case.

Giolitti's reforms

Giolitti hoped that increasing wealth and prosperity would make the country's Liberal institutions more acceptable and secure. After 1900 there was a major expansion of industry. At last, some of the benefits of economic change seeped down to ordinary people. Real wages (wages considered in terms of how much they could buy) rose by 25 per cent between 1890 and 1913. This was combined with a series of social reforms, with laws controlling female and child labour, and the establishment of social insurance and pensions schemes. The franchise (or right to vote) was extended to all males aged 30 and over.

Giolitti's aim of bringing all groups together was fine in theory, but did not work in practice. In trying to please one section he alienated another. Thus in trying to win over moderate Catholics and Socialists to the Liberal system, he only succeeded in upsetting some Liberals who feared any increase in the influence of the Church or workers.

He also tried to make the state more neutral in industrial disputes, instead of automatically using its power against workers. But this shift in approach failed to satisfy the unions, and the growth of Socialism continued. However, at the same time, Giolitti's policy worried some industrialists who feared that the Liberal system would no longer defend their interests. To them a neutral government appeared to be a government on the side of the workers. This growing fear influenced their actions in the turbulent post-war period. Industrialists began to look for a more authoritarian form of government which would vigorously resist any challenge from workers.

The growing role of the state led to an increase in the number of civil servants and other professional groups. These joined the PETTY BOURGEOISIE of small traders and shopkeepers who were also increasing as the economy developed. Some of these groups were concerned about the dangers of Socialism, the power of big business, and the weakness of the government. They too were beginning to look for an alternative to Liberalism.

As part of his attempt to win over all key groups Giolitti fell back on the old policy of foreign expansion to win support. He gave way to nationalist pressure and in 1911 attacked Libya, then ruled by Turkey. Italian forces defeated Turkey (by then known as the 'sick man of Europe'). At last Italy had won a war! However, many ordinary Italians resented the war. They were CONSCRIPTED to fight in a conflict they did not understand, and paid for it through increased taxation. The victory may have reduced criticism from the nationalist Right, but it strengthened the radical Socialists' criticism of Giolitti.

Giolitti had tried to encourage Italians to identify with the state by passing laws to assist them. However, his attempts at social reform were to some extent undermined by the fact that he used the methods of the traditional corrupt politicians, TRASFORMISMO (see page 14). In attempting to stay in office by gaining support from a variety of political groupings he appeared to be just another unprincipled schemer, and even became known as the 'master of the underworld'.

Despite Giolitti's reforms, 1914 saw the worst outbreak of mass unrest since 1898. In June the shooting of three demonstrators sparked off riots or demonstrations in most major cities. Some radicals seized control of government buildings. In 'Red Romagna' (see Chart 1D on page 11) two areas proclaimed themselves independent REPUBLICS. A general strike was called but the various Socialist groups failed to organise their protests effectively. The government used thousands of soldiers to restore order. After a week, unrest subsided. However, 'Red Week', as it became known, had frightened the bourgeoisie, and seemed to show that Giolitti's policy of trying to 'absorb' the workers into the system had failed. However, attention soon turned to international crises as war broke out in Europe. Politically aware Italians became embroiled in the debate over whether Italy should enter the war.

One could argue that Giolitti had pointed the way to what Liberal Italy could do to strengthen its position; others claim that his failure shows how the Liberal regime had still not satisfied key groups. It is clear that Italy's position was finely balanced when the First World War erupted and transformed its future.

■ **Activity**

1 After reading Sources 1.5 and 1.6, draw up a list of points showing

   a) evidence of considerable unity
   b) evidence of little unity.

2 Which historian do you consider to be the more optimistic over Italy's future? Explain your choice.

FOCUS ROUTE

How secure was Liberal Italy by 1914? To assess how strong a modern nation state is, you might consider if it has the following features:

a) Territorial
 • Definite and undisputed national borders

b) International
 • Successful diplomacy supported by military might
 • International respect

c) Political
 • A stable governing system
 • The mass of the population identifying with the state
 • Weak enemies of the state

d) Economic and social
 • A strong and growing economy
 • Social policies satisfying people's needs

e) Cultural
 • A broad intellectual consensus accepting the state
 • A sense of cultural identity

Using pages 19–21, draw up a chart and give Liberal Italy marks out of five as to the extent it had achieved this in each of the five categories. Discuss your response with a partner.

D Review: How secure was Liberal Italy in 1914?

Let us now return to our central theme for this chapter. For Liberal Italy to be on a more secure basis by 1914, you could argue that one vital ingredient would be a greater sense of national unity amongst Italians. Let us first look at two historians' conclusions on this issue, and then see if we can work out how different groups of Italians might have felt in 1914.

Historians' assessments

SOURCE 1.5 M. Clark, *Modern Italy, 1871–1982*, 1984, p. 177

Can we conclude that Italians had been made into a nation state by 1914? Urbanisation and growing literacy were certainly having some effect. 'Italian' had become a lingua franca [a language used for communication among people of different mother tongues] in the army and the towns, and perhaps six or seven million people spoke it (the rest spoke dialects). Most people, too, had gone through some patriotic propaganda at school. A national economy existed, linked by roads and railways. Many institutions – trade unions, CATHOLIC ACTION, newspapers – had become larger ... more national; and some national institutions, e.g. the CARABINIERI, had become fairly popular. Above all the state had existed, for good or ill, for 50 years. People had grown used to it. Even the Church appeared reconciled.

But one should not exaggerate. Nation states are ... very rare beasts indeed, and certainly pre-1914 Italy was not one. There was ... no Liberal hegemony [dominance], no agreement on basic IDEOLOGICAL, educational or social aims. Most people still spoke only dialect; nearly 40 per cent of adults were illiterate. A popular press barely existed. Marconi had invented the wireless in 1896, but as yet there was no broadcasting, no central control of the people's information. The social and economic gap between North and South was all too evident; so too was the chasm between town and country ... Italy was still run by ... a small elite, with little title to rule except its BELLIGERENT patriotism and its historical myths.

SOURCE 1.6 M. Robson, *Italy: Liberalism and Fascism*, 1992, pp. 34–35

Socialists condemned the [Giolitti] regime as a guise for capitalist exploitation of the Italian working classes. Wages were still very low and hours were very long compared with the rest of Western Europe. Welfare benefits such as sickness and pension payments also compared unfavourably. Any benefits in the life of the Italian worker had been wrung out of a state always too willing to use the army to crush strikers and opposing political groups. The wealth of the country had been squandered on imperialist adventures in Ethiopia and Libya. Chronic poverty was still widespread ...

To the nationalists on the Right the regime was equally contemptible. It had lacked the will to make Italy a major force on the European scene. Italian interests had been neglected at Tunis in 1881 and government incompetence had caused a disaster at Adowa in 1896 ... emigration was also a national disgrace ... Liberalism through its weakness had only exacerbated [worsened] the struggle between classes. The state had neither crushed Socialism effectively, nor provided a relevant alternative creed for Italian workers to believe in. Liberalism had never instilled an Italian 'national spirit', not least because its politicians lacked all principle. They were only concerned about their own careers and private interests and they made deals with anyone who could further their selfish aims ...

The Liberals ... were proud of what they had achieved. They had held Italy together for over 40 years, they had sponsored education for the masses, and had presided over industrialisation. Education, military service and economic growth had helped to forge Italians out of the masses who, for generations, had been locked in poverty and superstition, ignorant of anything outside their immediate locality. The task was not complete, and dangers from the far Left and far Right had not disappeared, but most Liberals were not despondent.

■ Activity

1 What did Italians feel about their position by 1914?

Match up statements 1–9 with these Italians in 1914:

a) Southern peasant   b) Northern industrial worker   c) Shopkeeper
d) Futurist painter   e) Nationalist journalist   f) Industrialist
g) Catholic bishop   h) Southern aristocrat   i) Liberal member of Parliament

1 *This Liberal regime is illegitimate and has stolen our territory, but we've got to face reality. I'm concerned about these radical socialist ATHEISTIC ideas, and so we'd better get more involved in the state.*

2 *At last I think we've got a chance of getting somewhere. My union and party have made a difference. You can see the government's frightened, as they're hurrying to give us more crumbs from the cake. But we want a complete redivision of the cake, and they can't stop us for long.*

3 *I've worked hard to get where I am, and I'm proud of my position. If only the government had worked as hard to defend Italy's interests. Instead it seems to be giving more and more concessions to the lazy masses, and encouraging big business to expand, regardless of the effects. Somebody needs to stand up for Italy and honest, hardworking Italians.*

4 *Life is continuing as normal. My peasants occasionally moan, but they can't do much. Life is hard and they must accept that as God's will. I must admit I'm pleasantly surprised how successful this new kingdom has been.*

5 *How long can this go on? We sold out our brothers in Italia Irredenta during the Risorgimento, and these feeble governments have been more concerned with appeasing the masses than really asserting Italy's power. We should be proud of our country. I suppose Libya was something, but I still can't forget Adowa. With tension building in Europe this is our chance to really make a mark on the world scene, but I can't see this spineless lot acting decisively.*

6 *Just when my business is really expanding, the government, instead of helping me, seems to be favouring the masses too much. Look what happened when our factories were occupied. They've got some dangerous new ideas, but I expect the government to follow its traditional policy of acting firmly in defence of property and law and order. This Giolitti's a bit too shifty for my liking.*

7 *Life gets no better. I still wonder whether I'm ever going to be able to support my family properly. I've heard some talk of protest, but I can't see that getting anywhere. Look what happened to old Fabrio when he tried. I could emigrate, but I don't really want to leave my village where my family has always lived. The priest is right, we'll just have to accept God's will, I suppose.*

8 *Whilst not feeling complacent, I think we've done fairly well over the last decade or so. Social reforms are gradually improving the position of the masses, and they can be trusted with more of a say in the country. Balance in all things.*

9 *I'm bored. This government is pathetic; the masses are superstitious and ignorant; the middle classes think of nothing but their pockets. We need action, excitement, some purpose.*

2 Which of these people would have voted for Giolitti in 1914?

3 Who might the others have voted for?

FOCUS ROUTE

Looking back on your work in Chapter 1:

1 Write a paragraph about each of the following failings of Liberal Italy 1870–1914: trasformismo; the gulf between real and legal Italy; Church–state tension; North–South divide; economic and social problems; growth of Socialism; Adowa, Italia Irredenta and assertive foreign policy; impact of Giolitti's reforms; Red Week.

2 Essay: 'To what extent had Liberal Italy satisfied the needs of Italians by 1914?'

■ Activity

Look at this list of four developments in pre-war Italy (D1–4), and the reactions they caused (R1–4). Match them up, and then link them with one of the four aspects of Fascist appeal (A1–4).

Development

D1 Failure of Liberal Italy to live up to Risorgimento expectations
D2 Giolitti's reforms
D3 Masses alienated from state
D4 Economic advance

Reaction

R1 Growth of insecure petty bourgeoisie
R2 Economic elite concerned about losing control of the state
R3 Growth of Socialism
R4 Growth of assertive nationalism

Fascist appeal

A1 End class warfare
A2 Smash Socialism
A3 Establish strong state
A4 Make Italy great

Let us now try and pull together the key issues from this chapter.

Key points from Chapter 1

1 United Italy had been created without involving the mass of the Italian people.
2 Liberal politicians represented a narrow, educated elite, and their quarrelling led to frequent changes of government.
3 Liberal Italy failed to make sufficient social reforms to win the support of the masses. Nationalism remained weak amongst the masses.
4 The powerful Catholic Church remained opposed to the Liberal state.
5 Formal unification failed to overcome the historic North–South divide.
6 When unified, Italy had failed to gain Italia Irredenta.
7 In her search for Great Power status, Italy suffered a humiliating defeat at Adowa in 1896.
8 Giolitti's limited reforms tried but failed to overcome fully Italy's deep-seated problems.
9 Italy was wracked by major crises in the 1890s, and again in 1914.
10 By 1914 the Liberal regime was being challenged by the socialist Left and nationalist Right.

A look ahead

As well as examining how united Liberal Italy had become, we have also been encountering points that help explain the later appeal of Fascism. The activity should help pull these ideas together.

In the 1920s many Italians were to be attracted to Fascism as it offered:

a) to smash Socialism and end class warfare
b) to establish a strong state
c) to make Italy a great power.

You have seen some trends in Italy before the First World War which help explain the appeal of these ideas. Without these developments it is unlikely that Fascism would have become a powerful force. A historian might call these factors PRECONDITIONS for the growth of Fascism.

How great a challenge did the First World War and Socialism pose to the Liberal state?

'Radiant May', 1915 – Italy goes to war!

SOURCE 2.1 King Victor Emmanuel III waves the Italian flag in celebration of Italy's entry into the war, May 1915

SOURCE 2.2 The nationalist poet d'Annunzio, May 1915 (see page 27)

Companions, here is the dawn. Our vigil is over. Our gaiety begins ... After so much wavering the incredible has happened. We shall now fight our war, and blood will flow from the veins of Italy. We are the last to enter the struggle but will be among the first to find glory. Here is the dawn. Let us kiss one another and take leave ...

You may find it amazing that anyone could greet Italy's declaration of war so enthusiastically. However, even if d'Annunzio had had our benefit of hindsight in seeing the mass slaughter the war caused it is unlikely he would have taken a different view. To d'Annunzio and others like him this was an exhilarating moment and an opportunity for Italy to assert itself and at last win glory.

When war broke out in Europe in July 1914 thousands of Italians shared d'Annunzio's excitement, but many others were bitterly opposed. The politically aware classes engaged in heated debate over what Italy should do. A large vocal minority favoured entering the war; most supported joining Britain and France, while a few favoured Italy's ally, Austria. Large crowds of noisy NATIONALISTS held meetings in the piazzas (squares), demanding that Italy join the conflict. Although the majority in Parliament favoured peace, the King and some ministers opened negotiations with both sides, to see who would offer the best terms. In April 1915 the government made the secret Treaty of London with Britain and France (see page 26), and the next month declared war on Austria.

Mussolini later claimed this was the founding moment of Fascism. In Mussolini's mind a group of heroic nationalist Italians, following his lead, had forced a dithering government to act to assert Italy's nationhood.

This chapter considers the extra strains caused by the First World War, both at the time and afterwards, and assesses how these weakened Liberal Italy. It then examines how the fears aroused by the growth of SOCIALISM encouraged the ELITE to support Fascism, and how Socialist weakness helped Mussolini and the Fascists gain power.

CHART 2A CHAPTER OVERVIEW

> **2 How great a challenge did the First World War and Socialism pose to the Liberal state?**
>
> **A** How was Italy affected by the First World War 1914–18? (pp. 23–25)
>
> **B** Why were the post-war years so turbulent? (pp. 26–30)
>
> **C** Could there have been a Socialist revolution in Italy 1919–20? (pp. 31–34)
>
> **D** Review: How great a challenge did the First World War and Socialism pose to the Liberal state? (p. 35)

A How was Italy affected by the First World War 1914–18?

■ **Talking point**

What did Trotsky mean? Can you think of other examples to support his assertion?

'War is the locomotive of history.' Trotsky's description was certainly true in Italy at this time. The all-pervading effects of the First World War were to open up new opportunities and experiences, and generate new ambitions and fears among sections of the community. The war was to divide Italy deeply, to lead Mussolini to break with his socialist past, and to create the conditions which allowed the Fascists to gain power.

The mass MOBILISATION of twentieth-century warfare ensured that nearly everyone in Italy was affected in one way or another by involvement in the war. At the front we can find groups who gloried in warfare and the new-found camaraderie of the trenches (trincerismo); others suffered demoralisation and mutilation. On the Home Front some people were to make financial gains from the war, while others were left feeling exploited.

Two key battles

When you think of the First World War, you think of the horror of the trenches on the Western Front, and perhaps the fighting on the Eastern Front in Russia. But there was also a Southern Front, where Italy faced Austria for three years. For most of that time, this was a stalemate, but there were two key battles that influenced Italy's history.

In October 1917 Italy suffered a major defeat at Caporetto, partly attributed to low morale. The government responded by promising major reforms when the war was over. So expectations were raised.

In October 1918, when the Austro-Hungarian Empire was on the verge of disintegration, Italy won a victory at Vittorio Veneto. It was a far smaller battle than Caporetto, but Italians remembered this victory rather than the defeat, and considered they deserved major rewards for their success. So, once again, expectations were raised.

■ **Activity**

1 Write out a list, from the choices below, of those developments which you think might have occurred during the war. Check your responses when you discover what actually happened (see pages 23–25).

   Consider whether any of these developments would be affected by whether the war was going well or badly.

Political developments
a) Increased power for the King and government
b) Greater role for Parliament debating issues
c) Upsurge in nationalism
d) Increase in strikes and discontent
e) Major social reforms
f) Government promises of reforms once the war is over

Economic and social developments
a) Growth of heavy industry
b) Expansion of small, luxury trades
c) Increased taxation
d) Falling government debt
e) Inflation
f) Increased foreign trade
g) Increased unemployment
h) Increased demand for labour
i) Women gaining more opportunities
j) Closer ties between the state and big business
k) Increased wages (in real terms)
l) Growth in trade unionism

Now read pages 23–25 about Italy's experience of war.

2 'Italy made a major contribution to the war.'
  'Italy's performance in the war was embarrassing.'
  As you work through this section, note down evidence that supports each of these statements.

The soldiers

Most of the soldiers were southern peasant CONSCRIPTS who did not understand why the war was being fought. Most skilled industrial workers were required to stay in their factories to produce war equipment. Soldiers were bitter about the 'shirkers' left at home. Low rations (600 grams bread, 250 grams meat, and 150 grams of pasta a day), low pay (½ lira a day to each soldier, and the same to his family), and the lack of modern equipment undermined morale. Thousands were killed by cholera, typhus and frostbite.

SOURCE 2.3 FUTURISTS at war. Futurists like Marinetti (seen here standing on the left) welcomed the war: 'We glorify war as the sole hygiene of the world … the world needs only heroism … an aesthetic [theory of beauty] of violence and blood'

SOURCE 2.4 Police with captured deserters. Around 290,000 soldiers were court-martialled, 4000 sentenced to death, and 750 shot

CHART 2B   Italy at war 1915–18

Summary of the war effort

Military
- Five million conscripted
- Generally trench stalemate
- Eleven offensives in two and a half years
- Maximum advance twelve miles
- 600,000 Italians killed
- 1,000,000 wounded

Political
- Government powers increased
- Parliament was just a rubber stamp
- Close state–industry links
- Caporetto led to reorganisation and promise of major social reforms
- PSI advocated 'neither support nor sabotage'
- Pope criticised 'useless slaughter'

Economic
- State spent 148 billion lire
- National debt
   1914 16 billion lire
   1919 85 billion lire
- Price index 1914 = 100
                1918 = 413
Major industries saw massive expansion, e.g. Fiat, Ansaldo (steel)

Social
- Strict discipline in war industries
- Long hours: up to 75 hours a week
- Increased employment of women
- Real wages fell approximately 25%
- Rents frozen
- Some peasants paid off debts
- Bread riots, Summer 1917: 50 killed

SOURCE 2.5 Mussolini on trincerismo (the camaraderie of the trenches)
The war had taught us one lesson, the great community of the front. All class differences disappeared under its spell. There was only one people, no individuals. Common suffering and common peril had welded us together.

Timeline of the war

August	1914	Great Powers go to war. Italy remains neutral.
May	1915	Italy joins war on the side of the Allies.
October	1917	Italian army badly defeated at Caporetto
October	1918	Italians triumph over the exhausted Austrians at Vittorio Veneto.
November	1918	Armistice signed
September	1919	Peace terms with Austria finalised at the Treaty of St Germain

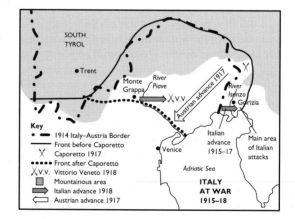

Comparative war costs

Country	Total mobilised forces (millions)	Deaths
Italy	5.6m	600,000
France	8.2m	1,500,000
British Empire	9.5m	1,000,000
Russia	13.0m	1,700,000
USA	3.8m	116,000
Germany	13.2m	1,950,000
Austria–Hungary	9.0m	1,050,000
Turkey	2.8m	325,000

The General

General Cadorna

General Cadorna was the autocratic, stubborn leader of the Italian army from 1915 to 1917. He implemented a series of massed infantry attacks against entrenched positions and ordered that not a yard gained should be given up. Cadorna was scornful of the soldiers' welfare. He sacked 217 generals; banned politicians from the war zone; and blamed failings on the weak government and its toleration of subversives (people plotting to overthrow the government). He was sacked after the defeat at Caporetto.

Historians assess the impact of the war

SOURCE 2.6   P. Morgan, *Italian Fascism 1919–45*, 1995, p. 7

Italy's involvement in the First World War was the first great collective and national experience for literally millions of Italians, especially the largely peasant conscript army. But, partly because of the imperfect nation forming since unification, and partly because of the way Italy entered the war in 1915 and the way the war was conducted, the Great War did not bring about national integration and unity. There was no ... temporary national and political truce for the duration of the war. Italy's wartime experience was extremely divisive; it increased popular alienation from the LIBERAL parliamentary state while heightening expectations of transforming it. Italy's national war was 'waged in an atmosphere of civil war'.

SOURCE 2.7   Clark, p. 200

The Italians had been divided before, but by November 1919 they were more divided than ever: 'combatants' against 'shirkers', peasants against workers, patriots against defeatists. No conceivable form of government could suit them all.

The war left other major legacies. They included a thirst for justice ('land for the peasants') and a transformed industrial economy. The war also produced tens of thousands of new officers, drunk with patriotism and greedy to command. They had won the war, and did not intend to let anyone forget it.

SOURCE 2.8   D. Mack Smith, *Italy, A Modern History*, 1969, p. 313

The final figure for the cost of the whole war had been 148 billion lire, that is to say twice the sum of all government expenditure between 1861 and 1913.

This total is a symbol for an enormous consumption of energy and natural resources, in return for which Italy obtained little joy and much grief. A great deal of idealism had gone into the war on Italy's part, and much elevated patriotism, but one need not look many years beyond 1918 to see that it had been one of the great disasters of her history. [As a result] Italy suffered 25 years of revolution and tyranny.

SOURCE 2.9   M. Blinkhorn, *Mussolini and Fascist Italy*, 1984, p. 9

War also brought profound changes to Italy herself. Most significant was the rapid growth and increased concentration of those industries most closely linked with war production: metallurgy, engineering, shipbuilding and automobiles. Any suggestion of a lasting boom was nevertheless misleading, for Italy's war machine consumed industrial products of a kind and at a rate no peacetime economy was likely to match. A distorted economy potentially short of raw materials, export outlets and a healthy domestic market was a sure recipe for post-war difficulties. Returning soldiers likely then to be the sufferers would scarcely be mollified [feel calmed or compensated] by the sight of those who had got rich while they were at the front: not only financial and industrial profiteers but also ambitious peasants who had seized opportunities to buy more land. Meanwhile the political situation looked more and more discouraging ... To many Italians, Liberal government was coming to seem ineffectual and irrelevant.

FOCUS ROUTE

1 Using pages 23–25, write a summary of the main effects of the war on Italy 1914–18. Classify your notes under these headings: military, political, economic and social.

2 This section opened with d'Annunzio's view of the 'new dawn'. Marinetti and Mussolini remained enthusiasts for war (see Sources 2.3 and 2.5). Other soldiers hated their experience of it. How can these differences be explained?

■ Learning trouble spot

Which peace treaty? What did Italy gain?

Two aspects of the peace treaty often confuse students. First there is the problem of names! The various treaties were named after the chateaux outside Paris where the negotiations took place. The peace treaty most affecting Italy was called the Treaty of St Germain and was signed with Austria on 10 September 1919. Consequently you would be wrong to refer to the Versailles 'Treaty', when discussing Italy's concerns. It would, however, be all right to refer to the Versailles 'Settlement' because this term covers all the treaties signed at the end of the war.

More significantly, students often think that Italy did not receive Italia Irredenta at the peace settlement because so much emphasis is placed on the 'mutilated' victory. A glance at the map (Source 2.10) shows that all of Italy's nationalist claims to Italia Irredenta were met, as it gained Trentino, South Tyrol and Istria. In fact, Italy got more than was strictly justified on nationalist grounds. Around 200,000 German-speaking Austrians now lived in land ruled by Italy. The principle of self-determination did not apply to them, partly, it seems, because they belonged to a defeated power, but also in order to give Italy the security of the natural frontier of the Brenner Pass. Italy also gained 250,000 Slavs in the mixed territory of Istria.

Despite these gains, most Italians felt bitter, as they had not gained what had been promised in the Treaty of London. This was partly because Dalmatia was now claimed by the new Yugoslav state, which was justified on the grounds of self-determination.

Most historians consider that in the circumstances Italy got fair rewards at the peace conference, but what matters is how people felt at the time. Millions of Italians considered Italy had been cheated.

B | Why were the post-war years so turbulent?

The end of the war brought no respite for Liberal Italy. The regime was soon beset with difficulties from all sides. You can find tasks to guide you through this section in the Focus Route on page 30.

Was Italy's victory in the First World War 'mutilated'?

Italy was on the winning side in the First World War. However, one of the great claims of the Fascist movement was to be that the government mishandled the war and then 'lost' the peace. How true was this claim?

In 1915 Italy had been secretly promised major territorial gains, mainly at the expense of the then Austro-Hungarian Empire. However, this was during the era of secret diplomacy and Great Power land grabbing. By 1919 the world had changed. The United States had entered the war in 1917 and saw it as a struggle for DEMOCRACY. Europe was to be rebuilt using President Wilson's FOURTEEN POINTS, the most important of which was national self-determination.

Italy was thwarted in some of its territorial and colonial ambitions. During the peace negotiations the Prime Minister Orlando walked out in protest at the terms offered to Italy. It had no effect, and after the final peace settlement the Liberal government was saddled with the blame for the 'mutilated victory'. Many Italians now felt another grievance at their limited rewards for their 600,000 war dead, massive debts and a huge increase in the cost of living.

SOURCE 2.10 Italy's territorial gains

Key

—— North-east boundary of Italy in 1914

- - - Boundary in 1919

CHART 2C | Italy and the peace settlement

What Italy claimed	Promised at Treaty of London, May 1915?	Did Italy receive it in the St Germain Treaty, 1919?
South Tyrol	yes	yes
Trentino	yes	yes
Istria	yes	yes
Fiume	no	no
Dalmatia	yes	no
Colonies	yes	no

27

HOW GREAT A CHALLENGE DID THE FIRST WORLD WAR AND SOCIALISM POSE TO THE LIBERAL STATE?

Gabriele d'Annunzio

Gabriele d'Annunzio, 1863–1938

- As a student he wrote poems and novels
- 1897 he was elected as an extreme RIGHT-WING candidate
- 1900 he briefly joined the extreme LEFT WING of the PSI, then he became a nationalist
- 1914–15 powerful INTERVENTIONIST speaker
- Volunteered for army aged 52
- August 1918 he dropped leaflets from plane over Vienna
- 1922 Possible rival nationalist leader; after Mussolini's appointment, he concentrated on writing
- 1937 he was made President of Royal Academy of Arts

What did d'Annunzio and Fiume give to Fascism?

- Heroic speeches to mass audiences from his balcony
- Rhythmic war cries, which were often incomprehensible, e.g. Eja, Eja, Alala
- His followers wore blackshirts, adopted the skull and cross-bones, and used castor oil to humiliate opponents (see page 51)
- The Roman straight-arm salute
- The song 'Giovinezza' ('Youth')
- Plans for a new organisation of all producers in a corporative state (see page 135)
- Spoke of 'our Mediterranean', and 'Italy or Death'
- Discussed a march on Rome
- Overall, d'Annunzio put on a great display, and made great claims for his mini-state; much of this was make-believe

How significant was d'Annunzio's occupation of Fiume?

The failure of the Italian government to gain Italy's expected rewards was highlighted by dramatic events that occurred at the Adriatic port of Fiume. Italy claimed the city, but was not granted it. The nationalist poet d'Annunzio seized Fiume and ruled it for a year. D'Annunzio's seizure of Fiume is a potentially confusing incident which is often given a lot of stress, but it can also be seen as an eccentric side-show. Was it really significant?

The events

Fiume was a major Adriatic port. Until 1919 it was part of the Austro-Hungarian Empire. The majority of its inhabitants were Italian, but the suburbs and hinterland were mainly Croat. It had not been mentioned in the Treaty of London. After the war was won, Italian nationalists clamoured for the port to be part of Italy, but in 1918 it was occupied by Allied troops. The Italian government failed to gain Fiume at the Versailles Settlement. It became an illustration of what d'Annunzio described as the 'mutilated victory'.

In September 1919 d'Annunzio, at the head of 300 ex-soldiers, seized control of the city. The Allied troops left, although some Italian troops who supported d'Annunzio remained. The Italian government did nothing, reinforcing the image of both its weakness, and its willingness to submit to violence. D'Annunzio theatrically kissed the Italian flag and proclaimed: 'In this mad, vile world, Fiume is the symbol of liberty.' His new state has been described by the historian Mitchell as a 'mixture of MANIFESTOS, harangues, fireworks, pageants, military concerts and overstretched nerves'. It was a true 'theatre of revolution', but one probably not appreciated by the locals!

For a time it had seemed as if d'Annunzio might exploit his position to seize power in Rome. However, in December 1920 Giolitti's new government decided to reassert its authority, and sent in troops. D'Annunzio and his veterans fled (fearing either shells or an influenza epidemic that was raging) and the Italian army quickly took command. It had previously agreed with Yugoslavia that Fiume should be an international free city. Fiume remained under international supervision until Mussolini took it over in 1923.

The Fiume incident showed that force could be used to try and achieve political aims in post-war Italy. The government's inadequacy was shown as it took over a year to respond to d'Annunzio's COUP. In addition, Italians could contrast d'Annunzio's vigorous action to defend Italy's interests with the government's apparently inadequate performance at the peace conference. In the end, perhaps d'Annunzio's chief significance was as an inspirer of many of the features, both of IDEOLOGY and symbols, of Fascist Italy.

D'Annunzio: a potential rival to Mussolini?

Until 1922 d'Annunzio was a far more famous leader than Mussolini, and the latter considered him a rival. He was a nationalist poet, who glorified Italy's past, and condemned its existing political system as 'a heap of filth which cannot even serve to manure the nation's cabbages'. During the war, despite being over 50, he had led heroic air raids, and lost an eye. His fame peaked as Commander of Fiume, and for a time he considered marching on Rome to overthrow the decadent (decaying and corrupt) parliamentary system.

With his retreat from Fiume his prestige fell, but he remained a dangerous rival. He had criticised Mussolini for his lukewarm support over Fiume, and told his followers not to join 'thug Fascism'. Many, however, still did. In the Autumn of 1922 various politicians contacted him asking that he join a national government. Mussolini was worried about him as a possible rival. In October 1922 d'Annunzio conveniently 'fell' from a balcony, so he was out of action for some time. Mussolini gained power first. From then on, there was room for only one nationalist DEMAGOGUE and d'Annunzio became Italy's 'lost leader'.

Why was there an economic and political crisis in post-war Italy?

SOURCE 2.11 D'Annunzio, speaking in 1919

Whatever happens, one thing is certain after the war. The future will bring something quite new to us, such as we have never seen before. Something stronger, more beautiful, will be born from this blood and sacrifice. All forms of art and politics will be overthrown; the new ones will be healthier. I believe we are entering a new era.

D'Annunzio's comment (Source 2.11) reflected a widespread desire in post-war Italy for a new beginning, but which way would such a divided society turn? The Italians had been divided before the war. The debate over whether to join, and then the experience of war 1915–18 had created further divisions. Government promises to help rally the nation after the humiliation of Caporetto had aroused great expectations of a better life, which it would be difficult to fulfil. The hopes of nationalists for major territorial gains were also dashed, leaving considerable bitterness. The war also produced tens of thousands of new officers, who were determined to assert themselves. They believed *they* had won the war, and did not intend to let anyone forget it. Some soldiers found it hard to settle down after the war. They felt the task of making Italy great was unfinished and were scornful of many of their compatriots who had not played a positive role in the war. They missed the comradeship of the trenches and some formed themselves into squads to fulfil their desire for action. Many were to be drawn into Fascism.

The Liberal regime was under attack from the Left as well as the Right. The Soviet Revolution in Russia inspired many Socialists. Workers, determined to improve their position, launched a series of strikes, whilst returning peasant soldiers seized unoccupied land. Socialists made major gains in local and national elections. The government made concessions, but this upset those on the Right, without stemming the unrest.

There were also severe economic problems. Heavy industry was hit by the end of major war orders, and the demobilisation of over two million soldiers put added strains on the economy. Continuing inflation undermined many people's living standards.

Whereas unions were able to force increased wages, and many industrialists benefited from higher prices, the PETTY BOURGEOISIE were particularly badly affected. The self-employed had no muscle to press for higher income. Those who had lent money to the government during the war found the value of their savings hit by inflation, and became especially bitter.

CHART 2D   **Summary of the post-war turmoil**

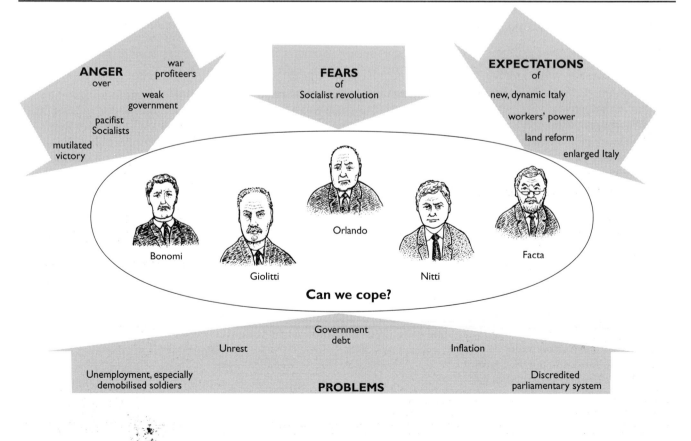

THE ADVANCE OF SOCIALISM

① Growth of **unions** 1919–20 wave of **strikes** in industry, agriculture

② **Factory occupations**
- Aug–Sept 1920 over 300 factories occupied

③ **Land occupations**
- 1919–20 returning ex-soldiers occupied uncultivated land, and some landlords' land. Government legalised these occupations. 1918–21 over 1m hectares transferred to peasants

④ **Socialist power in the agricultural economy**
- In Emilia-Romagna, powerful Socialist agricultural union (Federterra), labour exchanges and Chambers of Labour developed (see page 32)
- 1920 wave of strikes forced employers to improve workers' terms

⑤ **PSI success in local elections**
- November 1920 PSI won control of 2162 of 8059 communes, and 25 of 69 provinces, mainly in North and Centre

⑥ **Successful Russian Revolution**
- 1917 Soviet Revolution helped inspire many socialists
- 1919 strikes in solidarity with Soviet Russia

THE FASCIST REACTION

⑦ **Growth of Fascism**
- Founded in Milan, March 1919
- Cities taken over by Fascists, October 1922
- March on Rome, October 1922

⑧ **Civil War: Socialists v Fascists**
- 1919–22 violent clashes between Fascists and Socialists; over 2000 killed

TERRITORIAL PROBLEMS

⑨ **'Mutilated' victory**
- Italy failed to gain Dalmatia and Fiume
- No colonies in Africa, Middle East, Dalmatia

⑩ **Fiume** (see page 27)
- Nationalist d'Annunzio seized control 1919

ECONOMIC PROBLEMS
- Rising unemployment from 1920 as 2.5m soldiers demobilised, and industry hit by post-war recession 1920–21
- National debt in 1918 was 85 billion lire (1914 was 16 billion)
- Wartime inflation continued:
  1913 price index 100
  1918   413
  1920   591

GENERAL SITUATION
- Great hopes and fears
- Disillusionment, and hostility towards war profiteers
- Flu epidemic, killed nearly as many as the war

GOVERNMENT
- Weak Liberal governments continued in Rome. Failure of PSI and PPI to co-operate meant return to trasformismo-style politics
- Prime Ministers 1918–22
  Orlando   Oct 1917–June 1919
  Nitti   June 1919–June 1920
  Giolitti   June 1920–July 1921
  Bonomi   July 1921–Feb 1922
  Facta   Feb–Oct 1922

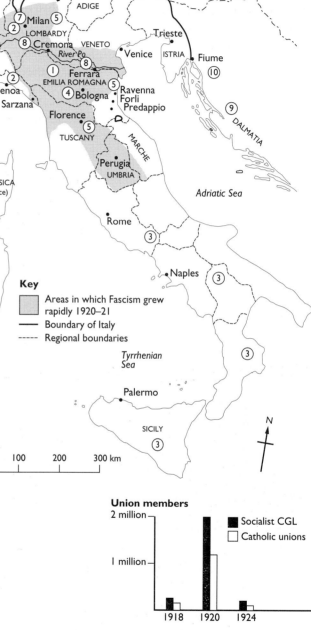

Key

▨ Areas in which Fascism grew rapidly 1920–21

— Boundary of Italy

---- Regional boundaries

GOVERNMENT REACTION TO PROBLEMS	
Problem	**Government reaction**
Modest gains at Versailles	→ Walked out of Treaty negotiations
D'Annunzio seizure of Fiume	→ Did nothing
Food riots	→ Set up commission and authorised price cuts
Land occupations	→ Legalised them
Factory occupations	→ Promised reforms
Powerful labour exchanges	→ Officially recognised and given state subsidies

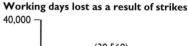

Union members

- Socialist CGL
- Catholic unions

2 million

1 million

1918 1920 1924

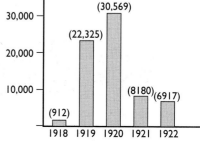

Working days lost as a result of strikes

40,000

30,000 — (30,569)

(22,325)

20,000

10,000 — (8180) (6917)

(912)

1918 1919 1920 1921 1922

30

HOW GREAT A CHALLENGE DID THE FIRST WORLD WAR AND SOCIALISM POSE TO THE LIBERAL STATE?

Were the 1919 elections a lost opportunity?

Some political developments seemed to offer hope for the future. A real opportunity existed in 1918 to strengthen the Liberal system by making it more democratic and susceptible to public opinion. There were key changes in the electoral system and the development of new political parties. In 1918 full universal male SUFFRAGE and a new system of PROPORTIONAL REPRESENTATION was introduced. A new party, the Popolari, approved by the Pope but independent of Church control, was set up representing Catholic views. The effect of these changes was that for the first time the Italian Parliament might reflect the views of the whole of (male) Italy.

The two mass parties, the Socialists (PSI) and Catholic Popolari (PPI), did well in the 1919 elections (see Chart 2F). It is extraordinary to those used to democratic systems that the election results you see displayed in the pie chart led to neither the PSI nor the PPI playing a role in government. Had they co-operated they could have had a majority in Parliament. However, they did not. Before the war Giolitti failed to gain the co-operation of both moderate Catholic and Socialist opinion, and this did not change. The Popolari were split between reformers and conservatives, and the Socialists between reformers and revolutionaries. The extreme wings could not co-operate.

CHART 2F   Election results, 1913, 1919 and 1921

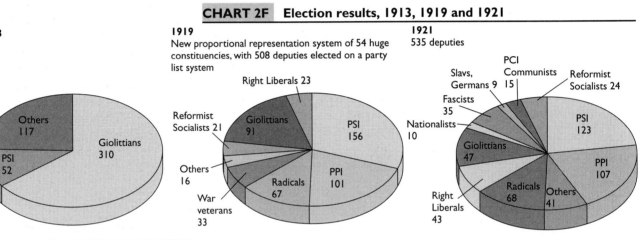

1913

1919
New proportional representation system of 54 huge constituencies, with 508 deputies elected on a party list system

1921
535 deputies

In the absence of agreement between the two mass parties, the old Liberal politicians remained in power, cobbling together enough support in Parliament to form five brief governments between 1918 and 1922. It was TRASFORMISMO again, not democracy. Such governments were largely unrepresentative of opinion in Parliament and in the country. Only if they achieved some outstanding successes would they gain credibility and consolidate the Liberal regime. The government did pass various measures to try to help the masses, such as bread subsidies and the eight-hour day, and began to make the tax system fairer. But once again these reforms did not satisfy RADICALS, and worried some of the elite. Generally, the succession of weak Liberal governments failed to solve Italy's social, economic and political problems (see Chart 2E).

Italy's post-war turmoil and the ineffectiveness of the governments in dealing with its problems gave an opportunity to radical forces on the Right and Left. Would any of these groups be able to take the opportunity?

CHART 2G   Divided Italy

Pre-war divisions		Post-war divisions
Class Regional Political	**WAR**	Class Regional Political INTERVENTIONISTS v NEUTRALISTS Financial gainers v losers

C Could there have been a Socialist revolution in Italy 1919–20?

CHART 2H The Socialist challenge

Municipal Socialism	Parliament 1919
• Control of northern and central local government	• 156 PSI deputies

The Socialist challenge

Soviet Revolution in Russia, 1917
• Communist International, 1919

Power in the countryside	Industrial struggle
• Labour exchanges	• Strikes
• Federterra	• Occupations

'Is this Italy or Russia?' remarked one landowner in post-war Italy. One can understand his concern as he walked around Cremona. He would have seen red flags flying over town halls, postage stamps showing the hammer and sickle, and Socialists making blood-curdling speeches about revolution.

In 1920 the PSI, the Italian Socialist Party, won elections to many town councils and so controlled local taxes and services. It claimed over 200,000 members, and its paper *Avanti!* was read by over 300,000. Italy was swept by a wave of strikes. Was the country close to a Socialist revolution? Many politicians and members of the elite thought so during the Biennio Rosso ('Two Red Years') of 1919–20 – but how dangerous was the threat from the Left?

Even if you decide that the danger was not great, that does not mean that the Biennio Rosso was not important. It can be argued that Italian Socialists played a major role in the success of their bitter enemies, the Fascists. The threat of Socialist revolution drove many of the elite to support Fascism, and the Socialists' weakness helped the Fascists come to power.

Let us now examine Italian Socialism; you will learn about a moment in history when what people *thought* was true was more important than the reality. Use the chart below to help organise your ideas about whether a Socialist revolution was likely.

■ Talking point

Can you think of another historical example of what people *thought* was happening being more significant than what was actually happening?

FOCUS ROUTE

Complete an assessment chart on Italian Socialism like the one below. In each box:
a) note the key features
b) put a tick if this made revolution likely or a cross if it made it unlikely.

Programme	Leaders
Support	**Divisions/Rivals**
Attitude of elite	**Effect of war on Socialism**
Actions/Strategy	**Other points**
CONCLUSION: Could there have been a Socialist revolution in Italy?	

32

HOW GREAT A CHALLENGE DID THE FIRST WORLD WAR AND SOCIALISM POSE TO THE LIBERAL STATE?

Italian Socialism

1 **Maximalists:** revolutionaries controlling the party versus
2 **Minimalists:** moderate MPs for parliamentary reform
3 **Communists:** formed own party in 1921

■ **Talking point**

What do you think Marx meant when he described religion as the opium of the masses? Can anything now be seen as serving this function?

How well organised were the Socialists?

The Socialists' difficulties began with their programme, which was uncompromising. They pronounced themselves a MARXIST party, aiming for a Socialist REPUBLIC. Thus they spoke of the eventual withering away of the state, after a period of DICTATORSHIP of the PROLETARIAT. There would be workers' control of industry, and the NATIONALISATION of all land. Religion, described by Marx as the opium of the masses in CAPITALIST societies, would no longer be needed and would wither away in their new socialist society.

However, although the party officially stood united behind this programme, it was deeply split between Maximalists and Minimalists. Maximalists, who controlled the party organisation, urged revolution to enact their full programme. Minimalists, who dominated the parliamentary party, were more prepared to use Parliament to enact reforms on the way to full Socialism. In January 1921 the PSI split into three. An even more radical group, prepared to join the Communist International on Lenin's terms, broke away from the Maximalists to form the Communist Party, PCI.

Matters were further complicated by the fact that alongside the divided Socialist party, there was also an industrial wing, with unions combined in the General Confederation of Labour (CGL). These also organised Chambers of Labour, and Socialist Leagues to protect workers' interests. Socialist support was challenged by rival Catholic unions, organised in the CIL (Italian Confederation of Workers).

The PSI controlled many local councils (see Chart 2E), but these failed to co-operate. The three main wings of the Socialist movement (the national PSI, Socialist unions, and Socialist councils) were all internally divided, and failed to work together effectively. Perhaps a powerful leader could have overcome these problems, but one of their potentially most effective leaders, Mussolini, had been expelled in 1914. They had a series of worthy leaders, such as Turati and Bissolati, but no one who could unite a majority.

The PSI looked set to pose the greatest threat to the Liberal state after the 1919 elections (see Chart 2F), either through a legal challenge or through revolution. Their prospects for power looked good, but they failed to agree a coherent strategy. The Socialists benefited from the pressure for change after the war, but also frightened many Italians. Farmers, manufacturers, landlords, professional men, shopkeepers and tradesmen felt under attack from the MUNICIPAL 'Dictatorships of the Proletariat'.

Many patriots already harboured a grudge against the Socialists because of their neutral 'neither support nor sabotage' position during the war. When the war was over, many returning soldiers (peasants and workers) felt bitter about the PSI. They resented how many Socialists had stayed working for higher wages in factories, whilst they had risked their lives at the front. The war thus split groups, most of whom might otherwise have been Socialist supporters.

What strategies did the Socialists adopt?

In the important rural areas there were significant developments too. The South was where the PSI was weak, but land occupations were taking place, organised by Catholic land leagues. In the more commercialised Po Valley, the Socialist agricultural unions of the Federterra were not only making the traditional economic demands on wages and hours, but were also looking to control the supply of labour and employment: in effect, challenging the owners' property rights and right to manage. The Federterra aimed to gain MONOPOLY control over the labour supply, to force employers to employ their workers, even during winter months. The Socialist unions were prepared to use violence against any employer using BLACKLEG labour. They also intimidated peasants and labourers who would not co-operate with their pressure tactics on employers. Some of these victims of Socialist strong-arm methods later supported Fascism.

The increased power and membership of unions encouraged a series of strikes in 1919–20. However, some workers went beyond using this traditional form of struggle. In September 1920 half a million workers in Turin and Milan responded to a LOCKOUT threat by occupying over 300 factories, and running

33

HOW GREAT A CHALLENGE DID THE FIRST WORLD WAR AND SOCIALISM POSE TO THE LIBERAL STATE?

SOURCE 2.12 Socialist Red Guards during the occupation of the factories, September 1920

SOURCE 2.13 Postcard advertising a Socialist meeting, 1904

■ **Activity**

1 What did the landowner mean when he asked (page 31) 'Is this Italy or Russia?'

2 How does Source 2.13 help to explain the Church's hostility to Socialism?

3 Would all Socialists have agreed with the writer of Source 2.14?

4 Malatesta (Source 2.15) was:
   a) correctly analysing Socialist weaknesses
   b) trying to provoke the Socialists into action
   c) correctly predicting the future.
   Which of these statements is correct?

5 Why, according to Source 2.16, was there no revolution?

6 Hold a debate in summer 1922 between a frightened industrialist who sees Socialism as a major threat, and a radical journalist who argues that the Socialists are too weak to have any chance of gaining power.

them for a month without the involvement of the bourgeoisie. Red flags flew, and armed workers protected 'their' factories. Some saw this as the first step to revolution; others saw it as a means to gain concessions.

Much to the annoyance of the employers, Prime Minister Giolitti took a conciliatory approach. After three weeks, supplies of raw materials and money were low. Eventually both sides accepted government mediation. After promises of reform, the workers withdrew. This turned out to be the peak of Socialist unrest because the onset of mass unemployment weakened the Socialist movement. After 1920 the number of strikes fell. An attempted general strike in August 1922, in protest against Fascist violence, fizzled out after 24 hours, partly put down by the Fascists themselves.

The PSI had talked revolution but had had no strategy for achieving it. The party proved to be incapable of carrying out either reform or revolution. Workers became disillusioned after the Biennio Rosso. However, the whole period had created a traumatic fear of 'BOLSHEVISM' among groups who had most to fear from it. This situation was to be skilfully exploited by Mussolini and the Fascists, who attacked the Socialists. The 'revolution of words' was about to be drowned in a 'revolution of blood'. The Fascists later claimed that they had saved Italy from Bolshevism, but with hindsight historians can see that the main danger of Socialist revolution was over before the Fascists grew strong.

SOURCE 2.14 Bologna PSI Congress, 1921

The proletariat must have recourse to violence for the conquest of power over the bourgeoisie ... The existing institutions of local and national government cannot in any way be transformed into organs which will help to liberate the people. Instead we must use new and proletarian organisations such as workers' soviets.

SOURCE 2.15 The anarchist Malatesta

If we let the right moment slip we will pay with tears of blood for the fright we have given the bourgeoisie.

SOURCE 2.16 Major northern newspaper, *Corriere della Sera*, September 1920

Italy has been in peril of collapse. There has been no revolution, not because there was anyone to bar its way, but because the General Confederation of Labour has not wished it.

■ **Activity**

1 Read Source 2.17.
   a) Summarise in a sentence the author's views of the Socialist threat.
   b) What evidence does he use to support his views?
2 Repeat question 1 for Source 2.18.
3 How did the Socialists make it easier for Mussolini to take power?

Historians and the Socialist revolution

SOURCE 2.17   A. Cassels, *Fascist Italy*, 1969, pp. 24–25

The threat of Bolshevism was exploited cunningly by Mussolini and it is difficult to overestimate its importance in bringing Fascism to power. Yet in truth, the threat in Italy was almost entirely illusory. No master plan of revolution existed; peasants and workers acted without premeditation and on a local basis only. Even during the occupation of the factories, when a pattern of action seemed to emerge, there was no real co-operation between the strikers in one town and those in the next. The Socialist Party signally failed to provide a national organisation to take advantage of the working-class distress. Whenever the PSI called for a general strike, which it did more than once between 1919 and 1922, the response was half-hearted and far from revolutionary. The Socialist leaders spent too much energy quarrelling among themselves, which led Lenin to dub the whole Italian proletarian movement as too immature for revolution, so no direction was forthcoming from Moscow. Furthermore, lower-class disorders and revolutionary sentiment waxed [grew] and waned [declined] in accord with fluctuations of the Italian economy. Hence, the danger years were 1919 and 1920. By the last quarter of 1921, the worst of the post war depression was past; so was the worst of proletarian unrest. By the time, a year later, that Mussolini arrived in office to save Italy from Bolshevism, the threat, if it ever existed, was gone.

SOURCE 2.18   Mack Smith 1969, pp. 327–28

Italy's misfortune was that Socialism lacked responsible leadership, and from the benches of the Left hardly a single constructive step was proposed which went beyond the vaguest generalisation. The only constant factor among the Socialists was their association of violent language with a timid uncertainty in deed. They refused to collaborate against Fascism with the governments, and in so doing they made a right-wing victory almost inevitable. Yet they had little idea of effecting a Communist revolution on their own. They simply sat back under the cosy illusion that time was on their side and that universal suffrage inevitably signified the approaching end of Liberalism and the dictatorship of the proletariat . . .

Despite their great number, despite the sporadic general strikes and local peasant revolts, the Italian Socialists were just waiting for the bourgeois state to fall into their lap instead of trying to coerce [force] events . . . With the expulsion of the SYNDICALISTS and Mussolini they had lost much of their revolutionary zeal . . .

One must conclude that Socialism did not believe wholeheartedly in either revolution or collaboration, and hence it was merely going to provoke Fascism and antagonise all straightforward patriots, without taking the only sort of action which could defend Italy against the inevitable counterattack from the Right.

35

HOW GREAT A CHALLENGE DID THE FIRST WORLD WAR AND SOCIALISM POSE TO THE LIBERAL STATE?

D # Review: How great a challenge did the First World War and Socialism pose to the Liberal state?

You have now studied how the First World War increased divisions and discontent in Liberal Italy, and led to a period of great social unrest and political instability. The Liberal regime faced a major threat from a potentially powerful but essentially disorganised socialist movement. This was too weak to gain power, but sufficiently strong to arouse great fears.

°FOCUS ROUTE

Look back at your work in Chapter 2 and explain the impact of each of the following on the Liberal state.

a) The 'mutilated victory'
b) Fiume
c) Economic developments, during and after the war
d) The 1919 elections
e) Socialism

Key points from Chapter 2

1 Italy was divided over whether to enter the war.
2 Some Italians profited and others suffered from the war.
3 During the war great expectations were raised of social reform and territorial gains.
4 There was great anger over the so-called 'mutilated victory'.
5 D'Annunzio in Fiume anticipated many aspects of Fascism.
6 The war left severe economic problems.
7 In 1919 the mass parties (PPI and PSI) gained a majority in the elections but did not form a government.
8 A series of Liberal governments struggled to cope with mounting problems 1919–22.
9 There was a wave of post-war Socialist-inspired unrest.
10 The Socialists raised great hopes but failed to take their opportunities, and just frightened the elite.

■ **Activity**

In the context of Italy in 1920, a wide variety of people might find aspects of Fascism attractive. Explain how each of the following might be attracted to Fascism, either through fear of the alternative or through positive attraction.

a) A demobilised officer
b) An industrialist
c) A small landholder
d) A large rural landowner
e) A Catholic bishop
f) A Futurist

A look ahead

It was within this context of continued Liberal weakness, post-war discontent and the growth of socialism that Fascism was to develop.

Remind yourself of the main features of Fascism (Chart 2I). These should suggest why it was able to gain support.

CHART 2I **What is Fascism?**

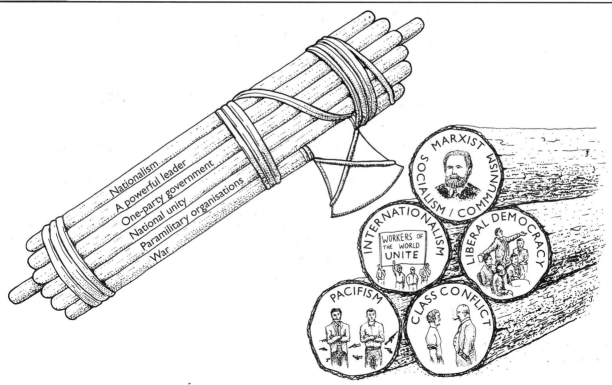

Why was Mussolini, the Fascist leader, appointed Prime Minister of Italy in 1922?

In 1922 King Victor Emmanuel III asked Benito Mussolini, the wayward son of a blacksmith, to become Prime Minister of Italy. This seems a remarkable offer to a man who in 1902 had stolen food from two English ladies in Geneva; who was subsequently expelled from Switzerland for trade-union activity, and who in 1913 edited a revolutionary SOCIALIST newspaper called *Avanti!* He and his new Fascist movement had then failed abysmally in the elections of 1919. Three years later he achieved his ambition of becoming Italy's leader.

How far was his rise the product of the skills of this extraordinary man and of the appeal of Fascism; and how far was it a product of the post-war circumstances, and the longer-term weaknesses in Liberal Italy that you have already studied?

CHART 3A   CHAPTER OVERVIEW

3 Why was Mussolini, the Fascist leader, appointed Prime Minister of Italy in 1922?

A Why did Mussolini become a Fascist? (pp. 36–43)

B Fascism 1919–22: an overview (pp. 44–45)

C How did Fascism develop 1919–21? (pp. 46–55)

D How did Mussolini gain power in 1922? (pp. 56–61)

E Review: Why was Mussolini, the Fascist leader, appointed Prime Minister of Italy in 1922? (p. 62)

A   Why did Mussolini become a Fascist?

Although Fascism was more than just the creation of one man, it is still true to say that Fascism was shaped by the extraordinary career of its creator. As you read about Mussolini's background, consider what features of his early life might have helped mould the movement he created.

Pages 36–43 chart Mussolini's career from his childhood to his role as a leading Socialist by 1914, to his quarrels with other Socialists over Italy's role in the First World War. This will help you to understand both Mussolini's qualities as a politician and his motives for gaining power. Was he motivated by principles, personal ambition, or both?

FOCUS ROUTE

As you study Mussolini's early life and the extracts from his autobiography (on pages 41–43), make notes on aspects of:

a) Mussolini's background
b) his most significant experiences
c) his character
d) his abilities
e) his views

which might make him successful in politics. Also note any weaknesses he might have to overcome.

Activity

1 Using pages 36–39, list the reasons why Mussolini became a leading Socialist.
2 Do you think he was more interested in action and leadership than in the principles and politics of Socialism? What evidence supports your views?

A born revolutionary?

Mussolini's birthplace

Birth

- Born July 1883 in Predappio, Romagna (see the map on page 29), a region of marked class conflict and strong anarchist and REPUBLICAN political traditions.
- Son of a blacksmith and a schoolmistress. He absorbed revolutionary ideas from his father: 'Socialism is an open and violent rebellion against our inhuman state of things.'
- Alleged not to have spoken until he was three; then he never stopped.
- Mussolini always emphasised, 'I am a man of the people. I understand the people because I am one of them.'

School experience

- As the local school found it hard to control him, at the age of nine he was sent to a boarding school run by Catholic priests. There he was involved in fights, threw an inkwell at a teacher, and stabbed an older boy with a penknife. He was suspended four times, and expelled. However, he still achieved the highest marks in History, Literature and Singing, and decided to become a teacher!

Mussolini's early life

38

WHY WAS MUSSOLINI, THE FASCIST LEADER, APPOINTED PRIME MINISTER OF ITALY IN 1922?

Mussolini's early life

Character

■ Disobedient, self-willed, quarrelsome and moody. Easily lost his temper. Restless and ambitious. A dreamer. He once said to his mother: 'One day I shall astonish the world.'

Jobs

■ Elementary school teacher for six months. Like Hitler, he experienced the humiliating struggle of the lower middle class or PETTY BOURGEOISIE.
■ 1902–4 he fled to Switzerland to escape his debts. Held a series of brief jobs. Experienced foreign contempt for Italians and helped organise Italian migrant workers.
■ 1904–6 conscripted into the army. Responded well to military discipline.
■ 1906–10 journalist and strike organiser in Italy and amongst Italians in Austrian Trentino. Gained support through his lively oratory and writing. 1909 he was expelled from Trentino.

Marriage

■ 1910 began living with Rachele Guidi, a local peasant girl.
■ In 1915 they married in a civil ceremony.

Politics

■ 1910 became Secretary to the Socialist Party in Forli (see map on page 29). He was on the extremist wing of the party and put all his energies into provoking a Socialist revolution. Soon nicknamed 'E'matt' (madman).
■ 1911 organised protest against the Libyan War. Led an attack on Forli railway station which blocked the movement of troops to Libya for three days. Jailed for five months. He frequently referred to the need for violence.
■ 1912 led demands for the expulsion from the Socialist Party of moderates who had co-operated with Giolitti. Became Editor of Socialist Party newspaper *Avanti!* (in two years its circulation rose from 28,000 to 100,000).

Personal qualities

■ A forceful and authoritative speaker, with a powerful voice, vigorous gestures and dramatic phrases. Developed an ability to arouse emotion by building up a series of apparently disconnected sentences. Realised the importance of cultivating a mood in an audience. Boasted of his virility (manliness). Had several violent relationships with women.

Influences

■ Read quite widely, especially
  –Marx (Socialism)
  –Sorel (need for an ELITE; role of violence)
  –Nietzsche (role of a superman who can impose his own laws)
  –Le Bon (how a brave leader could channel power of the crowd)
  –Prezzolini (need to create a modern assertive Italy).

39

WHY WAS MUSSOLINI, THE FASCIST LEADER, APPOINTED PRIME MINISTER OF ITALY IN 1922?

For a man who always put 'mood and action' before anything else, the following comments by contemporaries are revealing.

SOURCE 3.1   From Mussolini's last report from Faenza school, when he was twelve

Has a lively intelligence, and unusual memory but a character quite out of the ordinary ... passionate and unruly he cannot adapt himself to the life of the school ... He placed himself in opposition to every rule of the school ... One personal motivation guides him and this is the principal streak in his character ... He cannot tolerate an injury; he wants revenge ... he rebels against every punishment to a point which obliges the Headmaster reluctantly to ask his parents to withdraw him.

SOURCE 3.2   Angelica Balabanoff, a MARXIST Socialist who had a strong influence on Mussolini, gained this insight into his character

I soon saw that he knew little of history, of economics, or of Socialist theory and that his mind was completely undisciplined ... Mussolini's RADICALISM and ANTI-CLERICALISM were more the reflection of his early environment and his own rebellious egoism than the product of understanding and conviction; his hatred of oppression was not that impersonal hatred of a system shared by all revolutionaries; it sprang rather from his own sense of indignity and frustration, from a passion to assert his own ego and from a determination for personal revenge.

■ **Talking point**

Is it important to study the childhood of political leaders such as Mussolini, or should we simply study their policies once in power?

SOURCE 3.3   A police report by Inspector Gasti of the Milan branch of the security police in 1919 concluded

He is emotional and impulsive ... He is a bold organiser and personally brave, makes quick decisions, but is less firm in his beliefs and aims.

He is most ambitious ... He wants to lead and dominate ... Mussolini's political ideas are changeable ... and it cannot be ruled out that in certain conditions, whether for fear of being outbid by others, or as a result of fresh events, or for other subjective or objective reasons, he may take a new line and co-operate in undermining institutions and principles that he previously believed in and supported.

SOURCE 3.4   A reporter in 1912

I don't know what to make of this queer fellow Mussolini. But I know one thing – he's going to get somewhere.

As the First World War approached, Benito Mussolini was firmly established on the revolutionary wing of the Socialist Party. His journalism was aggressive; he supported violence and he promoted a revolutionary socialist takeover. However, he was also an unpredictable individual who loved action, and it was far from clear what his likely response to the outbreak of war would be.

The First World War: Mussolini's dilemma

At the outbreak of the First World War the Socialist Party's view was that the war was an IMPERIALIST struggle fought at the expense of the working classes of Europe. Unlike most other Socialist parties, the Italian Socialist Party stuck to its principles and opposed Italy's entry into the war.

However, Mussolini, the man of action, soon developed an impatience with being sidelined from an event which might destroy existing political structures, provide exciting revolutionary options and give opportunities for personal glory. He once said to his mistress Margherita Sarfatti, 'I need glory and wealth, I am always looking for the tumultuous and new ...' and 'I want to be ... greater than Napoleon.' He was a natural rebel who did not find it easy to stick to the party line.

■ **Activity**

1 How did Mussolini's political views change during 1914 (see Sources 3.6–8)?
2 What part did each of these factors play in changing Mussolini's views?
   a) patriotism
   b) war experiences
   c) his ambitions and personality
   d) political principles

40

WHY WAS MUSSOLINI, THE FASCIST LEADER, APPOINTED PRIME MINISTER OF ITALY IN 1922?

SOURCE 3.5 Mussolini as Editor of *Avanti!*

SOURCE 3.6 From Mussolini's writings

a) 1911

> *The national flag is for us a rag to plant on a dunghill.*
> *Let us show that the fatherland does not exist just as God does not exist.*

b) 1913

> *Let us have no more talk of battleships, barracks, cannon, at a time when thousands of villages have no schools, roads, electricity or doctors, but still live tragically beyond the pale of civilised life.*

c) Commenting on the outbreak of war, *Avanti!*, 26 July 1914

> *Down with War! Down with arms and up with humanity.*

d) *Avanti!*, 10 October 1914

> *To offer the same kind of opposition to all wars ... is stupidity bordering on the imbecile. Do you want to be a spectator of this great drama or do you want to be its fighters?*

SOURCE 3.7 Mussolini writing in *Il Popolo d'Italia*

a) November 1914

> *Who has iron has bread. Revolution is an idea which has found bayonets.*

b) 24 May 1915

> *From today we are all Italians, nothing but Italians.*

SOURCE 3.8 Mussolini's office

41

WHY WAS MUSSOLINI, THE FASCIST LEADER, APPOINTED PRIME MINISTER OF ITALY IN 1922?

Mussolini was expelled from the Socialist Party for promoting intervention in the war. He set up his own newspaper in November 1914, partly financed by the French government and Italian industrialists. The paper was known as *Il Popolo d'Italia* and claimed still to be the supporter of socialist ideas, but advocated Italy's entry into the war.

Mussolini himself was CONSCRIPTED into the Italian army in August 1915. He acquitted himself well even though he was not involved in any serious fighting. He was invalided out of the army in February 1917 when a mortar training accident left him with 40 pieces of shrapnel in his body.

After four months in hospital he returned to the editorship of *Il Popolo d'Italia*. Writing soon after the disastrous defeat at Caporetto, he claimed Italy needed a strong leader to take command of the war effort. He significantly changed his paper: from calling itself a socialist daily, it became the 'paper of combatants and producers'. No longer would the emphasis be on class. Mussolini would welcome anyone prepared to fight and work to save the nation.

Alienated from the Socialist Party by the split over the First World War, and concerning himself with the creation of national wealth and not its distribution, the logic of Mussolini's position was that his socialist ideas would soon fade. Could he find an alternative way to gain power?

Mussolini's autobiography

Of all the sources available to a historian, an autobiography is one of the most exciting. It may tell us a great deal about the author – and not only what he intended us to know. On pages 41–43 you can read Mussolini's own description of his life before he gained power.

SOURCE 3.9   Extracts from *My Autobiography* by Benito Mussolini. It was first published in English in 1928 and never translated into Italian. Reprinted 1936, 1937 (twice)

a) Publisher's preface

It is a book that is historically valuable, giving us, as it does, intimate pictures of Fascism in theory and in practice ... There has been a tendency to belittle the magnificent achievements of a man who, whatever may be said about his IDEOLOGY, is undoubtedly great, and whom history will record as the saviour of post-war Italy.

b)   The foreword is by Richard Child, former US Ambassador in Italy. He describes how he persuaded Mussolini, 'the busiest single individual in the world', to dictate this autobiography to him

Of course, there are many things which a man writing an autobiography cannot say about himself, or will not say about himself. He is unlikely to speak of his own size on the screen of history ...

In our time it may be shrewdly forecast that no man will exhibit dimensions of permanent greatness equal to those of Mussolini.

c)   Extracts from Chapter 1, 'Youth', and Chapter 2, 'War and its Effect upon a Man'

Mussolini's character

I was then a restless being; I am still. Then I could not understand why it is necessary to take time in order to act. Rest for restfulness meant nothing more to me then than now.

I believe that in those youthful years, just as now, my day began and ended with an act of will – by will put into action.

The difficulties of life have hardened my spirit. They have taught me how to live ... Any comfortable cranny would have sapped my energies. These energies which I enjoy were trained by obstacles and even by bitterness of soul. They were made by struggle; not by the joys of the pathway. ➡

■ Activity

Read Sources 3.9 a) and b).
1   Why did the writers of these extracts want Mussolini's autobiography to be published?
2   Mussolini's autobiography was written after he came to power. How might this affect his account of events?
3   How would you expect Mussolini to portray
    a) his own character and qualities
    b) the politics of the war and post-war years?

42

WHY WAS MUSSOLINI, THE FASCIST LEADER, APPOINTED PRIME MINISTER OF ITALY IN 1922?

■ **Activity**

1 Using each section in turn ('Mussolini's character', etc.), consider what Mussolini wants the reader to believe about himself and his actions.
2 What can you learn about Mussolini from these extracts?

Whenever I took an extreme decision I have obeyed only the firm commandment of will and conscience which came from within. I do not believe in the supposed influence of books . . .

For myself, I have used only one big book.
For myself, I have had only one great teacher.
The book is life experience.
The teacher is day-by-day experience.
The reality of experience is far more eloquent than all the theories and philosophies in all the tongues and on all the shelves . . .

His career as a journalist and soldier

As a journalist

The itch of journalism was in me. My opportunity was before me in the editorship of a local Socialist newspaper. I understood now that the Gordian knot [complicated problem] of Italian political life could only be undone by an act of violence.

Therefore I became the public crier of this basic partisan warlike conception. The time had come to shake the souls of men and fire their minds to thinking and acting. It was not long before I was proclaimed the mouthpiece of the intransigent [not willing to compromise] revolutionary Socialist faction.

I worked hard to build up the circulation, the influence and the prestige of Avanti! *. . . I did not yield an inch to* DEMAGOGUERY. *I have never flattered the crowd nor wheedled anyone; I spoke always of the costs of victories – sacrifices and sweat and blood.*

(Sixty days after war broke out, Mussolini gave up the editorship of *Avanti!*)
I felt lighter, fresher. I was free! I was better prepared to fight my battles than when I was bound by the dogmas of any political organisations. But I understood that I could not use with sufficient strength my convictions if I was without that modern weapon, capable of all possibilities, ready to arm and to help, good for offence and defence, the newspaper.

I needed a daily paper. I hungered for one . . . I was mad to tell Italy and Italians the truth – their opportunity!

On November 15th, 1914, the first number of the Popolo d'Italia *appeared. Even now I call this newspaper my most cherished child: it is only through it, small as was its beginning, that I am able to win all the battles of my political life. I am still its director . . .*

My first article in the Popolo d'Italia *turned a large part of public opinion toward the intervention of Italy in the war, side by side with England and France.*

As a soldier

I liked the life of a soldier. The sense of willing subordination suited my temperament. I was preceded by a reputation of being restless, a fire-eater, a radical, a revolutionist . . . It was my opportunity to show serenity [calmness] of spirit and strength of character.

SOURCE 3.10 Mussolini as a corporal in the Italian army

43

WHY WAS MUSSOLINI, THE FASCIST LEADER, APPOINTED PRIME MINISTER OF ITALY IN 1922?

The war moulded me . . . I wanted to be a soldier, obedient, faithful to discipline, stretching myself with all my might to the fulfilment of my duty. In this I felt I succeeded . . . I still hold on to, as my life's dedication . . . that once a man sets up to be the expounder of an ideal or of a new school of thought he must constantly and intensively live daily life and fight battles for the doctrines that he teaches – at any cost until victory – to the end!

Within a few months I was promoted corporal by merit of war action with a citation from my superiors in these words, 'Benito Mussolini, ever the first in operations of courage and audacity'.

One of our grenades burst in our trenches . . . I was rushed to hospital . . . My wounds were serious . . . I faced atrocious pain; my suffering was indescribable . . . I had 27 operations in one month, all except two were without anaesthetics.

(After Caporetto)
Helped by the mutilated, the wounded, and the pro-war veterans I began an active campaign of 'Stand to a Finish'. . . This campaign developed by degrees in the newspaper, in public meetings, in gatherings at the Front. It brought results far beyond my highest hopes. The government seemed to be tugged after us by our efforts, towards resistance and victory.

His view of Italy

Those years before the World War were filled by political twists and turns. Italian life was not easy. Difficulties were many for the people. The conquest of Tripolitania [Libya] had exacted its toll of lives and money in a measure far beyond our expectation. Our lack of political understanding brought at least one riot a week.

During one ministry of Giolitti I remember thirty-three. They had their harvest of killed and wounded and of corroding bitterness of heart. Riots and upheavals among day labourers, among the peasants in the Valley of the Po, riots in the South. Even separatist movements in our islands. And in the meantime, above all this atrophy [wasting away] of normal life, there went on the tournament and joust of political parties struggling for power.

I thought then, as I think now, that only the common denominator of a great sacrifice of blood could have restored to all the Italian nation an equalisation of rights and duties. The attempt at revolution – 'the red week' – was not revolution as much as it was chaos. No leaders. No means to go on! The middle class and the BOURGEOISIE gave us another picture of their insipid spirit.

I do not choose to make posthumous recriminations. The weakness of internal politics in 1917, the feeble parliamentary situation, the hateful Socialistic propaganda, were certainly preparing the ground for events that could prove ruinous. And the blow came in October 1917; it took the name of Caporetto.

Never in my life as an Italian and as a politician have I experienced a sorrow equal to that which I suffered after news of the defeat of Caporetto . . .

The final victory was not only a victory of a war . . . It was a victory for the whole Italian race. After a thousand years we were again giving tangible proof of our moral and spiritual valour . . . Our love of country had bloomed again.

His aims and political evolution

For my supreme aim I have had the public interest. If I spoke of life I did not speak of a concept of my own life, my family life or that of my friends. I spoke and thought and conceived of the whole Italian life taken as a synthesis [joining together] – as an expression of a whole people.

Above all there was my own country. I saw that INTERNATIONALISM was crumbling. The unit of loyalty was too large.

My political evolution has been the product of constant expansion, of a flow of springs always nearer to the realities of living life and always further away from the rigid structures of sociological theories . . .

The organisation of Fascismo was marked and stamped with Youth. It has youth's spirit and it gathered youth, which like a young orchard has many years of productiveness for the future.

B Fascism 1919–22: an overview

Before we look in depth at how Mussolini managed to gain support and achieve power it will be worth reading the following overview of the complex development of Fascism from 1919 to 1922. This will provide you with a clear structure within which to locate some of the key issues, and help you master the more detailed survey which follows.

Some key questions to consider as you study these events in more detail

a) Why did the elite support the Fascists when their 1919 programme was so radical?

b) How did the Fascists get support by promising to restore order and discipline when they were chiefly responsible for the post-war violence?

c) Did Fascism move to the Right and then get elite support, or get elite support and then move to the Right? Or did it do both at the same time?

CHART 3B The development of Fascism 1919–22

Key groups in the rise of Fascism

The following symbols represent various groups who by active support, collaboration or lack of action assisted the growth Fascism. When their contribution becomes important, their symbol is added to the relevant stage.

- Mussolini
- Original Fascists, e.g. ex-soldiers
- The industrial elite
- The agricultural elite
- Ras and squads
- Petty bourgeoisie, e.g. peasants, public servants
- The Liberal establishment
- The local authorities, e.g. prefects, police
- The King

Stage 2 (1919)

The movement attracted a mixed collection of people dissatisfied with the status quo. The movement's main mouthpiece was Mussolini's paper, *Il Popolo d'Italia*. In April 1919 the Fascists burnt the *Avanti!* offices, and engaged in other acts of violence against the hated Socialists. Standing on a radical programme in the 1919 elections, Mussolini failed miserably, gaining only 2% of the vote in Milan. The radical vote went to the PSI.

Stage 3 (1920)

By Summer 1920 the industrial and rural elite were worried by the Socialist threat, and by government inaction. Some saw the Fascists as the best bulwark against Socialism, and started to give funds to Fascist squads who were fighting Socialists.

THE LEFT

Stage 1 (1919)

In March 1919 Mussolini set up a fascio di combattimento, or combat group, formed mainly from ex-soldiers. The Fascists said they would provide new leadership in a national revolution. They were a movement not a party, and sought support from all patriotic Italians.

Their programme expressed radical social ideas, stemming from their experience of war. It thus provided a nationalist, socialist alternative to the PSI who were seen as traitors.

Stage 4 (1920)

Mussolini saw an opportunity. He wanted change; he wanted power. It seemed he might achieve these by appealing to people frightened by the Socialists. This would mean playing down his left-wing ideas, and shifting his programme to appeal more to the Right.

Ras
The ras were powerful local leaders of the Fascist squads. The word comes from the name for Ethiopian tribal leaders.

FOCUS ROUTE

Key points on Fascism 1919–22
Study Chart 3B and choose the more appropriate end to the following sentences.

1 Fascism began
 a) as a broadly LEFT-WING, NATIONALIST movement
 b) as an attempt to create a mass RIGHT-WING party.
2 Fascist attacks on Socialists
 a) lost it much of its support
 b) attracted support from the economic elite and many peasants.
3 Fascism
 a) remained essentially left wing
 b) gradually moved to the Right, where its support was increasingly coming from.
4 Mussolini
 a) exploited the preparedness of LIBERAL politicians to co-operate with Fascism
 b) rejected any involvement with Parliament.
5 Mussolini's relations with the RAS
 a) were sometimes tense
 b) were good since they accepted his dominance as the founder of Fascism.
6 Mussolini
 a) used the threat of violent squads to be legally appointed Prime Minister
 b) took power through violence.

Stage 7 (1921)

Prime Minister Giolitti hoped he could absorb the movement, which was becoming a major force in the country. He gambled by including Fascists on the list of candidates recommended by the government in the May 1921 election. (This was the last election before Mussolini was appointed Prime Minister.) They gained 35 seats, and Mussolini entered parliament. Giolitti hoped to tame the Fascists by offering Mussolini a government post, but Mussolini refused to join the government as a junior partner. He was more ambitious.

Stage 10 (1922)

The Fascists planned the takeover of local governments and a march on Rome, in order to seize power. Meanwhile many in the elite were arguing that the Fascists should join the government. Mussolini would only accept becoming Prime Minister. On 29 October King Victor Emmanuel invited Mussolini to form a government. The Fascists marched on Rome to celebrate their victory.

tage 6 (1921)

me original Fascists were concerned out how the bourgeoisie were ining the movement and Mussolini's ove to the Right. Many dropped out the movement. Several ras, who ere not under Mussolini's control, otested. However, as the movement ew, they realised how important ussolini, with his paper *Il Popolo Italia*, was for unity and strength.

THE RIGHT

Stage 8 (1921)

Tension was developing between those Fascists wanting to gain power legally and those supporting seizure of power. Mussolini was concerned about the growing Fascist violence which threatened his position as a respectable member of parliament and his control over the Fascist movement. On 2 August 1921 he signed a 'pact of pacification' with the Socialists. Ras pressure forced him to back down. In November he formed the National Fascist Party, which acknowledged the role of the squads but recognised Mussolini as the indispensable Duce. Its new programme was right-wing. Mussolini was looking for power. This meant becoming more respectable.

Stage 9 (1922)

By 1922 the Fascist squads had broken Socialist power in many areas of the North and Centre. They were often assisted by the authorities, who were pleased to see the Socialists smashed. Mussolini was under pressure from some ras to seize power; he also realised that if Fascism did not gain power it could soon break up. He hoped to use ras pressure on the government to become appointed Prime Minister legally. In September 1922 he announced his support for the monarchy.

tage 5 (1920–21)

late 1920 Fascism took off, pecially in the rural areas in North d Central Italy. Local leaders, or s, set up their own squads of scists. They attracted not just the rarian elite, but also many small ndholders harmed by Socialist local vernment and worried about a ocialist revolution. Fascist anti-ocialist violence made Fascism a ass movement.

FOCUS ROUTE

1 List the groups which supported Fascism.
2 Explain why each group supported Fascism.
3 Explain from which areas and groups Fascism gained most support.

■ Activity

1 Why did Mussolini set up a *new* movement in 1919?
2 Why did he call it a movement and not a party?

C How did Fascism develop 1919–21?

Why did Mussolini set up the Fascist movement?

SOURCE 3.11 Mussolini, *Il Popolo d'Italia*, 24 March 1919

The existing regime in Italy has thrown open the succession. There is a crisis which leaps to the eyes of all. Throughout the war we heard of the incompetence of the people who govern, and knew that if the war was won, it was solely by the virtue of the Italian people, not at all by the intelligence and the capacity of the governors. As the succession to the regime is open, we must not vacillate [hesitate]. We must run. If the regime is to be overthrown, it must be we who occupy its place. Therefore we create Fasci: organs of creation and agitation, capable of descending into the streets and crying: 'We, we alone, have the right to the succession, because we, we were the men who forced the country into war and into victory . . .'

Mussolini made this speech at a meeting of about a hundred men and a handful of women assembled in the hall on the Piazza San Sepolcro in Milan on 23 March 1919. These early joiners became the proud bearers of the title 'Fascists of the first hour'. Few rational observers would have predicted that they were witnessing the birth of a movement which within three years would take control of Italy. Indeed the early signs were that they would be little more than another splinter group on the political extreme.

Fascism was not intended as another party, but as a movement appealing to all Italians. Mussolini possessed no clear political ideology. His approach was a peculiar mix of socialist and nationalist ideas cemented by the concept of the powerful leader or DUCE.

Fascism can be seen as a means to an end. Mussolini made it abundantly clear that his prime aim was to gain power. He boasted that he had saved Italy in 1915. He declared war on all political parties but most strongly against the Socialists: 'We declare war on Socialism not because it is socialist but because it has opposed nationalism.' At this stage he still advocated REPUBLICANISM and hostility to the Church. Using nationalism as their ideological weapon and PARAMILITARY formations to strike at their enemies, the Fascists embarked on an ambitious and vigorous process of gaining support.

It is difficult to categorise the 'Fascists of the first hour'. Their specific beliefs and aims were less important than their desire to act and restore Italy to greatness. It was Mussolini's daunting task to emphasise the common aims without tying himself too closely to a programme which might alienate any of the groups or potential supporters.

Fascism remained small, with little over one thousand members in 1919. This was largely explained by the fact that the Fascists were still viewed as a leftist movement and left-wing support was going to the PSI. In the 1919 elections in Milan the Fascists only gained 5000 votes (compared with 168,000 for the PSI, and 70,000 for the PPI). Fascism seemed doomed to failure.

Who supported Fascism?

To understand how Mussolini gained the support in Italy which put him in a position to seek power we need to consider how he re-positioned his movement. Early Fascism was a rag-bag of ideas, very localised in its support and committed to violence as a political weapon; not the obvious credentials for success.

Mussolini's great skill was to exploit the fear of the middle and upper classes during the Biennio Rosso in 1919–20 and move Fascism to the Right. This lost some early supporters but these were replaced by young, lower-middle-class recruits from the universities, the civil service and 'respectable' bourgeois families. It must also be remembered that Fascism was far more than just Mussolini. The movement grew as a series of locally formed fasci, led by RAS, some of whom had different ideas to Mussolini. Historians are increasingly stressing the importance of local developments in Fascism at this time, reducing the importance of Mussolini in its growth. Where he was important was in providing a nationally recognised leader. It was, however, going to be several years before Mussolini was able fully to control Fascism.

The key group of active supporters came from the petty bourgeoisie (see Chart 3C). This group, containing a wide range of people in between the working class and middle class, felt a collective sense of insecurity, and were prone to turn to radical groups, outside traditional parties. Many were ex-soldiers proud of the military victory they had won, but who felt humiliated by not receiving what they considered their 'due' from the government. They thought themselves entitled to substantial rewards for their war services, but none were forthcoming.

CHART 3C   Why did the petty bourgeoisie support Fascism?

Trying to join the bourgeois elite – but unable to compete

Big business

The threatened petty bourgeoisie

Solution = Fascism

Smash Socialism. Everyone will be part of a great nation

Fear of falling back into the proletariat

Position threatened by proletarian advance

Who are the petty bourgeoisie? Shopkeepers, artisans, small merchants, small business owners, low-ranking civil servants, teachers, small landowners etc.

The Fascists also won a rural lower-middle-class base among small farmers in parts of Romagna, Lombardy and Venetia. Some of these farmers had recently improved their position and extended their landholdings. They believed that rural Socialism threatened these gains. This fear allowed Fascism, which had originated in the towns, to develop a mass base in the countryside during 1920. Here there was considerable resentment over the power of Socialist Land Leagues (Socialist organisations which controlled the rural labour market), who bullied farmers to hire labourers when they were not really needed. Many of these smaller peasant farmers welcomed groups who were prepared to fight against Socialist power. The AGRARI, or large landowners, also welcomed and were prepared to finance any movement that would resist the Socialists. This agrarian support made Fascism a mass movement. Fascism also attracted support from industrialists who were frightened by Socialism, but were also concerned that Liberal governments were making too many concessions to workers. (See Source 3.12.)

Large numbers of students and youths, eager for adventure and action, were embittered about the rising wages of unpatriotic workers and their own lack of prospects. They detested the boring routine of their daily lives, and many joined the Fascist squads. Finally, Fascism attracted some of the semi-criminal elements of Milan and other towns.

Increasingly as the Fascists smashed Socialist and Catholic unions, demoralised workers found they had to join Fascist SYNDICATES to get employment. Mussolini was not the only ex-Socialist who joined the Fascists. Several of its original members were ex-SYNDICALISTS, who believed that workers should be organised into unions to protect their members and contribute to the industrial growth of Italy. Some workers also resented the strong-arm methods against BLACKLEGS which Socialist unions used, and were

48

WHY WAS MUSSOLINI, THE FASCIST LEADER, APPOINTED PRIME MINISTER OF ITALY IN 1922?

■ **Activity**

Look at Sources 3.12–15 and Chart 3D. What do they reveal about:
a) who supported the movement and why
b) the areas of greatest Fascist strength
c) the influence of the war on the development of Fascism
d) why Fascists were prepared to use violence?

attracted to a rival organisation. The Fascists also attracted working-class support by retaining some aspects of their original social radicalism. They could still talk of giving land to the peasants, and fair wages and prices. Employers tolerated such talk as it served to weaken support for Socialism by attracting some workers; and in practice little came of these ideas.

It is useful at this stage to distinguish between two groups vital to Fascism's development: those who actually joined the Fascist movement (the real Fascists) and those who were prepared to support it for their own ends, but not through commitment to its cause (these can be called tactical Fascists, or users of Fascism). Many of the joiners were disaffected, looking for change. The users, the elite, were discontented since they feared change, and wanted to preserve the threatened status quo. The lower middle class provided a mass basis for power, but Fascism was to gain power through the support it won from industrialists and landowners.

An interesting insight into the nature of the Fascist movement is given by the following contemporary analyses (Sources 3.12–15).

SOURCE 3.12   The Milan prefect, describing the reaction of the Director of the Milan Tramway Company in 1921

[He] deplored the actions of the government [over a draft bill on workers' control over factories] and explained that the industrialists supported the Fascists in order to fight against the government and hinder its activity which was harmful to industry's interests.

SOURCE 3.13   An article in the Liberal newspaper *La Stampa* in May 1921 describes the composition of a Fascist crowd

[Demobilised ex-officers] who have sought and not found employment; [it is] a compound of repressed hope and desperation, [of forgotten heroes] convinced that they can harangue [speak angrily to] a community as they harangued a battalion in the field; [of] public employees scarcely able to eat compared with whom a peasant, a league organiser, a trade-union secretary is a gentleman; of swarms of brokers, shopkeepers, and contractors, hit by the slump, who detest with a deadly hatred the labour and consumer co-operatives, [of] students and young graduates with no clients and grandiose ideals, convinced that their misfortunes were due to the sinister plots of senile [old] politicians; [of bands of] incredible adolescents, aged 16–19, envenomed [made bitter] by bad luck which made the war finish too soon . . . because they wished to . . . do great deeds; [and finally of] bands of ex-revolutionaries who had become war enthusiasts in 1915 . . . anxious to recapture a position of command.

SOURCE 3.14   The Fascist Lanzillo analysed the growth of Fascism in his book *The State and the Post-War Social and Financial Crisis*, 1920

The fasci of Milan are composed, in the very great majority, of employees, small RENTIERS and lesser and middling professional men . . . Fascism is composed in the large cities of new men. They formed the crowd which before the war watched political events with indifference and apathy and which has now entered the contest. Fascism has MOBILISED its forces from the twilight zones of political life, and from this derives the unruly violence and juvenile exuberance of its conduct.

SOURCE 3.15   Mussolini acknowledged the importance of rural Fascism in 1922

The SHARECROPPER or leaseholder tries with all his strength to become an owner . . . The peasants are conquering the land by their own strength. It is clear that these serried phalanxes [close ranks] of new small owners cannot but detest Socialism. Instead, they have everything to hope for from Fascism and nothing to fear . . . During the RISORGIMENTO the rurali [the agricultural population] were either absent or hostile . . . But the great war of 1915–18 recruited the rurali in their millions. However, their participation in events was on the whole passive . . . Now Fascism has transformed this rural passivity . . . into active support for the reality and sanctity [holiness] of the nation.

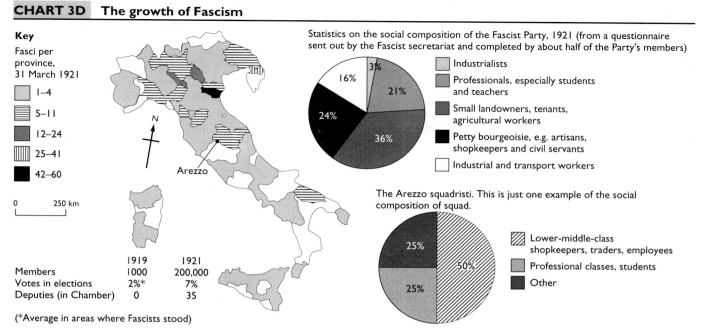

Key

Fasci per province, 31 March 1921

- 1–4
- 5–11
- 12–24
- 25–41
- 42–60

0   250 km

Arezzo

N

Statistics on the social composition of the Fascist Party, 1921 (from a questionnaire sent out by the Fascist secretariat and completed by about half of the Party's members)

- Industrialists
- Professionals, especially students and teachers
- Small landowners, tenants, agricultural workers
- Petty bourgeoisie, e.g. artisans, shopkeepers and civil servants
- Industrial and transport workers

3% / 21% / 36% / 24% / 16%

The Arezzo squadristi. This is just one example of the social composition of squad.

- Lower-middle-class shopkeepers, traders, employees
- Professional classes, students
- Other

50% / 25% / 25%

	1919	1921
Members	1000	200,000
Votes in elections	2%*	7%
Deputies (in Chamber)	0	35

(*Average in areas where Fascists stood)

What did Fascism offer?

From 1920 Mussolini began to drop his more radical policies. He presented a more acceptable face of Fascism: a movement and a party pledged to restore Italian power and prestige; to develop the economy by increasing productivity; to abolish harmful state controls; to re-establish strong leadership and law and order by curbing left-wing subversives. The abandonment of republicanism was announced in September 1922, closely followed by the ending of ANTI-CLERICALISM, and the dropping of the demand for votes for women and for taxes on war profits. Increasingly the emphasis was placed on nationalism, an active foreign policy and a strong state.

Mussolini never spoke favourably of party political programmes. He claimed Italy had had enough of politics and programmes and wanted action instead. Furthermore, it would be difficult to unite his diverse collection of supporters around a detailed political programme. In temperament, too, he was more interested in action than being tied to a specific party MANIFESTO. However, the Fascists did draw up various programmes and you can see the evolution of the Fascist programme between 1919 and 1921 on page 50.

CHART 3E   The appeal of Fascism in 1922

Unite all Italians

Strong leadership

Law and order

National greatness

Smash Socialism

Duce! Duce!

But on reflection...

Aren't they causing the chaos? Isn't the threat of Socialist revolution over? Aren't many Fascists former Socialists? Has Italy got the resources to be great?

SOURCE 3.16   D. Mack Smith, 'Sleeping Car to Power', a 1990 article

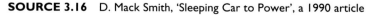

Fascism had elements of both [Left and Right] ... It was revolutionary, but could also sometimes claim to be conservative. It was MONARCHIST but also republican, at different times. It was Catholic, but also anti-clerical; it claimed to be Socialist, but could also be strongly CAPITALIST whenever it suited the Duce to be so.

Fascism was not a doctrine, not ideas, not ideology, but was really a means for winning power by a single man.

■ Activity

Read Source 3.16. Which aspects of the programmes on page 50 support this view?

50

WHY WAS MUSSOLINI, THE FASCIST LEADER, APPOINTED PRIME MINISTER OF ITALY IN 1922?

Fascist programmes, 1919 and 1921

In June 1919 Fascism was promising:	November 1921 it promised:
1 a republic with universal male and female SUFFRAGE	1 no specific commitment on political structure except one designed to ensure Italy's historic destiny
2 an eight-hour working day and guaranteed minimum wage	2 an eight-hour day with exceptions for agricultural or industrial requirements
3 workers' participation in the management of industry through National Councils of Labour	3 corporations to express national solidarity and increase production
4 common education for all	4 schools to train the governing elite and to provide Italy's future soldiers with physical and moral training
5 liberty of opinion and conscience	5 citizens' freedom limited in the interests of the nation
6 abolition of obligatory military service	6 obligatory military service
7 heavy and progressive tax on capital; confiscation of unproductive income	7 taxes proportional to income, not confiscatory
8 the NATIONALISATION of all arms and munitions factories; confiscation of 85 per cent of war profits	8 nationalised firms privatised; encouragement for national wealth through individual initiative; government spending cuts
9 the confiscation of all property belonging to religious organisations	9 no reference to Church property
10 a foreign policy of peaceful competition among the civilised nations.	10 complete unification for Italy with a major role in the Mediterranean.

FOCUS ROUTE

1 Compare the Fascist programmes of 1919 and 1921 with regard to the following areas:

a) Political structure
b) Social policy
c) Organisation of industry
d) Individual freedom
e) Conscription
f) Taxation
g) Church
h) Foreign policy.

2 To what extent can the 1919 programme be classified as left-wing, and that of 1921 as right-wing?

3 Match up the groups of people below with the various reasons for support.

Group of people

a) Industrialists
b) Agrari
c) Small landowners
d) Industrial workers
e) Rentiers
f) Ex-ARDITI

Reasons for supporting Fascism

i) Felt weak; hit by inflation; threatened by powerful organised groups; critical of weak state not protecting them

ii) Fear of workers' revolution

iii) Bitter at mutilated peace

iv) Hostile to Socialist pressure and COLLECTIVISATION programme; concerned to hold on to recent land gains

v) Might join Fascist syndicate; best way of staying in employment

vi) Wish to break stranglehold of Socialist Leagues

4 What overall conclusion emerges from these questions about the nature of support for Fascism?

The Fascists: bootboys or saviours?

SOURCE 3.17   Mussolini

For my part I prefer 50,000 rifles to 5 million votes.

Rarely has a political movement depended so greatly on violence for its growth. The history of Fascism is a history of violence. Fascism developed out of the feelings generated by the First World War; it grew through violence against its opponents, and was overthrown when facing defeat in the Second World War.

SOURCE 3.18   The sheer force of Fascist violence is well conveyed by these extracts from the ras Balbo's diary in early 1922

We are the masters of the situation. We have not only broken the resistance of our enemies, but we also control the organs of state. The PREFECT has to submit to the orders given by me in the name of the Fascists.

July in Ravenna
We undertook this task in the same spirit as when we demolished the enemy's stores in war time. The flames from the great burning building rose ominously into the night. The whole town was illuminated by the glare. We had to strike terror into the heart of our enemies. I announced to [the police chief] that I would burn down and destroy the houses of all the Socialists in Ravenna, if he did not give me within half an hour the means required for sending the Fascists elsewhere. I demanded a whole fleet of lorries. The police officers . . . told me where I could find lorries already supplied with petrol. Some of them actually belonged to the office of the police chief . . . I was organising a 'column of fire' . . . to extend our reprisals throughout the province . . . We went through . . . all the towns and centres in the provinces of Forli and Ravenna and destroyed and burnt all the red buildings, the seats of the Socialist and COMMUNIST organisations . . . The whole plain of the Romagna was given up to the reprisals of the outraged Fascists determined to break for ever the red terror.

Activity

Study Source 3.18. What are the most significant points about the nature of Fascist violence which emerge from this source? (Refer to the prefect, police, war and Socialism.)

Castor oil
The Fascists developed the sadistic policy of humiliating their political enemies by forcing them to drink castor oil. This laxative was designed to purge (cleanse) them of their sins. However, the real physical danger came from the other potential features of this treatment. Sometimes the victim was beaten on the kidneys or the oil was made into a dangerous cocktail which might include petrol, benzene or tincture of iodine. Serious illness or death could follow from such treatment.

SOURCE 3.19   The anti-Fascist Lussu, writing in 1936, had this to say about Fascist violence

The rebel having been reduced to impotence [powerlessness], had his mouth forced open, often by means of a special form of gag . . . In cases of obstinate resistance, recourse was had to the stomach pump as in hospital. The dose of castor oil was scrupulously proportioned to the obstinacy of the victim and the measure of his treason.
*   A further method of intimidation involved the forced eating of live toads!*

The Fascists smashed the organisational framework of the Socialist movement. Party and union buildings and members were attacked. An estimated 2000 opponents were killed by Fascists between 1920 and 1922, with about one-tenth as many Fascist casualties. Many Socialist councils were so disrupted that they had to be replaced by PREFECTS to re-establish order. By the end of 1921 the great power Socialists had exercised in many central and northern provinces had virtually disappeared.

   The irony is that a political group that was responsible for far more violence than any other came to win support from the elite and the authorities for its claim to be able to restore order and discipline to Italy. How was it able to do this?

Why was Fascist violence so successful?

Whereas many ordinary Italians could only see Fascism as political hooliganism, others welcomed it as a crude but necessary antidote (way of curing or getting rid of something) to Socialism. A major reason why the punitive expeditions were so successful was because the elite and agents of the government, disgusted by the weakness of the government, actually co-operated with the Fascists. Giolitti's inclusion of the Fascists in his government bloc

52

WHY WAS MUSSOLINI, THE FASCIST LEADER, APPOINTED PRIME MINISTER OF ITALY IN 1922?

electoral list in 1921 hardly encouraged local officials to take strong action against them! Giolitti was trying to use the old practice of TRASFORMISMO; he hoped to tame the Fascists by incorporating them in his government. In fact, this misjudgement just served to weaken opposition to Fascist violence. In December 1921 his successor Bonomi merely authorised, rather than instructed, prefects to take firm action against paramilitary groups. Most prefects avoided such a potentially dangerous course of action.

However, there is evidence that if the authorities had been prepared to stand up against the Fascist bullies, they might have easily put down the squads. In July 1921 at Sarzana twelve policemen, by firing, routed a band of 500 Fascists. But such incidents were rare. Right up until the final March on Rome in October 1922, the authorities generally preferred to tolerate and collaborate with Fascism rather than oppose it. As Cassels writes (p. 32), 'By 1922 there was hardly any segment of the Italian establishment not ready to collaborate with Fascism either for nationalist or anti-BOLSHEVIK reasons, or both.'

Although Mussolini was wary of the danger of uncontrolled squad violence, he also realised how Fascism's success to a large extent depended upon it. Here he seeks to defend Fascist violence:

SOURCE 3.20 Mussolini speaking to Fascists, Bologna, April 1922

We Fascists have a clear programme: we must move on led by a pillar of fire, because we are slandered and not understood. And, however much violence may be deplored, it is evident that we, in order to make our ideas understood, must beat refractory [obstinate] skulls with resounding blows . . . But we do not make a school, a system or, worse still, an aesthetic [theory of beauty] of violence. We are violent because it is necessary to be so . . .

Our punitive expeditions, all those acts of violence which figure in the papers, must always have the character of . . . legitimate reprisal: because we are the first to recognise that it is sad, after having fought the external enemy, to have to fight the enemy within . . . The Socialists had formed a state within a state . . . [and] this state is more tyrannical, illiberal and overbearing than the old one; and for this reason what we are causing today is a revolution to break up the Bolshevist state, while waiting to settle our accounts with the Liberal state which remains.

Not surprisingly, others saw it in a different way.

SOURCE 3.21 Cartoon by the Socialist Scalarini The authorities named at the bottom are (left to right) the police, local government and the judiciary

Activity

1 What different attitudes to violence are displayed in Sources 3.20, 3.21 and 3.22?
2 Explain in your own words:
   a) whom the Fascists used violence against
   b) what forms it took
   c) why it was successful.
3 'A revolution of blood against a revolution of words.' Do you think Turati's comparison of Fascist and Socialist policies was justified? (You may need to refer back to pages 32–34.)

How strong a contender for power was Fascism by 1922?

Because we know that Mussolini gained power in 1922 it is easy to read this success back into earlier events, and exaggerate Fascist strength by 1922.

The Fascists certainly had many assets. They had about half a million party members, and a quarter of a million Blackshirts. They virtually controlled several regions. They offered to give Italians firm leadership, end class conflict and gain national greatness, at a time when many Italians felt disillusioned. Their violence had helped to smash Socialism, and had attracted support from the elite and other worried groups. They thus had an aura of power far beyond their numbers.

They also benefited greatly from their opponents' weakness and divisions. They had been allowed to develop into a serious threat by Liberal governments that offered no firm leadership in the face of major economic and political problems. Recent historians have put great stress on what has been called the collapse of government both at the centre and, especially, in the provinces between 1920 and 1922. By the Autumn of 1922 the government either had to take a firm stand against Fascist violence, or try to tame it by incorporating the more moderate Fascists into the government.

Liberal, Socialist and Catholic opponents of Fascism were unable to co-operate against the growing threat. When in July 1922 moderates in the PSI and PPI at last agreed to join with Liberals in an anti-Fascist coalition government, Giolitti withheld his support, and the plan collapsed. Liberal politicians were still putting personal animosities (hatred or resentment) above the need for united action.

The Socialists' power had peaked in 1920. Since then they had been weakened by growing unemployment, demoralisation and Fascist attack. Interestingly, the diminished power of Socialism might have been a problem for Fascism, as a lesser threat of Socialist revolution meant less need for Fascism! But the decline of the Socialist threat was more real than apparent. Historians can now see the revolutionary peak as the occupation of the factories in September 1920; but contemporaries were still worried in 1921–22. Once again, as with the 'mutilated victory', what mattered was what people believed, rather than the reality.

People's fears of Socialism seemed confirmed in August 1922 when the Socialists called a 'legalitarian general strike' to protest at Fascist violence. This was a classic own goal. The strike collapsed after one day, largely through lack of support. However, the Fascists, who had mobilised to resist this renewed threat, took the credit and confirmed how vital they were.

■ **Activity**

1 Look at Chart 3F. Identify aspects that seem to be in conflict with each other. Why do you think Fascism as a movement had so many different strands?

2 What aspects might serve to unite the movement?

3 Read 'How strong a contender for power was Fascism by 1922?' above and list points suggesting it was a strong contender, then counterpoints.

4 Look back at the key questions on page 44. Discuss these issues, and note down the key points that emerge.

But Fascism was by no means an unstoppable movement. True, it offered to satisfy a growing desire for firm leadership and the restoration of order, yet it was largely responsible for the disorder. It contained many diverse elements (see Chart 3F). It was divided as to how to achieve power. Many of the ras wanted to seize it. Mussolini, impressed by the support the movement was gaining from the elite, considered he might achieve power legally. In 1922 various Liberal politicians were exploring the formation of a new government. Some favoured involving d'Annunzio, a potential nationalist rival to Mussolini. Others felt Fascists must be included.

However, Mussolini's weak base in Parliament must not be forgotten. Unlike Hitler, who had gained over 30 per cent of the Reichstag seats before he was appointed Chancellor, Mussolini, with seven per cent of the Deputies, had nowhere near enough support in Parliament to demand that the King make him Prime Minister. Mussolini had to use the threat of the ras to reinforce his claims. In Autumn 1922 tension within both the Fascist movement and the governing groups over the best way ahead was to form the vital background to Mussolini's appointment, a process which illustrated the ambiguity of the Fascists' approach to gaining power.

CHART 3F   The 'Fascist Cocktail'

What did Mussolini bring to the Fascist movement?

At the beginning of this book we stressed Mussolini's enormous ambition. His lowly origins would make it difficult for him to achieve his goals, and yet in 1922 he was on the verge of being appointed Prime Minister. Although recent historians have put great stress on Fascism as a broad movement, developing independently from Mussolini, this is not to deny his crucial contribution to its eventual success. Chart 3G will help to consolidate your understanding of his role.

CHART 3G   Mussolini's rise to power (>> = setbacks)

1883		Born
1910		Joined Socialist Party
1912		Editor of *Avanti!*
1914		Switched to support for First World War
		Expelled from PSI **>>**
		Created new newspaper *Il Popolo d'Italia*
1915		Pressurised for intervention in war
1917		Wounded in First World War
1919		Founded Fascism
		Fascism gained few votes in elections **>>**
		D'Annunzio at Fiume took limelight **>>**
1920		D'Annunzio expelled from Fiume; a potential rival weakened
1921		Elected to Parliament as one of 35 Fascists, part of the government bloc
		Gained 125,000 votes, as compared to 4,800 in 1919
		Briefly resigned as Fascist leader **>>**
		Forced to end pacification pact with Socialists **>>**
	Nov	Turned Fascism into PNF, more under his control
		New Fascist programme switched to the Right
		Dropped anti-clericalism
1922	Sept	Dropped republicanism
	Oct	Rejected offer of post in government
		Agreed with (or forced into) ras plans for march on Rome
		Planned to escape to Switzerland if COUP went wrong
		Called to Rome to become PM
		Appointed PM

Activity

Which of the qualities listed here under 'character' and 'abilities' help to explain why some saw Mussolini as a potential national leader in Italy at this time?

FOCUS ROUTE

Using pages 46–55,
Either:
Complete a political movement assessment chart (like the one on Socialism on page 31) for Fascism in September 1922.
Or:
You are a foreign journalist in Spring 1922. Write a report explaining what this new Fascist movement is and assessing its chances of gaining power.

His character

- Assertive
- Ambitious
- A natural rebel

But ... counterpoints

- Nervous
- Hesitated at key moments
- Did not initiate all Fascist action

His abilities

As a journalist

- Wrote in powerful, extreme way
- Sensed the popular mood
- Put need for impact above consistency
- *Il Popolo d'Italia* was the focal point for the whole movement

As a leader

- Sensed the mood of many Italians
- Skilfully held heterogeneous Fascist movement together
- Seen by ras as indispensable for gaining national power
- Portrayed himself to elite as a controlling influence on ras
- Politically flexible
- Pragmatic
- CHARISMATIC speaker

56

WHY WAS MUSSOLINI, THE FASCIST LEADER, APPOINTED PRIME MINISTER OF ITALY IN 1922?

FOCUS ROUTE

You can find the Focus Route for 'How did Mussolini gain power in 1922?' on page 61. You may find it helpful to look at this now to guide your reading of this section.

■ **Coup d'état**
A coup is a sudden seizure of power, normally by a small group such as army officers or a party. It comes from the French word for 'blow' ('to the state').

■ **Talking point**

What are the requirements for a successful coup?

D How did Mussolini gain power in 1922?

Which way to power? Coup or King?

By 1922 many Fascists considered their hour had come. The pressing question was not whether they should take control of Italy, but how. Mussolini was under great pressure from the ras to seize power. He, however, was still considering trying to be appointed legally. In October 1922 he was in contact with most major politicians over the formation of a new government, which would include Fascists.

Mussolini becomes leader of Italy, October 1922

On 29 October Rachele Mussolini received a telephone message that was to change Italy's history. The King needed to see her husband as soon as possible to discuss a new government. Mussolini said he wanted the offer in writing! Shortly after, the following telegram arrived:

'Very urgent. Top priority. Mussolini, Milan. H.M. the King asks you to proceed immediately to Rome as he wishes to confer with you.' It soon emerged that Mussolini was being offered the job of Prime Minister.

SOURCE 3.23   The telegram sent to Mussolini

Mussolini's strategy had worked. The leader of a recently formed party, that had for three years indulged in violence in the name of saving the country and making it great; of a party that had only 35 MPs, was being asked to lead the country!

How had this extraordinary situation come about? For some time the tide of events had been favouring the Fascists. They had been gaining control of local government. Squads in several towns had expelled Socialist councils and seized power. Since September rumours of a Fascist march on Rome had been rife. Alongside this, various politicians were thinking of incorporating Mussolini within a new government, perhaps with two to five Fascist Cabinet members. Mussolini made it clear he wanted a major role or nothing.

On 16 October Mussolini and six leading Fascists met in Milan and decided the time was right to take power. On the 24th a Fascist Congress was held in Naples. Forty thousand Blackshirts chanted 'A Roma' ('To Rome'). The leaders proclaimed their intention to organise a march on Rome in the tradition of Garibaldi (see page 9), and seize power. They drew up plans. First, Fascist squads were to seize public buildings in northern and central Italy. Others, led by QUADRUMVIRS, were to assemble outside Rome on 27 October, ready to march into the city on the next day. Mussolini proclaimed, 'Either the government will be given to us or we shall take it, descending upon Rome. It is now a question of days, perhaps hours.'

■ Activity

1 **Either**:

You are an adviser to Mussolini. Present the case for and against either:

a) seizing power; or

b) trying to be appointed legally.

You will need to consider these issues, amongst others:

i) How likely is each strategy to succeed in making Mussolini Prime Minister?

ii) What will be the longer-term consequences of each tactic for Mussolini's power? For example, how will each strategy affect his chances of retaining power, and fulfilling his long-term aims?

His relationship with the squads/ras, and with the elite are central issues in these assessments.

Or:

Prepare briefing papers for the King, for and against inviting Mussolini to lead the government. Half the class should take each side. Present your view to the teacher (the King!).

2 How did the existence of two possible routes to power strengthen Mussolini's position?

Mussolini himself was having grave doubts about the march, and hoped that he might be appointed legally. But he felt unable to resist his more aggressive Fascists. Besides, the mere threat of a Fascist march might intimidate the King into appointing him.

And so it proved. About 10,000 of the planned 50,000 squadristi began to assemble at three points about 20 miles from Rome. They had been told to avoid clashes with the army. During the night of 27 October local Fascists tried to seize control of key government and public buildings in many towns in North and Central Italy. They met with mixed success, but frightened prefects sent reports to Rome of the Fascist advance.

Many of the squads failed to meet at their assembly points for the March on Rome, as their trains were stopped by sabotage of the lines. Those that did meet were in a bad shape, poorly armed, drenched by rain, with sinking morale. They hardly looked like an irresistible force!

Prime Minister Facta, who, like many of his Liberal colleagues, for so long had failed to take a stand against the Fascist threat, now had to decide whether to organise firm government action against these blatant threats, or to capitulate. His government resigned, but he was asked to stay on. He requested that the King declare MARTIAL LAW, so that the army could take steps to crush the revolt. Was the Fascist bubble at last going to be burst?

The fate of Italy now rested in the hands of King Victor Emmanuel, a weak man quite incapable of providing firm leadership. As historian Lyttleton has said, 'The only man who could do anything was convinced of his impotence [powerlessness].'

Like many others in the elite, he overestimated the strength of Fascism. His mother sympathised with the movement, as did his cousin, the Duke of Aosta, who was in close contact with the Quadrumvirs. The King feared the Fascists might replace him with Aosta. He received conflicting reports from his generals as to the attitude of the army to a Fascist march. Some generals were deeply involved with the Fascists. The army and country might split apart; he might provoke civil war.

The King hesitated. Then at 2 am he agreed to Facta's request for martial law. Italy would be saved from the Fascist thugs. Twelve thousand troops began to be deployed around key buildings, behind sandbags and barbed wire. But this decisive action was short-lived. Eight hours later Victor Emmanuel changed his mind, and refused to agree to martial law. He had decided to try to compromise with Mussolini.

Facta resigned, and the King persuaded ex-Prime Minister Salandra to lead a government which included Mussolini. However, Salandra failed to gain support, and Mussolini himself refused to join Salandra's government. Mussolini insisted he would join the government as Prime Minister or nothing. For some time business circles had been advocating this solution. To the King there seemed no alternative but to ask Mussolini to be Prime Minister. So he sent the fateful telegram.

Mussolini, who had plans to escape to Switzerland if the march failed (as he thought it well might), had won. He caught the overnight train to Rome.

It arrived in Rome at 10.42 am on 30 October and Mussolini, wearing his blackshirt, was taken to meet the King. He apologised for his appearance, explaining, 'I have come straight from the battle, which, fortunately, was won without bloodshed.' He was formally asked to form a government.

The next day, wearing a borrowed morning coat and spats (ankle covering worn by the upper classes), he attended the King at his palace and was sworn in as Prime Minister, as well as Foreign and Interior Minister. There were only three other Fascists in a coalition government.

His squads now travelled to Rome by train, to celebrate 'their victory'. Fifty thousand Blackshirts, interspersed with regular army troops, paraded in front of their leader, and the King. This was the real March on Rome, which was to go down in Fascist history as the heroic revolution by which they had seized power. The Fascists expected Italy now to be handed over to their tender care. Things were not, however, going to be that simple.

Fascist local takeovers

- Generally authorities allowed Fascists to take over key
  buildings, as they waited for the national government to take lead in opposing the Fascists

Successful takeovers 27–28 Oct
- Alessandria, Bergamo, Brescia, Como, Venice, Padua, Vicenza, Trieste and virtually all
  Po Valley, e.g. Parma, Ferrara, Modena
- Pisa, Florence
- Some in South: Foggia, Apulia

Failed to gain full control
- Turin, Milan, Cremona, Bologna

The March on Rome

2 Assembly points

Perugia, Quadrumvirate's
headquarters
- 27 Oct Prefect agreed
  to hand over power

Foligno
- Reserves
- 3000 assembled;
  only 300 armed
- 5000 eventually marched

Civitavecchia
- 28 Oct 4000 assembled,
  no rail transport
- 30 Oct 6000 left
  for Rome

Tivoli
- 8000 assembled
- 31 Oct left

Monterotondo
- 28 Oct 2000 assembled
- 30 Oct 13,000 left

3 The Marchers

- 28 Oct total 14,000 met
- Poorly armed, inadequate food, pouring rain
- By 30 Oct over 30,000; impatient to move; eventually
  did so on 30 and 31 Oct, mainly by special trains
- 31 Oct paraded through Rome

1 The plan

Naples
- 24 Oct 40,000 Fascists met to plan
  seizure of power
- 27 Oct plan to mobilise at various
  local bases, then 27–28 Oct seize power in their
  areas; some squads would stay in their home base,
  others would meet at four concentration points
  for March on Rome

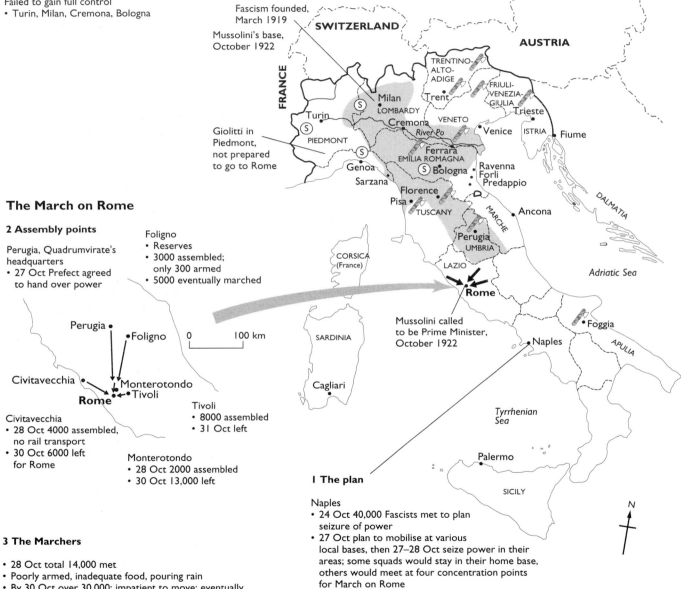

Fascism founded,
March 1919

Mussolini's base,
October 1922

Giolitti in
Piedmont,
not prepared
to go to Rome

Mussolini called
to be Prime Minister,
October 1922

Key

(S) Socialist strongholds

Fascist takeover of local government,
October 1922

→ March on Rome

Areas of growth of Fascism, 1919–21

59

WHY WAS MUSSOLINI, THE FASCIST LEADER, APPOINTED PRIME MINISTER OF ITALY IN 1922?

The March on Rome: a detailed chronology

There are some events in history when it is important to be clear what was happening day by day, and even hour by hour. This detailed chronology is designed to help clarify events during the crucial period 27–31 October.

Background

Liberal politicians quarrelling; many considered bringing Mussolini into the government. Some favoured d'Annunzio as a potential new strong ruler.

Summer 1922

Squads controlled several areas, e.g. Ferrara, Ravenna, Parma, Alto-Adige. Government took no action.

1 Aug Socialists called a general strike. Poor response, called off after one day. 'Caporetto of Italian Socialism'. Raised spectre of Socialist revolution, and allowed Fascists to portray themselves as protectors of the state.

March on Rome

16 Oct Mussolini and other Fascist leaders agreed to plan an insurrection.

24 Oct Fascist Congress in Naples. Mussolini publicly told squads that Fascism would either be appointed or would seize power. Authorities took no action.

Power in four days, 27–30 October

27 Oct Mussolini seemed on the verge of accepting a ministerial post in a new government. He was persuaded to hold out for more by other Fascists, and by government inaction.

Fascists concentrated in three main areas within marching distance of Rome. Blackshirts were under secret orders not to clash with the army. Quadrumvirs at Perugia (see Chart 3H) issued a proclamation, 'against a political class of half-wits and idiots which in four long years has been unable to give a true government to our nation'.

(Overnight) Fascists tried to seize control of telephone exchanges, police stations, government offices. In some areas, e.g. Milan and Bologna, they failed. In others, they took control, then lost it, e.g. Pisa. In many provincial cities, they succeeded.

(Midnight) PM Facta agreed to take military action against the Fascist threat; he asked the King to use the army.

28 Oct (2 am) King agreed to martial law. Some measures taken. Mussolini's arrest ordered. Milan prefect Lusignoli refused to act.

(9 am) King refused to sign martial law decree. Facta resigned. Salandra tried to form a government; Mussolini refused to join.

29 Oct Salandra advised that Mussolini be appointed PM. King agreed.

(Midday) King told de Vecchi to phone Mussolini to invite him to form a government. A telegram was sent confirming the offer. Mussolini left by night train.

30 Oct Mussolini arrived in Rome. Victor Emmanuel appointed him PM. The squads started arriving. Twelve were killed in minor skirmishes.

31 Oct Most squads arrived by train for a parade before the King and Mussolini.

SOURCE 3.24 Mussolini with the Quadrumvirs: General de Bono, 58, old-style nationalist; Balbo, 26, violent extremist, ras; de Vecchi, 37, ultra-conservative landowner, monarchist; Bianchi, 39, Syndicalist, ex-Socialist, journalist

60

WHY WAS MUSSOLINI, THE FASCIST LEADER, APPOINTED PRIME MINISTER OF ITALY IN 1922?

King Victor Emmanuel

He told a confidant he had refused to agree to martial law 'to save a Cabinet of poltroons [idiots]' and that in Mussolini he had a Prime Minister who was 'really a man of purpose who will last sometime and has the will to act and act well'

Mussolini in 1922

Giovanni Giolitti

Chief of Staff Badoglio

He was prepared to oppose the Fascists with force. Commander of Rome, Pugliese, said the army was loyal. His 12,000 well-armed troops in Rome would succeed against an estimated 17,000 badly armed squadristi. He made military preparations against the Fascists

Pope Pius XI

CHART 31   Who mattered in Mussolini's appointment? The key people

The King
- Disillusioned with parliamentary leadership
- Accepted, then rejected unanimous government advice to enact martial law; first time he had acted against his ministers' advice in 22 years
- Feared civil war and Duke of Aosta, his pro-Fascist cousin, as a rival monarch
- Queen Mother Margherita was pro-Fascist
- Doubted whether the army would be able to resist the march
- Cowardly, pessimist; lacked confidence
- Appointed Mussolini PM as Salandra advised

Mussolini
- Wavered over idea of march
- Used threat of coup to gain power
- Remained in Milan whilst march organised as it was the centre of Fascism, or because it was near to Switzerland
- Rejected offers of becoming a minister; wanted to be PM
- Realised his success rested as much on the ineptitude (failings) of his opponents as on his own strength

Facta
- Led a weak government Feb–Oct 1922
- Failed to act against Fascist threats and violence
- Asked King for martial law and when it was refused, resigned

Salandra
- Unable to persuade Mussolini to join his government, so advised his appointment as PM to stop his rival Giolitti

Giolitti
- 80-year-old master of Italian politics, and the politician Mussolini most feared
- Failed to come to Rome from Piedmont in October to be directly involved in negotiations over a new government
- Eventually supported Mussolini's appointment

Liberal politicians in general
- Facta, Salandra, Giolitti, Nitti, Orlando intrigued against each other, all looking to include Fascists in a new government led by themselves.
- Governments left it to prefects to take action against the Fascists.

The army
- Some generals sympathised with the Fascists.
- Six generals involved in the March
- Marshal Diaz told Victor Emmanuel, when asked about the army putting down the Fascists, 'The army will do its duty. However, it would be well not to put it to the test.'

The squads
- Thirty thousand squadristi gathered for the march, some unarmed.
- Other squads took over some local councils but failed elsewhere.

The Left
- Socialists did not call a general strike in response to Mussolini's appointment.
- Some saw Fascism's success as a sign of the collapse of the Liberal state, and a prelude to Socialist revolution.

The elite
- Leaders of the General Confederation of Industry, the Confederation of Agriculture, and the Bankers Association telephoned Rome asking for Mussolini as PM, 28 Oct.
- Pirelli and Olivetti (industrialists) urged a Mussolini government.

Pope Pius XI
- Friendly with Mussolini
- As bishop of Milan, allowed Fascist banners in church
- Oct: urged need for a peaceful settlement

The press
- Liberal press, e.g. *Corriere della Sera*, justified Fascist violence as the only alternative to anarchy.

Intellectuals
- Croce (see pages 120–21) and others sympathised with Fascism as a form of Italian renewal.

■ Learning trouble spots

1 The March on Rome and the Fascist seizure of cities

Many people have believed Fascism's claim that Mussolini was appointed Italian leader after the heroic Fascist March on Rome. They also ignore the Fascist seizure of provincial cities.

In fact, the March happened after Mussolini was appointed. It was still important in his appointment; but it was the (exaggerated) threat that mattered.

However, the Fascist threat did not just come from the planned march; the actions of the squads in the provinces, where they actually took control in many cities, were vital in persuading the King not to resist the Fascists.

2 The appeal of Fascism

Many students exaggerate the support for Fascism between 1919 and 1922. Mussolini is often regarded as the leader of a vast movement which appealed to millions of Italians, similar to the Nazis in Germany in 1932.

In fact, Mussolini had won no more than seven per cent of the vote in the 1921 election. Fascist propaganda stressing a great national renewal in 1922 must not be taken at face value. It seems likely that many Italians (far more than seven per cent) did welcome the promise of a more vigorous form of government under Mussolini, standing up for Italy's interests. However, he was clearly not swept to power primarily through the mass appeal of Fascism.

Later on, as we shall see, Mussolini became genuinely popular, and Fascism increased its appeal far beyond its limits in 1922. Even then, it was more a case of the great popularity of Mussolini as an individual rather than great commitment to Fascism.

FOCUS ROUTE

1 After reading the account of how Mussolini became leader of Italy, and looking at the chronological chart, note down what you consider to be the key steps from 24 October to his appointment.

2 With which of the following points do you agree? Note down evidence to support your choice.
   a) Mussolini was not in full charge of the Fascists.
   b) Mussolini was hesitant over the potential for a march to succeed.
   c) Mussolini brilliantly masterminded the Fascist seizure of power.
   d) Mussolini used bluff to gain power.
   e) The Fascists would have been far too weak to seize power if the authorities had been determined to resist.
   f) The King had good reasons to appoint Mussolini.

3 a) Complete a chart like the one below about the role of various groups in Mussolini's appointment.
   b) Then write a brief explanation of who you think was most responsible.

Person/ group	What he/they did (or did not do) that contributed to Mussolini's gaining power	Mark out of 5 for degree of responsibility 1 = low, 5 = high
King		
Facta		
Giolitti		
Army generals		
Prefects		
Economic elite		
Pope		
Socialists		
Others		

4 Note down several points where events could have taken a different course, resulting in Mussolini not being appointed Prime Minister.

62

WHY WAS MUSSOLINI, THE FASCIST LEADER, APPOINTED PRIME MINISTER OF ITALY IN 1922?

E Review: Why was Mussolini, the Fascist leader, appointed Prime Minister of Italy in 1922?

In this chapter you have looked at the growth of Fascism and the development of Mussolini's career from humble origins to his appointment as Prime Minister. You should now know the following points:

FOCUS ROUTE

1 To ensure you have understood the key features about Fascism, summarise what you have learnt about:
   a) Fascist programmes
   b) Fascist violence
   c) Their supporters (joiners and users)
   d) Attitude of authorities
   e) Role of Mussolini.
2 What were the main problems Mussolini had to face in achieving power, and what skills did he employ to overcome them?
3 Do you think Fascism would have come to power without Mussolini? Jot down three points where Mussolini's role seems indispensable, and then any counterpoints.

Key points from Chapter 3

1 Mussolini, a radical Socialist, broke with the PSI over his support for the war.
2 In 1919 he set up his own Fascist movement with a nationalist but left-wing programme; it gained little initial support.
3 Fascism began to attract support from groups frightened by the threat of Socialism. It moved to the Right politically.
4 Fascism's genuine mass base was in the petty bourgeoisie, but it also had key tactical support from the elite.
5 Fascist squads, led by ras, attacked Socialists, often with the compliance of the authorities.
6 In the 1921 elections the Fascists gained seven per cent of the vote, and 35 MPs were elected to Parliament.
7 In 1921 Mussolini formed the PNF (Fascist Party), with a right-wing programme.
8 In October 1922 the Fascists planned a march on Rome; and seized control of some northern cities.
9 King Victor Emmanuel hesitated to take firm action, and decided to appoint Mussolini as Prime Minister.
10 The March on Rome happened after Mussolini's appointment.

CHART 3J   The rise of Benito Mussolini: power in four stages

1 'Enter stage left'
- Leader of Revolutionary Socialists
- Inspired by his father and humble background, becomes a radical Socialist
- His extremism and powerful oratory increase his influence.
- Leads opposition to reformists at 1912 PSI Conference
- 1912 becomes editor of *Avanti!*

2 'A national editor: from anti- to pro-war'
- Under his editorship, *Avanti!* circulation rises dramatically.
- Supports PSI line opposing First World War, then changes his mind
- Abandons stress on class for new force, the nation; switches from anti-war to pro-war
- Resigns from *Avanti!* and becomes editor of new *Il Popolo d'Italia*

3 'Mix and match: a new alignment'
- Founds Fascism. Builds up movement from 1919 electoral failure on the Left, to major force in Italy, attracting support from the Right

4 'From Blackshirt to top hat'
- Uses threat of Fascist coup to be appointed Prime Minister in October 1922

Section 1 Review: Why did Mussolini come to power in 1922?

You have now looked at the last important element to explain Mussolini's rise to power: the nature of Fascism 1919–22. This review aims to pull together the key areas you have covered in this whole section, so that you can attempt to answer the central question: Why was Mussolini, the Fascist leader, appointed Prime Minister of Italy in 1922?

■ Activity

Why did Mussolini become leader of Italy?

I The following reasons have been suggested. As they stand, they are just a list. They need classifying. One way would be by estimating their comparative importance. Code them in the following way:

✓✓✓ Very important reasons   ✓✓ Important reasons   ✓ Less important reasons.

Be prepared to justify your views.

Factor	Importance	Chapter
I Nature of RISORGIMENTO		I
2 Failings of Liberal Italy		I
3 Impact of First World War		2
4 Versailles peace terms		2
5 D'Annunzio and Fiume		2
6 Economic dislocation 1918–22		2
7 Threat of Socialism 1919–21		2
8 Socialist weakness		2
9 Appeal of Fascism		3
10 1921 election and Fascist representation in Parliament		3
11 Fascist violence		3
12 Support from the ELITE		3
13 Attitude and actions of national and local governments		3
14 Mussolini's own qualities		3
15 Fascist takeover of local government, October 1922		3
16 Role of King		3
17 March on Rome		3
Others		

■ Talking point

What are the advantages and disadvantages of historians discussing hypothetical questions?

2 Was the rise to power of Mussolini in 1922 inevitable? Historians are often tempted to feel that because a particular event happened, it was bound to happen. However, if certain events or people are hypothetically removed from the historical scene, it can be interesting to speculate how events might have turned out differently. Would, for example, Fascism have come to power, if Mussolini had decided to emigrate in 1919, as he nearly did? Or if the King had kept to his original decision to declare MARTIAL LAW in October 1922? Debate the conclusion 'Mussolini's rise to power was inevitable'.

The rise of Fascism

The following exercise is designed to give you practice at reading some major extracts from different historians to help comprehension and evaluation skills.

SOURCE 1 M. Clark, *Modern Italy 1871–1982*, 1984, pp. 221, 260

Thus Mussolini did not really seize power. He did not, by 28 October, need to use force. He won by threatening to use it, and by having the squads ready to obey. Formally, he became Prime Minister constitutionally, appointed by the King; the 'March on Rome' happened afterwards ... Mussolini won by being 'brought into the system' by a king and a governing elite that could see no other way of containing organised violence. Although it is right to stress the longer-term causes of his victory – the 'mutilated victory' of Versailles, agrarian class conflicts, ex-officers seeking social promotion, PROPORTIONAL REPRESENTATION *and so forth, there was nothing inevitable about it. If there had been a 'respectable' conservative able to exploit anti-union sentiment in 1920–21, if Giolitti had not made Fascism respectable in May 1921, if the Popolari had not been so opposed to a new Giolitti government in February 1922, if the reformist Socialists had not called a general strike in August 1922, if Facta had resigned earlier in October, if Giolitti had been in Rome instead of Piedmont later in the month, or if the King had not been worried about his cousin, all might have been different. And the idea of 'absorbing' the Fascists into the Establishment, of allowing them a few posts in someone else's government, may have been ignoble but was not foolish. It might have worked – Mussolini himself recognized on 17 October that 'they would like to imprison me; joining a government would be the liquidation of Fascism'. 'Absorbing' troublemakers is normally sound Italian politics; on this occasion it misfired, but the politicians cannot be blamed too harshly for trying it ...*

All crises can have multiple outcomes. Fascism was not inevitable, nor was it bound to succeed. The only way to understand why Italy became Fascist is to study its detailed history.

SOURCE 2 M. Blinkhorn, *Mussolini and Fascist Italy*, 1984, p. 44

As the volume of serious historical literature on the different aspects of Italian Fascism increases, and as the passage of time makes possible a clearer perspective and greater objectivity, it becomes evident how complex a phenomenon it was. The underlying conditions – which did not, of course, constitute a cause – arose from the failure of Italian liberals, during and immediately after the Risorgimento, to involve more of the population in the nation's affairs. Even as the years passed the country's leaders were slow to move resolutely towards a broader-based political system. When greater DEMOCRACY *did arrive, it did so with explosive suddenness – between 1912 and 1922, when Italy was faced with the convulsive effects of war, post-war economic crises, mass demobilisation, frustrated* NATIONALISM *and acute social unrest. Such problems, of which social unrest was probably the most important, might have been more easily absorbed by an already established parliamentary system. It was Liberal Italy's misfortune to confront acute social conflict and the arrival of the 'masses' on the political stage at the same time. Worse still, in post-war 'democratic' Italy, hundreds of thousands, perhaps millions of Italians had no habitual or obvious political allegiance. Among them were two large and overlapping groups: war veterans, unrewarded for their sacrifices and belittled by the left, and assorted middle-class elements, some conforming to de Felice's picture of a rising and ambitious class, others, especially in the countryside, more closely resembling the fearful, declining* PETITE-BOURGEOISIE *of* MARXIST *accounts. These Italians, attached neither to traditional* LIBERALISM, *nor to political Catholicism, nor yet to Socialism, comprised Fascism's mass base.*

Fascism obtained power not through revolution but as the result of Mussolini's compromise with conservative and ostensibly liberal interests.

■ Marxist historians

There is a great variety of Marxist historians, but generally a historian influenced by the writings of Karl Marx might show some or all of the following characteristics. (NB These characteristics are not exclusive to Marxists.)

a) A belief that history is developing in a broad general direction, towards Communism

b) A stress on economic developments and class struggle as key forces in explaining history and the downplaying of the role of individuals

c) Sympathy towards the cause of the workers, and hostility to the bourgeoisie and elite

SOURCE 3   E. Tannenbaum, *Fascism in Italy*, 1973, pp. 6–7

There are perfectly plausible reasons for the behaviour of all the parties and factions concerned, but these do not shift the responsibility elsewhere. The point is that a liberal political system can only work when the majority of people with anything to say agree to make it work. This consensus simply did not exist in Italy. Thus the first well-organised attack against the liberal regime succeeded in destroying it altogether. Fascism was no mere 'parenthesis' [interlude] in the history of Italian liberalism, as Benedetto Croce maintained both during and after his own collaboration with Mussolini. Nor was it the last-ditch stand of capitalism against the PROLETARIAT, *as the Marxists used to claim. The argument that Italy was too underdeveloped economically to sustain a liberal regime discounts the fact that the main attacks against this regime came from some of the most advanced areas of the North, not the poverty-ridden South. The most that can be said is that Italy's liberal leaders did not adequately prepare the people for participation in the nation's political life . . .*

What went wrong? It is easy to argue that the war itself was what went wrong . . . The war and its immediate aftermath aggravated existing tensions and created new ones in other victorious nations without seriously threatening their liberal parliamentary regimes. One must therefore assume that there was something different about the Italian setting, at least since unification . . .

SOURCE 4   G. Carocci, *Italian Fascism*, 1974, pp. 26–27

The conservatives' wish for legality (sincere while at the same time more or less hypocritical) was mingled with another, profounder wish which is the key to an understanding of why Fascism was able to achieve power even when the situation of post-war crisis and revolutionary danger which had justified its success at the beginning no longer existed. This was the wish of conservatives and of the BOURGEOISIE *to halt the advance of democracy which had occurred since the war and to restore the old balance between the ruling classes and the mass of the people. In order to achieve this, they had to suppress the challenge of working-class parties, lower the level of wages, and restore total freedom to the entrepreneurs by abolishing the controls and attempts at control which had been introduced in those years . . .*

The March on Rome, like the intervention of 1915, was a show of strength against a parliamentary majority. This show of strength would have failed if the King had opposed it. But, as in 1915, the King felt it was right not to oppose it.

SOURCE 5   H. Kedward, *Fascism in Western Europe*, 1969, p. 43

Any account of European Fascism in the twentieth century must begin by saying that its strength lay in the willingness and enthusiasm with which large numbers of ordinary people welcomed its ideals, believed in its claims and endorsed its methods. In Italy in 1921 this was historical reality. In Germany in 1933 it was even more true. The wide appeal and attraction of Fascism is something which must first be admitted before any understanding of it can emerge.

SOURCE 6   T. Abse, 'The Rise of Fascism in an Industrial City: the Case of Livorno 1918–22', in D. Forgacs, *Rethinking Italian Fascism*, 1986, p. 52

Any analysis of the Italian political crisis stretching from the Armistice to the March on Rome which ignores or even minimises the role of class conflict is absolutely valueless. The mire into which even the most intelligent of self-consciously anti-Marxist historians are liable to sink is brilliantly exemplified by the notion propounded by Martin Clark in his Modern Italy 1871–1982 *that the rise of Fascism was merely a series of accidents and that if only the King had woken up in a different frame of mind one morning in October 1922 there would have been no Fascist regime.*

■ **End of Section test**

(Marks are given in brackets.)

Basic comprehension questions

1 Source 1. How inevitable does Clark consider Mussolini's appointment?   [2]

2 Source 2. Why, according to Blinkhorn, are interpretations of Fascism changing?   [2]

3 Source 3. What does Tannenbaum consider was wrong with the Italian Liberal system?   [2]

4 Source 4. What does Carocci argue the middle classes wanted?   [2]

5 Source 5. What does Kedward see as the main strength of Fascism?   [2]

6 Source 6. What does Abse see as the central issue in Fascism's rise to power?   [2]

Comparison of historians

7 To what extent do Blinkhorn and Tannenbaum agree on the weaknesses of Liberal Italy?   [5]

8 To what extent do Blinkhorn, Tannenbaum and Carocci agree on the importance of the First World War in explaining the rise of Fascism?   [6]

Explanation of historians' views

9 Referring to the provenance of Source 5, how might Kedward's stress on the popularity of Fascism be explained?   [3]

10 Which two historians do you consider most likely to be Marxist historians? Explain with close reference to the text.   [4]

Assessing historians

11 Which piece of historical writing do you find most persuasive? Which least convincing? Why?   [5]

Historical debate

12 How well do these extracts illustrate how historians disagree about the reasons for the rise of Fascism?   [5]

(Total: 40 marks)

Section 1 review: key points

Chapter 1

1 Italy was not unified through mass, nationalist action.
2 Liberal Italy failed to integrate the masses and the Catholic Church into the state.
3 Giolitti's reforms were too little, too late.

Chapter 2

4 The First World War increased divisions in Italy.
5 Italy after the First World War was wracked by economic, social and political tension.
6 Liberal Italy failed, especially in 1896 and 1919, to achieve its IMPERIAL ambitions.
7 Socialism posed a potential threat, but in practice suffered major weaknesses.

Chapter 3

8 Fascism started as a form of nationalist Socialism, but moved to the Right.
9 It gained support from the petty bourgeoisie, and the elite welcomed its attacks on Socialists.
10 Mussolini exploited the fear of a Fascist revolt to get himself legally appointed Prime Minister in October 1922.

A look ahead

In this section we have talked about 'Fascism coming to power'. However, as you will see, this was more a case of Mussolini, the Fascist leader, being appointed Prime Minister, than of a full takeover of the state by the Fascist movement. The nature of Mussolini's government will be a major theme to analyse in the next section.

FOCUS ROUTE

1 **Concluding essay**: 'Did Fascism come to power more through its own strengths or through the weakness of its opponents?'

You will need to discuss the nature of Fascism, and its opponents. This is more complex than you might think. Clearly the Socialists were opponents, but you will also need to consider other groups who perhaps might have opposed Fascism, but did not.

You might want to round off the essay by referring to other factors that contributed to Fascism's success.

You could also briefly consider whether 'Fascism' did come to 'power' in 1922. You will be able to understand the doubts about this after you have studied what Mussolini did when appointed Prime Minister, but you might already be able to challenge the assumptions in the question.

2 It could be argued that there were three broad political possibilities for Italy in the post-war period:
a) The consolidation of a Liberal regime
b) The creation of a socialist state
or, what actually occurred,
c) The creation of an AUTHORITARIAN or Fascist state.
Choose one of these alternatives to Fascism and explain how it might have occurred, and why it didn't.

How did Mussolini secure his regime?

Benito Mussolini, Il DUCE, ruled Italy from 1922 to 1943. During that time he became tremendously popular, perhaps the most popular Italian leader ever.

This section (Chapters 4–7) investigates how Mussolini established the Fascist regime and implemented his economic policies.

CHART A **SECTION OVERVIEW**

Section 2 How did Mussolini secure his regime?

4 How did Mussolini establish his dictatorship 1922–27? (pp. 71–84)

5 Was Mussolini an all-powerful dictator? (pp. 85–104)

6 How did Mussolini use propaganda to strengthen his regime? (pp. 105–24)

7 How successful were Mussolini's economic policies? (pp. 125–49)

Mussolini's Italy – an overview

Before you plunge into a detailed examination of Mussolini's domestic policies, it is useful to build up a clear overview of how the Fascist state developed. The next three pages provide this overview, and also give you a timeline for future reference. Chart B divides the period into four stages. Such division can help to give a neater structure to your study of a complex and evolving regime. However, as is usual in history, these do not represent stages with clear starting and ending points. Generally, each stage identifies a broad trend that some historians argue became more dominant at that time. However, you need to note that there are no precise dates when Mussolini moved from one stage to the next.

SOURCE 1   Mussolini encouraging farmers to grow more grain

CHART B The key events of Mussolini's Italy

Stages in the development of the Fascist state

1. Consolidation of Mussolini's government 1922–24

Initially, Mussolini's chief concern was to strengthen his position, so he acted fairly cautiously. He exercised strong government, but within the existing system. He thus disappointed the hopes of RADICALS for a full Fascist revolution.

2. The creation of dictatorship 1925–27

Mussolini moved to set up his own personal DICTATORSHIP as Duce, rather than one giving power to the Fascist Party. Basic freedoms, already restricted, were abolished.

STAGE 1		CONSOLIDATION
1922	Oct	New coalition Cabinet, led by Mussolini, with only four Fascists
	Nov	Parliament passes vote of confidence in new government by 306 to 116. Mussolini granted emergency powers for one year
	Dec	Fascist Grand Council created, controlled by Mussolini
1923		Continuing economic recovery
	Jan	Decree creates Fascist Militia, incorporating the Fascist squads
	Feb	NATIONALIST Association joins Fascist Party. Concessions to Pope
	Apr	Catholic Popolari Party dropped from government
	July	Acerbo Law guarantees two-thirds of the seats in Parliament to the largest party
	Aug	Foreign policy success in Corfu
1924	Jan	Italy gains long-claimed port of Fiume
	April	In election Fascists win 66% of vote, gaining 374 of 535 MPs

STAGE 2		DICTATORSHIP
1924	June	SOCIALIST leader Matteotti murdered. Opposition MPs walk out of Parliament
	July	Press censorship introduced. Opposition parties' meetings banned
1925	Jan	Mussolini accepts responsibility for Fascist violence. Wave of arrests and forced closure of hostile organisations
	May	DOPOLAVORO, mass leisure organisation, created
	Oct	'Battle for Grain', to increase grain production, launched
	Dec	Press censorship strengthened
1926	Jan	Law passed giving Mussolini right to issue decrees
	Feb	Elected mayors replaced by new appointed officials, the PODESTAS
	Apr	Strikes forbidden. Balilla, Fascist youth organisation, founded
	July	Ministry of Corporations created
	Oct	Opposition parties banned
	Nov	Special Tribunal for the Defence of the State and OVRA (new secret police)
	Dec	Value of lira raised to 90 to the pound
1927	Apr	Labour Charter issued granting workers' rights
1928	May	New electoral law replaces election of individual MPs with PLEBISCITE system

■ Activity

1 Study pages 68–69. What can you learn from them about:
   a) Mussolini's dominance of Italy
   b) the nature and aims of Fascist propaganda
   c) collaboration by the ELITE with Fascism
   d) the unattractive aspects of Fascism?
2 Try to find some early indications:
   a) why Mussolini was extremely popular at some times
   b) why he was overthrown.
3 Find evidence which supports the descriptions of the phases of Mussolini's rule as:
   a) Consolidation
   b) Dictatorship
   c) Consensus
   d) Radicalisation and collapse.

SOURCE 2 Fascist Blackshirts await the arrival of Mussolini

STAGE 3   CONSENSUS

1929	Feb	Concordat agreement with the Pope
	Mar	Plebiscite overwhelmingly approves government list of Deputies. National Council of Corporations
1931		Tension with Church over Catholic Action New penal code drawn up by Justice Minister Rocco
1934	Feb	Mixed Corporations of employers and employees set up. Again, plebiscite overwhelmingly approved government list of Deputies
	July	Mussolini defends Austrian independence
1935	Oct	Italy invades Abyssinia

STAGE 4   RADICALISATION AND COLLAPSE

1936	May	Victory proclaimed in Abyssinia
	July	Italian troops sent to help Franco in Spanish Civil War
	Oct	Axis agreement with Nazi Germany
1937	May	Ministry of Popular Culture to organise propaganda and culture
	Nov	Italy joins Anti-COMINTERN Pact against USSR with Germany and Japan
	Dec	Italy withdraws from League of Nations
1938		Reform of Customs aimed at changing Italians' behaviour
	July	Racial Laws discriminating against Jews
1939	Mar	Chamber of Fasces and Corporations created to replace Parliament
	Apr	Italy invades Albania
	May	Pact of Steel: formal alliance with Germany
1940	June	Italy declares war on France and Britain
	Oct	Italy invades Greece
	Nov	Italy invades Egypt
1941	June	Italy declares war on USSR
	Dec	Italy declares war on USA
1942		Series of Italian defeats in Africa
1943	July	American/British troops land in Sicily. Mussolini dismissed by King, and arrested. Fascism dissolved
	Sept	New government declares war on Germany. Germany invades North Italy. Mussolini installed as head of Salo Republic
1945	Apr	Mussolini killed by Italian COMMUNIST guerrillas
1946	June	Republic proclaimed after a referendum

3. Consensus: the development of the Corporative State 1929–35

This period has been called the 'years of consensus'. Mussolini achieved great popularity as a result of an agreement with the Church. He claimed his new Corporative State was the ideal form of government. In practice, it achieved little.

4. Radicalisation and decline 1936–45

Mussolini adopted more RADICAL domestic and foreign policies in a concerted attempt to change the nature of Italians. This move alienated many of his former supporters. Failure in war from 1940 increased discontent and led to his eventual overthrow in 1943.

SOURCE 3   Posts held by Mussolini

Head of Government 1922–43
Foreign Minister 1922–29, 1932–36, 1943
Interior Minister 1922–24
Minister for Colonies 1924, 1928–29, 1935–36, 1937–39
Minister for War 1925–29, 1933–43
Minister for the Navy 1925–29, 1933–43
Minister for the Air Force 1925–29, 1933–43
Minister for Public Works 1929
Minister for Corporations 1926–29, 1932–36

SOURCE 4   Comments on Mussolini by his colleagues

a) Socialist ex-colleague Serrati

He is a rabbit; a phenomenal rabbit! He roars. Observers who do not know him mistake him for a lion.

b) Fascist minister Balbo

Living in isolation, hearing nothing of reality, surrounded only by flatterers who told him only what he wanted to hear. If a man is told a hundred times a day that he is a genius, he will eventually believe in his own infallibility.

SOURCE 5   Mussolini and the King reviewing the army

SOURCE 6 Mussolini's sayings

a) *This people ... must ... accept obedience ... They must and they will believe what I tell them, and then they will march in compact ranks at my command.*

b) *It is really simpler to give orders myself instead of having to send for the minister concerned and convince him about what I want done.*

c) *You can usually get away with 97 cents worth of mere public clamour and three cents of solid achievement.*

d) *The nation is in our hands now, and we swear to lead her back to her ways of ancient greatness.*

e) *I shall defend the Italian lira to my last breath.*

f) *I often would like to be wrong, but so far it has never happened and events have always turned out as I foresaw.*

SOURCE 7 A Fascist Youth movement march

SOURCE 8 Fascist poster: 'We will go forwards'

SOURCE 9 Election posters during the 1934 plebiscite

SOURCE 10 Fascists marching past a hoarding with the slogan 'Believe, Obey, Fight'

How did Mussolini establish his dictatorship 1922–27?

FOCUS ROUTE

1 Use pages 71–75 to summarise the problems and pressures Mussolini faced once appointed Prime Minister in 1922.

2 Explain how Mussolini consolidated his position in 1922–24.

A   Normalisation or revolution? How did Mussolini consolidate his position between 1922 and 1924?

What problems and choices faced Mussolini in November 1922?

'I am here to stay.' That was Mussolini's confident declaration in October 1922 when he became Prime Minister, but very few people shared his confidence. He was not expected to stay in government long – not as Prime Minister and certainly not as the DICTATOR of Italy for nearly two decades. Italy did need a fresh, vigorous government but Mussolini faced many problems:

a) He was one of only four Fascists in the Cabinet.

b) There were only 35 Fascists in the 535-member Chamber of Deputies.

c) Fascism had won the support of only seven per cent of voters, achieving power partly through threats and violence.

d) Previous Italian governments had lasted on average under two years and Mussolini's new coalition government faced the same problems that the previous ones had failed to solve.

e) Mussolini had no detailed programme of policies and little experience of running anything except a newspaper.

f) Mussolini's own supporters were divided between moderates and RADICALS (see Chart 4B).

CHART 4B   Moderate and radical pressures on Mussolini

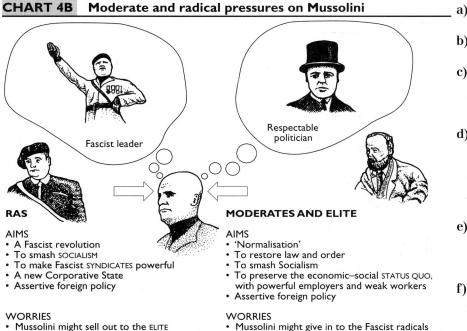

Fascist leader

Respectable politician

RAS

AIMS
- A Fascist revolution
- To smash SOCIALISM
- To make Fascist SYNDICATES powerful
- A new Corporative State
- Assertive foreign policy

WORRIES
- Mussolini might sell out to the ELITE

MODERATES AND ELITE

AIMS
- 'Normalisation'
- To restore law and order
- To smash Socialism
- To preserve the economic–social STATUS QUO, with powerful employers and weak workers
- Assertive foreign policy

WORRIES
- Mussolini might give in to the Fascist radicals

How could Mussolini overcome these problems and turn 'office into power'? His survival would be determined by his own strengths and weaknesses in 1922, the strengths and weaknesses of his opponents, and by the actions he and his opponents would take. In order to become Prime Minister Mussolini had had to achieve a balance between radicals who favoured a violent seizure of power, and those in the Fascist movement and their supporters in the elite who wanted Mussolini to gain power legally. As Prime Minister he was still under pressure from these two contrasting sides. The radicals in the Fascist movement now looked for revolutionary change, and moderate Fascists and their supporters advocated 'normalisation': strengthening the authority of the state and restoring law and order, but otherwise defending the status quo (see Chart 4B). Which way would Mussolini turn?

■ **Talking point**

What do you think is the distinction between holding office and having power?

■ **Activity**

1 Using your existing knowledge and Chart 4B make a list of:
   a) the problems Mussolini might face, including his weaknesses and potential opponents
   b) his likely allies, strengths and other advantages.
2 Below are some of the options Mussolini could have taken after his appointment. Write down which options you think he would choose. Discuss your answers in pairs, then report back your suggestions to the class.

	MORE RADICAL OPTION	MORE MODERATE OPTION
a) **Victory march?**	Allow Fascist squads a victory march through Rome	Immediately order the squads to return home
b) **Parliament**	Abolish Parliament	Alter electoral system
c) **Mussolini's own power**	Declare DUCE all-powerful	Get Parliament to grant emergency powers
d) **Political parties**	Ban other parties, create a one-party state	Allow other parties, but use state power against hostile ones
e) **The Church**	Take over control of the Church	Appease the Catholic Church
f) **Local government**	Strengthen power of PREFECTS	Restore and respect local DEMOCRACY
g) **The King**	Replace King	Appease King
h) **Civil Service**	Replace all top officials with Fascists	Use existing officials
i) **Cabinet**	Establish all-Fascist Cabinet	Keep existing coalition Cabinet
j) **Fascist Party**	Give Fascists top jobs in state	Try to tighten control of Fascists
k) **Fascist squads**	Allow squads free rein	Incorporate many squads into a new state militia
l) **Trade unions**	Ban free trade unions	Encourage development of Fascist trade unions
m) **Industry**	Establish state control of industry	Reduce government economic regulations
n) **Opponents**	Threaten to use force against opponents	Promise to respect individual liberties
o) **Programme**	Stress radical programme	Stress reconciliation and new national awakening

3 Are there any other measures Mussolini could take to strengthen his position? For example, what might he try to do in foreign policy?
4 Which of the following describes the overall approach you think Mussolini would take?
   a) Embark on a full-blooded Fascist revolution
   b) Reassure the elite and strengthen the power of the state
   c) Abandon revolution and run the existing system
5 Discuss your decisions. You can compare these with what Mussolini actually did by reading pages 73–75, and looking at Chart 4F on page 83.

■ **Talking point**

Why is it important to understand the options facing Mussolini rather than just learning what he did? Will this, for example, help to improve the quality of your essays?

How did Mussolini consolidate his position 1922–24?

To help us understand how Mussolini went about consolidating his power, let us look at his first important speech to Parliament.

SOURCE 4.1   An extract from Mussolini's first speech as Prime Minister to the Chamber of Deputies, 16 November 1922, as recorded in the official parliamentary record

Gentlemen! What I am doing now in this hall is an act of formal deference [respect] to you, for which I ask no special sign of gratitude ... To the melancholy zealots of super-constitutionalism [politicians who believe that every small detail of the CONSTITUTION should be kept to] I shall leave the task of making their more or less pitiful lamentations [moans] about recent events. For my part, I insist that revolution has its rights. And so that everyone may know, I should like to add that I am here to defend and enforce in the highest degree the Blackshirts' revolution, and to inject it into the history of the nation as a force for development, progress and equilibrium (lively applause from the right).

I could have abused my victory, but I refused to do so. I imposed limits on myself. I told myself that the better wisdom is that which does not lose control of itself after victory. With 300,000 youths armed to the teeth, fully determined and almost mystically ready to act on any command of mine, I could have punished all those who defamed [criticised] and tried to sully [harm] Fascism (approval from the right). *I could have transformed this drab silent hall into a camp for my squads ...* (loud applause from the right; noise, comments; Modigliani: 'Long live Parliament! Long live Parliament!'; noise and shouts from the right; applause from the extreme left)

... I could have barred the doors of Parliament and formed a government exclusively of Fascists. I could have done so; but I chose not to, at least not for the present.

Our enemies have held on to their hiding places; and they have emerged from them without trouble and have enjoyed freedom of movement. And already they are profiting from this by spitting out poison again ...

I have formed a coalition government, not indeed with the object of obtaining a parliamentary majority – which I can now get along very well without (applause from the extreme right and extreme left) *– but in order to rally to the support of this suffocating nation all those who, regardless of nuances of party, wish to save this nation.*

From the bottom of my heart I thank my collaborators, ministers and under-secretaries ... And I cannot help recalling with pleasure the attitude of the labouring masses of Italians who have strengthened the Fascists' motto by both their active and passive solidarity.

I believe that I also express the thought of a large part of this assembly, and certainly the majority of the Italian people, when I pay warm homage to the SOVEREIGN who refused to take part in futile, last-minute REACTIONARY manoeuvres, who averted civil war and allowed the new and impetuous Fascist current springing from the war and inspired by victory, to flow into the weakened arteries of the parliamentary state (shouts of 'Long live the King'; ministers and many Deputies rise to their feet for warm, prolonged applause).

Before attaining this position I was asked on all sides for a programme. Alas! It is not programmes that are lacking in Italy; it is the men and the willingness to apply the programmes. All the problems of Italian life, all of them I say, have been solved on paper. What is lacking is the will to translate them into fact. Today the government represents this firm and decisive will.

SOURCE 4.2   A cartoon from the Fascist newspaper *Il Popolo d'Italia* by Sironi, inspired by Mussolini's first speech to Parliament, 16 November 1922

Mussolini's speech, with its mixture of references to legality and to intimidation, well illustrates the ambiguity in the nature of the new government. Had Mussolini come to power through a revolutionary march on Rome in order to embark on a Fascist revolution; or had he been chosen constitutionally by the King to provide effective government? This ambiguity remained during the first three years of Mussolini's government.

Moderates within the Fascist Party were strengthened when the NATIONALISTS joined the PNF. Rocco and Federzoni, in particular, were to play a major role in establishing a strong, though not really Fascist, state. Mussolini realised the support of the elite was more important for his chances of staying in power than that of radical Fascists. He had used their violence to attack the Socialists and win power, but now the squads were less important. He could use the power of the state against his enemies. However, he could not ignore the Fascists. His formal power base was not that strong, and his control over the RAS had never been complete.

In November 1922 Parliament granted him limited emergency powers for one year to deal with the country's problems. Although his first political actions were a move to AUTHORITARIANISM he was neither just tightening up the existing system, nor embarking on a revolution. In strengthening his position he made some concessions to the Church and passed measures favourable to industrialists and agrarians. He also benefited from a general European economic recovery and consolidated his position through asserting Italy's rights abroad, in the Corfu and Fiume incidents (see page 212).

Mussolini also took account of the Fascist movement. He created two new Fascist bodies, the Fascist Grand Council, potentially a rival Cabinet, and a new militia, paid for by the state, largely recruited from the Fascist squads. Though superficially these might be seen as moves to fascistise the state, it was more a case of Mussolini extending his control over the Fascist movement.

Mussolini's position as Prime Minister was still potentially weak. The King could dismiss him at any stage, and Parliament, with only a small minority of Fascist MPs, would be likely to co-operate with any successor. If he could get a Fascist majority, however, Parliament could obstruct any successor. So he changed the electoral system, arguing the need to create a secure government by replacing the PROPORTIONAL REPRESENTATION system which had caused a series of coalition governments. In July 1923 the Chamber, surrounded by Blackshirts, passed the Acerbo Law (named after the Fascist deputy who introduced it) by 303 to 40. Henceforth the party gaining most votes in an election, provided they obtained at least 25 per cent of the votes, would take two-thirds of the seats.

This electoral reform was put into action in the elections of April 1924. The government drew up its list of approved candidates, and many non-Fascists were eager to be included. In Sicily 60 per cent of the government list were ex-LIBERALs. Conveniently for Mussolini the opposition remained split and the COMMUNIST Party rejected a PSI proposal for a joint Left list. The various Liberal factions also failed to agree on one list.

The voting exhibited some of the traditional features of Italian elections with government influence being heavily employed. This was reinforced by militia violence. One Socialist candidate was killed; meetings were stopped and hostile voters intimidated. Some Fascist voters were allowed to vote many times each! The ras had a virtually free hand in intimidating opponents in the small towns in the provinces, but less so in larger cities where workers' organisations were still strong. Lyttleton argues in his book *The Seizure of Power* that 'the use of violence, police repression and electoral fraud was on such a large scale that the expression of popular will was radically falsified'.

The government list won 66 per cent of the vote, with over 80 per cent of the vote in the South, while attracting less than 40 per cent in the industrial cities like Milan and Turin. The Fascists now had 275 Deputies, with another 100 supporters. The Socialists and Catholics were both reduced to under 50 Deputies.

By 1924 Mussolini was in a much stronger position. His Socialist opponents had been weakened by their failure to exploit their strength in 1920–21 and by the violent Fascist onslaught in 1921–22. The Fascists now had the power of the state behind them. Alongside 'official' militia pressure on critics, unofficial squad violence continued. Socialist meetings, individuals and buildings were attacked, as were hostile newspapers. Other potential critics kept silent.

However, a full-scale Fascist revolution had not taken place and Fascist violence could not solve all Mussolini's problems. In fact, violence was about to create a crisis that was the greatest threat to Mussolini's position before his final fall from power in 1943.

Why did so many Italians support Mussolini's government?

Even allowing for intimidation, once in power Mussolini's government attracted a lot of support, as the following comments show.

SOURCE 4.3   Pope Pius XI to the French ambassador Beyens

Mussolini alone has a proper understanding of what is necessary for his country in order to rid it of the anarchy to which it has been reduced by an impotent [powerless] parliamentarianism and three years of war. You see that he has carried the nation with him. May he be able to regenerate Italy.

SOURCE 4.4   Former Liberal Prime Minister Giolitti, November 1922

Mussolini's is the only government that can restore social peace . . . The Cabinet must be supported. The country needs a strong government that looks beyond living from day to day. Italian political life needs new blood, new energies.

SOURCE 4.5   Newspaper owner Conservative–Liberal Albertini, in public and private comments

He has saved Italy from the Socialist danger which had been poisoning our life for 20 years.
Once he is in Rome, he will be more subject to influence.

SOURCE 4.6   A 1923 cartoon by Max Beerbohm entitled 'The Beneficent Despot'. The figures on the right are Victor Emmanuel III and King George V. The caption was 'One constitutional monarch to another: "He has worked wonders for my people. If you'd like me to lend him to you . . ."'

SOURCE 4.7   Senator Frassati, the Liberal Editor of *La Stampa*, identified positive signs in an article in May 1923

The incorporation of the squadristi into the national militia, the punishment of the awkward, the elimination of men who were very well known in the party, the clear assertion that the authority of the state resides in the prefects and not in the representatives of the party, the recognition of the statute [constitution] and the authority of the King . . .

SOURCE 4.8   *The Times* reviews the first year of Fascism, 31 October 1923

Italy has never been so united as she is today . . . Fascismo has abolished the game of parliamentary chess; it has also simplified the taxation system and reduced the deficit to manageable proportions; it has vastly improved the public services, particularly the railways; it has reduced a superfluously large bureaucracy without any very bad results in the way of hardships or unemployment; it has pursued a vigorous and fairly successful colonial policy. All this represents hard and useful work, but the chief boons it has conferred upon Italy are national security and national self-respect . . .
Fascismo has had a great deal of courage, very considerable wisdom and immense luck . . . it has deserved the sincere birthday greetings of the world.

■ Activity

In the 1921 election the Fascists had won seven per cent of the vote. In the next election of 1924 they gained 66 per cent. How can this increased electoral support be explained?

1 Read Sources 4.3–5 and 4.7.
   a) List the various reasons why these members of the elite supported Mussolini's government.
   b) What other reasons might explain why the elite supported Mussolini?

2 In 1924 one politician explained his decision to join the government list as due to 'safety' and 'office'. What do you think he meant?

3 a) Match up the group whose support Mussolini won, with the description of how he achieved this. (Refer to Chart 4F on page 83.)

Group	Measures taken
1 MONARCHY	a) Raised priests' salaries and made minor concessions
2 Workers	b) Respected its role
3 Landowners	c) Relaxed state controls and adopted LAISSEZ-FAIRE policies
4 Industry	d) Fascist trade unions encouraged
5 Fascists	e) Abandoned agrarian reform plans
6 Church	f) Assertive foreign policy
7 All	g) Jobs provided in growing bureaucracy

   b) Might any members of these groups be disappointed with Mussolini's policies?

4 Study Sources 4.6 and 4.8.
   a) Explain the reference to 'parliamentary chess'.
   b) What does *The Times* see as Fascism's greatest achievements?
   c) How does Source 4.8 help us understand Source 4.6?

B How important was the Matteotti crisis?

SOURCE 4.9   Giacomo Matteotti

SOURCE 4.10   The car in which Matteotti was assassinated

FOCUS ROUTE

Using pages 76–81, write structured notes on the Matteotti crisis.

i) Describe what happened.
ii) Explain why Mussolini survived.

Find evidence to support each of the following:

a) Attitudes/actions of the King
b) Attitudes/actions of the elite
c) Nature, actions of the opposition
d) Mussolini's actions
e) Fascism's strengths
f) Other reasons for Mussolini's survival.

On 30 May 1924 Giacomo Matteotti rose to his feet in the Italian Chamber of Deputies. Outraged by the Fascist violence in the recent elections, the Socialist leader had prepared a 30-minute speech denouncing the violence and calling for the annulment (cancelling) of the election results. He began to speak but within moments the interruptions began. Fascist Deputies were determined to stop Matteotti. Again and again they disrupted his speech but Matteotti struggled on. It took him two hours to complete his speech. Matteotti knew the likely cost of opposing the Fascists. As he left the Chamber of Deputies he turned to colleagues saying, 'Now you can prepare my funeral oration.'

Matteotti was right. He had predicted his own death and his prediction came true. Eleven days later, Matteotti (for once not under surveillance by the police) found his way to the Chamber blocked by a gang of ex-squadristi. They bundled him, desperately resisting, into a car. 'You may kill me,' he shouted, 'you will not kill the ideal. The workers will bless my dead body.' As the car screeched off, his abductors, armed with guns and knives, repeatedly stabbed him.

It was two months before Matteotti's death was confirmed. Dogs found his naked body, lying in a shallow grave 23 kilometres from Rome. A file was still sticking in his chest. An investigation was set up. The initial incident had been seen by a passer-by who noted down the car's licence plate registration. The car was found to belong to Filipelli, a leading Fascist. From this lead, many people linked to the government were implicated. The murder was traced to Dumini. He was a member of a secret hit squad called the Cheka (named after Lenin's secret police) that Mussolini had set up. Deservedly nicknamed 'nine homicides', Dumini was the personal assistant to Mussolini's press secretary and confidant, Cesare Rossi.

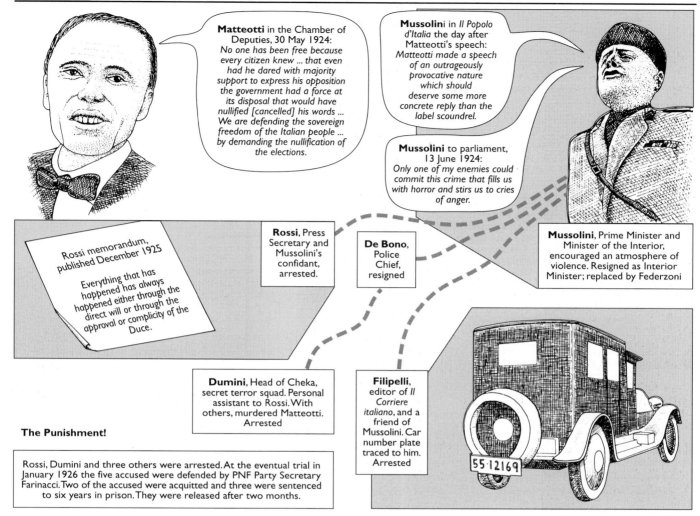

Matteotti in the Chamber of Deputies, 30 May 1924: *No one has been free because every citizen knew ... that even had he dared with majority support to express his opposition the government had a force at its disposal that would have nullified [cancelled] his words ... We are defending the sovereign freedom of the Italian people ... by demanding the nullification of the elections.*

Mussolini in *Il Popolo d'Italia* the day after Matteotti's speech: *Matteotti made a speech of an outrageously provocative nature which should deserve some more concrete reply than the label scoundrel.*

Mussolini to parliament, 13 June 1924: *Only one of my enemies could commit this crime that fills us with horror and stirs us to cries of anger.*

Rossi, Press Secretary and Mussolini's confidant, arrested.

De Bono, Police Chief, resigned

Mussolini, Prime Minister and Minister of the Interior, encouraged an atmosphere of violence. Resigned as Interior Minister; replaced by Federzoni

Rossi memorandum, published December 1925

Everything that has happened has always happened either through the direct will or through the approval or complicity of the Duce.

Dumini, Head of Cheka, secret terror squad. Personal assistant to Rossi. With others, murdered Matteotti. Arrested

Filipelli, editor of *Il Corriere italiano*, and a friend of Mussolini. Car number plate traced to him. Arrested

The Punishment!

Rossi, Dumini and three others were arrested. At the eventual trial in January 1926 the five accused were defended by PNF Party Secretary Farinacci. Two of the accused were acquitted and three were sentenced to six years in prison. They were released after two months.

55·12169

Mussolini now faced a crisis that threatened to topple him from power. There was a widespread belief that Mussolini was personally involved in the murder of his chief political opponent. Fierce criticism came from many sections of the press. Large crowds gathered in the streets to protest. People tore up Fascist membership cards. Communists called for a general strike.

The murder of Matteotti raised in a stark form the question of the nature of the new Fascist government, which had not been clarified during the previous two years. Was it a terrorist regime where opponents were at the mercy of Fascist thugs, or was it merely a strengthened form of parliamentary government that operated within the law? Mussolini had wavered between the two approaches. Now he had to make a decision between one approach or the other, or face removal from power.

How did Mussolini respond to the crisis?

Mussolini was initially unsure what to do: 'My position is untenable. It is impossible to remain in power with a dead man at one's feet,' he said. For a time he was paralysed by depression, partly caused by severe ulcers. Most opposition Deputies walked out of Parliament, in a move known as the Aventine Secession named after a group of ancient Roman politicians who had set up a rival assembly on the Aventine Hills above Rome. They met elsewhere and declared themselves to be the true representatives of the Italian people. They expected the King to dismiss Mussolini.

King Victor Emmanuel, however, wanted others to take the lead and, fortunately for Mussolini, his opponents were divided. Despite most Deputies' opinions, many in the elite still considered a Mussolini government the best

78

HOW DID MUSSOLINI ESTABLISH HIS DICTATORSHIP 1922–27?

CHART 4D **Benito finito? Those who would decide his fate**

Ras
- Wanted to set up a Fascist dictatorship, smash the Liberal state.
- Farinacci: 'Duce, untie our hands.' 'All that is needed to solve the Italian problem is a few hundred thousand deaths.'

Elite
- Not entirely happy with Mussolini, but thought he'd been doing a good job – especially when faced with the alternatives.

King
- Unwilling to act, thinking it safer to keep Mussolini in office and that he'd learnt his lesson.
- 'I am not a judge. I should not be told such things.'
- 'I am blind and deaf; my eyes and ears are the Senate and the Chamber of Deputies.'

Church
- Mussolini had saved Italy from Socialism.
- Cardinal Gaspari: 'The overthrow of Mussolini could plunge the country in fire and blood.'

- Can I survive?
- Will the Left force me out?
- Shall I get swept away by the ras?
- Is this my opportunity to create a personal dictatorship, to control the Fascists, and establish my own power?

Opposition leaders
- Turati: 'Everyone feels that something ought to be done, but no positive decision can be reached.'
- Giolitti: 'Mussolini has all the luck; the opposition was always very troublesome to me, but with him it just walks out and leaves the field free.'

Army
- Would obey the King.

Moderate Deputies
- Now Mussolini was weak, believed they'd be able to control him.

Parliament
- Senate vote of confidence 225 v 21. Most opposition MPs left Chamber; large Fascist majority remained.

■ **Learning trouble spot**

Students sometimes come away with the impression that:

a) **The Matteotti murder led straight away to a Fascist dictatorship.**

b) **Mussolini admitted direct responsibility for the murder in his January 1925 speech.**

In fact, it is more complex:

- **Matteotti was murdered in June 1924; this led to a prolonged crisis, during which Mussolini was uncertain how to act.**
- **He finally asserted himself six months later with his speech to Parliament in January 1925.**
- **In this he took responsibility for Fascism (and its violence) but denied ordering Matteotti's murder.**
- **Although this speech was followed by a wave of arrests and repressive action that marked the beginning of dictatorship, the major formal decrees were made gradually over the next two years.**
- **The most important of these, giving Mussolini power to rule by decree as Head of Government, was not passed until December 1925, eighteen months after Matteotti's murder.**

option, and thought that as he was in trouble he would be easier to control. While the opposition hesitated the Fascist radicals demanded that Mussolini seize the initiative, abandoning his conciliatory approach and setting up a full Fascist dictatorship.

Mussolini's first response was a policy which combined repression and concession. The militia was MOBILISED and tighter controls were imposed on the press, but there were concessions when the militia was integrated into the armed forces, with a new loyalty oath to the King. The suspects Rossi and Chief of Police de Bono were sacked, and the conservative Federzoni replaced Mussolini as Interior Minister.

However, this was not enough to take the pressure off Mussolini. Criticism from his opponents mounted as new evidence emerged implicating him in Fascist violence. On 27 December a newspaper published Rossi's testimony, directly implicating Mussolini in Fascist murder. However, the King refused to read the incriminating report, let alone act.

Mussolini was also under pressure from his own party. The Fascist radicals were equally critical, fearing that if Mussolini lost power their chances of a Fascist revolution would disappear. The ras pressured Mussolini to act, culminating in a tense meeting on 31 December 1924. Finally Mussolini took the plunge.

On 3 January 1925 he addressed the Chamber of Deputies. He took responsibility for Fascism (though not for the actual murder of Matteotti), and announced he would act within 48 hours to set up a dictatorship. The speech was followed by a wave of arrests, and measures against opponents. Over the following year a series of increasingly repressive DECREES and laws were issued. Mussolini was given the power to issue decrees, which he used to increase government controls. In January 1926 alone, over two thousand decrees were issued, and the powers of the government to act against critics were vastly extended. A new secret police, the OVRA, was established. Other parties were banned, and elected councils were replaced by appointed officials (see Chart 4F). The government ceased to be a mere ministry, and became a regime, as Mussolini established his dictatorship. However, contrary to the wishes of the ras, it was a personal dictatorship, rather than a fully Fascist one. Although Mussolini appointed the radical ras Farinacci as Party Secretary in February 1925, he cleverly used him to centralise the party (see page 94), and then dismissed him in March 1926. Thus Mussolini survived the Matteotti crisis due both to the actions he took, and the limitations of his opponents. In the end he gained considerably from a potentially fatal setback.

■ Activity

1 Read the following historians' assessments (Sources 4.11–16). Fill in a chart to record what each historian says about each of the following areas:
   • Attitudes/actions of King
   • Attitudes/actions of elite
   • Nature, actions of opposition
   • Mussolini's actions
   • Fascism's strengths

2 What points do all the historians make?

3 Are there any actual disagreements?

4 Which historians put more stress on Mussolini and the Fascists controlling their own fate?

5 Hold a discussion, set in early 1926, amongst a group of politically aware Italians (ranging from a Fascist sympathiser to a Socialist) over what you feel about Mussolini's government.

SOURCE 4.11   M. Gallo, *Mussolini's Italy*, 1974, pp. 189–91

The Aventine was undermined by its own contradictions. For the members of the opposition, genuine democrats who had not understood that Fascism represented a radically new element in political life, there was no choice but to await the constitutional monarch's pleasure and to continue making broad statements. Therefore, and as much in order to avoid frightening the King as out of fear of revolution, they rejected the call for a general strike and the proclamation of the Aventine as the sole legal Parliament of the country. Thereupon the anti-Fascist tide receded ... Turati [the Socialist] noted: 'We feel that it is essential to do something, but we cannot decide on anything positive. We feel that with the passage of time the enemy is catching his breath and that without doubt the Matteotti affair has now been drained of its possibilities.'

[After the Rossi memorandum was published] The Liberals of the Aventine thought that this indictment [damning report] would be read by at least one person, the King. They hoped to bring about a Cabinet crisis and the dismissal of Mussolini. It was now December, seven months after the murder of Matteotti, and the Aventine moderates had not yet learned that on the parliamentary battleground Mussolini was bound to win because the King was determined to uphold him and a comfortable majority in the Chamber supported him. Furthermore, the battle was already lost because disillusion had swept the Italian masses once roused by hope and rebellion. In addition, the Fascists everywhere were arming themselves and reinforcing the militia.

SOURCE 4.12   Cassels, p. 47

The reluctant attitudes of King and Pope summarised the problems in a nutshell: the Italian power structure was slow to admit that its creature, Fascism, was out of control, and without leadership from the power structure, the anti-Fascist opposition remained fragmented and embryonic.

SOURCE 4.13   R. Eatwell, *Fascism, a History*, 1995, p. 52

Visitors to Mussolini at this time found him red-eyed and unshaven; he clearly feared his days were numbered. Yet the King declined to act ... He had quickly come to value Mussolini ...

Mussolini was under considerable pressure, but he was far from resigning. He countered by making changes in the government to reassure moderates ... Damage limitation was helped by the Vatican ... Many leading members of the clergy were grateful to Fascism for breaking the Left ... Industrialists too stayed largely faithful, reflecting their basic satisfaction with government policy ... Other prominent figures rallied to Mussolini ... many clearly believed that Mussolini deserved a further chance to show he could provide firm government. Mussolini too played his part, shrewdly exploiting the fear that if he resigned the result would be further political chaos, and a squadristi wave of violence.

SOURCE 4.14   Blinkhorn, p. 19

Mussolini panicked and would have resigned had the King required it. The King did not [make Mussolini resign], demonstrating the unwillingness of conservatives even now to abandon Mussolini, partly from fear of a LEFT-WING revival and partly in the hope of exploiting Mussolini's vulnerability to increase their influence over him.

SOURCE 4.15   Clark, pp. 227–28

His victory, once again, owed much to the militant squads and to their power in the provinces; and, once again, it owed much to the King's unwillingness to use the army against the Fascists. Yet once again, it was not inevitable. If the opposition parties had been present in the Chamber ... or if the Rossi memorandum had not been published when it was (on 27 December, the holiday period) ... or if the militia 'consuls' [leaders] had not conveniently put pressure on in late December, or if the elder statesmen ... had shown more initiative, then Mussolini might have fallen ... The King had decided, and Mussolini was safe.

SOURCE 4.16   E. Wiskemann, *Fascism in Italy, Its Development and Influence*, 1969, p. 16

Mussolini lost his confidence for months. By the end of the year he recovered it partly because of the hopeless divisions among his enemies. Most of them left the actual Chamber to form the Aventine Secession ... but most of the Liberals disapproved of this as contrary to parliamentary principles. The King disliked the Aventine people because most of them were REPUBLICANS. The decisive voices, however, were those of the Church and of industry. The Pope expressed approval of the regime ... Industrialists were opposed to another fresh beginning, all the more so since Mussolini had gone all out to propitiate them [win them over] by reducing the state's interference in the economy.

■ Activity

(Marks are given in brackets.)

1 Explain the references in Source 4.17 to:
   a) 'from the days of intervention' (2)
   b) 'castor oil and the club'. (2)

2 What do the extracts from Mussolini's speech suggest about his attitude to violence? (3)

3 Explain Orlando's description of the role of Fascist violence and state power (Source 4.18). (3)

4 What can you learn from Source 4.20? (2)

5 Study the cartoons (Sources 4.19 and 4.21). Compare the impression given of Mussolini in the two cartoons. What message is conveyed by each cartoon? (5)

6 'These sources illustrate how force and violence helped Fascism gain and keep power, but also the dangers for Mussolini of such an approach.' To what extent do you agree with this comment? (8)

Source exercise: The Matteotti crisis

SOURCE 4.17   Extracts from Mussolini's speech to the Chamber, 3 January 1925 (reported in the parliamentary record)

The speech I am going to make may not be classifiable as a parliamentary speech . . .

I here declare, before this chamber, and before the whole of the Italian people, that I, I alone, assume full political, moral and historical responsibility for all that has happened. (Most lively and repeated applause; many shouts of 'We are all with you! We are all with you!') . . . If Fascism has been nothing more than castor oil and the club and not a proud passion of the best Italian youth, the blame is on me. If Fascism has been a criminal association, then I am the chief of this criminal association (vigorous applause). If all the violence has been the result of a particular historical, political, and moral atmosphere, the responsibility is mine, because I have created this atmosphere with a propaganda from the days of intervention down till today . . .

When two irreducible elements are in conflict, the solution is force . . . In history there never has been any other solution, and there never will be . . .

You thought Fascism was finished because I was restraining it, that it was dead because I was punishing it and because I had the audacity to say so. But if I were to employ the hundredth part of the energy in unleashing it that I have used in restraining it, you would understand then (vigorous applause). But there will be no need for this, because the government is strong enough to break the Aventine's sedition completely and definitely (vigorous, prolonged applause). Gentlemen, Italy wants peace and quiet, work and calm. I will give these things with love if possible and with force if necessary (lively applause).

You may be sure that within the next 48 hours after this speech, the situation will be clarified in every field (vigorous, prolonged applause). Everyone must realise that what I am planning to do is not the result of personal whim, of a lust for power, or of an ignoble passion, but solely the expression of my unlimited and mighty love for the fatherland (vigorous, prolonged and reiterated applause. Repeated cries of 'Long live Mussolini!').

SOURCE 4.18   From a speech given on 16 January 1925 by Orlando, former Liberal Prime Minister who had joined the Fascist list in 1924, but then broke with Fascism during the Matteotti crisis

You say that the country is calm. Well, if you are willing to be content with that kind of calm! . . . During these last two and more years of government we have gone through various phases. In some of these there prevailed what I would call the private violence of the Fascist party and its organisations. This violence was deplored, even by the government. Then there followed governmental restrictions on personal freedom, with the justification that this was the way to contain the aforementioned violence. And thus pressure from the government replaced that of the party . . . Now we have both; we have both governmental reaction and party violence.

SOURCE 4.19   A 1924 cartoon from the Italian underground newspaper *Becco Giallo*

SOURCE 4.20 Italians placing a wreath on the spot where Matteotti was assassinated

SOURCE 4.21 A British cartoon from *Punch*, 26 November 1924

BLACK JERSEYS AND BLACK SHIRTS.

Signor Mussolini. "I SOMETIMES WISH *MY* 'ALL BLACKS' WERE ONLY FOOTBALLERS!"

The significance of the Matteotti crisis

This question, like the question of who was responsible for the Reichstag fire in Germany in 1933, and whether Stalin ordered the assassination of Kirov in 1934, has intrigued many historians.

In reality, the results of the Matteotti murder were far more important than the question of Mussolini's involvement. However, if Mussolini did order the murder, it could be used as evidence for those who question his political judgement.

The Matteotti crisis marked the turning point of Mussolini's regime. Until 1925 his ministry had appeared as just a stronger form of constitutional government. Mussolini eventually used the Matteotti crisis to set up a dictatorship, under which liberal freedoms and safeguards were replaced by a system concentrated on the power of one man.

C Review: How did Mussolini establish his dictatorship 1922–27?

Study the two charts in this conclusion. Chart 4E portrays the development of Mussolini and the Fascist regime 1922–27 from its roots before 1922, identifying the two trends, legal–normalising and violent–revolutionary, which operated within the Fascist movement and then the regime. This ambiguity was largely resolved after the Matteotti crisis, with the establishment of a dictatorship. However, it was not really a Fascist dictatorship, but more a personal dictatorship of Mussolini himself. The chart suggests that from its beginning Fascism can be partly explained as a vehicle for Mussolini to gain power.

Chart 4F summarises how the regime developed between 1922 and 1927, both chronologically and thematically. It thus centres on key stages in Mussolini's rise to power. Around this central image, it looks at what happened in important political areas, in the two key stages between 1922 and 1924, and 1925–27.

CHART 4E The ambiguous nature of Fascism

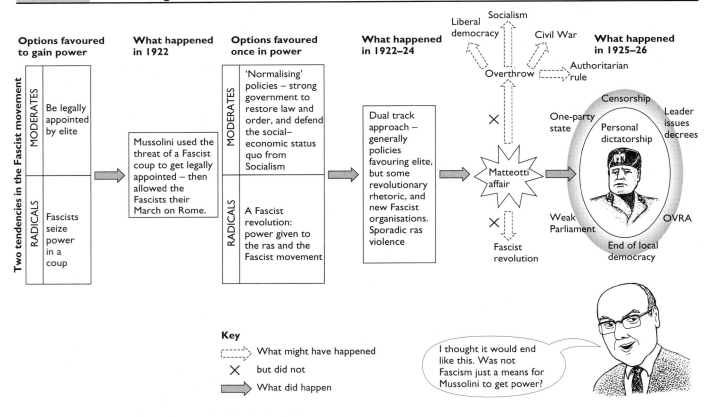

Key

- ┄┄▶ What might have happened
- ✕ but did not
- ⟹ What did happen

I thought it would end like this. Was not Fascism just a means for Mussolini to get power?

FOCUS ROUTE

1 **Either:**
Explain what Chart 4E shows about the two strands in Fascism 1922–25, and how they developed into Mussolini's personal dictatorship.
Or:
Choose to be either the ras Farinacci, or the moderate Fascist Rocco in 1927. (You may like to refer to Chapter 5 page 96 for more details on Farinacci.) Using Chart 4E as a guide, explain your view of how Mussolini should have gained power, what policies he should have adopted, and how you now view the regime.

2 From the list of measures in Chart 4F, identify examples of:
   a) increasing control by Mussolini over the Fascist Party
   b) the strengthening of the power of the state
   c) policies reassuring the elite.

3 Did the creation of dictatorship after 1924 mark a complete change of approach, or an intensification of earlier policies?

4 Write an essay with the title 'How and why did Mussolini set up a dictatorial regime in Italy in 1922–27?'.

Key
Stage 1 1922–24
Stage 2 1925–27

Government/Parliament
- Cabinet initially included representatives of every party except PSI and PCI. By mid-1923 most had left.
- 1922 7% MPs Fascists, Apr 1924 66%
- **Mussolini given great powers; could legislate by decree**
- **Responsible to King not Parliament**
- **Parliament lost power to initiate laws.**
- **1925 All-Fascist Cabinet**

Administration/Local government
- Immediate purge of opponents in civil service but no major change
- Local Socialist councils replaced
- Mussolini proclaimed the prefect supreme over the local party
- **Judges, civil servants, teachers purged**
- **Elected municipal councils eliminated**
- **7000 government-appointed** PODESTAS **replaced elected mayors**
- **Powers of prefects extended**

The steps to dictatorship

1 Oct 1922 Mussolini appointed Prime Minister of new 'National Government' with three other Fascists.
2 Nov 1922 Government easily wins vote of confidence in Parliament, and is voted emergency powers to reform the administration and tax system.
3 Dec–Jan Fascist Grand Council and Militia set up
4 Feb 1923 Nationalists join Fascist Party.
5 July 1923 Acerbo Election Law
6 April 1924 New elections. Government wins 66% of the votes.
7 June 1924 Matteotti murdered. Major crisis
8 3 Jan 1925 Mussolini addresses Parliament, and takes responsibility for violence. Series of arrests Most MPs withdraw in opposition. Mussolini under attack from all sides; major crisis, then …
9 Dec 1925 Law on powers of Head of Government; Mussolini given great executive powers. Greater control of press, followed by purge of civil service. Podestas replace mayors
10 Nov 1926–Jan 1927 Exceptional Decrees increase repression, with new Special Tribunal, secret police (OVRA).

10

9

8

7 Matteotti crisis

6

5

4

3

2

1

The Fascists
- Fascist militia, MVSN, set up from squads. Paid by state; took loyalty oath to Mussolini
- Fascist Grand Council set up as rival to Cabinet
- Fascists merged with Nationalists
- **Mussolini centralised the Party.**

Other parties
- Mussolini exploited tension between PPI and Pope, to weaken them; 1923 they left the government.
- PSI, PCI were tolerated, but activities liable to disruption.
- **All non-Fascist parties suppressed**

Judiciary/repression
- Existing court system used
- Hostile press, politicians intimidated
- **Judiciary lost independence**
- **Special Tribunal for political crimes**
- **Law for Defence of State**
- **Administrative powers widely used (a government official could order an arrest without justification)**
- **Secret police OVRA created**
- **Free press ended**

Trade unions
- Tolerated but intimidated
- Number of strikes fell
- **1926 Law on Corporations (see page 137)**
- **Fascist unions recognised as sole representatives of workers**
- **Strikes, lockouts illegal**

Other policies 1922–27
Church
- Concessions to Catholic Church (see pages 174–75)

Economy
- From 1922, economic recovery
- Laissez-faire policies favouring industrialists (see page 128)

Foreign policy
- Intimidated Greece by invading Corfu, 1923 (see page 212)
- Gained Fiume, 1924 (see page 212)

■ Learning trouble spot

Explanations

You were asked on page 82 to write an essay explaining why Mussolini set up a dictatorial system. Your first concern may be to gather lots of information and to get the story of the events of 1922–27 clear in your mind. This is vital, but the task does not just need knowledge. Even if you know every detail of all the events you have studied in this chapter you could still score a low mark if you just tell the story of what happened in chronological order. If you do that, you may not fit in the explanation that is needed.

So what do you need to think about in terms of explanation? Here are some issues that are central to this essay. They aren't the answers, but they may help you think along the right lines.

a) Did events turn out the way they did because Mussolini planned them that way?
b) Did the actions of his opponents – or their failure to act – affect the way the regime developed?
c) Was there a key point when several different outcomes were possible? If so, why did a dictatorship develop rather than the other possibilities?
d) Did anything happen to influence events that was outside the control of Mussolini or his opponents?
e) Who was most responsible for the development of a dictatorship – Mussolini or his opponents? Where did the balance of responsibility lie?

Key points from Chapter 4

1 Mussolini was in a potentially weak position on his appointment.
2 He was under pressure from radicals for a Fascist revolution, but he was concerned to reassure the elite.
3 He carefully mixed conciliation and threats in his early actions, and worked largely within the existing system from 1922 to 1924.
4 He set up new Fascist bodies, the Grand Council and MVSN, but exercised tight control over them.
5 His restoration of firm government, and economic growth, won the support of the elite.
6 A mixture of genuine support, a modified electoral system and intimidation helped the government win a large majority in the 1924 elections.
7 The murder of Matteotti in June 1924 provoked a prolonged political crisis.
8 His opponents failed to exploit the situation, and he eventually used it to establish a personal dictatorship.
9 Between 1925 and 1927 Mussolini gained the power to issue decrees; elected local government was replaced, other parties abolished and the OVRA was created.
10 By 1927 the key features of Mussolini's dictatorship had been established.

A look ahead

You have now studied how Mussolini established his personal dictatorship. After 1927 there were some some political changes, but none of them were very significant. The overall structure was established. So we can now leave this largely chronological account of political developments, and look at how Mussolini's personal dictatorship really operated during the Fascist regime.

5

Was Mussolini an all-powerful dictator?

■ **Activity**

Which of these three models do you think was most likely to develop? Give reasons for your opinions and then use the rest of the chapter to come to a firm decision.

'Mussolini is God'

No dictator could hope for a more loyal statement than that! However, was Mussolini really completely in control as the statement suggests? Was he an all-powerful DICTATOR, or did he share power with others? In this chapter we will investigate which of the three models of government below was the real form of government in interwar Italy. We will also examine how Mussolini exercised power, and the extent to which his power depended upon the use of repression.

SOURCE 5.1   Mussolini in 1925

SOURCE 5.2   Mussolini and his circle of leading Fascists

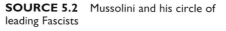

SOURCE 5.3   Mussolini and the King, November 1923

<u>Model 1</u>
Mussolini, as DUCE, was in sole control of Italy and its government.

<u>Model 2</u>
Mussolini had to share power with the Fascist Party that had helped him into power.

<u>Model 3</u>
Mussolini shared power with the King and the ELITE who were still too powerful to ignore.

CHART 5A   CHAPTER OVERVIEW

5 Was Mussolini an all-powerful dictator?

A What role did Mussolini play? (pp. 87–93)

B What was the role of the Fascist Party in Mussolini's Italy? (pp. 94–96)

C Did Mussolini share power with the elite? (pp. 97–99)

D How far did Mussolini's power depend upon repression? (pp. 100–01)

E Review: Was Mussolini an all-powerful dictator? (pp. 102–04)

■ **Learning trouble spot**

Using photographs as sources
In this chapter you will see a good many photographs that were used to boost Mussolini's popularity and power. It would be easy to dismiss these photographs as propaganda and therefore as being of little or no use to historians. However, if we treat them carefully and ask the right questions, they can be of considerable use – in ways that Mussolini never intended!

This picture may be such a propaganda photograph. Unfortunately photographs like this which are owned by photograph libraries are often short of the information historians need, such as when they were taken. However, we may be able to squeeze out some conclusions – even if they are tentative ones that make careful use of words such as 'possibly' and 'probably'.

1 Which of these statements could the photograph be used as evidence to support?
 a) Mussolini was popular with church leaders.
 b) Mussolini used church leaders as part of his propaganda campaign.
2 Can you suggest any other tentative conclusions you could draw from this source?
3 What would you need to know in order to use this photograph most effectively as historical evidence?
4 Why is it important to use words such as 'possibly' and 'probably' in your essays and other work in History?

SOURCE 5.4   Mussolini and Roman cardinals

SOURCE 5.5   Official photograph of Mussolini, used at the beginning of his autobiography

■ **Activity**

1 Which qualities of Mussolini was Source 5.5 trying to convey?
2 This, like many other photographs of Mussolini, was taken looking slightly upwards at him. Why do you think this was?
3 What can you learn from this photograph, apart from what Mussolini looked like at the moment it was taken?

FOCUS ROUTE

1 Using pages 85–93, make notes on the nature and effects of the Mussolini cult.

2 Draw up a list of Mussolini's good qualities as a ruler; then his bad points. What do you consider his greatest political ability and his greatest weakness?

3 How closely did the real Mussolini correspond to the image projected by Ducismo?

Myth
The cult of the Duce has been likened to the Hitler myth. The word myth is often taken to mean 'make believe', a complete fabrication. However, it can be used to mean a strong feeling, partly based on reality, which is so widely believed that it helps to explain events.

What was the cult of the Duce?

If you had asked a government official which of the models on page 85 was correct, his answer would have been immediate. Mussolini alone was the ruler of Italy. This image was propagated in posters, newspapers and in official statements. Italy, having endured years of political weakness, was now firmly under the control of a wise, all-powerful statesman. 'Mussolini is always right', as the slogan ran. Another claimed: 'Duce, you are all of us.' This was part of the cult of the Duce.

Let us now try to understand how it was that many Italians in the 1930s could hold such exaggerated opinions of the qualities of their leader. Study Chart 5B. This should help you to understand more about how Mussolini was viewed, and the importance of this official image.

CHART 5B   The Mussolini myth

How was Mussolini portrayed?
As a statesman

- Saviour of Italy
- Sent by God, and protected by Him
- Supreme patriot
- Symbolised the nation
- Heir to Julius Caesar and Augustus
- All-wise ruler
- World statesman
- Great thinker; inspirer of the Corporative State
- Had a paternal love for his people

As a man

- Likened to St Francis and Jesus
- War hero, who despite 40 wounds did not need anaesthetics when operated upon
- Man of action
- Worked up to 20 hours a day
- Great lover
- True Fascist man; virile, cultured
- Incorruptible; unconcerned about money
- True man of the people

2

How was this image projected?
- Through all the media, especially press, posters, film
- Through government pronouncements
- Public buildings carried pictures and sculptures of him
- Even the Catholic Church periodically referred to Mussolini as a man sent by providence (see page 174)

3

What was the role of the myth?
- To provide a focal point for the people to rally around

4

What were the effects of the myth?
- Helped win mass support
- Mussolini's personal prestige sustained the regime when it got into difficulties. Corruption and other minor problems could be blamed on the Fascists, not Mussolini.

However,

- Mussolini came to believe his own image; he became a victim of his own propaganda; his belief in his infallibility cut him off from reality.
- As the gap between myth and reality grew, more Italians came to see through the myth. Once the Mussolini myth died, it was possible to replace Mussolini.

This cult of Mussolini emphasised his infallibility (that he could never fail or be wrong), and used the glorification of Mussolini to unite the whole nation. He was the saviour of Italy. The myth, begun in the 1920s, reached its zenith, or height, in the 1930s under Party Secretary Starace when Mussolini was referred to as 'magnificent', 'sublime', and 'divine Duce'. A whole industry of articles, books and speeches was devoted to the cult of the Duce. But what was the truth behind the image of the superhuman ruler?

SOURCE 5.6   Fascist Youth leader Scorza, in a letter to Mussolini, 1931

It is necessary to give a Myth to the youth, because youth needs to believe blindly in something. The Mussolini Myth equals LOYALTY COURAGE THOUGHT LIGHT BEAUTY HEROISM ETERNITY.

Did foreigners believe in the cult?

Your immediate answer might be no, but this is too simple. Although the people and governments of other states were not subjected to the same relentless propaganda as Italians, it should be realised that well into the 1930s Mussolini won considerable respect abroad.

SOURCE 5.7   British Foreign Secretary Sir Austen Chamberlain in 1924 and 1926

[Mussolini is] a wonderful man working for the greatness of his country.

The fortunes of Italy are directed by a very remarkable man . . . he became the founder of a new political system, and the creator of a new Italy.

SOURCE 5.8   In 1927 Winston Churchill on a visit to Italy was widely reported to have said

If I were an Italian I would don the Fascist Black Shirt.

In 1933 he described Mussolini as

. . . the Roman genius . . . the greatest lawgiver among living men.

And *The Times* reported this comment by Churchill at a press conference

I could not help being charmed, like so many other people have been, by Signor Mussolini's gentle and simple bearing and by his calm and detached pose in spite of so many burdens and dangers. Anyone could see that he thought of nothing but the lasting good, as he understood it, of the Italian people . . . It was quite absurd to suggest that the Italian government does not stand upon a popular basis or that it is not upheld by the active and practical assent of the great masses. If I had been an Italian I should have been wholeheartedly with you . . . in your triumphant struggle against the bestial [beast-like] appetites and passions of Leninism.

■ Activity

1   You are a young journalist working for *Il Popolo d'Italia*. Write a caption or slogan to go with each of the pictures that illustrate the official view of Mussolini (Source 5.9).
2   In what ways are these pictures valuable to historians of Mussolini and Fascist Italy?
3   Explain why some foreign statesmen admired Mussolini.

■ Talking points

1   In what sort of societies, and at what times, might cults of great leaders develop? Can you think of other examples?
2   Why might it be easier to rally a people around an individual leader than around a set of political ideas?

SOURCE 5.9 Propaganda pictures of Mussolini

CHART 5C Mussolini in his own words

a) *(1922) Today in Italy is not the time for history. Nothing is yet concluded. It is the time for myths. Everything is yet to be done. Only the myth can give strength and energy to a people about to hammer out its own destiny.*

g) *(1944) Fascism is Mussolinism ... As a doctrine Fascism contains nothing new ... I have made dictatorship noble. I have not, in fact, been a dictator, because my power was no more than the will of the Italian people.*

b) *To govern you need only two things, policemen and bands playing in the streets.*

c) *The crowd does not have to know, it must believe; it must submit to being shaped.*

f) *You must always be doing things and obviously succeeding. The hard part is to keep people always at their window because of the spectacle you put on for them. And you must do this for years. Now I have succeeded in never boring the Italians; I have kept them tensed up in a state of exaltation by always offering them something new.*

d) *One must know how to strike the imagination of the public: that is the real secret of how to govern.*

e) *If only we give [the masses] faith that mountains can be moved, they will accept the illusion that mountains are moveable, and thus an illusion may become reality.*

■ Activity

1 Study Mussolini's statements about how to rule. Summarise in your own words his views on leadership.
2 What are
   a) the strengths
   b) the weaknesses
   of this style of leadership?

■ Activity

Does Chart 5D suggest that one of the models on page 85 was correct?

How much power did Mussolini have? Chart 5D shows how Mussolini by 1927 had been granted great formal powers. He had the power to issue DECREES with the full authority of the law. He appointed and dismissed his ministers, and was able to take over these positions virtually at will. He was not challenged over any major decision. He also increased his control over the Fascist movement, although some of the RAS remained a cause for concern.

CHART 5D Mussolini's role in government

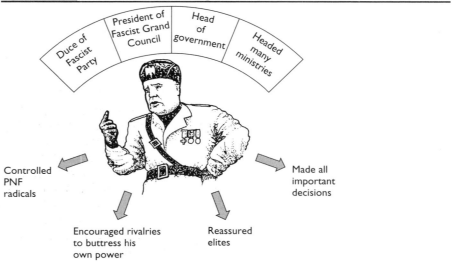

Duce of Fascist Party

President of Fascist Grand Council

Head of government

Headed many ministries

Controlled PNF radicals

Made all important decisions

Encouraged rivalries to buttress his own power

Reassured elites

■ **Talking point**

How useful to a historian are a politician's own statements about their role in government for understanding their methods?

■ **Activity**

Either:
As an ambitious Italian journalist, write an assessment in 1930 of Mussolini's qualities as a ruler.
Or:
As a non-Fascist career civil servant, write a letter to an English friend trying to correct the widespread view of Mussolini as a wise statesman.

Let us now try to penetrate beneath the image to get closer to reality. Mussolini believed that communication was at the heart of the political process. He was skilled at inspiring crowds, and devoted much time to propaganda. His exhibitionism fascinated many Italians, impressed by his supermasculinity and sexuality. Unfortunately his gesturing did not produce the policies and actions which his ambitions for Italy required.

He did not lead an efficient government team. His advisers served one key function: to bolster his own image of himself. He did not want to hear contrary opinions. Discussion was not part of the 'Fascist style'. He wanted acclaim not criticism. He was increasingly protected from unpleasant truths. This was especially so after 1931 when his brother Arnaldo, one of the few people prepared to tell Mussolini the truth, died.

Like many dictators, Mussolini sowed discord amongst his ministers and encouraged them to tell tales about each other. Distrustful, he failed to train any deputy leaders, or a successor. By 1933 he had dismissed arguably his most able ministers – such as Rocco, Federzoni, Bottai, Grandi and Turati – replacing them with more subservient (submissive) officials. He treated officials with contempt, requiring them to run the twenty metres to his desk in his office.

His reliance on his intuition (instinct), his MONOPOLISING of so many positions, and his concern for trivia all militated against effective policy making. The chasm between his portrayal as a superhuman ruler and his administrative inadequacies says a lot about Fascist Italy – strong on style and weak on substance. Mussolini, indeed, considered the former more important. His orders were meant to impress; he frequently failed to check whether they were carried out.

However, when you consider the career of Mussolini, both how he became Prime Minister, and how he then held power for far longer than any other modern Italian leader, you have to acknowledge his political skill. As well as his obvious abilities as a speaker, he was able to hold together a heterogeneous movement (one made up of many different parts). He knew how to compromise with the traditional elites by satisfying their essential self-interest, yet led a potentially revolutionary movement. He won domestic and international praise for his work.

Historians' assessments of Mussolini

Let us now consider how some historians have assessed Mussolini's qualities as leader.

SOURCE 5.10 A. de Grand, *Italian Fascism, its Origins and Development*, 1982, p. 42

Mussolini was an extraordinary political tactician, but his skill at manoeuvre was due in part to the absence of any ethical foundation or an overall political vision. Every individual or institution became an instrument to be used only as long as it served his immediate purpose. Unlike Adolf Hitler, he was not mentally unbalanced. He operated on the level of ordinary calculation and rationality. In his case, however, the myth of his own indispensability corroded and corrupted to the point that during the 1930s he had to be consulted when the Roman police wanted to wear summer uniforms earlier than usual.

SOURCE 5.11 T. Koon, *Believe, Obey, Fight*, 1985, pp. 4, 9, 245

Mussolini's greatest talent, perhaps his only genuine talent, was his ability to manufacture and communicate myths and slogans that captured the popular imagination ... Mussolini was a consummate [very skilled] propagandist, actor and stage manager. His political style reflected his thought processes, which were less intellectual than instinctual. In politics he relied on his own understanding of group psychology and his intuition, what he referred to as his 'animal instinct', rather than on strict adherence to IDEOLOGY and logic ... His approach to politics was not based upon principles, at best useful nails on which to hang a particular policy, but rather on an intuitive grasp of what he perceived as the psychological needs of the masses ...

Mussolini was a man tragically out of touch with reality. He had no tolerance for real administration but an inexhaustible capacity for trivial detail. He was supposed to be all-powerful, and yet he constantly changed his mind. He wanted no bad news, but because after a certain point the news was almost all bad, he heard little truth.

SOURCE 5.12   A. J. P. Taylor's video, *Men of Our Time: Mussolini*

He liked the glamour of his public appearances. Others did the work . . . Mussolini only appeared when treaties had to be signed and the cameras began to run . . . The one thing that Mussolini worked at was the strengthening of his own power . . . There was only one man in Italy, Mussolini.

SOURCE 5.13   Cassels, p. 54

DEMAGOGUERY [whipping up popular feeling] came easily to him . . . The facial contortion and the trick of rolling his eyes . . . proved effective when viewed from the piazza . . . His voice was his major asset. Trained in hundreds of street-corner speeches, it was at once powerful and flexible . . . It was a series of sharp, usually unconnected statements, declamatory rather than persuasive . . . The presentation was everything. All who heard him, friend and foe alike, have testified to his unerring ability to establish rapport with a crowd and to stimulate it. He possessed that mystic quality of leadership known as CHARISMA.

Although he might move men to action, Mussolini himself shied away from it . . . It was not that he was devoid of physical courage . . . but in a crisis his habit was to stand aside. He seemed to lack self-confidence . . . The picture of the strong, resolute Duce that was sold to the world was the work of a superb public relations expert whose forte [strength] lay in words and images, not in deeds and actuality.

SOURCE 5.14   Clark, p. 240

Mussolini proved to be a rotten manager. He had a lively journalistic intelligence, but he was impulsive. He oversimplified and dramatized everything, and had no patience for prosaic [matter of fact] long-term planning. He was also distressingly vulgar and vulnerable to flattery. Corruption and incompetence were tolerated, even encouraged. Intensely suspicious of rivals, he dismissed most of his competent subordinates . . . He deliberately isolated himself . . . He worked long hours, but to little purpose. Much of his time was spent reading newspapers, or deciding trivial questions . . . His initial M was needed on every document, and it was rarely refused. Senior civil servants and ministers pursued their own policies, often quite contradictory to those of their rivals, and each of them would produce an initialled paper from the Duce to overcome his colleagues' opposition. The Council of Ministers met only once a month, and even then did not co-ordinate policy. Perhaps Mussolini had grown bored; perhaps he was simply too contemptuous of arguments and of men to keep everyone dependent on him. At any rate, it was no way to run a country.

SOURCE 5.15   R. Lamb, *Mussolini and the British*, 1997, p. 1

His popularity with ordinary Italians, particularly during his early years of power, cannot be overestimated. He had considerable personal charm and a hypnotic personality; large crowds filled the piazzas whenever he spoke, listeners raptly awaiting every word. His technique was superficial, flamboyant and vulgar, but it worked – though not always with people of taste and culture, who often abhorred him . . .

Mussolini's principal weakness as head of state was that he based his decisions on whether they would increase his own popularity and that of the Fascist Party; the well-being of the Italian nation came only second.

■ **Talking points**

1 Historians may neglect the ageing of politicians. Mussolini ruled Italy from the age of 39 to 63. How might that affect the nature of his rule?

2 How important is the personality of a ruler when trying to explain the nature of a regime?

Finally, what was Mussolini like as a person? Did Mussolini the man fit the image created by Ducismo (the cult of the Duce)?

Physically he was no superman. He was only 5ft 6ins (1.67m) tall, (fortunately still 6 inches [15cm] taller than the King!) so he tried to be viewed whenever possible from below. This action man was actually a heavy sleeper, needing nine hours a day, and suffered from periods of mental paralysis when under stress. Although when appointed in 1922 he was Italy's youngest-ever Prime Minister (aged 39), and though the Fascist movement cultivated an image of itself as youthful and dynamic, age caught up on Mussolini and his regime. By the 1930s the press was not allowed to refer to Mussolini's age nor to other apparent blemishes.

He suffered from several medical problems. In his youth he had contracted syphilis, and after 1926 he increasingly suffered from a gastric ulcer. This led his doctor to virtually ban him from eating meat and drinking wine. He relied increasingly on eating grapes and drinking three litres of milk a day. By 1942 his medical problems were acute and he was confined to his bed for long periods.

Mussolini was very superstitious and stored charms to ward off evil spirits. Although he has been viewed as sharing some personality traits with Hitler and Stalin, such as an inferiority complex and a craving for power, he was far less cruel than his fellow dictators.

Finally, let us consider Cassels' assessment:

SOURCE 5.16 Cassels, p. 52

Since he was young, his hairline had receded rapidly; this threw into relief his sallow, round face whose main features were a jutting jaw, large mobile mouth, and dark protuberant eyes. This less than impressive appearance he contrived to offset by his mannerisms. To disguise his short stature he always stood ramrod straight, pushed out his lower lip and jaw, and tilted back his head; thus his eyes seemed to look down, never up, at a person ...

He had a sentimental attachment to his children ... yet he was anything but a family man. [His wife] Rachele was a plain, honest country woman with no interest in politics ... She bore him five children. She put up stoically [bravely and resignedly] with his neglect and his endless infidelities [unfaithfulness]. Mussolini was openly proud of his sexual prowess. He was never at a loss for a mistress. His office was his favourite trysting [meeting] place. He would seize his partner roughly, throw her to the hard floor, and make love to her there and then; apparently many of his conquests relished his primitive approach.

Almost certainly Mussolini suffered from an outsized inferiority complex. His outward self-assertiveness was doubtless a psychic compensation for his inner timidity. This personality trait seems to have been reflected in the policies which he imposed on Italy. For the most part, they were pretentious [seemed impressive] when first announced but tended to be lethargically executed.

■ **Activity**

Now that you have read pages 87–93, do you think it is likely that Model 1 (page 85) describes the real structure of power in Italy? Give reasons for your answer.

B What was the role of the Fascist Party in Mussolini's Italy?

Mussolini had used the Fascist movement to gain power, but would he share power fully with his supporters once he became dictator? The statements in column 1 of the table below describe possible roles for the Fascist Party. Make your own copy of the table and complete column 2 after reading about the role that the Fascist Party actually played.

Potential roles for PNF (National Fascist Party)	Whether the PNF actually fulfilled this role
1 Forming a new ruling elite	
2 Implementing a Fascist revolution	
3 Ras controlling their own areas of the country	
4 Means to get good jobs in the administration	
5 Propaganda	

Fascistisation of the state or statisation of the Party?

Many Fascists hoped that Fascists would take over all the key positions in the state, and the Fascist Party in effect would run Italy. Thus the state would be fascistised. However, more moderate Fascists, such as Rocco, wanted a strong state that would control key areas, including the Fascist Party. This would become a tool to be used by the state; thus the PNF would be statised.

Mussolini's relationship with his party was never easy in the years before he was appointed Prime Minister. Achieving power made the situation even more difficult because there were important decisions to be made about the role in government of this 'revolutionary' party. Mussolini was worried about the idea of a 'revolution from below' and believed that the radicalism of the ras might frighten his industrial and landowning backers. He also feared that the squads could not provide people of sufficient quality to run the state bureaucracy. Mussolini preferred the traditional state organs of the police and PREFECTS to administer his regime. The Fascist Party had to be subjected to the state. Some Fascists wanted the reverse (see left).

Making this happen in practice was another matter: Mussolini had to tread warily since the party, despite his centralising efforts from 1921, was far from under his total control. He was, however, helped by the heterogeneous nature of Fascism. From 1922 he gradually increased his control of the PNF (see Chart 5E). Now that he had control of the state machine, he did not regularly need the intimidatory activities of the squads. For a few years they were still able to indulge in periodic violence, but especially after squad violence in Florence in October 1925 Mussolini was determined to neutralise the party. He cleverly appointed the ras Farinacci as party secretary and then used him to centralise the party. He then dismissed him to block Farinacci's more radical ambitions for the Fascist revolution. The powers of the ras were gradually clipped, whilst the prefects' powers were enhanced. In October 1925 the Fascist Grand Council ordered the disbandment of the remaining squads, telling members to join the MVSN.

In a party statute (rule) of October 1926 the Duce became permanent leader and all party posts were appointed, not elected. Top jobs came to be held by people Mussolini could easily dominate, such as Starace, who was Party Secretary from 1931 to 1939. Thus Mussolini bureaucratised and devitalised (took the life out of) the party he had used to gain power.

As a result of Mussolini's tactics the Fascist party did not make political decisions, neither at the centre where Mussolini was supreme, nor locally where prefects were powerful. The Fascist Grand Council might have become a key agent of a Fascist revolution, but Mussolini maintained power in his own hands. The Grand Council became less important as he developed his personal dictatorship. Nor did the party play an administrative role. Instead, Mussolini used the existing state machinery, reorganised in a more AUTHORITARIAN structure, to run the country. This can be clearly seen in Mussolini's circular to prefects in 1927 which insisted that the party was 'simply the instrument of the state's will' and 'must collaborate in a subordinate fashion' with the prefect, 'the highest authority of the state in the province'. In some ways, however, the

Activity

1 The historian Seton-Watson has commented: 'Having used the support of the radicals to consolidate his personal power, Mussolini abandoned their programme.' What evidence would you use to support this historian's statement?

2 Look back at page 85. Can you now discount model 2?

administrative machinery did become Fascist as, increasingly, civil servants joined the party, but they were not really genuine Fascists (see Chart 5E).

The party was, however, directed to undertake new functions within the state. It was to be used as a vehicle for propaganda and parades to try and reform the Italian character, and secure positive commitment to the state (see Chapter 8). It served as the 'capillary organisation' of the regime, conveying Mussolini's will to the people by organising and indoctrinating them. As Koon says, 'The party was increasingly visible and audible but liquidated as a political force, incapable of taking real initiatives, and reduced to the role of choreographer [someone who arranges a performance] for the cult of the infallible leader.'

CHART 5E   The Fascist Party in Mussolini's Italy

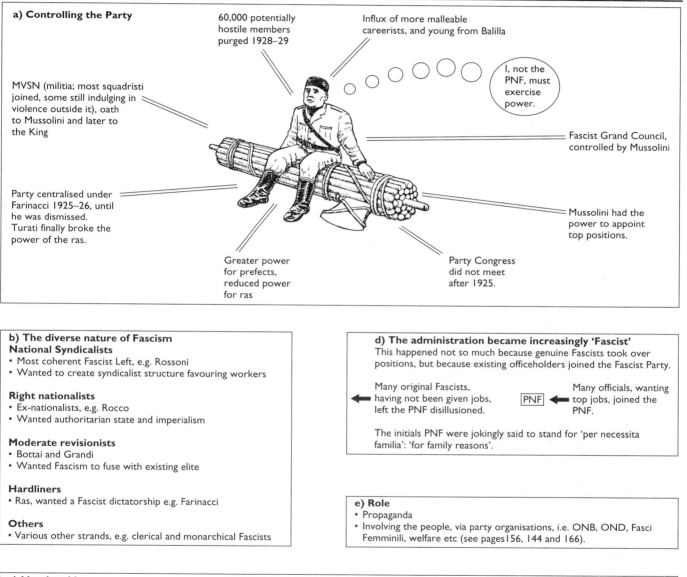

a) Controlling the Party

60,000 potentially hostile members purged 1928–29

Influx of more malleable careerists, and young from Balilla

I, not the PNF, must exercise power.

MVSN (militia; most squadristi joined, some still indulging in violence outside it), oath to Mussolini and later to the King

Fascist Grand Council, controlled by Mussolini

Party centralised under Farinacci 1925–26, until he was dismissed. Turati finally broke the power of the ras.

Mussolini had the power to appoint top positions.

Greater power for prefects, reduced power for ras

Party Congress did not meet after 1925.

b) The diverse nature of Fascism
National Syndicalists
• Most coherent Fascist Left, e.g. Rossoni
• Wanted to create syndicalist structure favouring workers

Right nationalists
• Ex-nationalists, e.g. Rocco
• Wanted authoritarian state and imperialism

Moderate revisionists
• Bottai and Grandi
• Wanted Fascism to fuse with existing elite

Hardliners
• Ras, wanted a Fascist dictatorship e.g. Farinacci

Others
• Various other strands, e.g. clerical and monarchical Fascists

d) The administration became increasingly 'Fascist'
This happened not so much because genuine Fascists took over positions, but because existing officeholders joined the Fascist Party.

Many original Fascists, having not been given jobs, left the PNF disillusioned.

PNF ← Many officials, wanting top jobs, joined the PNF.

The initials PNF were jokingly said to stand for 'per necessita familia': 'for family reasons'.

e) Role
• Propaganda
• Involving the people, via party organisations, i.e. ONB, OND, Fasci Femminili, welfare etc (see pages156, 144 and 166).

c) Membership
Party membership changed considerably after 1922. About one-third of the original party members were workers or small farmers; by the late 1920s the party membership was overwhelmingly middle class.

More radical elements were replaced by mainly pliable officials. The membership became increasingly middle class as Italians realised their job opportunities were closely linked to party affiliation.

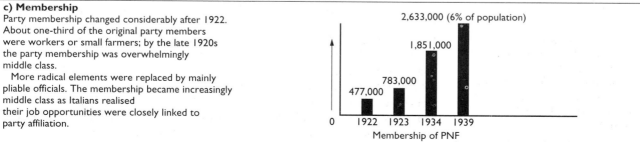

2,633,000 (6% of population)

1,851,000

783,000

477,000

0   1922   1923   1934   1939
Membership of PNF

Roberto Farinacci

None of the other Italian Fascist leaders are as famous as their Nazi counterparts. Here we look at the career of just one of them, Roberto Farinacci, as it sheds a fascinating light on the nature of the regime.

Roberto Farinacci

Born to humble parents in 1892, he became a railways telegraph operator in Cremona. He joined the PSI, but, like Mussolini, he broke with it over its hostility to the war. In 1919 he joined Mussolini in founding the Fascio di Combattimento in Milan. He became the Fascist ras in his home town of Cremona. There he ran his own newspaper. He proved to be a good organiser, and built up a strong base of Fascist support amongst tenant farmers. He led squad violence against the Socialist threat, and was considered one of the most powerful of the Fascist ras. In October 1922 he organised the Fascist seizure of Cremona.

Farinacci was on the extreme wing of the movement, and Mussolini saw him as a dangerous radical. So he was not initially given a major post in the new government. Instead, he was used as a general trouble-shooter, and in 1923 he reorganised the Fascist Party in Rome. He studied to become a lawyer, and qualified in three months, after plagiarising (copying) his thesis. (His own proposed title *Dowsing Subversives with Castor Oil on the Part of Fascists cannot be considered an Act of Violence* had unsurprisingly been rejected as insufficiently academic!)

He supported Mussolini during the Matteotti affair, and defended Matteotti's killers at their trial. He helped push Mussolini into repressive actions, hoping to see the creation of a genuine Fascist state. In a somewhat surprise move, Mussolini, who personally disliked Farinacci, appointed him PNF Secretary-General in January 1925, in charge of the party organisation. This in fact was a wise move by Mussolini; he used this powerful ras to centralise control of the PNF, thus weakening the power of the ras.

As Party Secretary 1925–26 Farinacci played a crucial role in establishing the dictatorship. He directed from the centre a series of local terror campaigns against opponents. He wanted, however, to establish the party as dominant over the state, favouring the 'strictest dictatorship of the party in the nation'. Here he disagreed with Interior Minister Federzoni's and Rocco's view that law and order should be enforced by state organs, i.e. the police and prefect. Mussolini supported their view of the state being dominant over the party, not Farinacci's view.

Having skilfully used the radical Farinacci to weaken the party, Mussolini removed him as party secretary to prevent him becoming too powerful. From 1926 to 1933 Farinacci concentrated on being a journalist and lawyer in Cremona. From there he criticised what he saw as the transformation of revolutionary Fascism into a BOURGEOIS establishment.

In 1934 he was appointed to the Fascist Grand Council, and became a junior minister. He briefly fought in the invasion of Abyssinia, where he 'heroically' lost a hand (actually when using a grenade to fish with!). He continued to criticise weaknesses in the regime. In 1939 he was appointed to the largely ceremonial Chamber of Fasces and Corporations, and became a Lieutenant General in the MVSN. In 1939 he published a three-volume history of the Fascist revolution.

Farinacci became increasingly attracted to Nazism which he saw as more like the revolutionary Fascism he had wanted in Italy. He was a strong supporter of the 1938 ANTI-SEMITIC laws.

When the Second World War broke out Farinacci advocated fighting alongside Germany. In 1941 he was sent as a military official to Albania.

In July 1943 at the Grand Council meeting he criticised Mussolini for betraying Fascism and voted against him, alongside moderate critics. When Mussolini was arrested, Farinacci fled to Germany, but returned under the Salo Republic to rule Cremona, on behalf of the Germans. In 1945 he was captured by anti-Fascist partisans and shot.

■ **Talking point**

Is it more appropriate to call Italy 1925–43 Fascist Italy or Mussolini's Italy?

■ **Activity**

1 What does Farinacci's career illustrate about the nature of Fascism as
   a) a movement
   b) a regime?
2 Split into two groups, one representing Farinacci, the other Mussolini. Debate the motion 'Mussolini has betrayed his most loyal supporters.'

King Victor Emmanuel III

C Did Mussolini share power with the elite?

Mussolini used Fascism to get into office but then he made certain that the Fascist Party did not rival his own power. However, Mussolini also had to deal with other, more traditional bodies who had long held and shared power in different ways – the monarchy, the Catholic Church, Parliament and the courts amongst them. Was Mussolini strong enough to subdue these elites as effectively as he dominated the Fascist Party?

What part did the King play in Fascist Italy?

People often forget that Italy remained a monarchy during the Fascist era. Mussolini certainly did not, and he felt increasingly hostile to the King.

Victor Emmanuel became King in 1900 when his father was assassinated by an anarchist. He was weak and indecisive, and lacked self-confidence, partly due to his small size (5 ft/1.52m). He acted correctly as constitutional monarch. His greatest formal role was appointing and dismissing the Prime Minister, and in signing parliamentary laws.

In October 1922 he had appointed Mussolini Prime Minister, partly because he was afraid of being replaced, or of civil war, if he resisted Fascism. He also felt no confidence in Liberal politicians, so he was prepared to sacrifice LIBERALISM for authoritarianism.

His most significant 'act' before 1943 was his refusal to dismiss Mussolini during the Matteotti crisis, when he could easily have done so. Instead he acquiesced in the establishment of Mussolini's dictatorship, though he could have dismissed him at any time. He held twice-weekly meetings with Mussolini. He signed most decrees, and only opposed a few, such as a plan to incorporate the fasces into the Italian flag. In 1928 he reluctantly agreed to extra powers for the Fascist Grand Council, and in 1938 to Mussolini sharing the new title of First Marshal of the Empire with him. He supported the Abyssinian, Spanish and Albanian wars (1935–39), though he favoured Italy's traditional policy of balance between two power blocs, and was wary of closer links with Nazi Germany. He was critical of Mussolini's anti-semitic decrees, though he signed them, as he did the declaration of war in June 1940.

By 1930 he had largely retired from public affairs, and had virtually abdicated in all but name. From 1939, however, several politicians began looking to the King to resume his powers, and to prevent the drift to war alongside Nazi Germany.

When the war started going badly, he secretly explored ways of removing Mussolini. He eventually ordered his arrest on 25 July 1943, after the Fascists themselves had initiated the move against Mussolini.

Although he declared war on Germany, the Allies refused to let him return to liberated Rome. In May 1946 he reluctantly abdicated in favour of his son, Umberto II, in an attempt to save the monarchy. However, in June 1946 Italians voted in a referendum for a republic. He left Italy and died in December 1947.

The following sources give further insight into the relationship between the Duce and the King.

SOURCE 5.17 Mussolini's (private) views of Victor Emmanuel

a) 1939
It has needed all my patience to tow this tiresome monarchy along. It has never done anything which would commit it to the regime. I am still biding my time, because the King is seventy and I hope that nature will come to my rescue.

b) After his overthrow in 1943
I made one great mistake, and have had to pay the price. I never understood that the Italian Royal House was my enemy and would remain so. I should have made Italy a republic after the end of the Abyssinian campaign.

■ **Activity**

1 Summarise Victor Emmanuel's role in, and attitude to, the Fascist state.
2 Why do you think Mussolini did not establish a republic?

■ **Talking point**

Do you think the Italian monarchy deserved its fate? Why/not?

FASCIST INSTITUTIONS

Duce
- Appointed Prime Minister by the King and could have been dismissed by him
- Head of Government (and by 1933 head of seven ministries)
- Mussolini headed all three military ministries 1924–29, 1933–43
- Great personality cult

Fascist Grand Council
- Mussolini its President. Had the right to choose its members and the timing of meetings
- By 1928 could exclusively decide who should become a Deputy or Senator
- Could determine successor to throne and to Mussolini
- In theory the highest organ of the Fascist regime, in practice subordinate to Mussolini

PNF
- Subordinated to state bureaucracy
- Increasingly used just for propaganda purposes, not as policy-making body

MVSN and OVRA
- Fascist squads incorporated into new militia
- New secret police but limited impact

Corporations (see Chapter 7)
- Complex system developed from 1926
- System extended until 1934 mixed corporations
- Regulated labour contracts but little say in economy
- 1939 new Fasces and Corporations Chamber powerless

FOCUS ROUTE

1 Study Chart 5F, which explains the roles and functions of each institution in the Fascist state. Make and complete an assessment grid like this one. Discuss your results, as there could be more than one useful answer.

Code	Assessment of its role	Example
T	Traditional major institutions/groups with potential power but not prepared to use it against Mussolini	
O	Old institutions/practices either kept as a powerless facade or abolished	
N	New institutions with little real power	
C	The centre of power	
E	Existing state organisations which were little changed	
I	Institutions which are supposed to support the rights of the individual but did not in Fascist Italy	

2 **a)** Place the following in order of the power they exercised:
   King Duce Parliament Fascist Party.
   b) Did the situation change over time?
3 Using the information in Chart 5F, explain the role of the key institutions in Mussolini's Italy.

TRADITIONAL INSTITUTIONS

CENTRAL GOVERNMENT

King
- Mussolini kept with protocol (formal custom) and visited him twice a week, but did not ask his advice
- Privately protested that Mussolini infringed his prerogative (the rights attached to his office), but publicly remained silent
- Accepted all Mussolini's major decisions
- Mussolini considered 'the functions of the monarchy [were] withering away . . .'
- Proclaimed Emperor of Abyssinia 1936
- 1938 Given title First Marshal of Empire (equal with Mussolini)

Cabinet
- Formally kept, but no real Cabinet team. Mussolini made all the decisions

Parliament
a) Senate survived
Membership changed as existing Senators (appointed for life) died, and were replaced by Fascist nominees
b) Chamber of Deputies
  i) Changes in elections

   - 1923 Acerbo Law
   - 1928 Electoral Law: 800 candidates nominated by worker and employer organisations. Four hundred of these were then selected by Grand Council, submitted in single constituency to PLEBISCITE. 1929, 1934 plebiscites

  ii) Membership

   - 1922–24 overwhelmingly non-Fascist
   - 1924–26 66% Fascist, with declining opposition members
   - 1926 no opposition party members

  iii) Institutional changes

   - 1938 Chamber abolished
   - January 1939 replaced itself with Chamber of Fasces and Corporations (see page 137)

  iv) Role

   - Approved laws, en bloc, without debate

Police
- Remained largely traditional career profession, e.g. Bocchini, Police Chief 1926–40, was a non-Fascist

ADMINISTRATION

Civil service
- Dominated by career officials sympathetic to authoritarian government
- 1927 only 15% of the civil service were Fascists
- Postholders increasingly joined Fascist Party; compulsory after 1935
- Implemented government policy, didn't initiate policy

Judiciary
- Purged of 'undesirable' elements; some sacked
- Independent judiciary undermined, but basic system kept
- Mussolini intervened in some cases
- Imprisonment without trial common
- New special tribunal

Prefects
- Powers enhanced; most not Fascists

Elected local government
- Abolished; replaced by PODESTAS, officials from Rome

ELITE

Army
- Owed loyalty to King; he refused to allow army to use Fascist salute
- Top positions increasingly given to Fascists, but no major reorganisation
- Potential to replace Mussolini, but passive
- Mussolini shared his generals' interest in expanding the army, and assertive foreign policy
- Army resented the Fascist militia

Church
- Major influence on mass of population
- Initially welcomed firm, anti-Socialist government
- 1929 compromise with government; avoided politics in return for support from the state

Traditional elite
- Administrative, economic and social elite remained in place. Old politicians generally adapted or retired.

D How far did Mussolini's power depend upon repression?

How many people did Mussolini's government kill and imprison? If this question is asked of Stalin's Russia or Hitler's Germany one gets an immediate response of several millions. Mussolini's record was quite different from those of Stalin and Hitler. Comparatively few people died because of their opposition to his regime. The best estimate seems to be around 400 killed, 'legally' and through murder, during the Fascist regime (considerably fewer than those killed in 1919–22). However, it would be unwise to conclude from this that Italian Fascism was 'just another despotism' which was 'really not so bad after all'.

Fascist violence was generally more prominent between 1920 and 1925, but although less obvious afterwards, the regime still used repression. As Morgan has said, 'Repressiveness was not the most distinctive feature of the Fascist TOTALITARIAN system, but it was an essential and inescapable component of it'. The police's preventive and repressive powers were extensive and sought to create a real climate of fear. Policing increasingly came to involve information gathering and comment on practically everything which talked or moved.

It is hard to assess accurately the extent to which Mussolini's power depended on repression. In Chapter 8 you will be looking at the comparatively small amount of opposition in Fascist Italy. This could be used to support either the view that this reflected considerable repression, or that little repression was needed. Clearly Mussolini had an array of legal powers and repressive institutions which buttressed his power, but there is evidence to suggest that several broadly popular policies and successful propaganda were more important than repression in sustaining the regime, at least until the 1940s.

FOCUS ROUTE

1 Using pages 100–01 make notes on the system of repression covering

- the informer society
- organs of repression
- types of punishments
- deaths attributed to the state.

2 Draw up two columns, and jot down evidence to support the view that the government was
   a) a very repressive regime
   b) a comparatively mild dictatorship.

3 Study Sources 5.18–25. What does each source show about the nature of repression in Fascist Italy?

CHART 5G   How repressive was Fascist Italy?

Special Tribunal
- Applied summary justice (immediate judgments, without a full trial) outside normal court system
- 21,000 people tried 1926–43, mainly for trivial political crimes; three-quarters acquitted
- 1927–39 3596 sentences were passed, totalling 19,309 years – so the average sentence was approximately five years

Censorship
- Anti-Fascist propaganda viewed as treason
- Journalists had to be registered with government; critics removed
- Hostile newspapers liable to be shut down

MVSN (militia) and squads
- 50,000 armed militia, intimidated opponents
- Although squadrist violence was severely reduced after 1925, Fascists were still able to beat up and threaten selected victims, and to destroy property.

OVRA (secret police)
- Operated independently of the regular police authorities
- 20,000 actions weekly. Hundreds of arrests and detentions per week
- Vast network of informants and agents
- Morgan: 'Police harassment and surveillance became habitual and continuous, affecting even the most mundane areas of daily life, especially in working-class districts'

Political prisoners
- 1922–43 about 5000 imprisoned
- About 10,000 in 'confino' (internal exile), many on islands, especially Lipari and Lampedusa

Exiles
- Many opponents forced into exile; some were killed there by Fascist agents, e.g. Rosselli brothers (see page 185).

Controls
- Internal migration had to be approved

Deaths
- About 400 people killed by the state for political reasons
- 1922–40   9 political executions
- 1940–43   17 political executions

SOURCE 5.18 Public Safety Decree, November 1926

If they are a danger to public safety, the following persons may be assigned to compulsory domicile under police supervision [house arrest], with an obligation to work:

i) Those who have received a warning

ii) Those who have committed or have shown a deliberate intention of committing any act calculated to bring about violent disturbance to the national, social or economic regulations of the state ... or to impede the carrying out of the functions of the state in such a manner as to injure in any way the national interests either at home or abroad.

A sentence of compulsory domicile will last no less than one nor more than five years, and will be carried out either in a colony or a commune [village or small town] of the kingdom other than the normal residence of the sentenced person.

SOURCE 5.19 Police Chief Bocchini

Without an efficient police the dictatorship would not be able to continue to exist.

SOURCE 5.20 The exiled Socialist writer Ignazio Silone, in his 1936 novel *Bread and Wine*, describes the atmosphere in Fascist Italy

It is well known that the police have their informers in every section of every big factory, in every bank, in every office. In every block of flats the porter is by law a stool pigeon [informer] for the police ... Informers are legion [very many], whether they work for a miserable pittance or whether their only incentive is the hope of the advancement of their careers. This state of affairs spreads suspicion and distrust throughout all classes of the population. On this degradation of man into a frightened animal, who quivers with fear and hates his neighbour in his fear, and watches him and betrays him, sells him and then lives in fear of discovery, the dictatorship is based. The real organisation on which the system is based is the secret manipulation of fear.

SOURCE 5.21 The Socialist politician Salvemini describes squad violence

When the Militia is on regular service, or in attendance on official ceremonies, its members wear a uniform. But when they are out to burn, beat and kill, uniforms are left behind. They are no longer militia but squadristi.

SOURCE 5.22 Mussolini in a telegram to the Turin Prefect, March 1924

I hear that Gobetti [a critical editor] who was recently in Paris is now in Sicily. Please keep me informed, and be vigilant in making life difficult again for this stupid opponent of the Government and of Fascism.

SOURCE 5.23 Sarto, a Roman worker, describes intimidation by the authorities

During the last ten years I have been arrested hundreds of times, charged with being a conspirator, a dynamiter, a dangerous criminal. Every time they used to keep me in prison a couple of days and then let me go. In consequence I wasn't able to work regularly and soon I could no longer find any work at all. People were afraid to employ me because of the suspicion with which the police surrounded me.

SOURCE 5.24 Salvemini describes a trial

On 3 May 1926, the case was heard of a Communist, Achille Pepe, who had already spent five months awaiting trial. The accused was acquitted of criminal conspiracy, but received six months imprisonment for inciting class hatred. As the defence lawyer left the court a crowd of Fascists overwhelmed him with insults and threats ... He was beaten and wounded ... It would be naive to ask whether the assailants were ever brought to justice.

SOURCE 5.25 A French cartoon, 1929, copied from the Italian underground newspaper *Becco Giallo*. The caption was:

Voter: 'Excuse me, where do I go to vote against?'

Polling officer: 'Opposite, to the cemetery.'

E Review: Was Mussolini an all-powerful dictator?

You have now studied the political structure of Fascist Italy, and should be in a position to respond to the original question at the beginning of this chapter on where power lay in Fascist Italy.

SOURCE 5.26 A cartoon showing the King, the Pope and Mussolini

SOURCE 5.27 'The Face of Fascism' by John Heartfield. This was the title page *for Italien in Ketten*, a 1928 German Communist publication. The original subtitle included a quotation from Mussolini: 'In the next fifteen years I will change the face of Italy so that no-one will be able to recognise it'

■ Activity

Study Sources 5.26 and 5.27.

Source 5.26

a) How does the cartoonist view the three main characters?

b) How does he view Italy?

c) Do you think the cartoon is an Italian or foreign one? Explain your answer.

d) What is the overall message the cartoon is trying to convey?

Source 5.27

e) Who seems to be supporting the Fascist regime?

f) What unattractive features of Fascism are portrayed?

g) What is the overall message of the illustration?

h) Does the origin of the illustration devalue its use as evidence?

Overall

i) To what extent do the two illustrations convey similar messages about the nature of Fascist Italy?

Historians' assessments of the nature of the regime

SOURCE 5.28   Blinkhorn, p. 22

Power ... resided ... in the traditional apparatus of the state, to which ... the police system remained subordinate; in autonomous centres of influence such as private industry and the Church; and of course in the Duce, an essential ingredient of whose role was his ability to deal personally and separately with these interests ...

The rising cult of the Duce did not ... mislead: by the 1930s Mussolini's regime was as personal as propaganda suggested.

SOURCE 5.29   Tannenbaum, 1973, p. 93

Although it failed to produce a new ruling elite, the Fascist regime had brought about a political revolution whose effects were immediate, obvious and enduring. Parliamentary DEMOCRACY, *such as it was, was destroyed, and most of the old political class went into retirement or exile. Mussolini gave the impression of being all powerful, but he could not rule alone, and the Fascist Party as such was little help to him in running the country. The civil service, the courts, the armed forces and the police remained in the hands of career officials whose commitment to Fascism was usually nominal. Chief of Police Bocchini had far more power than Party Secretary Starace. Indeed the party and the Militia tended increasingly to become ceremonial leftovers from the days of the 'revolution', much like the soviets in the USSR. The bigger and more ostentatious [showy] they became, the less they had to do with the way in which Italy was ruled.*

SOURCE 5.30   S. Payne, *History of Fascism 1914–45*, 1995, pp. 116–17

The new system was a personal dictatorship under Mussolini, yet still legally a monarchy ... The government ruled by decree ... Local elections were eliminated; all mayors were now appointed by decree.

Yet the basic legal and administrative apparatus of the Italian government remained intact. There was no 'Fascist revolution', save at the top ... At one point [Mussolini] was nominally in charge of eight different ministries. In fact, he personally administered almost none, leaving them to be run by senior officials. State administration changed comparatively little; the provinces were still administered by state prefects, not by the Fascist ras, and on the local level affairs were still dominated more often than not by local notables and conservatives. Purging of civil servants was minimal, and there was little interference with the courts ...

■ Activity

1. Read the historians' assessments of the nature of the Fascist regime (Sources 5.28–31). What view do they hold on the power of each of the following:
   - **a)** Mussolini
   - **b)** Fascist bodies
   - **c)** Traditional institutions?
2. What evidence can be used to:
   - **a)** substantiate (support)
   - **b)** refute (reject)

   the view that under Fascism Italy experienced a 'political revolution'?
3. Copy and complete the following chart of parallel structures in Fascist Italy.

Traditional institution	Fascist body
Head of Government	
	MVSN
Prefect	
CARABINIERI	
	Special Tribunal

FOCUS ROUTE

1 **a)** Where did power lie in Fascist Italy?
   Return to our original question at the beginning of the chapter. Consider the three models, and write a paragraph explaining your final choice.

b) Draw up two lists of points to support and oppose the view that Mussolini was an all-powerful dictator.

SOURCE 5.31   C. Seton-Watson, *Italy from Liberalism to Fascism 1870–1925*, 1967, p. 701

Neither did the state absorb the party nor the party the state. Italy continued to be governed by two parallel hierarchies of institutions, each deeply influencing the other but remaining distinct. Mussolini stood at the apex [head] of both, as Head of Government and Duce of Fascism. Beneath him the party militia co-existed with the regular armed forces, the prefect co-existed with the provincial party official. Even in the police and judiciary a certain distinction lingered on, between the royal carabinieri [police] and the ordinary courts of law on the one hand, and the secret police and the Fascist Special Tribunal on the other . . . With time the process of Fascistizzazione ['Fascistisation'] did diminish the independence and esprit de corps [pride in belonging to a particular group, sense of purpose] of the old state institutions. From 1927 the Fascist prefect, the Fascist diplomatist and the Fascist judge became more common. In the armed forces, especially the army, a display of Fascist enthusiasm could accelerate promotion. The character of the Senate, too, was transformed; as elder statesmen died and new Fascist blood was injected, it became indistinguishable from the lower house in its black shirts and well-drilled unanimity. The schools, the press and sport were special targets for Fascist penetration. Nevertheless even dedicated Fascists, appointed to infuse a new spirit into old institutions, did not always escape the influence of tradition. It was also Mussolini's policy . . . to strengthen the authority of officials such as the prefect, even at the party's expense. If Fascistizzazione dello stato [Fascists taking over the state] had its successes, there was also the process of statizzazione del Fascismo [the state taking over the Fascist Party, see page 94].

In this chapter you have studied the roles of Mussolini, the Fascist Party and the elites in government and how repressive Mussolini's regime was. By this stage you should know the following points.

Key points from Chapter 5

1 After a period of cautious consolidation in 1922–24, from 1925 to 1927 Mussolini established a personal dictatorship.
2 Italy remained a monarchy, but Mussolini held real power.
3 Mussolini was a skilled politician but lacked many of the attributes of a strong and effective leader.
4 Mussolini's power was sustained by a personality cult.
5 The chasm between his portrayal as a superhuman ruler and his performance says a lot about the nature of Fascist Italy: strong on style, and weak on substance.
6 The Fascist movement was taken over by the state, not vice versa.
7 Many from the traditional governing groups joined the Fascist Party to benefit their careers.
8 The Fascist Party was used primarily as a propaganda machine, not as a party of rule.
9 Mussolini's policies gained the support of the elites. Their interests were not threatened, and they tolerated his considerable power.
10 Individual liberty was suppressed but violence was not so extensive or systematic as in other dictatorships.

A look ahead

You could argue that in order to stay in power a government may have to use a mixture of wise **policies** and skilful **propaganda** to win support, and **repression** to weaken opponents.

We have looked at the political structure of Fascist Italy and considered the extent of Mussolini's power. Repression was an important element in buttressing his power, but so too were his policies and propaganda. You will need to assess these (Chapters 6–8) before being able to assess fully how successful a leader Mussolini was. First, though, let us consider how he used propaganda to help secure his regime.

How did Mussolini use propaganda to strengthen his regime?

Propaganda and DICTATORS seem to go hand in hand. Both Hitler and Stalin established complete control of the media in their countries, using it to win support and also to ensure that opponents had no means of communicating their views effectively. Did Mussolini succeed in doing the same? He certainly saw the opportunities when he said to an American film crew, 'Your talking newsreel has tremendous possibilities. Let me speak through it in twenty cities in Italy once a week and I need no other power.'

■ Activity

1 List ten methods the Fascist government might have used to spread its ideas and win support.
2 Now study Chart 6B and compare this list with your own.

A What were the aims and methods of Fascist propaganda?

CHART 6B   Fascist propaganda. Aims and means

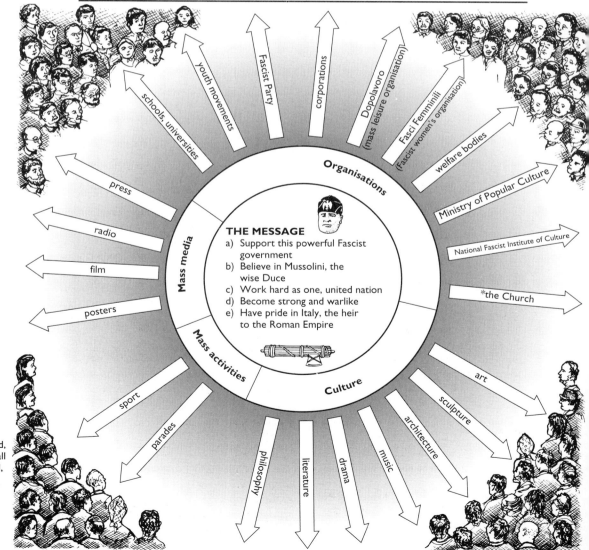

THE MESSAGE
a) Support this powerful Fascist government
b) Believe in Mussolini, the wise Duce
c) Work hard as one, united nation
d) Become strong and warlike
e) Have pride in Italy, the heir to the Roman Empire

*Unlike the other organisations listed, the Church did not try to inculcate all Fascism's ideas in the people, but did, especially after 1929, serve as a powerful body fostering support for the regime (see page 174–76).

Support was also maintained by censorship and suppression of criticism, not itself propaganda.

FOCUS ROUTE

Using pages 106–07, explain how the Fascist regime exploited Italy's Roman past.

Fascism and Ancient Rome

'Italians, you must ensure that the glories of the past are surpassed by the glories of the future.'

These words of Mussolini were engraved on the imposing entrance to the Mostra Augustea della Romanita exhibition in 1937, which was to celebrate the 2000th anniversary of the birth of Augustus. Over one million people attended the exhibition of 30,000 items, designed to display Rome's IMPERIAL might, and show Mussolini as the heir to Augustus. 'Romanita', or the cult of Ancient Rome, was a major theme in Fascist propaganda.

Italy's Roman past was used both as the inspiration of, and the justification for, Fascist policies. For a country which recently had suffered from disunity and an inferiority complex, the regime's exploitation of this once glorious past was hardly surprising.

In Fascist Italy, symbols of Ancient Rome were everywhere. Hundreds of medieval buildings were demolished in Rome to allow imperial Roman ruins to be better displayed, and new public buildings were largely classical in design. Mussolini was increasingly portrayed, both in appearance and in action, as a new Roman leader who, like Augustus, had established order out of chaos; who was restoring Rome's grain production and improving drainage; who was building up Italy's military might and leading the country to imperial glory.

CHART 6C How Fascism used Ancient Rome

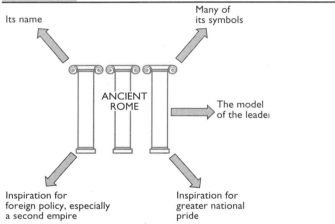

Its name

Many of its symbols

ANCIENT ROME

The model of the leader

Inspiration for foreign policy, especially a second empire

Inspiration for greater national pride

SOURCE 6.1 Mussolini speaking in 1935

Rome is our point of departure and our point of reference. It is our symbol and, if you like, our myth. We dream of a Roman Italy, an Italy that is wise and strong, disciplined and impersonal. Much of the spirit of Ancient Rome is being born again in Fascism; the Lictorian fasces are Roman, our war machine is Roman, our pride and our courage are Roman too. Civis Romanus sum [I am a Roman citizen].

SOURCE 6.2 Extract from a schoolbook for ten-year-olds

If you listen carefully . . . you may still hear the terrible tread of the Roman legions . . . Caesar has come to life again in the Duce; *he rides at the head of numberless cohorts, treading down all cowardice and all impurities to re-establish the culture and the new might of Rome. Step into the ranks of his army and be the best soldiers.*

SOURCE 6.3 From a speech made by Mussolini in May 1936, which was then inscribed in stone for the 1937 exhibition

The Italian people have created the Empire with their blood, will make it fertile with their labour and defend it against whomsoever with their arms. In this certain hope, raise high, legionaries, the standards, the steel and your hearts, and salute, after fifteen centuries, the reappearance of the Empire on the fated hills of Rome.

■ **Talking point**

Chart 6D is a reconstruction drawing combining various features of Ancient Rome which were adopted by the Fascists. What are the strengths and weaknesses of presenting information through reconstruction drawings?

■ **Activity**

1 Look at the drawing in Chart 6D. List all the references to Ancient Rome.
2 Study Sources 6.1–3. How is the cult of Ancient Rome being used by the regime here?

Dictatorship and technology

The role of technology is often neglected by political historians. One could, however, argue that it would have been very difficult for the totalitarian regimes of the 1930s to have existed without modern technology. This allowed governments and parties to convey their ideas directly to the masses for the first time.

The Fascist regime still made use of generally supportive parish priests and bishops' circulars to influence the rural masses, but radio and, to a lesser extent, film allowed Mussolini to bypass these intermediaries. The microphone and loudspeaker also helped bring Mussolini's voice directly to the masses.

In other ways, technology enhanced the Fascist regime. Fascist architecture, also used to impress the people, benefited from improved technology, such as reinforced concrete, and improved transportation for massive pieces of stone.

Other products of improved technology such as electrification, planes, railways, cars and tanks all in their way gave added power to the regime.

■ Activity

Read pages 108–11. In a chart like the one below assess each area of the mass media and give it a grade (5–0). Make sure you note down the evidence you would use to back up each judgement.

This is necessarily a simplified assessment; make a note where relevant alongside your chart of any changes over time.

Area of the mass media	How effectively was it used for propaganda purposes?		
	State ownership 5–0 (5 = complete, 3 = considerable, 0 = none)	State control of content 5–0 (5 = complete, 3 = considerable, 0 = none)	Effective propaganda use 5–0 (5 = effective, 3 = some use, 0 = not used)
Newspapers			
Radio			
Cinema			
Posters			

The development of propaganda

Mussolini had begun his rise to power through his talents as a journalist, and throughout his life he paid great attention to the press. The historian Tannenbaum has described the Fascist regime as 'in some ways the reign of journalists'. Newspapers were the most important information and propaganda instrument in Fascist Italy, especially in the 1920s. Mussolini was determined first to suppress criticism, then to ensure the press followed official views. After a slow start, radio became a major propaganda tool of the regime, as did film, especially newsreels. In addition to these formal media, the government fostered enthusiasm by involving the masses in vast parades and sporting activities. Italy's sporting achievements were used to heighten national pride.

The development of a propaganda machine was a gradual process, and the Fascist regime never achieved the impact of Goebbels' efficient machinery. Tannenbaum has described its approach to propaganda as 'amateurish', and this reduced its effectiveness, certainly compared to that of the Nazis. Mussolini's Press Office gradually extended its original role in the 1930s to cover radio, film and eventually all aspects of culture. It was made a ministry (in imitation of Nazi Germany) in 1935. It launched a major propaganda campaign during the Abyssinian War (see pages 214–20) which helped rally support for the war. In 1937 it was renamed the Ministry of Popular Culture, to symbolise its increased effort to bring all Italians into the NATIONAL, Fascist experience. Its sarcastic nickname, 'Minculpop', suggests it had a limited effect, which was not surprising given its bureaucratic inefficiency. This is confirmed by the failure of the Fascist propaganda machine to win popular support for the German alliance and the government's ANTI-SEMITIC policies in the late 1930s. On the other hand, most Italians believed, and some still do despite evidence to the contrary, that Fascism reduced crime, vice and poverty.

The key instruments of propaganda

1. Mass media

Newspapers

SOURCE 6.4 The *Domenica del Corriere* newspaper announcing the beginning of the Abyssinian War

Initially, hostile newspapers were attacked by Fascist squads. In 1923 a law made PREFECTS responsible for censorship. The Fascist Party organised boycotts of some critical papers. By 1926 the last opposition party papers had been suppressed; others conformed, through commitment or fear of the consequences of criticism. Many were bought up by Fascist sympathisers. Hostile journalists and editors could be arrested or replaced, but most popular journalists remained in their posts, helping to reinforce readers' acceptance of what the press said. The government gave grants to favoured journalists and papers.

The state controlled what the papers said, and, more importantly, what they did not say. Most censorship was carried out by editors themselves, with prefects only rarely needing to intervene. Reporting of most crime, disasters, unemployment, and disorders was forbidden. The majority of foreign papers were banned. The only press agency was run by a Fascist. Mussolini's Press Office sent out detailed instructions on the 'correct' version of events. Journalists had to be registered by the state, and join a Fascist association.

Fascist Party newspapers never had more than ten per cent of overall circulation. Mussolini was far more concerned with the content of newspapers than with their ownership. The Vatican's *Osservatore Romano* increased its daily circulation from 20,000 to 250,000 in the late 1930s. The Milan-based *Corriere della Sera* had a circulation (600,000 in 1933) five times that of the Fascist *Il Popolo d'Italia*. The greater variety permitted in newspapers in Italy meant readership grew, unlike in Nazi Germany. Furthermore, some underground anti-Fascist newspapers continued to circulate.

SOURCE 6.5 In July 1923 prefects were charged with ensuring that

[no] articles, comments, notes, titles [might be published which would] impair the nation's interest . . . provoke alarm among the people or disturb public order. [Anything that led to] crime, inspired class hatred, provoked disobedience, or compromised discipline [was to be suppressed].

SOURCE 6.6 Extracts from Minculpop instructions to the press

- *Report that the Duce was called back to the balcony ten times.*
- *Stress that the Duce was not tired after four hours on a threshing machine.*

Radio

SOURCE 6.7 An advertisement for 'Radio Balilla' at the National Exhibition of Radio, Milan 1920s

Radio was neglected initially as Mussolini was sceptical of its value. From 1924 onwards the rapidly expanding radio network was state run. The content of programmes was controlled by the state. It consisted mainly of music, both classical and American jazz, and drama. There were two hours a day of official broadcasts. The amount of official broadcasts increased in the 1930s. Their tone, stern and martial, made as much impact as their content. Other commentators whipped up excitement with evocative descriptions of events. Mussolini's major speeches were broadcast live. Large loudspeakers carried them to cheering crowds in piazzas throughout Italy. Private radio listeners, however, also had access to foreign programmes such as Vatican broadcasts, the BBC, and Rosselli broadcasts from Spain.

Few people had radios since they were expensive, though their numbers increased (from 40,000 in 1927, to 1 million in 1938). This number could be multiplied by five to give the approximate number of listeners of private radios. Far more listened in public. In the 1930s, the government provided sets for a new rural radio agency (ERR). It also gave radios to schools. Dopolavoro (OND) ran community listening meetings which helped spread Fascist ideas, especially in rural areas and to the illiterate.

Cinema

SOURCE 6.8 Mussolini laying the foundation stone of the new LUCE building, 1937. The banner proclaims 'Film is the strongest weapon'

SOURCE 6.9 Minister Bottai, 1931

Too openly propagandist films or those too overtly moralising perhaps will not meet with public favour. Even a production which is backing up religious or political ideas must concentrate on its artistic and commercial sides and not lose sight of what leads to success, the real reason for the cinema's existence.

SOURCE 6.11 'Italy has its empire at last'

As with radio, the government was slow to realise film's potential, but in 1924 a government agency, LUCE (L'Unione Cinematografica Educativa), was created to produce documentaries and newsreels (called cinegiornali). Mussolini frequently previewed them before release. They typically consisted of brief news from abroad, several sports items, a local colour item, such as a festival or an item on the Duce, with a happy story about animals, children or a film star to conclude. Cinemas had to show these before the main film. The state censored Italian and imported films and issued directives on style and content.

In the 1920s Italian cinemas were dominated by Hollywood imports, and the young Italian film industry languished. In 1934 the government decided to intervene, more as part of its AUTARKY policy than for propaganda reasons. A Director General in the Culture Ministry was appointed; he encouraged film production by restricting Hollywood imports, and providing subsidies and training.

In 1937 the IRI (the Institute for Industrial Reconstruction) helped fund Cinecittà, a series of major film studios, as a 'Hollywood by the Tiber'. This helped the revival of domestically produced films. Italian audiences thus had a mixture of state-produced documentaries, privately produced subsidised Italian films, and American imports. In 1938 three-quarters of ticket sales were for US films, with the most popular being *Snow White and the Seven Dwarfs*. Mussolini's favourite film was *Stanley e Olio* ('Laurel and Hardy').

Initially the government valued the commercial success of films over their propaganda role, and till the late 1930s most films were escapist, or historical drama. Only a few were self-consciously Fascist, dramatising the lives of a Fascist of the first hour struggling against Socialists (*Vecchia guardia*), or that of a pilot in the Abyssinian war (*Luciano Serra, pilota*). Thus there were few explicit propaganda films (apart from newsreels), though most feature films stressed Italy as a modern, technologically advanced country with social harmony.

Increasing numbers of Italians went to the cinema as Dopolavoro showed films, and mobile cinemas toured the countryside. Films offered people escape from their humdrum lives, and a false sense of security and national pride.

SOURCE 6.10 Freddi, Director of DGC (General Directorship of Cinematography), 1937

A nation that is able to avoid the harsher realities that involve all the world will be one where all the citizens, even the so-called private citizens, know how to think and act, not merely out of self-interest, but out of regard for the collective group, the nation ... The most powerful force, over the last three years, which has hastened the development of this attitude has been our film production. The new national film production is acquiring an international reputation and meaning because it expresses our time in history, which is truly Italian and Fascist.

Posters

Posters were the most visual means of propaganda, and many walls were plastered by the party and government agencies with simple slogans and striking images of the Duce. They were important as there was still considerable illiteracy. Occasionally opposition posters were displayed briefly, but generally the government had a MONOPOLY of this important medium (see pages 118–19).

2. Mass activities
Rallies

SOURCE 6.12 A rally to celebrate the seventh anniversary of the Fascist March on Rome

The Fascist Party organised a series of mass parades, both to inculcate discipline and collective identity in participants and to impress observers. Mussolini obtained from Stalin details on Soviet May Day parades which he imitated.

SOURCE 6.13 The art historian F. Whitford has powerfully described the role of such activities in *Art and Power*, 1995

All these events were quasi-religious and ritualistic. All instilled in their participants a sense of belonging to a whole greater than the sum of its parts. Everyone was a member of an organisation, wore its uniform, and knew his or her place in its clearly defined hierarchy. The state itself was seen both as a work of art and a perfectly functioning machine.

Sport

SOURCE 6.14 The Italian team that went on to win the World Cup, 1934. The sign at the back of the stadium reads 'Buy Italian products'

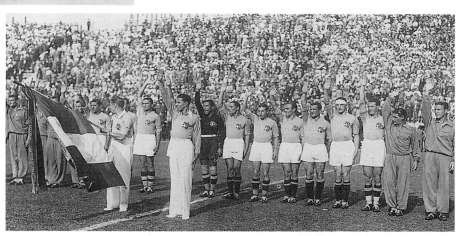

Sport was encouraged, both as a form of active participation and as a spectacle. Like rallies, mass sport was used to help discipline, and socialise the people, and to secure their commitment to the regime.

Many new stadiums were built, and these were also designed to impress the masses (see page 112). Successful national teams were seen as a way to increase national pride. The regime received a great boost from Carnera being world heavyweight boxing champion from 1933 to 1935. The importance placed on sporting success may be indicated by the rumours that the national football team received a telegram saying 'Win or Die' before the 1938 World Cup final! They won, as they had in 1934.

SOURCE 6.15 Fascist Deputy and newspaper editor Lando Ferretti in 1928

Sport is, for us, above all a school for the will which will prepare citizens in peace time to be heroic soldiers for Fascism in war time ... To be prepared, to confront the struggle, to behave with honour, to die for victory if necessary, this is the trajectory [direction] of sporting education and its supreme purpose.

SOURCE 6.16 D. Thompson, *State Control in Fascist Italy*, 1991, p. 84

The channelling of emotions into nationalistic competitiveness associated particularly with football, cycle racing and boxing, probably bound far more individuals to Mussolini and the regime than did any IDEOLOGY or the overt militarism of so much Fascist activity.

■ **Activity**

What were the strengths and weaknesses of the major means of propaganda in spreading the Fascist message?

■ **Talking points**

1 In what ways do modern governments try to use sport for political purposes?
2 Have you ever attended a public event where you were emotionally swept away by the power of the occasion? What long-term effects did it have on you, if any?

B How did Mussolini use culture for propaganda purposes?

SOURCE 6.17   F. Whitford, *Art and Power*, 1995

Culture mattered a great deal to totalitarian governments. They paid it obsessive attention because they believed in its power. They knew that it could, if directed, immensely enhance their authority. They also knew that, if uncontrolled, it could undermine and destroy their omnipotence [total power]. Culture could only serve their purposes if it were regulated as ruthlessly as every other aspect of life.

Whitford makes this comment in the book *Art and Power* about the use of culture by the dictatorial governments in the 1930s. Let us examine how justified this view is of Fascist Italy.

First, however, we need to consider what we mean by culture. Culture can be taken to mean both elitist works of art and intellectual discussion (high culture), and popular customs and behaviour (mass culture). Mussolini was concerned with both, though particularly the latter. As we have seen, the development of modern means of communication had given the regime the opportunity to reach and influence the masses far more effectively than previous governments. However, the regime also concerned itself with high culture, both as a means of propaganda, but also to increase the external prestige of the Fascist state.

Was there an official view of Fascist art?

If you have studied art in Nazi Germany and the Soviet Union, you will have an image of totalitarian governments seeking to impose an official style, 'Aryan' or Socialist Realist, and ban 'degenerate' (perverted) art in an attempt to control all aspects of life. You might expect to see the same in Fascist Italy.

SOURCE 6.19   The artist Mario Sironi, *Manifesto of Mural Painting*, 1933

In the Fascist state art acquires a social function; an educative function. It must translate the ethics [principles] of our times. It must give a unity of style and grandeur of contour to common life. Thus art will once again become what it was in the greatest of times and at the heart of the greatest civilisation; a perfect instrument of spiritual direction.

SOURCE 6.20   Alfieri, Minister of Culture, 1939

Art must be, in these times of noticeable social improvement, art for the people and by the people; such art as shall exalt the people and which the people, advancing towards higher aims, will understand.

FOCUS ROUTE

1   Using pages 112–22, make notes on the way Mussolini used the arts for propaganda purposes.
2   Why was there considerable cultural diversity in Fascist Italy?

SOURCE 6.18   Portrait of Mussolini by Dottori, 1933

SOURCE 6.21   The Stadium of the Marbles, Mussolini Forum

■ Activity

1 What do Sources 6.19 and 6.20 tell us about the Fascist regime's view of art?

2 Look at the examples here of paintings and buildings from Fascist Italy.
   a) Describe each source.
   b) What message might each one be trying to convey?

3 Do you think they would make an impact on ordinary people, as Alfieri wished?

SOURCE 6.22 Langoni, *Battle for Corn*, 1940. Submitted for the Cremona Prize

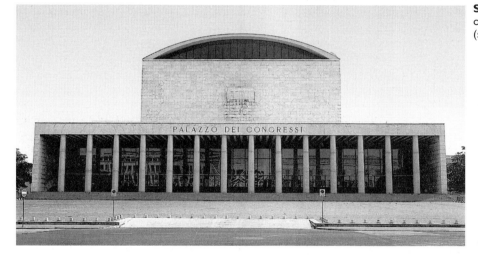

SOURCE 6.23   A modern photograph of the Palace of Congresses, EUR, 1938–42 (see page 116)

SOURCE 6.24   *Portrait of the Duce* by Amrosi, 1930. A FUTURIST aero-portrait of Mussolini, with a view of Rome and the via dei Fori Imperiali behind him

SOURCE 6.25   Sironi, *Shepherd*. Sironi was a strong Fascist supporter

Were other kinds of art allowed?

Alongside official Fascist art, painting which was more abstract, and sometimes potentially subversive art, was still created (see Sources 6.26 and 6.27). This was not just in private commissions, but even within state and party-sponsored works. Many artists officially conformed to enhance their career opportunities, but exploited the system to express their own artistic vision (see Source 6.28).

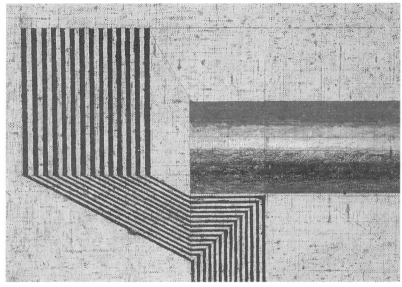

SOURCE 6.26 *Rhythm* by Licini, 1933, an example of abstract painting

SOURCE 6.27 *Crucifixion* by Manzù. This painting won the Bergamo Prize in 1939, and can be seen as an attack on Nazi brutality in Germany

SOURCE 6.28 Casa del Fascio, Como, by Terragni, 1936–40

SOURCE 6.29 Fascist Grand Council Member Farinacci, 1940

We cannot allow the consciousness of people to be expressed in art by disgusting nudes, Jewish hats, gaunt and emaciated [abnormally thin] faces, bodies suffering from elephantiasis [a disfiguring disease], by drunken and deformed expressions; in short by the rhetoric [exaggerated language] of monstrosity and deceit, the mania of novelty for the sake of it, and even of technical virtuosity which conceals, without success, the total absence of sentiment, thought and understanding of life.

How could you have this variety?

'Fascist art is the art of the masses.' This proud boast, reiterated by numerous Fascist officials, stemmed less from a desire to develop the cultural sophistication of Italians than the government's aim to use art as a means of propaganda. Thus 'Fascist art' had to have a clear message and be impressive. However, it was not that simple. There were, typically, divisions and debates amongst the Fascists as to what should be the 'Fascist style', or even if there should be one. Thus far more than in the fellow totalitarian regimes of Nazi Germany and the Soviet Union, there was considerable cultural diversity under Fascism. This also reflected the general variety of influence centres and greater toleration of diversity in Fascist Italy, provided this did not lead to direct opposition to the regime. Whether this greater diversity actually harmed the government's propaganda aims is open to debate.

SOURCE 6.30 Fascist Grand Council Member Bottai

Fascism does not want a state art ... For the state, it is important that both Bergamo and Cremona [two alternative art exhibitions] exist, as consenting and dissenting voices, that is, as expressions of a reality that is both vital and dialectic [progressive clash of opposites].

SOURCE 6.31 Bottai, speaking at the opening of the Venice Biennale Art Exhibition in 1940

Art which is directly controlled by the state, as an instrument of propaganda, not only results in illustration or documentation, but owing to the lack of expression loses all its effectiveness as propaganda.

There were broadly two main artistic tendencies. **Neo-classicists** looked to ancient Rome for inspiration, favouring realism and monumentalism (Sources 6.21, 6.22 and 6.23), whereas **modernists** experimented in more diverse, abstract styles (Source 6.26). Mussolini was himself torn; on the one hand he claimed to be modernising Italy, yet he, and most people, were not attracted to more abstract modernist architecture and art.

Given its claim to be a state that incarnated (embodied) the nation, and the government's desire to use art as a means of propaganda, it is not surprising that ultimately most Fascists (like the Nazis and COMMUNISTS) favoured the more classical, realist approach, especially as this could be seen as traditional Italian art as opposed to more cosmopolitan (international) modernism.

In common with other totalitarian regimes, the most favoured forms of art showed human beings as social stereotypes, not individuals. Thus sturdy rural or industrial workers, productive women, and virile youths striving to make Italy great were frequently portrayed (see Source 6.25). Even more dominant was, of course, Mussolini, in numerous paintings, posters and sculptures, shown as a firm, wise leader (see Sources 6.18 and 6.24).

In the late 1930s, a radicalisation evident elsewhere also affected art. Farinacci led the attack on Jewish influences in culture, which was used to attack abstract art which previously had been tolerated. As in other areas, this radicalisation aroused dissent (see Chapter 11). The tension between different Fascist views of painting is well illustrated by the establishment of two rival prizes in 1939, by two leading Fascists. In 1939 Farinacci, an admirer of Nazi Germany, set up the Cremona Prize to promote simple, propagandist art. Mussolini himself chose the themes, such as 'Listening to a speech by the Duce on the radio', 'The Battle for Grain' (1940), and 'Italian Youth of the Fascist Movement' (1941). Bottai, in opposition, set up the Bergamo Prize to encourage more creative freedom. The themes were more open, for example landscape in 1939, two figures in 1940, and there was no set theme in 1941–42.

The government tried to control art through promoting competitions, at regional, national and international level. Winners received government funds and commissions. Alongside this, however, private commissioning continued largely unaffected, until the late 1930s. Artists were expected to join the Syndicate of Professionals and Artists. They had to profess loyalty to the regime, but were not required to subscribe to an official view of art. This meant that unlike Nazi Germany Fascist Italy experienced no loss of major artists.

How was art used?

So far you have been looking at the nature of art in Fascist Italy; we now need to examine how it was used as a form of propaganda. When you have studied this next section, you can complete the chart on page 122, which you might like to look at now.

If art was to serve as an effective form of propaganda, it had not just to be easily understandable, it also had to reach the people. This was easier to achieve with architecture, certainly for urban Italians, than with painting. However, the government organised about 50 art exhibitions a year, with major ones every two to four years at Rome, Milan and Venice for which there were reduced train fares. These exhibitions helped increase familiarity with art. Other exhibitions more directly celebrated the achievements of the regime. Like the major 1932 Exhibition of the Fascist Revolution, these were often housed in newly constructed buildings, which themselves sent a message, as did the new stadiums, such as Rome's Stadium of Marbles (see Source 6.21).

Like other dictators, Mussolini wanted to demonstrate the stability and power of his regime, and the construction of monumental official buildings was one of the best ways of doing this. Public buildings were designed to impress. Most were decorated with sculpture or murals (see Source 7.16 on page 139), which the artist Sironi considered 'social painting par excellence'. A practice developed, formalised in 1942, that all public buildings had to have at least two per cent of their outside walls used to display some form of art. Probably one of the most effective ways in which art was used to gain support for the regime was in a series of striking posters (see pages 118–19).

All dictators plan grandiose restructuring of their capitals, or even have new cities designed to show, through their sheer scale, the power and permanence of the state. New motorways (even if there were not many cars) served the same purpose. Mussolini's new exhibition city EUR (Universal Exhibition of Rome) planned for 1942 was not completed, but the centre of Rome felt the impact of his new vision, with many old buildings being demolished for his new via dei Fori Imperiali (see Source 6.37).

Talking points

1 Benton entitled a chapter on totalitarian architecture (in *Art and Power,* 1995) 'Speaking without adjectives'. What do you think he meant?

2 Mussolini was far more interested in Italy's Roman architectural and military past, than he was in Italian Renaissance art. Why do you think this was?

SOURCE 6.32 The Gori sculpture on top of the Italian Pavilion, Paris 1937. Italy's pavilion faces that of Germany, with the Soviet Union's on the left. This major international exhibition, celebrating peace and technology, evoked great rivalry between the major states, especially between the Fascist regimes and the USSR

SOURCE 6.33 A sculpture of Mussolini standing on his own head, 1930

SOURCE 6.34 Mussolini monument, Abyssinia 1936. This was built by soldiers in 1936, near the battleground of Amba Aradam. All it needs is an adoring crowd!

SOURCE 6.35 The Palace of State and Work, EUR, 1942. The architects were Guerri, Lapadula and Romano. One of the few parts of EUR actually built, it echoes the grandeur of Roman monuments and combines it with the boldness of a modernist vision

SOURCE 6.36 The entrance to the Exhibition of the Fascist Revolution, 1932, a strikingly modernist design

SOURCE 6.37 Mussolini starts demolition work for the via dei Fori Imperiali, built 1928–32

CHART 6E The state and the arts in Fascist Italy

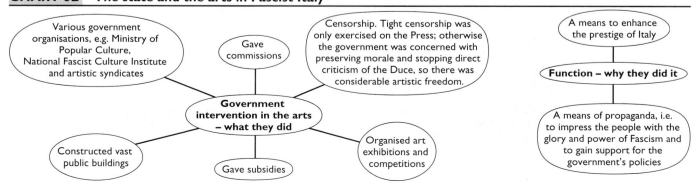

Various government organisations, e.g. Ministry of Popular Culture, National Fascist Culture Institute and artistic syndicates

Gave commissions

Censorship. Tight censorship was only exercised on the Press; otherwise the government was concerned with preserving morale and stopping direct criticism of the Duce, so there was considerable artistic freedom.

A means to enhance the prestige of Italy

Function – why they did it

A means of propaganda, i.e. to impress the people with the glory and power of Fascism and to gain support for the government's policies

Government intervention in the arts – what they did

Constructed vast public buildings

Gave subsidies

Organised art exhibitions and competitions

SOURCE 6.38 A poster for the 1934 plebiscite

SOURCE 6.39 'Buy Italian': a poster encouraging people to fight against the sanctions imposed during the Abyssinian War

SOURCE 6.40 A poster for the Olympic Games linking Italian prowess in sport with that in war

DUCE - DUCE - DUCE - DUCE - DUCE
DUCE - DUCE - DUCE - DUCE - DUCE
DUCE - DUCE - DUCE - DUCE - DUCE
DUCE - DUCE - DUCE - DUCE - DUCE
DUCE - DUCE - DUCE - DUCE - DUCE
DUCE - DUCE - DUCE - DUCE - DUCE
DUCE - DUCE - DUCE - DUCE - DUCE
DUCE - DUCE - DUCE - DUCE - DUCE

■ **Activity**

1 Comment on the style of Bot's poem.
2 What do you think is Bot's attitude to Mussolini?

■ **Talking point**

Why do you think there was no Italian equivalent to *Das Kapital* or *Mein Kampf?*

Literature and drama

Much less attention was paid to literature and drama, which did not reach the masses. Mussolini spoke of 'a theatre for twenty thousand', hoping to extend this art form to the masses, but drama remained a minority pursuit, despite the efforts of the OND and National Fascist Culture Institute. The latter had been established in 1926 to spread 'Fascist' culture to the masses. It had 94 provincial sections and organised conferences, free concerts and publications. It claimed 200,000 members by 1941, though these were overwhelmingly middle class. Music (apart from opera) had less potential for direct propaganda. Musicians were required to join the Fascist Union of Musicians, and were encouraged to reject foreign influences, and develop 'cultural AUTARKY'. However, considerable diversity was still maintained.

In theory the Ministry of Popular Culture was supposed to control music, but in practice music escaped major regimentation. The same can be said for literature. Initially some major writers, such as the dramatist Pirandello and the poet d'Annunzio, had been attracted by the bright future promised by Fascism, but as the regime degenerated into corruption and careerism (where people were motivated only by the desire to further their own careers), many writers tried to isolate themselves from the cynicism and hypocrisy of day-to-day life. No great Fascist literature was written, as is perhaps illustrated by Source 6.41! Provided writers included nothing directly hostile to the regime, they were left free, apart from being required to join the relevant Fascist syndicate. The poet Eugenio Montale probably spoke for many when he explained, 'I never was Fascist, nor did I sing to Fascism. Nor however did I write poems that might appear to oppose that pseudo-revolution.'

Philosophy and intellectual ideas

Mussolini was concerned about other aspects of culture, and was particularly concerned to develop a philosophy of Fascism. He considered this could boost the regime's international reputation, and help establish a new Fascist ELITE. Unlike COMMUNISM, which had the writings of MARX and Lenin, and even Nazism, which had *Mein Kampf*, Fascism had no corpus (body) of writing explaining its nature.

Mussolini had been a critic of dogmas (sets of beliefs or principles). However, now that he was the leader of a regime, not just a protest movement, he was keen to formulate a clearer doctrine of Fascism.

In 1925 over 200 intellectuals, presided over by the philosopher Gentile, met at Bologna to produce the MANIFESTO of Fascist Intellectuals. They grandly proclaimed that without Fascism there could be no true culture. Other intellectuals, led by Croce, responded with a Counter Manifesto declaring Fascism and culture incompatible.

Gentile in fact had a far more refined view of Fascist culture than many in the party. He wisely believed that higher culture could not be coerced, but only gradually absorbed into the new Fascist consciousness. The most famous product of this approach was the *Enciclopedia Italiana* which was published between 1929 and 1938 as a sort of rival to the *Encyclopedia Britannica*. It was a compendium (collection) of human knowledge, with particular stress on Italy's role. As editor, Gentile gained the collaboration of 2500 experts, whom he chose on the basis of their expertise rather than political views. This led to some criticism from more RADICAL Fascists, but interestingly Mussolini supported Gentile's approach as his main concern was to increase the prestige of Italy in the eyes of the world. (This concern for intellectual rigour did not, however, prevent Mussolini from co-authoring the long article on Fascism!) The diversity of perspectives in this official publication neatly illustrates the lack of rigid cultural controls under Mussolini's regime.

Indeed, the attempt to intellectualise the diverse and contradictory ideas in the Fascist movement had little impact. Amongst the educated, Fascism was seen primarily as a vehicle for career advancement rather than intellectual inspiration. Though the 60 eminent intellectuals who became members of the new Royal Academy of Italy in 1929 boosted the regime's prestige, most were not committed Fascists. The famous philosopher Croce retained his influence. He had initially sympathised with Fascism as a positive force that might reinvigorate Italy, but became increasingly critical. His renown was so great (and his mass influence so little) that the government took no action against him. In 1926 he was the victim of unofficial squad violence (Mussolini was suitably horrified), but his books were still published. Indeed, in the 1930s the circulation of his philosophical journal, *La Critica*, doubled.

The Liberal economist Einaudi also remained influential in academic circles, as, of course, did the Catholic Church, with its own students' federation, and Catholic University in Milan. The Italian intelligentsia, though politically conformist, did not become intellectually engaged with the regime. The historian Zaggario has argued that 'Italian academic culture was largely impervious [resistant] to Fascistisation'.

SOURCE 6.42 Extract from the *Enciclopedia Italiana* entry on Fascism, 1932, written by Gentile and Mussolini

Against individualism, the Fascist conception is for the state; and it is for the individual in so far as he coincides with the state, which is the conscience and universal will of man in his historical existence. It is opposed to classical LIBERALISM, which arose from the necessity of reacting against absolutism, and which brought its historical purpose to an end when the state was transformed into the conscience and will of the people. Liberalism denied the state in the interests of the individual; Fascism reaffirms the state as the true reality of the individual. And if liberty is to be the attribute [quality] of the real man, and not of that abstract puppet envisaged by individualistic Liberalism, Fascism is for liberty. And for the only liberty which can be a real thing, the liberty of the state and of the individual within the state. Therefore, for the Fascist, everything is in the state, and nothing human or spiritual exists, much less has value, outside the state. In this sense Fascism is totalitarian, and the Fascist state, the synthesis and unity of all values, interprets, develops and gives strength to the whole life of the people . . .

Therefore Fascism is opposed to SOCIALISM, which confines the movement of history within the class struggle and ignores the unity of classes established in one economic and moral reality in the state; and analogously [similarly] it is opposed to class SYNDICALISM . . .

Fascism is opposed to DEMOCRACY, which equates the nation to the majority, lowering it to the level of that majority; nevertheless it is the purest form of democracy if the nation is conceived, as it should be, qualitatively and not quantitatively . . .

It is not the nation that generates the state, as according to the old naturalistic concept which served as the basis of the political theories of the national states of the nineteenth century. Rather the nation is created by the state . . .

Above all, Fascism . . . believes neither in the possibility nor in the utility of perpetual peace. It thus repudiates [rejects] the doctrine of PACIFISM – born of a renunciation of the struggle and an act of cowardice in the face of sacrifice. War alone brings up to their highest tension all human energies and puts the stamp of nobility upon the peoples who have the courage to meet it . . .

Fascism carries over this anti-pacifist spirit even into the lives of individuals. The proud motto of the Squadrista, 'Me ne frego' ['I don't give a damn'], written on the bandages of a wound, is an act of philosophy which is not only stoical [self-sacrificing], it is the epitome [essence] of a doctrine that is not only political: it is education for combat, the acceptance of the risks which it brings; it is a new way of life for Italy . . .

If it is admitted that the nineteenth century has been the century of Socialism, Liberalism and Democracy, it does not follow that the twentieth must also be the century of Liberalism, Socialism and Democracy. Political doctrines pass; peoples remain. It is to be expected that this century may be that of authority, a century of the 'Right', a Fascist century . . .

In the Fascist state religion is looked upon as one of the deepest manifestations [products] of the spirit; it is, therefore, not only respected, but defended and protected . . .

■ **Activity**

1 What does the background information about the *Enciclopedia Italiana* indicate about Fascist Italy?

2 Read the extract from the *Enciclopedia* (Source 6.42). What is Fascism
   a) opposed to
   b) in favour of?

3 How influential do you think this definition of Fascism was in strengthening Mussolini's regime?

4 As a member of the Ministry of Propaganda, draw up a simple propaganda leaflet, conveying to the masses the key ideas from this encyclopedia entry.

To conclude, let us look at some historians' comments on culture and dictatorship.

SOURCE 6.43 Whitford, p. 5

The central message of totalitarian art and architecture was that individual identity had meaning only in terms of the larger identity of the state, embodied in the CHARISMATIC *person of the supreme leader.*

SOURCE 6.44 I. Golomstock, *Totalitarian Art,* 1990, p. 120

Totalitarianism as a whole effected its control of art through the use of both the carrot and the whip. Italian Fascism, however, used only the carrot: its cultural policy was executed through encouraging supporters rather than through destroying opponents.

SOURCE 6.45 V. Zaggario in *Historical Dictionary of Fascist Italy,* ed. P. Cannistraro, 1982, p. 149

It cannot be said that the Fascist regime forcefully channelled culture in a precise, well-defined direction ... In reality it is more accurate to consider the existence only of a general plan for organising an intellectual consensus through cultural agencies. The most important goal of this plan was to obtain subservience to the regime in exchange for relative autonomy of artistic and cultural forms, but not of content.

SOURCE 6.46 De Grand, p. 70

Control over culture was subject to the same fragmentation of power [as] ... in other areas of Fascist administration. The impact of the Ministry of Popular Culture was limited by rival power centres, e.g. Bottai in the Education Ministry from 1937 ... Outside of government, the Catholic Church developed its own cultural network. The old liberal culture survived under the protection of Croce ... and Einaudi ... The Fascist hardliner Roberto Farinacci used his provincial power base to foster the style of art favoured by the Nazis.

SOURCE 6.47 S. Fraquelli in *Art and Power,* 1995, p. 136

Its pluralistic cultural policy created a form of consensus, though ultimately it underscored the disunity and diverging factions that existed within the Fascist regime.

■ **Activity**

1 Read the historians' assessments (Sources 6.43–47), and note down points under these headings:
   • Aims
   • Methods
   • Degree of control/uniformity.
2 Draw a chart like the one below. Then assess each area of Italian culture and give it a grade to indicate the extent of the government's control. You will probably find this a challenging exercise. Discussion with others may be useful.

Area of the arts	How effectively was it exploited for propaganda purposes?		
	Degree of state intervention 5–0 (5 = major, 3 = some, 0 = none)	**Degree of individual artistic freedom** 5–0 (5 = virtually none, 3 = within certain bounds, 0 = virtually total)	**Effectiveness as propaganda** 5–0 (5 = effective, 3 = some exploitation, 0 = not used)
Art			
Architecture			
Literature			
Theatre			
Music			
Philosophy			

■ **Talking point**

Why do you think this chapter on propaganda has come before an examination of Mussolini's main policies?

C Review: How did Mussolini use propaganda to strengthen his regime?

This chapter has looked at the aims and methods of Fascist propaganda. Mussolini used it to try to strengthen his regime, but how far did he succeed?

This is a difficult question to answer. Propaganda is designed to affect people's attitudes, and this is hard to assess. (This issue is addressed in Chapter 8.) One must also be aware that different groups of Italians might react in different ways.

Secondly, propaganda was only one factor helping to sustain the regime. It seems probable that Mussolini was particularly popular in 1936, and became increasingly unpopular from 1940. But how far was the former due to the success of propaganda, and the latter to its failure? To what extent were propaganda successes due to the methods used, or to the message being conveyed?

It does, however, seem likely that propaganda played a major role in sustaining Mussolini's regime, and making him Italy's most popular leader ever. On the other hand, it is likely that propaganda helped reinforce support gained for other reasons, and that it was unable to prevent growing discontent caused for other reasons. It is also possible that the novelty value of having a supposedly all-wise leader wore off, and that the excesses of the cult of the Duce led to a decline in Mussolini's popularity.

It can also be argued that propaganda ultimately contributed to the downfall of the regime. This is based on the view that Mussolini, the great propagandist, himself came to believe his own propaganda, and lost his earlier grasp of reality. This led him in the late 1930s to adopt domestic and especially foreign policies that alienated powerful groups in Italy, culminating in his overthrow in July 1943.

Let us end by considering the tentative judgements of the historian Tannenbaum in his chapter 'Popular Culture and Propaganda'.

SOURCE 6.48 Tannenbaum 1973, pp. 246, 280, 282

Most modern dictatorships use various forms of mass culture to create the impression that life in their country is wholesome and that their citizens are all honest and patriotic ... the fact that the Fascists were more amateurish in their propaganda than the Nazis and the Communists did not limit their control over the mass media, though it did reduce their effectiveness in inculcating the public with a coherent new set of values. This ineffectiveness was also due in part to the lack of coherence or newness in the values the Fascists thought they had. The Italians tried to be sceptical towards overt propaganda and to trust their own personal experience. But most of them had no way of resisting the covert propaganda in the mass media, which pretended that crime, vice and poverty did not exist ...

The older generations of rural people, particularly in the South, were virtually untouched by the mass media, and their children, who were more exposed to them in the youth organisations and the schools, still preserved many of their traditional values beneath a veneer [thin coating] of Fascist gestures and slogans. Even most urban workers seem to have learnt little about the regime from the mass media, although they were presumably 'integrated' into it through their labour unions and the DOPOLAVORO. On the other hand, the educated classes tried to resist the media as a sign of their own superiority. It was the younger members of the urban middle and lower-middle classes who were most receptive to both the media and their messages, particularly their entertainment aspects.

The ineffectiveness of Fascist propaganda in changing people's attitudes was especially evident regarding the regime's two most important changes in policy in the late 1930s: racism and the alliance with Nazi Germany.

FOCUS ROUTE

1 It seems likely that Fascist propaganda had more effect on some groups than others. Try the following exercise to help you clarify your ideas. Take one of the Italians in the list, and try to judge how he or she would be affected by the various forms of propaganda. Make and complete a chart like the one below. Decide what impact (large, limited, none) each propaganda form might have had on that person.

Person	**Propaganda form**
Southern peasant	Literature
Teacher	Radio
Industrial worker	Cinema
Urban housewife	Newspapers
Industrialist	Posters
15-year-old schoolgirl	Art
Low-ranking civil servant	Architecture
	Spectator sport
	Rallies

Person:	
Form of propaganda	**Degree of impact**
	Large
	Limited
	None

2 You are the newly appointed Spanish ambassador in Rome in 1939. Your new ruler General Franco has asked you to report on Mussolini's propaganda methods. Write an assessment of his approach, making recommendations on the best methods to adopt.

3 'The history of Fascist Italy is a history of propaganda.' Mack Smith made this claim referring to Fascist foreign policy, but do you think it could be used more generally of the regime?

Key points from Chapter 6

1 Propaganda was a vital part of the Fascist regime; Mussolini took a great personal interest in it.
2 The cults of the Duce and of Ancient Rome were central features.
3 The PNF had a vital propaganda role.
4 The press, though mostly not Fascist-owned, realised it had to conform to the government's wishes.
5 Radio and film were used to gain support for Fascist policies, but they remained primarily forms of entertainment.
6 Mass activities, such as rallies and sport, were also used for propaganda purposes.
7 The organisation of propaganda developed piecemeal; it was only in 1937 that the Ministry of Popular Culture was established.
8 The regime tried to use art and architecture for propaganda purposes, but still allowed considerable diversity.
9 The attempt to establish a clear Fascist doctrine made little impact.
10 Fascist Italy's policy towards the media and the arts was far less totalitarian than that of Nazi Germany or the Soviet Union.

A look ahead

You have studied how Mussolini consolidated his regime, and seen the role of propaganda within this. It is now time to look at what role economic policies played in securing the regime.

How successful were Mussolini's economic policies?

At one time or another Mussolini probably plastered all his key economic policies in slogans on walls! You can see some possible ones below, conjuring up images of great successes. This chapter investigates the truth behind the slogans. What were Mussolini's economic objectives? How did he try to achieve them? How close did he come to success? And did he make the Italian people better off?

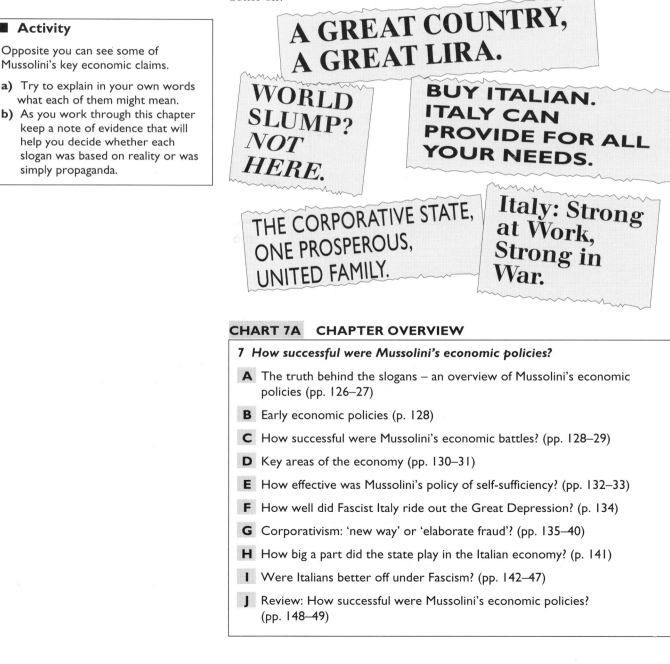

A GREAT COUNTRY, A GREAT LIRA.

WORLD SLUMP? NOT HERE.

BUY ITALIAN. ITALY CAN PROVIDE FOR ALL YOUR NEEDS.

THE CORPORATIVE STATE, ONE PROSPEROUS, UNITED FAMILY.

Italy: Strong at Work, Strong in War.

■ **Activity**

Opposite you can see some of Mussolini's key economic claims.

a) Try to explain in your own words what each of them might mean.

b) As you work through this chapter keep a note of evidence that will help you decide whether each slogan was based on reality or was simply propaganda.

CHART 7A   CHAPTER OVERVIEW

A The truth behind the slogans – an overview of Mussolini's economic policies

Unless you are one of the lucky few who can master the intricacies of economics you will probably find this a challenging area. Mussolini himself had no real understanding of or interest in economics, but he did understand the importance of a strong economy in consolidating his regime and making Italy great.

■ Activity

First let us try to understand what we mean by a strong economy, and how people are affected by economics.

1 What features do contemporary governments highlight when they talk about a successful economy?
2 What might prevent particular countries from developing a strong economy?
3 What might the people in the following groups want from the Italian economy?
   a) Make a list of groups and write next to each one the letter(s) of their chief wishes from the economy.
   b) Identify and briefly explain three features that might be desired by some groups and disliked by others.

Social group	Concerns
• Workers	a) Secure jobs
• Industrialists	b) Growing markets
• Landowners	c) Low taxes
• Public officials	d) Large civil service
• Peasants	e) Good standard of living
	f) LAISSEZ FAIRE
	g) High import duties
	h) Decent working conditions
	i) Controlled workforce
	j) Low inflation
	k) Increased ownership of land
	l) High food prices
	m) Good state welfare schemes

4 Would all the people within each group have the same economic interests? How might their interests differ?
5 Study the following evidence in this introduction to the Fascist economy. Make two initial lists, one of apparent economic successes, the other of failures.

CHART 7B Overview of the Fascist economy

A Aims
• To consolidate the political system
• To make Italy economically self-sufficient
• To provide the economic base for military might

B Mussolini's economic inheritance
• Very limited raw materials (see page 12)
• Industrialising North with modernising agriculture; more backward South, with large estates and mass poverty
• Tradition of close industry–banks–state links
• Limited literacy

C Key economic periods
1 **1922 onwards**. Economic recovery in Italy. Mussolini coming into office with no specific programme pursues traditional LIBERAL economic policies of lowering inflation, and limited government intervention.
2 **1927 onwards**. Economy begins to weaken. Some of the pain is self-inflicted due to problems caused by the overvaluation of the lira.
3 **1929 onwards**. Italy is hit by the Great Depression. Mussolini responds with growing government intervention to bail out industrialists. Efforts are made to establish the distinctly Fascist Corporative State.
4 **1936 onwards**. The economy is increasingly harmed by the stress on AUTARKY and the needs of war.

D Key figures on the Fascist economy

1 Agricultural production
• Value (in constant prices) of sold agricultural produce

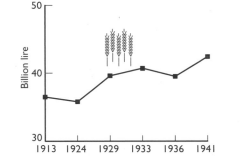

– Wheat production up 100% 1922–39
– Wheat imports fell by 75% 1925–35

2 Industrial production

- 1929–39 industrial production increased by 15%, lower rate than in other W. European countries
- By 1939 industry (34%) had overtaken agriculture (29%) as proportion of GNP (Gross National Product)

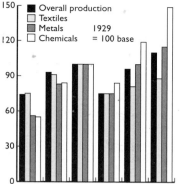

- Pig iron output

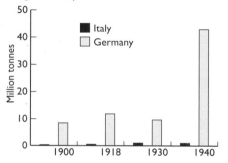

- Annual production of electricity (in million kilowatt hours)

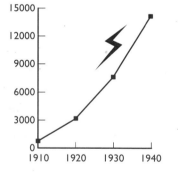

- Per capita growth rates % per year

	1897–1913	1922–38
Italy	2.7	1.9
Germany	2.6	3.8
UK	1.9	2.2
W. Europe average	2.1	2.5

3 Trade

- Balance of payments

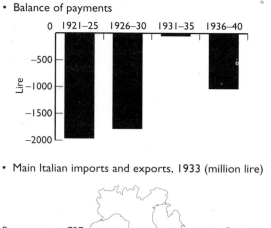

- Main Italian imports and exports, 1933 (million lire)

Raw cotton	737		Fruit, veg	1091
Coal	685		Silk	820
Wheat	504		Cotton	676
Machinery	365		Cheese	241

4 Transport

- Railways electrified

– 1927 14%
– 1939 31%

- Freight traffic on the railways

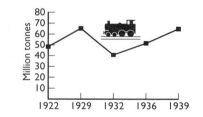

- Autostrada

– 500km built by 1940
– Only 290,000 cars on road by 1939

5 Government finances

- Public expenditure 1922–43

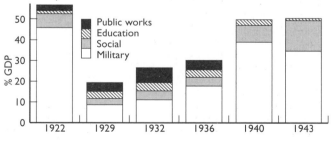

- Public debt

FOCUS ROUTE

1 Note down the main aims of each battle. Summarise the degree of success of each.
2 Which battle/s could be summarised as:
   a) a prestige success but economically harmful
   b) a propaganda success, which failed to really tackle the problem?

■ **Talking point**

Several government policies were called battles. Why do you think this was?

■ **Activity**

You are a radio journalist reporting for the BBC on Mussolini's economic policies. Prepare a five-minute talk on how successfully Mussolini has fought his economic battles and list the questions you propose to ask him if you are granted an interview.

B Early economic policies

Mussolini was initially fortunate. In the early years of Fascism the economy improved for a variety of reasons:

- A general European economic recovery
- Laissez-faire policies favouring industry
- The ending of the threat of SOCIALIST revolution, which increased the confidence of the economic ELITE
- The weakening of trade unions

Mussolini appointed de Stefani, an Economics professor, as his Economics Minister. He adopted Liberal policies, reducing government intervention in the economy, and trying to stimulate investment. Public spending was reduced, and efforts were made to balance the budget. Taxes on war profits were reduced or abolished. Industrialists were pleased with these actions.

Mussolini knew the economy was significant for his longer-term ambitions. The question was, should he continue with these policies, or follow the RADICAL Fascists, who wanted a major reorganisation of the economy, along SYNDICALIST lines? The creation of the one-party state after 1925 seemed to offer a new opportunity. However, when he dismissed de Stefani in 1925, Mussolini did not turn to the radicals but replaced him with the industrialist and financier Count Volpi. The DUCE later claimed that new economic structures were established in his state, but in practice CONFINDUSTRIA ensured that industry's interests were largely safeguarded.

C How successful were Mussolini's economic battles?

How were Mussolini's economic objectives to be met? Certainly not by the implementation of specific economic theories. As a DICTATOR he tended to believe in will power as the driving force of a society which could overcome all obstacles. Consequently the Italian people were MOBILISED in a series of battles, and exhorted to struggle to achieve their targets.

CHART 7C   The Battle for the Lira

SOURCE 7.1 A Fascist cartoon. The caption reads 'It was going down ... but something has stopped it and is pushing it up again'

Aims

- Fix lira at 90 to £ (as in October 1922; since then it had been falling rapidly, reaching 150 in 1926)
- Reduce inflation, which was harming sectors of the middle class
- Confirm image of Fascism bringing stability to Italy
- Show Italians and the world that the lira, and hence Italy, was a mighty power

Actions

- Banks instituted tight controls on money supply
- Economy deflated to drive up value of lira
- Quota 90 achieved in 1927 when lira was returned to GOLD STANDARD and exchange rate was fixed

Effects

- Showed authority of regime, and perhaps boosted Italy's prestige
- Harmed the economy by hitting exports as now Italian goods were more expensive abroad
- Undermined smaller firms, which were taken over by larger ones
- Helped industries dependent upon imports, e.g. chemical and steel
- Caused serious DEFLATION
- Government imposed 20% cut in wages
- 1936 government was forced to devalue lira

SOURCE 7.2 Mussolini, in a speech in 1926

We will conduct the defence of the lira with the most strenuous decisiveness, and from this piazza I say to the whole civilised world that I will defend the lira to the last breath, to the last drop of blood ... The Fascist regime is ready, from the chief to its last follower, to impose on itself all the necessary sacrifices, but our lira, which represents the symbol of the nation, the sign of our riches, the fruit of our labours, of our efforts, of our sacrifices, of our tears, of our blood, is being defended and will be defended.

CHART 7D   The Battle for Grain

SOURCE 7.3   A 1925 poster. The text reads 'National competition: the victory of grain'

Aims
- To boost cereal production to make Italy self-sufficient in grain
- To reduce the balance of trade deficit
- To free Italy 'from the slavery of foreign bread'
- To make Italy less dependent on imports when war came
- To show Italy as a major power

Actions
- Battle announced in 1925: high TARIFFS put on imported grain
- New marginal land used (land that was expensive to farm)
- Government grants to farmers to buy machinery and fertilisers

Effects
- Cereal production increased (doubled from 1922 to 1939) but at the expense of other forms of agriculture, e.g. animals and viticulture (vine growing)
- Wheat imports fell by 75% 1925–35
- Italy became almost self-sufficient in cereals by 1940, but not in fertilisers
- Raised cost of grain and bread in Italy
- Decline in quality of Italian diet
- Protection benefited Italian grain producers, especially inefficient southern landowners
- Increased imports of meat and eggs
- Cereal production fell during the war as imported fertilisers were restricted

SOURCE 7.4   D. Mack Smith, *Mussolini*, 1981, p. 140

Success in this battle was ... another illusory propaganda victory won at the expense of the Italian economy in general and consumers in particular.

CHART 7E   Battle of the Marshes

SOURCE 7.5   Extract from an official school textbook

Fascist land reclamation is not only defence against malaria which has depopulated our country ... and poisoned the race. It is the new duty of the state ... Fascist land reclamation is one of our major tasks, perhaps the most important part of that mobilisation in peace which Mussolini has known how to demand of all the Italians in the same spirit of the intervention in war, in the spirit of the trenches and that of victory.

Aims
- To show dynamic government in action; impress foreigners
- To increase land available for cereal production
- To provide more jobs
- To improve health by reducing malaria

Actions
- Laws passed (1923, 1928, 1933) on reclamation, extending previous schemes
- Private landowners encouraged to co-operate with drainage schemes

Effects
- 1928–38 only 80,000 hectares (hectare = 10,000 m^2) reclaimed, one-twentieth of propaganda claim of one-sixth of the land of Italy
- Pontine marshes near Rome drained
- Three-quarters of land reclaimed was in North; South neglected
- Ambitious plans blocked by southern landowners
- New towns – Latina and Sabaudia – created as showpieces
- Bigger impact in providing jobs and improving public health than in boosting farming

SOURCE 7.6   The new town of Sabaudia: people gather in the main square for Mussolini's visit, September 1934

D Key areas of the economy

Any government has to deal with certain key areas of the economy. The Italian government's policy is described in the following chart.

CHART 7F Key areas of the Fascist economy

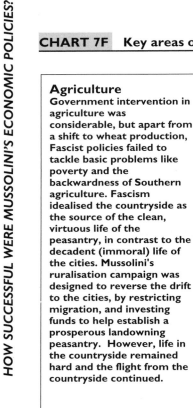

Agriculture

Government intervention in agriculture was considerable, but apart from a shift to wheat production, Fascist policies failed to tackle basic problems like poverty and the backwardness of Southern agriculture. Fascism idealised the countryside as the source of the clean, virtuous life of the peasantry, in contrast to the decadent (immoral) life of the cities. Mussolini's ruralisation campaign was designed to reverse the drift to the cities, by restricting migration, and investing funds to help establish a prosperous landowning peasantry. However, life in the countryside remained hard and the flight from the countryside continued.

North: considerable advances in yields, 50% more wheat per acre

See battle for grain (switch to grain from dairy production and viticulture) and battle of the marshes (new land farmed)
Government rhetoric stressed the importance of the peasantry and rural life
Poverty: Depression led to 20–40% cut in agricultural workers' wages
Flight from the land: 1.5 million left

Small farmers particularly hit by world slump in food prices

South
• Government's close ties to landowners restricted major agrarian reform
• Yields remained low
• 20% drop in cattle and sheep farming

Government help via:
• tariffs (1926 on imported grain)
• grants for fertilisers and machinery
• spreading scientific knowledge

FOCUS ROUTE

Look at Chart 7F.

1 a) What advances were there in agriculture?
   b) What problems remained?
2 a) What areas of industry developed?
   b) What role did the government play (see also page 141)?
3 a) What were the Fascist government's priorities in transport?
   b) What criticisms could be made of them?
4 a) Who bore the highest tax burden?
   b) How did this change over time?
5 What factors influenced the amount of imports and exports in Italian trade?

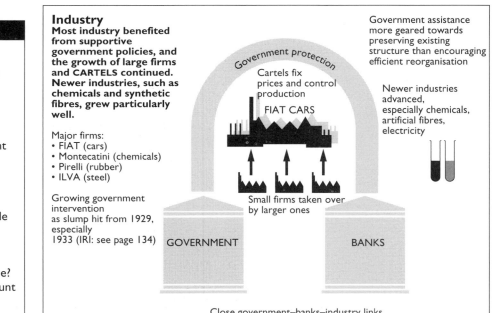

Industry

Most industry benefited from supportive government policies, and the growth of large firms and CARTELS continued. Newer industries, such as chemicals and synthetic fibres, grew particularly well.

Major firms:
• FIAT (cars)
• Montecatini (chemicals)
• Pirelli (rubber)
• ILVA (steel)

Growing government intervention as slump hit from 1929, especially 1933 (IRI: see page 134)

Government protection

Cartels fix prices and control production

FIAT CARS

Small firms taken over by larger ones

GOVERNMENT

BANKS

Government assistance more geared towards preserving existing structure than encouraging efficient reorganisation

Newer industries advanced, especially chemicals, artificial fibres, electricity

Close government–banks–industry links

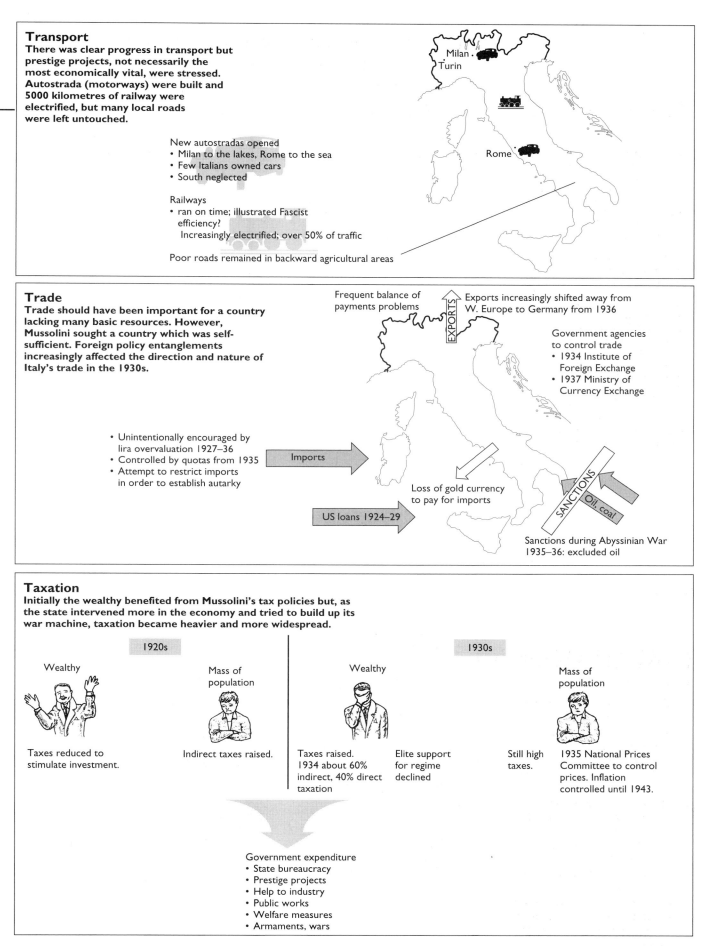

Transport

There was clear progress in transport but prestige projects, not necessarily the most economically vital, were stressed. Autostrada (motorways) were built and 5000 kilometres of railway were electrified, but many local roads were left untouched.

Milan
Turin

Rome

New autostradas opened
• Milan to the lakes, Rome to the sea
• Few Italians owned cars
• South neglected

Railways
• ran on time; illustrated Fascist efficiency?
   Increasingly electrified; over 50% of traffic

Poor roads remained in backward agricultural areas

Trade

Trade should have been important for a country lacking many basic resources. However, Mussolini sought a country which was self-sufficient. Foreign policy entanglements increasingly affected the direction and nature of Italy's trade in the 1930s.

Frequent balance of payments problems

EXPORTS

Exports increasingly shifted away from W. Europe to Germany from 1936

Government agencies to control trade
• 1934 Institute of Foreign Exchange
• 1937 Ministry of Currency Exchange

• Unintentionally encouraged by lira overvaluation 1927–36
• Controlled by quotas from 1935
• Attempt to restrict imports in order to establish autarky

Imports

Loss of gold currency to pay for imports

US loans 1924–29

SANCTIONS
Oil coal

Sanctions during Abyssinian War 1935–36: excluded oil

Taxation

Initially the wealthy benefited from Mussolini's tax policies but, as the state intervened more in the economy and tried to build up its war machine, taxation became heavier and more widespread.

1920s

Wealthy

Taxes reduced to stimulate investment.

Mass of population

Indirect taxes raised.

1930s

Wealthy

Taxes raised. 1934 about 60% indirect, 40% direct taxation

Elite support for regime declined

Mass of population

Still high taxes.

1935 National Prices Committee to control prices. Inflation controlled until 1943.

Government expenditure
• State bureaucracy
• Prestige projects
• Help to industry
• Public works
• Welfare measures
• Armaments, wars

How effective was Mussolini's policy of self-sufficiency?

SOURCE 7.7   Mussolini speaking in a debate on the SYNDICAL law, December 1925

I consider the Italian nation to be in a permanent state of war . . . To live for me means struggle, risk, tenacity [holding on] . . . not submitting to fate, not even to . . . our so-called deficiency in raw materials.

SOURCE 7.8   Mussolini speaking to a meeting of the National Council of Corporations, March 1936

Italy can and must attain the maximum economic independence for peace and war. The whole of the Italian economic system must be directed towards this supreme necessity, on which depends the future of the Italian people . . . The plan of control for Italian economic policy in the coming Fascist era . . . is determined by one single consideration: that our nation will be called to war.

As the regime became more established, Mussolini was freer to indulge in his own priorities. He wanted to establish the prestige both of the government within Italy, and of Italy in the world. Economic policy could be used to this end. Mussolini placed great stress on autarky. Such a policy was hardly surprising for a strongly NATIONALIST government which considered war inevitable. Put simply, a nation which was to fight needed to produce all the necessary materials itself, and should never be in a position to be held to ransom by being economically dependent on any other nation.

The first major move towards autarky was the Battle for Grain in the 1920s. The collapse of world trade in the early 1930s and the League of Nations' imposition of economic sanctions in 1935–36 further brought home the advantage of having a largely self-sufficient economy. In 1936 Mussolini formally announced his policy of autarky, accompanied by a vast propaganda campaign.

Mussolini's attempt to make Italy more self-sufficient was neither successful economically nor militarily. Although Italy became virtually self-sufficient in grain, it still depended largely on imports for other basic needs. Due to a lack of foreign currency (caused by the neglect of exports) during the 1930s Italy was unable to import the raw materials its military preparations required, which meant it was unable to join its ally Germany in the war in 1939, and then performed badly when it did join in 1940 (see Chapter 15).

However, Morgan has argued that the desire to achieve autarky was, as with Hitler, a reason for Mussolini's expansionism.

SOURCE 7.10   Morgan, pp. 168–69

Autarky was certainly an unattainable goal for a relatively poor and ill-resourced country like Italy, which would always need to import coal, oil and raw materials. But the fact that it was unrealisable in present conditions was the very reason pushing Fascist Italy towards war alongside Germany. Within the Axis bloc of Fascist powers, German resources were already making up for some of Italy's economic shortfalls. Whatever the illusions about Ethiopia's economic potential, the EMPIRE was an attempt to make Italy economically independent and powerful by war. Future expansion and conquest would achieve that redistribution of territory and resources which had always been behind Fascist 'REVISIONISM'. Talk of 'living space' (spazio vitale) was as common in Fascist Italy before and during the war as it was in Germany.

> **Autarky**
> This word is often misspelt. Autarky comes from the Greek 'aut' (self) and 'arkeein' (to suffice) and should not be confused with autarchy (which comes from the Greek for self-rule). Autarky means economic self-sufficiency. It requires that a country produces all of its resources itself, and does not need to import them. It is rare for a country to achieve total autarky.

■ Activity

1 What disadvantageous implications for economic policy might there be in Mussolini's statement (Source 7.7)?
2 What is typical of Mussolini in this speech?
3 What might be the purpose of the sculpture in Source 7.11?

SOURCE 7.9   'In this shop only Italian products are sold'

FOCUS ROUTE

Explain what a policy of autarky means. How successful was it in Italy?

THE DREAM
Self-sufficiency, i.e. Italy to produce for itself all its major needs, i.e. food, raw materials, manufactured goods

'Total self sufficiency is impossible, but we can move in that direction.'

THE REALIST

WHY?
- **Nationalism**: to make Italy great, and not dependent upon others
- **Militarism**: to prepare Italy for war
- Other factors:
  a) to justify imperial expansion, gaining 'spazio vitale' (living space)
  b) to avoid a repetition of the 1935–36 League of Nations boycott

MEASURES
- Increased controls on currency
- Quotas on imports
- Increased tariff protection
- Government assistance to develop new products as import substitutes, e.g. cheese-based lanital for wool, rayon for cotton; and to locate new mineral sources
- State agencies such as AGIP (the oil company) searched for new energy sources
- 1937 High Commission on Autarky to supervise policies

THE REALITY
- Virtually no coal supplies; little iron, no discovered oil
- Even by 1940 domestic production met only one-fifth of Italy's industrial raw material needs
- Grain Battle cut wheat imports, but other food imports rose
- Italy really needed to increase its exports to pay for essential imports
- Increased prices
- Some industries hit, e.g. textiles

Trade statistics

a)

	Exports	Imports
	(1922 = 100)	
1922	100	100
1925	194	100
1929	189	109
1932	142	72
1936	115	52
1938	162	58

b) Italy continued to suffer a balance of trade deficit which made it hard for it to import the raw materials it needed.

c) In 1939 domestic production met only one-fifth of its raw material needs, especially coal and iron ore.

d) Basic raw materials were very expensive – coal was three times the price it was in England, and steel twice the price.

SOURCE 7.11
Entrance to an exhibition on autarky

AVTARCHIA

MVSSOLINI HA SEMPRE RAGIONE

F How well did Fascist Italy ride out the Great Depression?

Italy, like other Western European countries, was unable to escape the effects of the world slump, sparked by the Wall Street Crash in 1929. Italy had received considerable investment from the USA following the post-First World War debt settlements of 1924–25. Much of this money was withdrawn. Farmers, unable to diversify from wheat due to the Grain Battle, were particularly hit by the collapse in grain prices. Industry, and their partner banks, suffered from the collapse of demand. Unemployment grew to two million, and wages fell.

The Depression led to greater government intervention, especially through the IMI (an organisation to support the banks) and the IRI. The IRI (Institute for Industrial Reconstruction) was a government agency set up in 1933 to help industry. It took over industrial shares previously held by banks, and those of other companies in trouble. It reorganised such companies to maintain production. Although intended as a temporary body to help private industry through a crisis, it became permanent in 1937 with extended powers to take over private firms. By 1939 the IRI controlled 75 per cent of pig iron production, 45 per cent of steel production, 90 per cent of ship building, and overall controlled 20 per cent of industry.

The IRI is an interesting feature of Fascist economic policy because it shows the pragmatic nature (dictated more by practical consequences than theory) of Fascist policy. It acted as a kind of hospital service for existing firms, and did not attempt broader policies of rationalisation (organising things in the most efficient way), which might have benefited the economy more. It is interesting to note that when the government intervened in a major way in the economy, it set up this new body, and bypassed the structures of the Corporative State (see page 136), a reflection of the latter's insignificance.

The government further helped industry by encouraging price-fixing and cartels and by imposing further wage cuts.

However, increased public works (land reclamation, housing, roads and electrification), reductions in the working day to help share out work, a lifting of the ban on emigration and extensions of welfare slightly reduced the misery caused by the Depression.

The government also claimed the developing structure of the Corporative State protected Italians from the slump which was devastating other countries. Italy certainly was not as badly hit as many other countries. And although none of their measures were particularly impressive (and the corporative system was largely irrelevant), government policies did cumulatively help prevent the widespread unrest and political turmoil seen elsewhere. Mussolini was one of the few European rulers who did not lose office during the Depression.

FOCUS ROUTE

1 Note down the significant points about the IRI. Do they suggest that Fascist economic policy was radical?
2 What evidence is there for and against the claim that Fascist Italy 'rode out the Great Depression'?

CHART 7H **The impact of the Depression**

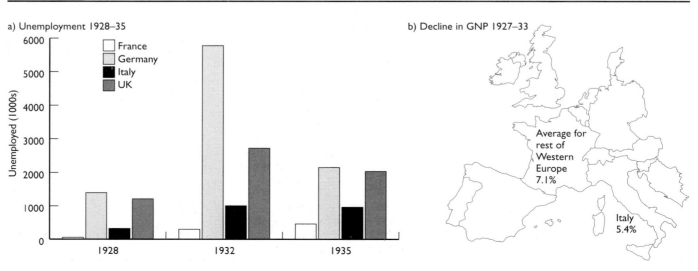

a) Unemployment 1928–35

France
Germany
Italy
UK

Unemployed (1000s)

6000
5000
4000
3000
2000
1000
0

1928   1932   1935

b) Decline in GNP 1927–33

Average for rest of Western Europe 7.1%

Italy 5.4%

The Corporative State

Have you ever tried 'looking in a dark room for a black cat that isn't there'? That was how the Italian politician Salvemini described trying to work out what the Fascist Corporative State actually was. The Corporative State, Mussolini's 'third way', was the feature of Fascist Italy which he was most proud to boast about. As the rest of the world seemed trapped in a battle between capitalism and Socialism, Italy was presented as an internally unified nation where everyone's interests were protected.

Many students of History have struggled like Salvemini to understand what the Corporative State actually was. This is partly because the meaning of the key word 'corporation' causes confusion. The form corporations took was complicated, and evolved over time. Although Mussolini made great claims for his new system, it is hard actually to pin down what it was, and even more so what it did. You may find by the end it was more important in terms of propaganda than actual performance.

Key terms causing confusion

1 Association Group of employers seeking to protect their members' interests, e.g. Confindustria.

2 Corporation Originally this term was used as an alternative to describe workers' unions/ syndicates or employers' associations. From 1934 these two types of organisations were merged into mixed corporations, consisting of both workers and employers in one branch of the economy.

3 Syndicate Another word for union; often used to describe Fascist unions.

4 Union Traditional organisation of workers to protect their interests from employers. Separate unions might be linked together in national organisations, like the CGL.

G Corporativism: 'new way' or 'elaborate fraud'?

Why was a new way of organising the economy needed?

The stability of post-war Europe seemed to contemporaries to be precariously balanced against the background of the tension between CAPITALISM and socialism. Would the interests of capitalists or the working class win out?

Fascists believed they had the answer in promoting the national interest above sectional interests. They wanted a society where all people involved in economic activity (i.e. both employers and workers) could all work together in the national interest, which in the end would bring the best for all. This was to be based on a system of corporations.

SOURCE 7.12 Alfredo Rocco, Minister of Justice, and a leading Fascist theorist

The corporation in which the various categories of producers, employers and workers are all represented . . . is certainly best fitted to regulate production, not in the interest of any one producer but in order to achieve the highest output, which is in the interests of all the producers but above all in the national interest.

Mussolini claimed that his Corporative State provided the advantages of both capitalism and Socialism, whilst avoiding each one's weaknesses. It was thus a new 'third way'.

■ Activity

1 Complete a chart like the one below, which at the moment just identifies the supposed benefits of Corporativism. Use the points below to fill in 1–4 in the table on the claimed benefits and disadvantages of capitalism and Socialism.
   a) Personal incentives
   b) Economy rationally planned
   c) Overpowerful state machine
   d) Selfishness
   e) Wealth unfairly distributed
   f) Creates wealth
   g) Economy prospers
   h) Weak go to the wall
   i) Harms individual enterprise
   j) Full employment ensured
   k) State welfare provision
   l) Employers do well
   m) Creates class conflict
   n) Eventually ends class divisions
   o) Economically inefficient

System	Supposed benefits	Supposed weaknesses
Capitalism	1.	2.
Socialism	3.	4.
Corporativism	• National interest advanced • Economy regulated • Class conflict ended • Everyone's interests protected • Problems solved by conciliation, not struggle	5.

2 Look at your completed chart. Does the idea of Corporativism look more attractive than capitalism or Socialism?
3 After you have studied Corporativism in practice, see what points you can add to the weaknesses of Corporativism (5).

How did the corporative structure work?

The concept of the Corporative State was not totally new. It brought together a variety of existing ideas and practices about the organisation of production (see Chart 7I).

An elaborate structure was built on the corporative principle. The corporations were:

- organisations consisting of all workers and employers in a particular field of economic activity
- self-governing, and supposed to discuss all matters concerned with production, working conditions, pay, etc. in their sector
- represented at the National Council of Corporations, and later the Chamber of Fasces and Corporations which made policy decisions affecting the entire country.

CHART 7I The ingredients of Corporativism

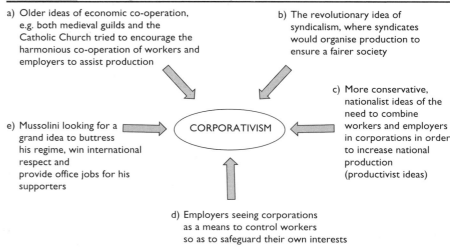

a) Older ideas of economic co-operation, e.g. both medieval guilds and the Catholic Church tried to encourage the harmonious co-operation of workers and employers to assist production

b) The revolutionary idea of syndicalism, where syndicates would organise production to ensure a fairer society

c) More conservative, nationalist ideas of the need to combine workers and employers in corporations in order to increase national production (productivist ideas)

e) Mussolini looking for a grand idea to buttress his regime, win international respect and provide office jobs for his supporters

CORPORATIVISM

d) Employers seeing corporations as a means to control workers so as to safeguard their own interests

CHART 7J The Corporative State: the final structure

Who represented whom?

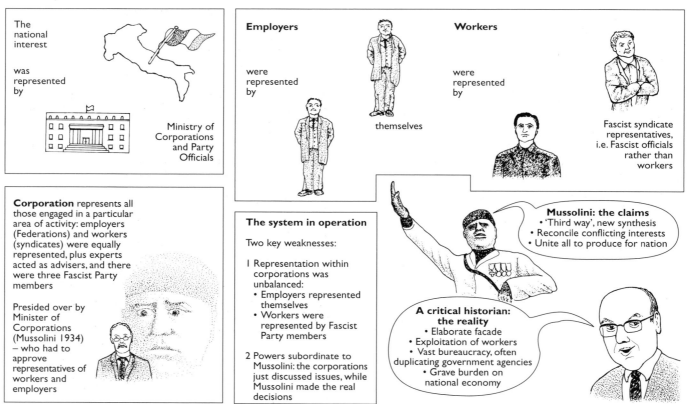

The national interest was represented by

Ministry of Corporations and Party Officials

Employers were represented by themselves

Workers were represented by Fascist syndicate representatives, i.e. Fascist officials rather than workers

Corporation represents all those engaged in a particular area of activity: employers (Federations) and workers (syndicates) were equally represented, plus experts acted as advisers, and there were three Fascist Party members

Presided over by Minister of Corporations (Mussolini 1934) – who had to approve representatives of workers and employers

The system in operation

Two key weaknesses:

1 Representation within corporations was unbalanced:
- Employers represented themselves
- Workers were represented by Fascist Party members

2 Powers subordinate to Mussolini: the corporations just discussed issues, while Mussolini made the real decisions

Mussolini: the claims
- 'Third way', new synthesis
- Reconcile conflicting interests
- Unite all to produce for nation

A critical historian: the reality
- Elaborate facade
- Exploitation of workers
- Vast bureaucracy, often duplicating government agencies
- Grave burden on national economy

How was the Corporative State set up? Key steps

Chart 7K gives the details of how the Corporative State was gradually set up. Initially, Fascist unions were favoured. Indeed, the syndicalist leader Rossoni had hopes of establishing powerful Fascist syndicates to improve workers' conditions, and in 1924–25 there was a series of successful strikes. But Mussolini's government would not tolerate such a potential threat to industrialists for long. Existing Socialist and Catholic unions, deprived of negotiating rights and harassed by the authorities, faded out of existence. Alongside this, workers were promised social improvements in the much heralded Labour Charter (see page 138) though this was more impressive on paper than in reality. Fascist syndicates proved unable to protect workers from powerful employers and the state. Rossoni's hopes of a powerful syndicalist organisation were dashed in 1928 when his confederation was split up. Labour was to be subordinate in the Fascist state.

Over the next decade the Fascist government gradually established a system which it claimed would protect the interests of the workers and employers. Economic development would proceed through harmonious co-operation in the interests of the state. A new chamber of representatives of all aspects of the economy eventually replaced the old Parliament, so the corporative approach finally covered the political as well as the economic organisation of Italy. In practice, the system amounted to a vast bureaucracy, with little real power.

It has been argued that Mussolini never took the system that seriously, except for propaganda purposes. He was concerned not to alienate the economic elite. So the Corporative State became little more than an instrument for exploitation in the workplace and a powerless sham as a national structure. Significantly Mussolini failed to 'launch a battle for corporations' and the slow and lethargic way in which the system was implemented reflected his caution.

CHART 7K   The nine key steps

Stage 1   The weakening of the unions

1. **Palazzo Vidoni Pact, 1925**
   - A pact between Confindustria and Rossoni's Fascist trade unions depriving other unions of bargaining rights
   - A great victory for industrialists

2. **Rocco Law, April 1926**
   - Confirmed position of Fascist syndicates
   - Strikes, lockouts illegal
   - Mixed corporations could be set up (but were not until 1934)

3. **Ministry of Corporations, July 1926**
   - To organise conciliation of disputes
   - Intended as central controlling and co-ordinating body, but was obstructed by the Economics Ministry
   - Mussolini was Minister, then 1929–32 Bottai

4. **1927 Labour organisations CGL and CIL dissolve themselves as powerless**

5. **Rossoni's national syndicalist organisation split up, 1928**
   - Independent workers' organisations had already collapsed; now Fascist unions were weakened

Stage 2   The creation of a vast Corporative State structure

6. **Charter of Labour, 1927**
   - Claimed as the MAGNA CARTA of Fascist revolution, and the 'greatest document in the whole of history'
   - Work was seen as a social duty
   - Private enterprise declared the most efficient
   - To counter image of exploited workers, workers' rights were proclaimed in employment, social insurance and welfare
   - Assumed mixed corporations would organise production (although they did not yet exist)
   - General indication of intent, not legally binding

7. **National Council of Corporations, March 1930**
   - Seven large sections, embryo corporations, of worker and employer organs covering main parts of economy were created
   - Not properly representative, e.g. a philosopher represented grain growers; a professor, textiles
   - Consultative role, discussing matters actually decided elsewhere; just a facade
   - Did not meet after 1937

8. **Twenty-two corporations of major economic sectors, 1934**
   - Issued regulations in their areas, e.g. fix prices; in practice they did little
   - 'Stillborn', as employers were suspicious
   - Decisions had to be approved and issued by Mussolini

9. **Parliament replaced by Chamber of Fasces and Corporations, 1939**
   - In practice this just meant one powerless body was replaced by another

Fascist views of the Corporative State

SOURCE 7.13   Extract from Mussolini's autobiography, 1928

Amid the innovations and experiments of the new Fascist civilisation, one interests the whole world: it is the corporative organisation of the state.

It was necessary to emerge from a base [immoral], selfish habit of the competition of class, and to put aside hate and anger. After the war, especially with the subversive [aiming to overthrow the government] propaganda of Lenin, ill will had reached perilous proportions. Usually agitations and strikes were accompanied by fights, and there were dead and wounded men . . .

However, five years of harmonious work have transformed in its essential lines the economic life, and in consequence the political and moral life of Italy. Let me add that the discipline that I imposed is not a forced discipline and does not obey the selfish interests of categories and classes. Our discipline has one vision and one end, the welfare and good name of the Italian nation.

Instead of the old trade unions we substituted Fascist corporations . . . Public order must never be troubled for any reason whatsoever. That is the political side. But there is also the economic side; it is one of collaboration . . .

We have solved a series of problems of no little importance; we have abolished all the perennial [long-lasting] troubles and disorder and doubt that poisoned our national soul. We have given a rhythm, a law and a protection to work; we have found in the collaboration of classes the reason for our possibilities, for our future power. We do not lose time in troubles, in strikes . . . which imperil . . . our strength and the solidity of the economy. We consider conflict as a luxury for the rich. We must save strength.

SOURCE 7.14   Some points from the Charter of Labour, April 1927

1. The Italian nation is an organism with objectives, life and means of action superior in power and duration to those of the individuals or groups which compose it. It is a moral, political and economic unit which is integrally [fully] realised in the Fascist state.

2. Labour in all its organised and executive forms, intellectual, technical and manual, is a social duty. In this aspect, and in this aspect alone, it is under the protection of the state. Production as a whole is a unit from the national point of view; its objectives are single and are summed up in the welfare of individuals and the development of national power.

3. Syndical or professional organisation is free. But only the syndicate which is legally recognised and subject to the control of the state has the right legally to represent the entire category of employers or workers for which it is constituted . . . to conclude collective labour contracts binding upon all belonging to the category, to impose contributions upon them.

4. In the collective labour contract the solidarity between the various factors of production finds its concrete expression through the conciliation of the opposing interests of employers and workers and their subordination to the higher interests of production.

6. The legally recognised . . . associations assure the legal equality of employers and workers, maintain discipline in production and labour, and promote their improvement.

7. The Corporative State considers private initiative in the field of production to be the most effective and most useful instrument in the national interest . . .

9. The intervention of the state in economic production takes place only when private initiative is lacking, or is insufficient or when the political interests of the state are involved. Such intervention may take the form of control, encouragement and direct management . . .

27. The Fascist state proposes to accomplish . . . the improvement of social insurance.

SOURCE 7.15 An exercise book cover celebrating the creation of the Charter of Labour

LA TERRA E LE CITTA

QUADERNO di

SOURCE 7.16 A cartoon study for a mosaic mural entitled *The Corporative State* by the Fascist Sironi. It illustrated all sections of society co-operating for the common good. The mosaic was displayed in the 1937 Paris Exhibition and alluded to the recent victory in Abyssinia in the figure of triumphant, all-embracing Italy, symbolic of the union of recent and imperial history

SOURCE 7.17 Extract from a speech by Mussolini on the Inauguration of the Corporations, November 1934

Today we affirm that the method of capitalistic production is superseded ... Capitalistic enterprise, having fallen into difficulties, throws itself desperately into the state's arms. This is the instant when the state's intervention becomes more and more necessary ... There is now no economic field in which the state is not obliged to intervene ... The Corporation is established to develop the wealth, political power and welfare of the Italian people ... Corporativism overcomes Socialism as well as it does LIBERALISM: it creates a new synthesis.

■ **Activity**

1 a) In Sources 7.13 and 7.14, what are the proclaimed aims of Corporativism?
   b) How are these to be achieved? How does this differ from the situation in Italy before 1922?

2 a) In the Charter of Labour, do workers and employers seem to be treated equally? Was this really the case?
   b) How are the ideals of Corporativism reflected in the Charter of Labour?

3 What does Source 7.15 show about one of the main purposes of the Charter of Labour?

4 Although other unions were not actually banned, can you see from Source 7.14 why they faded out of existence?

5 a) Can you see any difference in the Fascist attitude towards capitalism in Sources 7.14 and 7.17?
   b) What has happened in between the two comments that might explain this?

6 What idea about the Corporative State is Sironi trying to convey in Source 7.16?

7 Discuss the value of each of these five sources to a historian of Fascist Italy.

■ **Activity**

1 **Either:**
Draw up a Fascist poster proclaiming the marvels of the Corporative State in 1939.
Or:
Compose an underground Socialist leaflet exposing it as a fraud.

2 Read the four historians' assessments (Sources 7.18–21), and use their criticisms to complete your copy of the evaluation chart on page 135.

3 Do you agree that the importance (for the history student) of the Corporative State is not its effect on Fascist Italy, but what it illustrates about the nature of the regime?

Historians' assessments of the Corporative State

SOURCE 7.18   Tannenbaum, p. 101

Fascist Corporativism performed the function of a myth to solve the dual problems of class conflict and national economic poverty; in doing so it held the divergent forces [moving in different directions] within the party and the country together.

SOURCE 7.19   De Grand, p. 81

When it came to dealing with the effects of the depression, the corporative system proved totally irrelevant.

SOURCE 7.20   Blinkhorn, pp. 24–25

Corporativism in practice ... involved the thinly disguised exploitation and oppression of labour ... For the Duce Corporativism was ... an apparent social and political experiment useful for bestowing respectability on his regime in the eyes of foreigners; and an elaborate facade behind which corruption and exploitation could flourish.

SOURCE 7.21   Cassels, p. 58

Corporative theory constituted a not unintelligent reaction to the fragmentation of modern society. But its application in Fascist Italy was an elaborate fraud. In this, the Corporative State was a true child of Mussolini: the great poseur brought forth an organism that was a travesty of what it purported to be.

FOCUS ROUTE

1 Study Chart 7J, showing the final structure of the Corporative State. Explain how it was supposed to operate, and how it did so in practice.

2 Look at the following views of the Corporative State, and match up each view with a person.

a) A worker

b) An employer

c) A member of the Fascist Party

d) Mussolini

e) A British Conservative statesman

i) I was originally worried about some of the Fascist rhetoric, and the degree of government intervention in my business. But in practice my workers are well controlled, and the Corporations don't actually do a lot.

ii) It's a con; this sham structure does not represent our interests.

iii) Once again our country is leading the world with this grand new idea.

iv) What a fine idea. Italy seems to have solved the key problem of the twentieth century.

v) I'm proud of our new idea, and I've got a safe job out of it.

FOCUS ROUTE

1 Why did the Fascist state intervene in the Italian economy?
2 In what ways did it do this?
3 What were the effects?

H How big a part did the state play in the Italian economy?

Mussolini claimed to lead a TOTALITARIAN state, which implied the government had full control of all aspects of the state, including the economy. As we have seen, it did come to play an increasing role in the economy, with a wave of regulations and policies affecting economic performance (see Chart 7L). Mussolini did not, however, want to challenge the position of the industrial elites. Their freedom of economic activity was somewhat restricted, and they had to bend to state priorities, but their ownership of successful businesses was not challenged. The IRI marked a major extension of the state in the economy, but this only intervened to help industries that were in trouble. The impact of the Depression meant that by the late 1930s the state, via the IRI, controlled a higher proportion of industry than in any other country, except Stalin's USSR.

The Corporative State might appear to be great state intervention in the economy, but in practice its effect on the organisation of industry was small. With the banning of Socialist trade unions, and the weakening of Fascist ones (see page 137) employers gained increased control over their workforce, despite the official view that the Corporative State balanced the interests of workers and bosses.

From 1935 onwards, Fascist Italy was virtually permanently at war, and the government increasingly intervened to favour industries supplying military needs. This further distorted the economy, as well as massively increasing the budget deficit which rose from two billion lire in 1934 to 28 billion by 1939, despite increased taxation. This was mainly caused by increased expenditure on the military. These trends served to weaken the elite's commitment to the regime. An increased number of businessmen began to transfer funds to Swiss bank accounts. The writing was on the wall.

CHART 7L   Government and economy

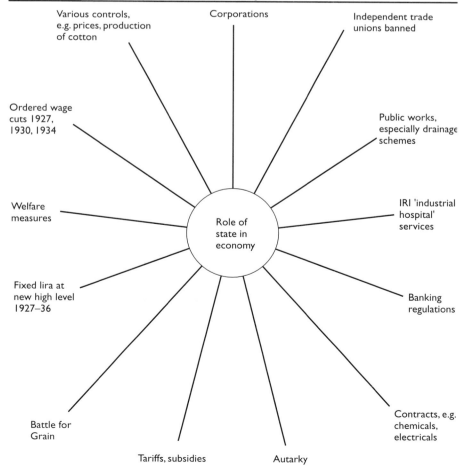

FOCUS ROUTE

'Welfare policy in Fascist Italy was typical of the nature of the regime.' Do you agree? Consider its aims, enactment and the claims as opposed to the reality.

■ **Talking points**

1 What do you understand by the term 'welfare state'? Would you expect Fascist Italy to be one?
2 Do you think the state or the individual citizen should take most responsibility for providing for people's welfare needs?

1 Were Italians better off under Fascism?

We have looked at the broad sweep of Mussolini's economic policies, but what did they actually mean for the individual Italian? Fascism did not have as a major aim the material improvement of people's lives. Mussolini's priority was to make Italians harder and better fighters; an easy material existence might weaken their spirit. However, bread and butter issues could not be ignored, not least to ensure there was no recurrence of the post-war economic unrest.

Was Fascist Italy a welfare state?

Most people associate a welfare state with governments concerned with the welfare of their citizens. In some ways this jars with the popular image of Fascist regimes as cruel DICTATORSHIPS. However, Fascism claimed to represent the interests of the whole community. The Fascist government did pass welfare measures, but as Chart 7M shows, its motivation was mixed.

The regime inherited a complicated system of welfare, provided by private bodies, the Church, and state schemes initiated by Liberal Italy. The party set up an umbrella organisation, the EOA (Agency for Welfare Activities), to control the distribution of funds. Most of these came from private bodies, though the party claimed the credit. Government welfare schemes, most notably family allowances, were extended in the 1930s. These were largely inspired by the Depression, but also by the increasing stress in that decade on 'going to the people', to make the mass of ordinary Italians more committed to Fascism.

Mussolini hoped welfare would allow Fascism to reach areas of life as yet little touched by the regime. Welfare provision would also demonstrate the national commitment and inter-class solidarity of the regime, with the rich contributing to help the poor.

CHART 7M Welfare in Fascist Italy: key aspects

A Aims
- To protect the interests of the people
- To reduce the danger of unrest
- As a form of propaganda to win support
- To demonstrate a united nation
- To prepare Italians for military success through a larger and more vigorous population

B How welfare was funded
- State taxation and levies on various organisations, e.g. syndicates, companies, banks

C Particular measures
  a) Health
  - There was limited sickness insurance in most employment contracts after 1928, but a government system was not established until 1943.
  - Great variations in hospital provision: there were some good hospitals in major cities, but many areas had no hospital facilities.

  b) Pensions
  - No extension of government scheme until minor improvements in 1939

  c) Working conditions/unemployment
  - No improvements in very limited unemployment insurance scheme
  - Shorter working hours 1934 (but due to the Depression)

  d) Childcare
  - 1934 family allowances to factory workers (to compensate for the reduction in working hours)
  - ONMI provided infant welfare schemes (see page 166).

  e) General welfare
  - Special payments, e.g. 1.75 million families in winter 1934–35 were receiving relief.

D Overall assessment
- Despite government boasts, welfare system was not particularly impressive.
- Government measures concentrated on strengthening the power of the nation.
- Some advances were not due to the regime, e.g. the incidence of tuberculosis fell, mainly due to scientific advances.

SOURCE 7.22 An assessment from the exile Salvemini in 1936

No more than a few fresh initiatives can be accredited to the Fascist dictatorship in the so greatly glorified field of social legislation, besides the bureaucratic centralisation of all those institutions which once battled against tuberculosis, assisted maternity and infancy, and aimed at promoting the recreation, education, and spirits of the workmen. To maintain those institutions, wages are subjected to deductions which amount to 4.5 per cent of the wage . . .

Fascists . . . affirm . . . that the iron hand of the 'man of destiny' has created all there is of good in Italy. Even one who does not accept this doctrine can recognise that in this field not all the merits which the dictatorship attributes to itself are imaginary. Only, one must not forget that sports and assistance to children have become vehicles of partisan propaganda, of nationalist exaltation, and of warlike drill.

SOURCE 7.23 V. Zamagni, *Economic History of Italy 1860–1990*, 1993, p. 317

The highly proclaimed Fascist social policy was a mixture of measures that had already been put into practice by previous Liberal governments, and others, badly co-ordinated and taken for IDEOLOGICAL *and pragmatical reasons, which demonstrates just how little real social progress was made.*

SOURCE 7.24 Tannenbaum, p. 129

The system of family allowances was based on humanitarian as well as nationalistic motives, even though it was a poor substitute for real wage increases and was not tied to any broader programme of social security.

SOURCE 7.25 Morgan, p. 114

By providing the moral and material benefits of welfare, the party was extending the regime's network of control and surveillance of the population.

SOURCE 7.26 Clark, p. 251

This was not exactly a Welfare state, rather a medley of different provisions and different 'semi-state' welfare bodies; but it was novel, and it helped defuse working-class unrest.

■ **Activity**

1 What does Salvemini (Source 7.22) see as the good and bad points about welfare provision in Fascist Italy?
2 To what extent do the historians (Sources 7.23–26) agree on the purposes and success of Fascist welfare measures?

How effective was the government's provision of leisure facilities?

The Fascist regime did not just concern itself with providing social services for Italians, but also encouraged the provision of subsidised leisure facilities. To some extent these replaced similar facilities previously provided by co-operative and labour organisations which the government had dissolved. In 1925 it created the Opera Nazionale Dopolavoro (OND) to provide state-sponsored afterwork entertainment. As with welfare schemes, this was not primarily motivated by a desire to make Italians' lives more enjoyable, but to improve their health and especially to gain their support for the regime. You have already seen how the Fascists exploited national success at spectator sports for propaganda purposes. Providing greater opportunities for participation in sport would also assist this cause.

The OND also illustrates the totalitarian aspirations of the regime, seeking to exercise control over all aspects of Italians' lives. It was particularly aimed at those groups, especially in rural areas, which might remain largely outside the influence of press, radio and cinema. The OND underwent a major extension in the 1930s, as part of the 'going to the people' policy of trying to integrate the masses into the state. As well as providing leisure facilities, it gave financial assistance to members in need. The OND undoubtedly helped win support for the regime, but this must be distinguished from turning Italians into committed Fascists; most accepted the regime but did not absorb the ideology (see Chart 7N on page 144).

CHART 7N Opera Nazionale Dopolavoro (OND)

a) Organisation
- Created in 1925, it was reorganised in 1927 under PNF control; it took over many existing clubs and activities.
- It was a huge agency providing social activities, holidays, entertainment, sport and welfare.
- Its role was extended during the Battle for the Lira to help workers suffering wage reductions.
- Firms developed their own Dopolavoro institutions, e.g. Dopolavoro Ansaldo (steel firm) had 50,000 members.

b) Aims
- To replace and extend services previously provided by labour organisations
- To provide compensation for low pay
- To help production by developing healthier workers
- To foster the image of caring employers
- To gain popularity and support by being largely non-ideological, i.e. geared to win support, not convert Italians to Fascism

c) Operation
Subscription dues were subsidised by the state, and employers were forced to contribute. It offered a range of activities, including:
- Library, films, and radios for communal listening
- A travel agency which subsidised trips, especially excursions
- Mobile cinemas, theatre and orchestras for remote areas
- Obligatory showing of newsreels produced by the government-controlled film agency, LUCE
- Sport and summer camps
- Welfare to families in distress

d) Impact
i) Extent
- Impressive membership: 281,000 in 1926, 1.7 million in 1931, 3.8 million in 1939 (about 80 per cent of salaried employees; 40 per cent of industrial workforce; 25 per cent of peasants). It was the largest and most active adult organisation. In the late 1930s it provided over four million holiday trips a year. Most villages, even in the South, had a Dopolavoro clubhouse.

ii) Influence
- It was the main point of contact with the industrial working class who were seen as potentially hostile; it was hoped that through it they might become more attracted to the regime.
- It diverted attention away from economic and social problems.
- It assisted management control over employees' leisure time.
- It placed less emphasis on self-improvement than its German equivalent Strength Through Joy.
- It did not foster a national community; often there was class segregation on trains, and cruise ships.
- The state helped develop mass leisure; elsewhere this was done by a consumer society.
- It was the Fascist state's most popular institution and survived the regime's collapse; in 1945 it was renamed the National Organisation for Worker Assistance.

SOURCE 7.27 Cyclists greet Mussolini during a rally organised by Dopolavoro

Historians' assessments

SOURCE 7.28   De Grazia, in Cannistraro (ed.), 1982, p. 176

The initial aims of the regime, that of eliminating the oppositional Socialist 'state within a state', bringing the working population into the organisational purview [reach] of the modern state, and blunting social tensions in a period of intense economic crisis, were largely achieved by such organisational policies.

SOURCE 7.29   Whittam, *Fascist Italy*, 1995, p. 75

If Fascism hoped to create a forceful, militaristic society and to transform the average Italian into a new 'uomo Fascista' [Fascist man] then the OND not only failed to fulfil this mission, it had proved decidedly counter-productive. It was so popular precisely because it enabled millions of Italians to enjoy resources without the obligation of any full commitment to Fascist ideals and practice.

■ Activity

1 The historian Tannenbaum has described the OND as 'the most popular of all Fascist institutions'. What evidence is there in Chart 7N for this? How might this popularity be explained?

2 A Fascist Party official once criticised the OND for not campaigning enough, but Mussolini said, 'The important thing is that people are able to meet in places where we can control them.'
   a) What does this show about Mussolini's priorities?
   b) Might greater stress on propaganda have actually reduced the success of Dopolavoro?

Talking point

Is it easy to make simple statements about Italians' living standards in 1922–43? Why/not?

Did Fascism improve Italians' living standards?

Elections these days are said to be won by 'the pound in your pocket'. This implies that if people feel their standard of living is rising they are likely to support the government. Mussolini did not have to worry about fair elections, but the acceptance of his regime would be influenced by people's day-to-day economic and social experiences. However, deciding how well off people are, or feel, is sometimes difficult.

Apart from the problem of what criteria to use when assessing living standards, there are difficulties with the nature of the available sources, and differing interpretations of them. This applies to both statistical and more impressionistic sources. The whole matter is further complicated by its political dimension. The Italian historian de Felice (see page 256) has substantiated his controversial claims about a pro-Fascist consensus by referring to rising working-class living standards. Both these assessments have been challenged by more recent historians like Corner and Abse who have found strong evidence of a decline in living standards from the revaluation of the lira through the Great Depression. The imposition by the government of wage cuts in 1927, 1930 and 1934 reduced wages below the cost of living; these were facilitated by the weakness of Fascist unions, and the unbalanced corporative structure. This serves to confirm the more negative assessment of Fascism's impact on working-class living standards.

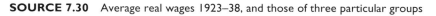

SOURCE 7.30   Average real wages 1923–38, and those of three particular groups

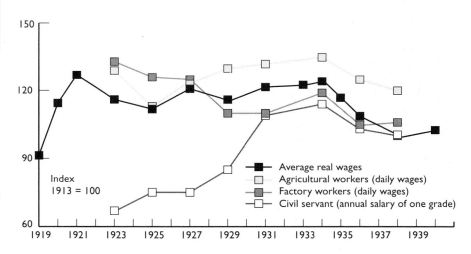

Index 1913 = 100

— ■ — Average real wages
— □ — Agricultural workers (daily wages)
— ■ — Factory workers (daily wages)
— □ — Civil servant (annual salary of one grade)

SOURCE 7.31   Annual per capita income and expenditure in lire (1938 prices)

	Per capita income	Private consumption	Public expenditure*
1926–30	2948	2545	179
1931–35	2902	2479	250
1936–40	3191	2522	369

*Covers government help to industry and armaments expenditure as well as welfare

SOURCE 7.32   Changes in government tax policy (% of revenue)

	1921–22	1931–32
Direct taxation	39%	28%
Indirect taxation	24%	29%

Overall personal consumption increased by six per cent between 1923 and 1939, but fell by fifteen per cent between 1939 and 1942, and fell more dramatically between 1943 and 1945. There was a decline in the per capita consumption of meat, fruit, vegetables, fats, tobacco and coffee.

Emigration fell, due to restrictions in the USA and the world slump. There were other factors which influenced standards of living:

• Increased social security contributions
• Decline in female employment in the 1930s
• Lack of genuine trade union representation
• Autarky

Activity

1 Study Source 7.30. What does it show about how hard it is to generalise about the Italians' standard of living under Fascism?

2 Explain how the 'other' factors (right) might have affected the standard of living.

SOURCE 7.33   D. Williamson, *Mussolini, from Socialist to Fascist*, 1997, pp. 67–68

Overall Italy was more prosperous in 1939 than in 1923. On average, the gross domestic product increased by 1.2 per cent per year, but this modest increase did not filter through equally to all sections of the Italian population.

The industrialists and the great landowners in the north of Italy profited most from Mussolini's regime, but the middle classes also gained stability and protection from Socialism and the threat of red revolution. Their savings, too, were guaranteed from inflation by Mussolini's stubborn insistence on defending the overvalued lira. By doubling the number of public employees, civil servants and teachers from 500,000 to one million, his regime was able to offer the more educated members of the middle classes secure jobs in the state service.

Mussolini was not so successful in helping the peasantry. Despite his constantly repeated slogan of giving land to the peasants, the low price of food in the inter-war period and the emphasis on growing grain at the expense of fruit, vegetables and wine ensured that in practice the number of small farmers declined from 3.4 million to slightly less than three million in 1931.

The industrial workers fared better under Fascism, although their unions were destroyed and the new syndicates were not nearly as effective in defending their interests against employers. In 1926 they had to work longer hours and between 1928 and 1924 there were wage cuts of about 25 per cent. Yet the workers did benefit from Italy's relatively speedy recovery from the Depression and the syndicates were successful in securing employment and welfare measures for their members . . . To compensate those who had lost eight paid hours of labour, family allowances were introduced. Employers also started to agree to Christmas bonuses and holiday pay by the end of the 1930s and to include accident and sickness insurance in pay settlements negotiated with their workers. These benefits, combined with leisure opportunities presented by the National Afterwork Agency (OND) helped allay working-class discontent with the regime. On the whole the workers accepted what was on offer without becoming supporters of Fascism.

For all Mussolini's claims to unify Italy the division between the industrialised North and the backward rural South continued to widen . . . The standard of living fell drastically in the South and by 1950 income per head was only 60 per cent of what it had been in 1924.

SOURCE 7.34   Tannenbaum, p. 100

The Fascist regime had virtually complete control over the labour movement and very little control over the nation's economic structure. Like the MONARCHY, *the Church and the armed forces, big business, both urban and rural, co-operated with the regime when it had to but never committed itself completely and ran its own affairs with very little outside interference. Neither Mussolini's government nor the Fascist corporations were ready to bully Fiat, Pirelli or the Bank of Italy. In collusion with these giants the regime destroyed Italy's independent labour movement and herded the nation's workers into its own unions. These unions were uniquely Fascist, not company unions and not really state unions either. They were the outstanding example of the way in which the regime pushed millions of little people around while merely barking, so to speak, occasionally at the rich and powerful.*

■ **Activity**

1   Study Sources 7.30–34. Draw up an assessment chart to show what each social group gained and lost from Fascist rule.

Social group	Positive impact	Harmful impact

2   Does Tannenbaum consider Mussolini balanced the interests of workers and employers as he claimed to?
3   Study Chart 70. How might the diagram be different for a peasant family? Which influences might be stronger, which weaker?
4   You are an international observer in 1939, researching living standards in inter-war Europe. Write a report on the achievements of the Fascist regime.

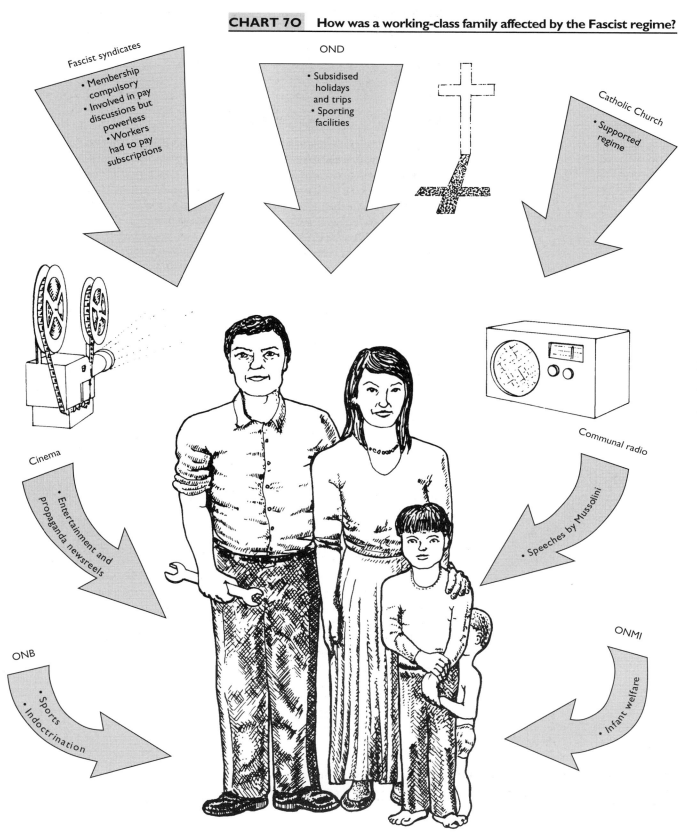

Fascist syndicates
- Membership compulsory
- Involved in pay discussions but powerless
- Workers had to pay subscriptions

OND
- Subsidised holidays and trips
- Sporting facilities

Catholic Church
- Supported regime

Cinema
- Entertainment and propaganda newsreels

Communal radio
- Speeches by Mussolini

ONB
- Sports
- Indoctrination

ONMI
- Infant welfare

PLUS
- Sense of belonging to a great nation/empire
- Family allowances (1934 onwards)
- Winning the World Cup!

MINUS
- Periodic wage cuts
- Strikes banned
- Hours periodically cut
- Expensive bread
- No political power

J Review: How successful were Mussolini's economic policies?

Historians' assessments

SOURCE 7.35   Tannenbaum, p. 128

Economically Fascism was a failure. The most serious ideological and constitutional innovation of the regime, the Corporative State, did nothing to reduce class antagonisms or improve economic conditions; in fact it never functioned at all except on paper ... Italy became almost self-sufficient in wheat production at the expense of the rest of her agriculture. IRI ... served mainly to perform a salvage operation (not to stimulate economic growth) ... Italy's performance (in conservation and recovery) was worse than that of any major country. The main reason for this bad performance was that Italy was poorer to start with, but the fact remains that the Fascist regime did more to hinder than to aid economic growth and modernisation ... Even before the disastrous losses of the Second World War, growth in national income was retarded by restrictive cartels, discouragement of urban growth, the Battle of Grain, the spread of autarky and promotion of war industry.

SOURCE 7.36   C. Maier, *In Search of Stability*, 1987, pp. 94–96, 113

The rhythm of Italian industrial development does not, therefore, seem particularly tied to the Fascist regime ... Fascist interventions were part of a longer pattern of periodic public initiatives ... Italian Fascism ... encouraged spurts of development when it came to power and as it switched to autarky. The Fascist experience produced few results in terms of modernisation that other governments might not have achieved ...

The Italian Fascists took charge of a country still dualist in structure, still ripe for the major transformations associated with industrialisation. Nevertheless, the Fascists did not really succeed in pushing through structural changes outside the regions already on their way to development. Moreover, the governments before and after the Fascist era chalked up more impressive records. The Italian Fascists, in effect, presided over further advances, at a moderate pace, in the already modernised regions of the country. Likewise, their performance in terms of quantitative growth rate was typical of other areas. The regime enjoyed two growth spurts, 1922–25 and 1935–39; between the two, the Fascists suffered from the same stagnation that afflicted all the capitalist economies and that had repeatedly hobbled long-term Italian growth.

SOURCE 7.37   S. di Scalia, *Italy, From Revolution to Republic*, 1995, p. 245

Fascist economic policies had their failures, particularly in agriculture and in the field of wages. But those policies also stimulated important modern industries such as electricity, steel, engineering, chemicals and artificial fibres. Italy's profile began to resemble that of modern European countries to a greater degree than in the past.

SOURCE 7.38   M. Vajda, *The Rise of Fascism in Italy and Germany*, 1972

Under Fascist rule, Italy underwent rapid capitalist development with the electrification of the whole country, the blossoming of automobile and silk industries, the creation of an up-to-date banking system, the prospering of agriculture ... Italy's rapid progress after World War II ... would have been impossible without the social processes begun during the Fascist period.

■ Activity

1 Read Sources 7.35–38.
   a) List the points made in support of the view that Fascism had a distinctively positive impact on the Italian economy.
   b) What counterpoints are made?
   c) What overall conclusions do you draw?
2 Look again at Mussolini's claims for the economy at the start of this chapter (page 125). Martin Clark has written of Mussolini: 'He relied on intuitions not appraisals; he mouthed slogans instead of analysing situations; he was obsessed with his own prestige rather than his country's interests ...' Was this true of Mussolini's economic policies? Give reasons for your answer.

■ Talking points

1 Why is it important when assessing Fascist economic policy 1922–43 to consider what happened in the economy before and afterwards, and in other countries at the same time?
2 Do you think most people place 'bread and butter' issues, and national greatness, above political freedoms? If so, can this be used to justify Mussolini's policies?

FOCUS ROUTE

Let us review Mussolini's economic policy, first by assessing the key areas of the economy, then by looking at specific Fascist policies.

1 Draw up an assessment chart like the one below, identifying achievements and criticisms.

	Achievements	Criticisms
Agriculture		
Industry		
Transport		
Trade		
Employment		
Economic growth		

2 Draw up and complete a chart like this of more distinctly Fascist economic policies.

Distinctly Fascist policies	Examples/Measures	Effects (positive and negative)
Boost Italy's prestige		
Establish a new way of organising economic life		
Autarky		
Strengthen rural life		

Key points from Chapter 7

1 There was no distinctly Fascist economic policy; initially Mussolini adopted laissez-faire policies; later there was more government intervention.

2 Mussolini was prepared to distort the economy for the sake of his own, often unwise, priorities.

3 The Battle for Grain increased grain production but at the expense of the rest of agriculture.

4 The Battle for the Lira raised the value of the currency at the cost of harming industry and lowering wages.

5 Autarky, the major policy of the 1930s, was unwise given Italy's limited resources.

6 In the 1930s the state was forced to intervene more in the economy. The IRI helped rescue industries.

7 Mussolini claimed the Corporative State was a new Third Way, but it was more important for propaganda purposes than in its actual effects.

8 Public works and extended welfare reduced the impact of the Depression, but there was no systematic welfare system. OND provided subsidised leisure facilities.

9 Workers' living standards suffered as the regime favoured the employers.

10 Overall there was modest growth but no major transformation of the economy.

A look ahead

You have now studied Mussolini's political and economic policies that helped him secure his regime. You are now going to examine how he tried to use his position to create a nation of Fascists.

How successful was Mussolini in creating a nation of Fascists?

Fate che le glorie del passato siano superate dalle glorie dell'avvenire.
MUSSOLINI

Quaderno

SOURCE 1 The cover of an exercise book including a quotation from Mussolini: 'Make sure that the glories of the past are surpassed by the glories of the future'

SOURCE 2 Fascist slogan

The thoughts and wishes of the DUCE must become the thoughts and wishes of the masses.

SOURCE 3 Mussolini saluting a crowd in Padua, 26 September 1938

151

HOW SUCCESSFUL WAS MUSSOLINI IN CREATING A NATION OF FASCISTS?

You have studied Mussolini's methods of propaganda and those features of his economic and social policies which affected the material side of life. Now we will complete the picture by examining the key areas where he tried to indoctrinate the Italian people and make them adopt Fascist values, attitudes and behaviour. We will assess whether he was successful in creating a nation of Fascists. Fascism aimed to develop a new national consciousness which would assume priority over class, regional and group identity. Everyone had to be MOBILISED behind the objectives of the regime. This was a remarkable and highly ambitious aim, particularly given the strength of Italy's traditional divisions which had hindered Liberal Italy's attempts to create 'Italians'.

The regime attempted this task partly by developing the concept of the heroic DICTATORSHIP, in which a single leader, Mussolini, became the embodiment of the ideals of the masses. In addition, the character of the Italian people was to be changed. They were to become proud warriors of a great Italy, working hard to increase their country's economic and military strength, and devoted followers of their Duce.

Mussolini did not intend to alter Italy's basic social structure. We must remember that the revolution Mussolini talked of was to be one of the spirit rather than a social and economic one.

■ **Activity**

1 What problems do you think Mussolini would face in trying to create a nation of Fascists?

2 What advantages did he possess for his campaign?

CHART A   SECTION OVERVIEW

Section 3 How successful was Mussolini in creating a nation of Fascists?

Did Fascism capture the hearts and minds of the young?

FOCUS ROUTE

As you work through this chapter, make notes under the following headings:
1 What values were the Fascists trying to indoctrinate in youth, and how did they try to do this?
2 What factors limited the impact of their policies?
3 How effective were their policies?

CHART 8A   CHAPTER OVERVIEW

8 Did Fascism capture the hearts and minds of the young?

A What values did the Fascists try to indoctrinate in young people?

SOURCE 8.1   Mussolini

There's no need to swamp their [children's] minds with past and present learning . . . what is really necessary is that the schools should develop the character of Italians.

The whole school . . . must educate youth to understand Fascism, to renew themselves in Fascism, and to live in the historic atmosphere created by the Fascist Revolution.

SOURCE 8.2   Starace, speaking in 1938

[The ideal young Fascist] tempers all enthusiasm with iron discipline . . . despises fear, loves the hard life, and serves with faith, passion and happiness the cause of Fascism.

SOURCE 8.3   Dictation exercise for eight-year-olds

One year has passed since November 1935: we have shown the world that we are the strong ones, the just ones, the best ones . . . They wanted to humiliate us, but our victory and sacrifice have raised us above them.

SOURCE 8.4   Extract from a textbook for eight-year-olds

The eyes of the DUCE are on every one of you. No one can say what is the meaning of that look on his face. It is an eagle opening its wings and rising into space. A child who, even while not refusing to obey, asks 'Why?' is like a bayonet made of milk. You must obey because you must. What is the duty of a child? Obedience. The second? Obedience! The third? Obedience. How can we ever forget that Fascist boy who, when near to death, asked that he might put on his uniform and that his savings should go to the party?

■ Activity

1 Before you study education in Fascist Italy, consider for a moment your own views on education.

   a) What are the main reasons why you attend school/college?

   b) Why do governments get involved in education?

   c) List in order of priority what you consider to be the most important subjects taught in school.

   d) Do you think your government would share this viewpoint?

2 **a)** What problems might a Fascist government face in trying to indoctrinate the young?

   b) How might a Fascist government use particular subjects in the school curriculum to achieve its aims?

3 Look at Sources 8.1–9. What beliefs and values is the regime trying to develop in the young?

4 Why were these beliefs and values important to Mussolini?

■ Talking point

Why do you think the Fascists chose 28 October as the beginning of the regime, rather than 30 October when Mussolini was actually appointed?

SOURCE 8.5   Extract from a textbook for seven-year-olds

'What is the twenty-eighth of October?'

'It is the anniversary of the March on Rome. The Fascists in their blackshirts enter Rome and put everything in order. Then the Duce arrives and says, 'Go away all nasty Italians who do not know how to do things for the good. Now I will see to putting everything right! Long live Italy!'

'Good,' said the mistress. 'You say it in your own way, but you explain yourself, all the same.'

'I know it too!' answered several children.

'Of course you do! All of you know already what Fascism is and what Benito Mussolini has done for Italy. On 28 October 1922 there began his great work of renewal, which is still not finished, but which has already changed the face of Italy. The first day we recall with gratitude, and therefore every year we want to solemnise it with great rejoicing. Listen, children: even if you have to make it with paper, tomorrow every window must have its flag.'

'Yes, teacher! Eia! Eia! Alala!'

SOURCE 8.6   What children learnt in particular subjects

a) **Third-grade Mathematics (eight-year-olds)**
The glorious war in Africa lasted seven months. How many days is that?

b) **Fifth-grade Geography, 1942 (ten-year-olds)**
The white race is the most civilised, that is the most capable of great ideas; to this group the Italic race belongs.

c) **Grammar**
Conjugate [give the different forms of] these verbs: 'Believe. Obey. Fight.'

d) **History: examination essay for entry to secondary school, 1930s**
Write an essay on the origins of squadrismo which ... struggled against subversives and the renouncers of the Fatherland and with the march on Rome saved Italy from certain ruin.

■ Talking point

How does the History essay title differ from those that you are set?

SOURCE 8.7   The Fascist creed, chanted by members of youth groups

I believe in Rome the Eternal, the mother of my country, and in Italy her eldest daughter, who was born in her virginal bosom by the grace of God; who suffered through the barbarian invasions, was crucified and buried, who descended to the grave and was raised from the dead in the nineteenth century, who ascended into heaven in her glory in 1918 and 1922. I believe in the genius of Mussolini, in our Holy Father Fascism, in the communion of its martyrs, in the conversion of Italians, and in the resurrection of the EMPIRE.

SOURCE 8.8   An illustration from a school textbook. The caption reads 'Benito Mussolini loves children very much. Italian children love their leader very much'

BENITO MUSSOLINI
ama molto i bambini.
I bimbi d'Italia amano molto il Duce.

VIVA IL DUCE!

Saluto al Duce:

A noi!

SOURCE 8.9   A 1935 dictation for nine-year-olds

These are the duties of a Balilla [young Fascist]. To love, fear and pray to God. To love your parents as much as your country and your country as much as your parents. To love the victorious king who personifies our free and united country and the Duce who has made it stronger and greater. To feel love and gratitude for all those who have given their blood for Italy and for the Fascism which saved us. To obey your superiors enthusiastically, to fulfil your duties meticulously as a son, brother, a scholar and a comrade. To endeavour to grow up good, strong, industrious, polite and educated so as to be able to contribute to the prosperity and the greatness of the nation.

B How did the Fascists use schools and universities for propaganda purposes?

There was no major change in the structure of Italian schools in the 1920s. Mussolini appointed the renowned intellectual Gentile as Education Minister, partly to reassure the ELITE. He encouraged the ginnasio/liceo (grammar school) which concentrated on Latin, philosophy and humanities. It was the type of school favoured by the middle classes and provided a route to a career in the professions. Gentile was not interested in technical and vocational reforms and believed in 'fewer but better' schools, and was content to see the weaker ones fall by the wayside. He set up a standardised system of examinations, which applied to state and private schools. He largely ignored the illiteracy rate (around 30 per cent in 1921), and discriminated against women. Attendance at school actually dropped by 100,000 in the first four years of Fascist rule.

Gentile aroused the anger of many Fascists, and his system was steadily dismantled after his departure in July 1924. However, a serious attempt at fascistising education was only really made in the 1930s. The government increasingly laid down what was to be taught, especially in elementary schools. Hence the standard textbook, the libro unico, was introduced for each school year. This was, as Mussolini explained, in order to mould in children 'a real awareness of their duties as Fascist citizens'. The whole system was centralised and teachers were required to take an oath of loyalty to the regime. These changes culminated in Bottai's 1939 School Charter. Bottai wanted to establish an organic union of party and school which would 'finish forever the age of the agnostic [sceptical, critical] school, which was indifferent to political life ... We decisively wish a Fascist school, a Fascist pedagogy [principles of teaching], Fascist teaching to create the Fascist man.' He looked to break down the class barriers in the system and placed more emphasis on science and technology. Special schools for the children of peasants and craftsmen were established to incorporate more fully the rural sector, and manual work became part of the curriculum at all levels. At last the regime was trying to create the 'new Fascist man and woman' and to create an education system befitting the Corporative State. But this potentially RADICAL idea worried some amongst the conservative middle classes. In any case, the experiment was disrupted by the outbreak of war.

Government control over what occurred in educational institutions declined the higher up the structure you went. It was more a case of adding courses, for example in military training and Fascist culture, and taking opportunities to highlight Italian and particularly Fascist achievements, rather than a wholesale reorganisation of the curriculum.

The same trend is seen with control over teachers. This was most extensive with elementary teachers (who tended to be younger and easier to replace). Despite the loyalty oath which all teachers were forced to take from 1929, secondary and university teachers were by no means all committed Fascists. Indeed the mass acceptance of the oath of loyalty probably prevented the purge of teachers which was really necessary for the regime to achieve its aims. The limited extent to which the Fascist regime dominated the higher levels of education may seem surprising for a regime claiming to be TOTALITARIAN.

SOURCE 8.10 Oath all university teachers had to take, 1931

I swear to be faithful to the King, to his royal successors, and to the Fascist regime, and to observe loyally the STATUTO and the other laws of the State, to exercise the office of teacher and to fulfil all my academic duties with the aim of training hardworking, upright citizens, devoted to the country and to the Fascist regime. I swear that I do not belong nor will belong to associations or parties whose activity is irreconcilable with the duties of my office.

■ **Talking point**

Do you think it reasonable for teachers to take an oath of loyalty to the state?

CHART 8B   The main changes in education

1 Curriculum changes

a) Religion
- Compulsory RE in elementary schools 1923; in secondary schools 1929

b) Cult of Mussolini
- Portrait of Mussolini provided in all classrooms.
- All pupils were given a notebook with Mussolini on the cover, and a free copy of the *Life of Mussolini* by Pini.
- The school day began with the raising of the tricolour flag, and there were prayers twice daily, and songs about the leader.

c) Government intervention
- In 1926 101 of 317 history texts were banned.
- In 1928 a single government textbook was introduced, the libro unico, in each year of all elementary schools, covering all subjects.
- Official course plans were produced.
- All dialects were banned.
- 1935 military education in secondary schools, covering history, weapons and tactics
- 1936 lessons in Fascist culture introduced in elementary schools
- 1938 ANTI-SEMITISM taught in schools

2 Control over teachers

- 1925 public employees with views 'incompatible with the general political aims of the government' could be dismissed.
- 1929 teachers took oath of loyalty, partly to try to counter the Concordat (which increased religious influence).
- 1931 all teachers' associations merged into a Fascist Association. Membership was made compulsory in 1937. It organised indoctrination courses; teachers had to take these if they wanted promotion.
- 1931–32 professors told to take loyalty oath. Only 11 of 1250 refused. Others took oath 'with fingers crossed'.
- 1933 all new teachers and professors had to be party members.
- 1934 teachers to wear Fascist uniforms for official occasions. Urged to join ONB as leaders.
- 1938 racial laws led to dismissal of Jewish teachers/students.

3 Fascism and universities

- Universities were generally left alone as long as they did not become involved in hostile political activity.
- By the late 1930s many teenage students were likely to be Fascist-orientated anyway as they had been indoctrinated in elementary schools and the Balilla.

SOURCE 8.11   Schoolgirls salute Mussolini's residence

■ Talking point

Do you think this History book would have been banned in Fascist Italy?

■ Activity

1 Wiskemann has said of the libro unico, 'It wove patriotism, Catholicism and Fascism into a mystical whole.' Why do you think each of these three elements was contained in it?

2 Why did Fascists focus on younger children rather than university students?

3 Write an account of Mussolini's rise to power for the libro unico. This extract from a third-grade History textbook will give you a good sense of the tone required: 'The deserters, traitors, cowards ... sought to render vain the sacrifice of our 600,000 dead ... Our beautiful tricolour was reduced to a rag by sacrilegious [disrespectful] hands ... while another one, a red one symbolising destruction, was waved and carried in triumph ... Then Benito Mussolini, the Man sent by God, decided to save the Fatherland from the COMMUNIST danger.'

C What role did the Fascist youth movements play?

Apart from in elementary education, it was probably the various youth organisations which were most successful in inculcating Fascist values into Italian youth. These bodies organised a range of activities, on Saturdays and in the evenings, which increasingly cut across school provision. Young people were probably more attracted to them for the facilities they provided than for their propaganda message, but they clearly did help strengthen the regime.

The new Fascist youth organisation was called ONB (Opera Nazionale Balilla) or Balilla. It was a party organisation, but in 1929 it was taken over by the Education Ministry. Some Fascists complained that this led to insufficient Fascist aspects in ONB activities. Party Secretary Starace criticised the influence of 'unregenerate [unreformed], lazy, bureaucratic' education officials and teachers unsuited to a Fascist outlook leading exercises that lacked true Fascist spirit. The regime also faced potentially rival youth organisations run by the Catholic Church. After much tension, the government finally gained the dissolution of the Catholic Boy Scouts in 1928, and restrictions on CATHOLIC ACTION youth groups (see page 175).

As in other aspects of the regime, there was an intensification of indoctrination in the late 1930s, and in 1937 the ONB was incorporated into a new party organisation, GIL (see Chart 8C). The law establishing this proclaimed it was the 'unitary and totalitarian organisation of the youth of the Fascist regime . . . instituted in the very heart of the party'.

CHART 8C The organisation of Fascist youth movements

Name	Age and membership	Nature
ONB/Balilla 1926 Subgroups:	6–18	Run by party till 1929, then by Education Ministry. Membership compulsory 1935
• Children of the She Wolf	6–8 boys and girls	
• Balilla	8–14 boys	
• Avanguardisti	14–18 boys	
• Piccole Italiane	8–12 girls	
• Giovani Italiane	13–18 girls	
Fascio Giovanile del Littorio 1930	18–21 youths not at university	
GUF (Gruppi Universitari Fascisti)	18–21 university students	Run by party
GIL (Gioventù Italiana del Littorio) 1937	All youth	Replaced ONB. Covered all groups, under party control

Balilla
Balilla was the general term for all youth groups, and the particular name for the subgroup of 8–14 year old boys. It was named after the legendary Genoese schoolboy who threw stones at the Austrian occupiers in 1746.

The following list indicates the range of activities organised by ONB:

- Sport, including skiing, riding, fitness training; particular importance was given to military drill.
- Propaganda lectures, especially nationalist indoctrination
- Parades
- Saturday afternoon rallies from 3.30 to 6 pm
- Local and national competitions
- Summer camps, attended by an estimated 700,000 for two weeks
- Week-long Campo Dux in Rome with tens of thousands of participants.

Girls enrolled, but on a smaller scale. They did some of the above activities, plus they did callisthenics (rhythmic exercises), watched films, gave music recitals, and did sewing, singing, handicraft, gardening, child care, hygiene, charity work, flower arranging and doll drills (passing in review holding dolls like babies).

GUF was a similar body, catering for university students. Most who joined did so for career or social purposes. It organised many activities, including the Littorialia in 1934–40, annual contests covering art and politics to help train a new elite. Here there was considerable freedom for dissent.

SOURCE 8.12   Order of the Day by the Secretary of the Fascist Party, 1930

The regime is and intends to remain a regime of the young... The regime intends to prepare spiritually all the youth of Italy, from whom by successive selections there must issue tomorrow the ranks of the governing classes of Italy, and for this purpose it has created, alongside the civil Militia of the party, the organisation of the Balilla, the Avanguardisti and the University groups. The totalitarian principle of the education of youth, systematically demanded by Fascism, responds to this supreme necessity of the Fascist Revolution which intends to last...

The young people... must be resolutely introduced from the beginning into the ranks of political, administrative, trade union, journalistic, co-operative, academic, military, sporting and Dopolavoro life...

The young must know how to obey, to acquire the right, or rather, the duty of commanding; above all they must know how to dare... they must despise an ideal life, whether individual or collective, of indifference, or what is worse, of comfort.

Provided this happens, the young of today and of tomorrow will be the ones to continue, in spirit and form, the Revolution of October 1922.

SOURCE 8.13   Fascist Hymn *Giovinezza* (Youth)

Hail, O people of heroes,
Hail, O immortal fatherland,
Thy children are reborn,
With faith in the ideal.

Within the Italian boundary,
Italians have been re-fashioned,
Re-fashioned by Mussolini,
For the war tomorrow,
For the joy of labour,
For the peace and the laurel,
For the shaming of all those
Who their country deny.

The poets and the craftsmen,
The gentry and the peasants,
With the pride of Italians,
Swear loyalty to Mussolini.
There is no poor district
Which does not send its tale,
Which does not unfurl its banners
Of Fascism the redeemer.

Chorus:
Youth! Youth!
Springtime of loveliness,
In the bitterness of life,
Your song rings out, and away!

SOURCE 8.14   'Children of the Wolf' relieving the guard at Mussolini's residence in Rome

■ **Activity**

1 According to Source 8.12:
   a) How did the party view youth?
   b) What role did the party claim in influencing the young?
   c) Why?
2 How do Sources 8.12–18 illustrate the methods the regime used to indoctrinate youth?
3 **a)** Re-read Source 8.7. Where might a young Italian have heard a similar creed?
   b) Why do you think the Fascists seem to have modelled their creed on this?
   c) How might some parents have reacted to this?

SOURCE 8.15
Cover of the magazine *Fascist Youth*. The quote from Mussolini reads 'Fascism promises you neither honours nor offices nor gains, but duty and struggle'

GIOVENTŮ FASCISTA

A. IX
ERA FASCISTA
ANNO 1 - N. 28
27 SETTEMBRE

IL FASCISMO NON VI PROMETTE NÉ
ONORI NE CARICHE NE GUADAGNI MA
IL DOVERE E IL COMBATTIMENTO
MUSSOLINI

■ **Talking point**

Read Sources 8.16 and 8.17. How would you react to being asked to take such an oath, and obey such a rule?

Even now British guides and scouts pledge obedience to the MONARCH. American schoolchildren take a daily oath of allegiance to the American flag. Does this affect your judgement of Fascist youth movements?

SOURCE 8.16 Balilla oath

In the name of God and of Italy I swear to carry out the orders of the Duce and to serve with all my strength and, if necessary my blood, the cause of the Fascist Revolution.

SOURCE 8.17 Rule 12 of the Balilla

When one finds one's self in the presence of people, even adults, who cast doubt on the fundamental political principles of the Regime, or who express lack of faith in its Leaders ... one must intervene to correct, and if necessary, scold and silence anyone who holds an offensive attitude towards the regime.

GIOVENTÙ FASCISTA

A. IX
ERA FASCISTA
ANNO I° N. 29-30
4-11 OTTOBRE ..

I° ANNUALE DEI
FASCI GIOVANILI DI
COMBATTIMENTO

D Review: Did Fascism capture the hearts and minds of the young?

To attempt to answer the question above, we need first to look at how extensive membership of Fascist youth organisations was. It increased considerably during the regime, helped by a 1928 decree saying only youths who had been in the ONB could join the Fascist Party. By 1929 about 60 per cent of northern youths were members; the proportion was far lower in the South. In 1935 membership became compulsory. However, passing a law was one thing; ensuring all youths joined was far harder.

Organisation was very tied to the school system. Teachers were urged to become ONB leaders. This close tie with schools meant membership of the ONB was disproportionately male and middle class, as many girls and poorer boys left school when they were 12–14 years old, and thus found it easier to escape the ONB system. This particularly applied to peasant children. The ONB was organised on a neighbourhood basis so there was little mixing of classes.

The strong position of Catholicism in Italy also served to limit the spread of Fascist youth movements. Catholic schools did not properly enforce membership until the 1930s, and Catholic Action youth organisations continued to exist, though they were not allowed to duplicate key ONB activities such as sports.

It is even more difficult to assess the IDEOLOGICAL impact of Fascist youth policies. There is some conflicting evidence, which partly reflects individuals' different responses to ONB membership and activities. Some contemporaries complained that male youths remained more lovers than fighters, and that they were just time-servers, not genuine enthusiasts. There was a growing number of reports from PNF secretaries and police of disaffection amongst youth in the late 1930s, and especially during the unpopular German alliance and war.

On the other hand, the sheer length of time the Fascists were in power meant that all Italians born between about 1910 and 1930 experienced Fascist propaganda at school during their formative period, and this probably served to strengthen the regime, if not necessarily convert millions to Fascism.

Certainly, the extent to which support for Fascism disappeared after the overthrow of Mussolini in 1943 adds weight to the arguments of those who believe that Fascist youth policies had limited success.

■ Activity

1 Study Chart 8D. What does it reveal about the impact of Fascist youth policies?

2 Study Chart 8E.
   a) Roughly what percentage of Italians by the late 1930s would have experienced over five years of 'Fascist' education?
   b) What does this suggest about the value of using the education system as a means of creating a nation of Fascists?
   c) What evidence does the chart provide as to how successful Fascist youth policy was?

3 Read the historians' assessments in Sources 8.20–24.
   a) Make notes in a chart like the one below.

Historian	Assessment of success or failure	Explanation	Evidence
Koon			
Tannenbaum			
Clark			
De Grazia			
Thompson			

   b) Do you detect any major disagreements between the historians?

4 You are a civil servant in the Ministry of Education in 1936. Mussolini has demanded
   a) a report on the success of his attempts to create young Fascists, and
   b) plans for ensuring further success.
   Your job is to prepare both documents using the material in this section.

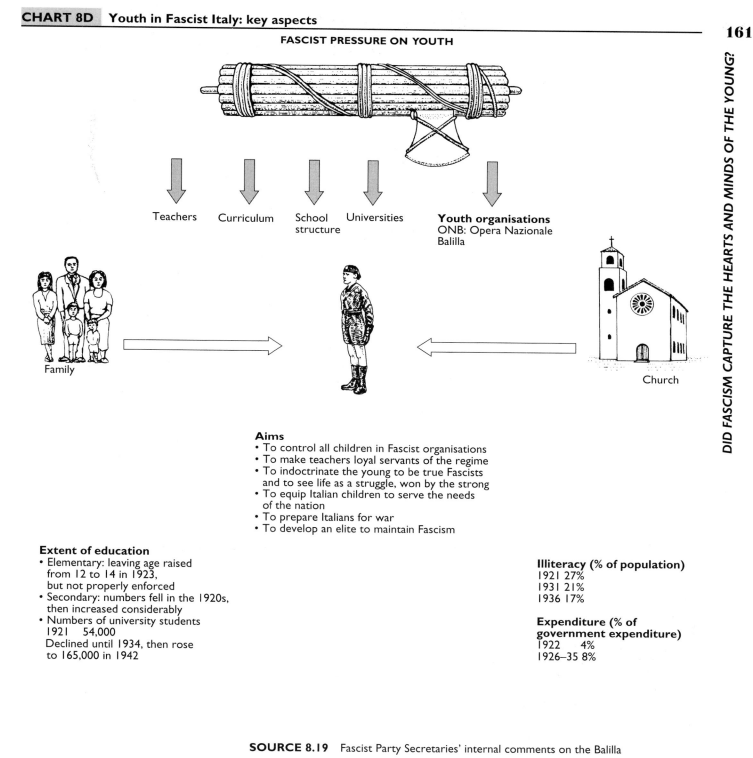

FASCIST PRESSURE ON YOUTH

Teachers Curriculum School structure Universities

Youth organisations
ONB: Opera Nazionale Balilla

Family

Church

Aims
- To control all children in Fascist organisations
- To make teachers loyal servants of the regime
- To indoctrinate the young to be true Fascists and to see life as a struggle, won by the strong
- To equip Italian children to serve the needs of the nation
- To prepare Italians for war
- To develop an elite to maintain Fascism

Extent of education
- Elementary: leaving age raised from 12 to 14 in 1923, but not properly enforced
- Secondary: numbers fell in the 1920s, then increased considerably
- Numbers of university students
  1921 54,000
  Declined until 1934, then rose to 165,000 in 1942

Illiteracy (% of population)
1921 27%
1931 21%
1936 17%

Expenditure (% of government expenditure)
1922 4%
1926–35 8%

SOURCE 8.19 Fascist Party Secretaries' internal comments on the Balilla

a) 1931 Turin provincial Party Secretary

Unfortunately instead of diminishing, the gap between Fascism and the youth sector seems to be growing... There is an aversion [hostility] to what Fascism represents.

b) 1936 Savona Party Secretary

The Fasci Giovanili were a joke from all points of view... Discipline did not exist and I was forced to resort to... severe punishments to get them to show up at meetings.

c) Turin Party Secretary 1937

The Young Fascists are deserting the meetings... only the books are full of members, but the truth is that the young no longer go to the groups.

CHART 8E The impact of Fascist youth policies

Membership of the ONB

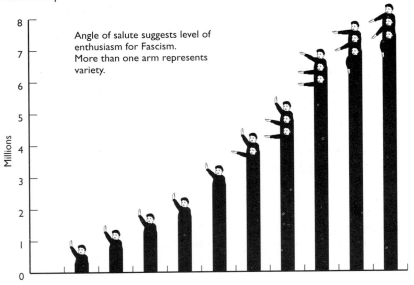

Angle of salute suggests level of enthusiasm for Fascism.
More than one arm represents variety.

Number of Italians educated under Fascism

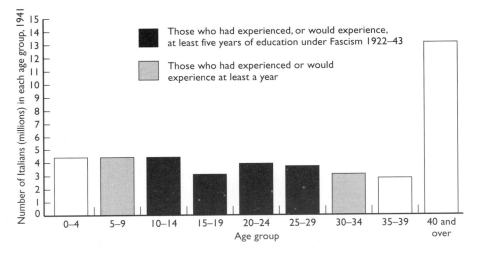

Those who had experienced, or would experience, at least five years of education under Fascism 1922–43

Those who had experienced or would experience at least a year

Historians' assessments of the impact of Fascist youth policy

SOURCE 8.20 Koon, pp. 86 and 251–52

Some teachers undoubtedly supported the regime; many more bowed to external pressure in prudent conformity; many were disillusioned and discouraged . . .

Most Italian teachers . . . performed the ritual obeisances [acts of devotion] the party required in order to keep their positions but did not become stalwart [strong] supporters of the regime . . . As they embarked on their 'long voyage through Fascism', many of the young born and raised in the 'new Fascist climate' realised that the regime had given them nothing to believe in, no one to obey, and nothing for which to fight.

SOURCE 8.21 Tannenbaum, p. 143

For the most part young Italians enjoyed getting together in their uniforms, shouting slogans and sharing the prescribed patriotic ritual.

As one would expect, there is wide disagreement about the extent to which Italy's teachers were fascistised . . . as in other walks of life, most teachers and professors saw in Fascism what they wanted to see . . .

All observers agree that the elementary school teachers were the most affected

by fascistisation ... By the outbreak of the Second World War it would have been very difficult indeed for most elementary school teachers not to have been convinced Fascists, reinforcing in the schools what the children learnt in the youth organisations and the mass media.

SOURCE 8.22   Clark, pp. 245–46

Superficially the Fascists were successful. They brought up a new Fascist generation, imbued from childhood with patriotic zeal and military fervour ... The Fascists probably succeeded in indoctrinating most children in primary school, but they did not create a really 'Fascist' elite via secondary or higher education, let alone create a Fascist intelligentsia ... Pupils were not hostile to Fascist ideas, indeed they accepted them as normal; but they were not committed enthusiasts either.

SOURCE 8.23   De Grazia, in Cannistraro (ed.), 1982, p. 572

The Fascist youth organisations had a powerful impact on youth growing up under the regime, although membership itself was by no means universal. An estimated 30 to 40 per cent of the population between the ages of eight and eighteen never joined at all, the vast majority of whom were probably working-class youth and young women, especially those who left school before the age of fourteen. However, even before enrolment was made compulsory, the overwhelming majority of middle-class children joined either out of conviction or because of the material advantages offered, or as a result of teacher pressure, parental fears, or a simple desire not to be excluded from such a highly visible form of sociability. The generation born after World War I in Italy thus experienced Fascist regimentation as something entirely routine. Having had little or no contact with alternative organisations or cultural models, it was inevitably susceptible to [likely to be influenced by] propaganda that identified everything pre- or anti-Fascist as decrepit or inept and the regime itself with dynamism and the energy of youth.

SOURCE 8.24   Thompson, p. 35

[Anti-Fascism] developed largely within the Fascist institutions amongst young people who saw themselves as Fascists but who gradually came to believe that their ideals were continually being thwarted or betrayed by the narrowness, inertia or corruption of those in positions of authority. It was a growing awareness of the chasm which separated Fascist rhetoric from action, as well as from the social and economic realities of life under the regime, culminating in the disasters eventually experienced during the course of the Second World War, which were responsible for the disillusionment, alienation and finally rebellion, which many of that generation were to experience.

■ **Talking point**

If you had grown up in Fascist Italy, what aspects of youth policy would you have liked? Which would you have disliked?

Key points from Chapter 8

1 Mussolini prioritised youth in his aim to create a nation of Fascists.
2 They were trained in Fascist values such as obedience, love of the Duce, nationalism and militarism.
3 There were no major changes in the structure of the education system until Bottai's School Charter of 1939 which was too late to make much impact.
4 The middle classes became increasingly concerned about the devaluing of education as manual work was introduced at the expense of traditional academic subjects.
5 The state influenced the school curriculum, and made teachers take a loyalty oath.
6 The state made less impact on universities, and some dissent was tolerated.
7 All children were encouraged to join Fascist youth movements, which eventually became compulsory, though membership was never total.
8 The ONB provided sporting and leisure activities besides being used for propaganda purposes.
9 Although the Catholic Boy Scouts were closed down, Catholic Action continued to provide youth facilities, especially for students.
10 Many youngsters absorbed Fascist ideas; others just conformed; increasing numbers reacted against the regime.

9

Did Mussolini succeed in imposing Fascist values on women?

FOCUS ROUTE

As you work through this chapter, complete a chart like the one below analysing Fascist policies towards women.

Aims	Methods	Successes	Failures

CHART 9A   CHAPTER OVERVIEW

9 Did Mussolini succeed in imposing Fascist values on women?

A How did Fascists see the role of women? (p. 165)

B How did the regime treat women? (pp. 166–68)

C Did Italy's women deliver? (pp. 169–70)

D Review: Did Mussolini succeed in imposing Fascist values on women? (pp. 171–73)

SOURCE 9.1   Schoolgirls in 1941. The text on the back wall reads, 'Woman should always be a decisive influence in determining the destiny of human society'

A How did Fascists see the role of women?

■ Activity

What do Sources 9.2–4 suggest about the role of women in Fascist Italy?

'DUCE, do you want to increase the number of suicides, prostitutes, and emigrations?' Thus wrote a 40-year-old Turinese spinster to Mussolini in October 1938. She was protesting at the latest government DECREE that laid down a limit of ten per cent on offices' employment of women. If she lost her job, her parents and nephews whom she supported would have to fall back on government welfare.

This decree illustrates one aspect of the regime's twenty years of discriminatory policies towards women. Women had a clearly specified role to play within Fascist doctrine. It was their task to run the home and maximise their child bearing so that the regime's DEMOGRAPHIC ambitions could be achieved. This chapter explores what actual effect this had on women's lives at the time.

SOURCE 9.2 An Italian woman displaying a portrait of Mussolini on her swimsuit

SOURCE 9.3 An image of motherhood: 'The destiny of nations is linked to their demographic power'

SOURCE 9.4 Fascist sayings

War is to the man what motherhood is to women. Wives and sardines keep best in sealed tins.

SOURCE 9.5 Mussolini's views

a) From a late 1920s interview with a female journalist

Women's place in the present as in the past is in the home . . .
Women are the tender, gentle influence that represents a pleasant parenthesis [interlude] in a man's life, the influence that often helps a man to forget his trials and his fatigue, but that leaves no lasting trace . . . Women are a charming pastime, when a man has time to pass . . . but they should never be taken seriously, for they themselves are rarely serious . . . My wife and family are my dearest possessions, but so greatly do I treasure them that I keep them apart from my duty.

b) Various statements from the 1930s
   - *Women must obey . . . In our state, she does not count.*
   - *Intellectual women are a monstrosity.*
   - *Higher education for women should just cover what the female brain can cope with, i.e. household management.*
   - *Child bearing is women's natural and fundamental mission in life.*
   - *Women should be exemplary wives and mothers, guardians of the hearth, and subject to the legitimate authority of the husband.*
   - *[Women's work] distracts from reproduction, if it does not directly impede it, and foments independence and the accompanying physical–moral styles contrary to giving birth.*

B How did the regime treat women?

Employment

During the late nineteenth century, as in other industrialising nations, some mainly middle-class women had begun to organise to advance their political and economic rights. The First World War had increased women's employment opportunities, but afterwards measures were taken to restrict their employment, especially after the rise in unemployment from 1927. The main target was women in 'unnatural' occupations (such as school teachers, office workers and professionals). From the mid-1920s women were excluded from certain teaching jobs. In 1933 the state imposed a limit of ten per cent on state jobs for women; in 1938 this was extended to many private firms, though it was reversed during the war. The Fascists did not, however, challenge women's traditional importance in agriculture, and had to accept that millions worked in industry. Indeed, to help women combine this with their chief child-rearing function, several laws were passed protecting women at work.

Education

Education for women was seen as training to stay at home, to be effective housekeepers and mothers. Women were excluded from the most prestigious posts in secondary schools – teaching Latin, Italian, History and Philosophy – so more taught Maths and Science. Perversely the lack of job opportunities led to an increase in women at university (from only six per cent of students in 1914 to fifteen per cent in 1938).

Personal life

The Fascists held firm views on what women should look like. Well-rounded and sturdy rather than thin, elegant women were required. Salvemini sardonically described Fascist pressure on women's appearance as the 'Battle for Fat'. The state criticised cosmetics, high heels, trousers for women, and Negro and rhythm dancing. Yet though the National Committee for Cleaning Up Fashion might campaign against the 'horrid vice' of indecent and scandalous dress, millions of Italians went to cinemas where they could catch glimpses of American actresses' breasts, and thousands of women performed scantily dressed in athletic parades.

Fascists had a confused attitude to female sport; it could promote health, vigour, discipline and national pride, but it also might distract women from their main job of child production, and encourage lesbianism, and female liberation. Mussolini feared female involvement in sports (riding, skiing, cycling) because it was believed they caused infertility!

Politics

The Fascists also had an ambivalent attitude to women's involvement outside the family. When the franchise was extended to all males in 1919, women still could not vote. In 1925 the Fascist-dominated Parliament gave women the vote in local elections; but then ended such elections! MOBILISING women politically might have distracted them from their primary role in the home. Some women set up female Fascist groups. An attempt by their secretary Elisa Rizzioli to increase their influence was blocked, and the Fasci Femminili remained a vehicle to spread the socially REACTIONARY policies of the regime's male politicians, under the slogan 'Woman into the home'. This was reinforced by Pope Pius XI in his 1930 ENCYCLICAL Casti Conubi. He criticised the decline in paternal authority, and stressed the role of women as obedient wives and caring mothers.

There were still opportunities for women to broaden their involvement, however. Women served on committees of ONMI, a state organisation designed to help mothers, particularly disadvantaged ones. They were encouraged to engage in charity work, and to run home economics courses for women workers. Women were enlisted in the campaign against the League of Nations' sanctions (1935), culminating in exchanging their gold wedding rings for tin bands (see Source 14.12). Women were encouraged to attend rallies, and help in

■ Talking point

Your attitudes to the position of women in society are probably very different to those held by Mussolini and most others in the 1930s. Does this make it hard for you to make an objective assessment of Fascist policies?

Activity

1 Study Chart 9B. Were Fascist policies the only major influence on women's position in society?
2 Were the other influences assisting or hindering Fascist policies?

propaganda and social work, but were not expected to campaign for their own policies. There was only one female member of the Council of Corporations – from the Midwives Corporation!

In the 1930s the PNF tried to 'reach out to the people', and in an effort to fascistise the nation hoped to involve groups as yet uncommitted. In 1935 they set up the Massaie Rurali (rural housewives) for peasant women, and in 1938 the Section for Factory and Homeworkers (SOLD). Thus alongside a conservative stress on women staying at home to raise children, the regime did, in its TOTALITARIAN quest for mass involvement, try to involve millions of women in wider affairs.

CHART 9B   Women in Fascist Italy: influences and policies

The position of women in Fascist Italy: the broader context
Factors influencing the position of women
• Fascist views and policies
• Mussolini
• Economic developments, especially Depression, decline of textile industry, growth in retail trade
• Wars
• Catholic Church
• Traditions
• Growth of mass culture (via urbanisation, radio, cinema, periodicals, department stores, advertising)

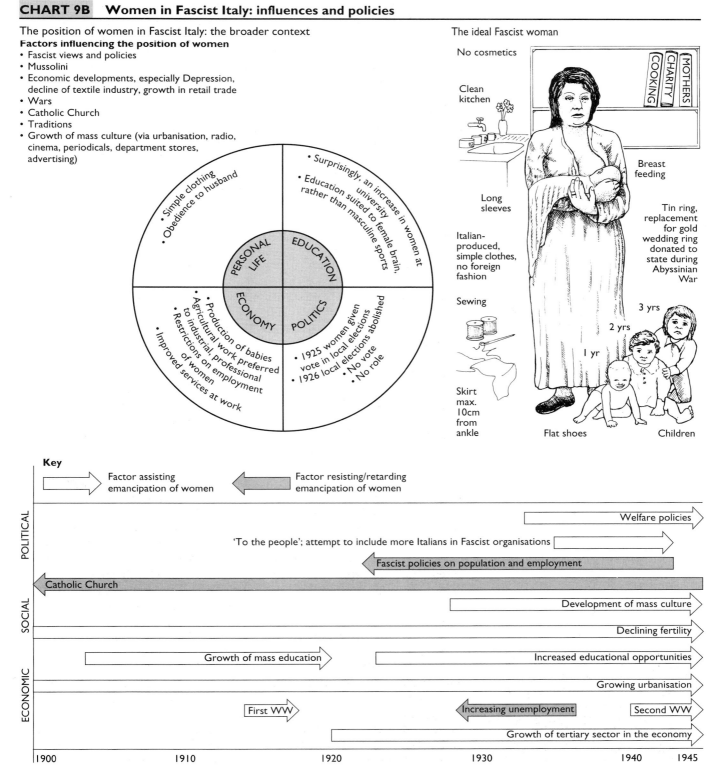

The women in Mussolini's life

Mussolini had a voracious sexual appetite, and had a string of mistresses whom he dominated. The following three women, however, he treated rather better.

Rachele Mussolini (1892–1979)

She came from a peasant family. From 1910 she lived with Mussolini, whom she married in 1915 in a civil ceremony, and in 1925 in a religious one. She was poorly educated, and unconcerned about politics. She bore Mussolini five children, and was extolled as the model Fascist housewife and mother. She concentrated on running the household, ignoring Mussolini's mistresses. She stayed loyal to him till the end. In 1945 she was arrested, but released after several months. She later ran a restaurant, and received a government pension until her death.

Margherita Sarfatti (1883–1961)

She came from a rich Jewish family, and became a RADICAL SOCIALIST and feminist. She supported Mussolini, first as a radical socialist, then as a Fascist. From 1915 she worked on *Il Popolo d'Italia* and other Fascist publications. She became his mistress. In 1926 she wrote Mussolini's biography which became a best seller. A passionate lover of art, she became an influential supporter of modernism, having a major influence on the government's cultural policy. For the first thirteen years of the regime she had a major moderating influence on Mussolini's domestic and foreign policy. Her biographer Cannistraro has called her 'the uncrowned Queen of Italy'. However, from 1935 her relationship with Mussolini and her influence were over. Her articles were suppressed after the 1938 ANTI-SEMITIC legislation. In 1938 she left Italy, only returning after the war.

Clara Petacci (1912–45)

She came from a rich family, and developed a schoolgirl crush on Mussolini. She became his mistress in 1936, and devoted her life to him. Their relationship was not widely known about, helped by the fact that Clara used a secret staircase in the Palazzo Venezia. In contrast to Sarfatti, she was unintelligent and pro-Nazi. She stayed loyal despite Mussolini's other mistresses, followed him to the Salo Republic and was with him when he was captured by partisans. Her wish to be shot with him was granted.

■ **Talking point**

Should the sexual behaviour of rulers and politicians affect the way historians assess their reputations?

SOURCE 9.6 Whittam, p. 72

The two women ... who wielded most influence, Margherita Sarfatti and Clara Petacci, also happened to be mistresses of Mussolini, a final sad commentary on male domination in all its aspects.

C Did Italy's women deliver?

'I'll do it again.' Thus responded a forty-year-old mother of thirteen, returning home from a prize ceremony in Rome for prolific mothers, when asked about her future plans. Her Duce would have been delighted with her response, but did most Italian women fulfil their leader's wishes of having large families?

In our age, when so many countries are concerned about the problem of over-population, and the need to control birth rates, it's hard to understand a government committed to massive population increase. However, this was the case with Mussolini's Italy. He once remarked that reaching his target of 60 million Italians would be the real test of his Fascist revolution. Mussolini wanted a larger population for reasons of national power. He wanted more soldiers to fight his wars, and more Italians to populate his expanding EMPIRE. In 1927 Mussolini proclaimed the great battle which was to achieve this aim, the Battle for Births. He told delegates from a Fascist women's organisation, 'Go back home and tell the women I need births, many births.'

Mussolini's Battle for Births was an extreme form of a policy other states adopted, and it had the support of the Catholic Church which saw women and marriage as rightfully preoccupied with procreation (reproduction). Both state and Church adopted a reactionary policy, attempting to reverse general trends they saw as corrupting women. They blamed the declining birth rate on female vanity, individualism, pleasure-seeking, godlessness, and a corrupting desire to be modern.

CHART 9C The Battle for Births

Aims
a) To increase Italy's population from 37 million in 1920 to 60 million by 1950
b) To make Italy great
c) To provide soldiers

Actions
Launched in 1927; measures intensified from 1936 as methods below had limited impact
a) Propaganda
  • Campaign stressing importance of marriage

b) Improved services
  • Better health care

c) Financial rewards
  • Marriage loans (repayments cancelled if mother bore four children)
  • Tax relief, e.g. no income tax if ten children

d) Ceremonies/prizes
  • Annual ceremony honouring the most prolific mothers (93 families in 1933 had a total of 1300 children)
  • 1939 medal with silver bar per child

e) Pressure and prohibition
  • Increased taxation of bachelors
  • Divorce remained illegal
  • Abortion banned, and distribution of contraceptives limited
  • In 1931 Penal Code included 'crimes against the wholeness and health of the race'
  • Civil service jobs and promotion reserved for fathers

Results
• Birth rate continued to decline
• Population rose to 45 million in 1940, and 47.5m in 1950 (short of the 60 million target)
• Average age of marriage rose, and marriage rate fell

■ **Talking point**

Why do you think the average age of marriage varies considerably over time? Why might women have delayed marriage at this time? Would the same reasons apply today?

SOURCE 9.7 A salute from prizewinning mothers, Rome 1930

SOURCE 9.8 A 1930s Turin paediatrician (children's doctor) reports some responses from her working-class clients

a) *The government is not going to get anything from us ... Let the government go ahead and talk about the ever bigger need to make the country greater, with an ever higher birth rate, to keep the stock healthy; in my opinion, it's all yack.*

b) *Let the priest feed the kid, if he's so keen on making babies.*

c) *Mussolini's not the one to raise it.*

SOURCE 9.9 Scorza, the RAS of Lucca

Society today despises deserters, pimps, homosexuals, thieves. Those who can but do not perform their duty to the nation must be put in the same category. We must despise them. We must make the bachelors and those who desert the nuptial bed ashamed of their power to have children. It is necessary to make them bow their foreheads in the dust.

SOURCE 9.10 Birth rates by region per 1000 inhabitants, 1921–45

Dates	Italy overall	North	South
1921–25	29.9	26.6	36.3
1931–35	24.0	20.3	30.8
1941–45	19.9	17.5	25.3

SOURCE 9.11 Infant mortality rates. There was a tendency for doctors, midwives and parents to report babies' deaths during and just after birth as still births (i.e. dead when born) rather than as infant deaths. However, the two groups of figures indicate the trend

a) Deaths of infants under one year per 1000 live births

1914	130
1918	196
1922	128
1926	127
1930	106

b) Still births in relation to live births

1922	45%
1926	39%
1930	35%
1934	33%
1938	32%
1942	28%

■ **Activity**

1 How might each of following have affected the birth rate?
   a) The First World War
   b) The Depression
   c) The Catholic Church
   d) The continued drift from the countryside to cities

2 What two other factors apart from the birth rate would determine the size of Italy's population?

3 a) Why, given Italy's economic resources, is it surprising that Mussolini tried to increase Italy's population?
   b) How might a Fascist argue for an increase in population?

4 What do the pictorial and statistical sources, and contemporary comments, suggest about the success of the Battle for Births?

D Review: Did Mussolini succeed in imposing Fascist values on women?

Study the following sources to help draw some conclusions as to the success of Fascist policies.

■ Activity

1 What are the main trends in women's employment that emerge from Source 9.12? What other factors besides government policies might help explain these developments?

2 Complete your own version of the following chart on the treatment of women:
How were women
a) discriminated against
b) assisted?

	in childbirth and in the family	in employment	in education	in politics
a) discriminated against				
b) assisted				

3 **a)** Draw up a chart of the attitudes of the girls in Source 9.14:

What they wanted	What they disliked

b) From this evidence, how successful do Fascist policies seem to have been?
c) Why must you be wary in drawing too many conclusions from this survey?

4 What limitations do the historians in Sources 9.16–18 identify in Fascist policies towards women?

SOURCE 9.12 Women in the labour force

	% of all working women employed in			Women as % of total labour force		
Year	Agric	Indust	*Other	Agric	Indust	*Other
1911	58.8	24.2	17.0	43.2	43.9	39.5
1921	52.2	23.6	18.2	44.7	39.0	38.5
1936	51.1	24.1	24.8	41.3	33.1	42.8
1951	41.4	28.0	30.6	32.6	28.0	42.7

* Clerical, professional, retail, etc.

SOURCE 9.13 Enrolment in Fascist women's organisations

SOURCE 9.14 Attitudes and actions of young women in Fascist Italy: points made in a 1937 official survey of 1000 Roman girls aged 14–18, mainly from the professional classes

- *'Extraordinarily vague' ideas about having families*
- *Regarded babies as burdensome*
- *Considered one or two children best*
- *Studied in order to qualify for a job*
- *Housework seen as tedious*
- *Didn't expect husband to support them*
- *Most uninterested in traditional female handicrafts like knitting and sewing*
- *Favourite pastime movies; half went to movies at least once a week*
- *Favourite reading novels, especially romances and adventures*
- *Preferred dancing to singing and painting*
- *Preferred company of peers [friends of the same age] to that of younger brothers/sisters*
- *Prized self-confidence*
- *Wanted to command more than obey*
- *Described as 'healthy, vivacious but not turbulent'*

■ **Talking point**

Do you think that a modern survey of young women's attitudes would produce similar results?

SOURCE 9.15 An account of the housework of a working-class woman who in 1930 spent an estimated 1500 hours working at home in addition to agricultural work

Household chores were a major undertaking given the lack of electricity and indoor plumbing. To prepare meals meant first cleaning out the hearth and drawing the fire, preceded by hauling water from the well or spring, and gathering kindling. Laundry was a twice-monthly enterprise which took days by the time heavy linen sheets had been lugged to the water source, ash applied several times, and the whole lot pressed with stove-heated irons. In addition to laying away lentils, tomatoes, capers and other stores, caring for chickens, and tending the orchard garden, at harvest time the women served the men in the fields and often laboured there themselves.

Finally, read the following analyses from historians.

Historians' assessments

SOURCE 9.16 A. J. Gregor, *Italian Fascism and Developmental Dictatorship*, 1979, p. 290

The demographic program, the ruralisation of the peninsula, and the effort to revive the traditional female virtues . . . all appear to have been unsuccessful . . . Fascism may have been instrumental in removing women from the job market, but the statistics are not unequivocal [don't prove it conclusively] . . . Fascist anti-feminism was not particularly successful and/or may not have been pursued with any special application. In any event, Fascist anti-feminism was, at best, a subsidiary concern of Fascist social policy, and made its appearance largely as a consequence of concerns with a declining birth rate and rising unemployment.

SOURCE 9.17 De Grazia, in *How Fascism Ruled Women*, 1992, pp. 269–70

Fascism's organisation of women rested on a fundamental paradox, one that can be traced back to Fascism's own contradictory definitions of female citizenship. Women's duty was maternity; their primary vocation was to procreate, nurture and manage family functions. Yet to perform this duty, they needed to be responsive to public well-being; they needed to be conscious of society's expectations and the effects of their essentially individual acts on the collectivity. This need required that women be engaged outside the household. Moreover, the PNF, mobilising ever-larger crowds to demonstrate public support, became obsessed with numbers. Women, though excluded from consultation in the PLEBISCITES of 1929 and 1934, could be tallied up to display totalitarianism's organisational might.

The mass organisations of women ultimately reflected unresolved tensions within the DICTATORSHIP over how to define women in the Italian state.

SOURCE 9.18 P. Willson, 'Women in Fascist Italy', in *Fascist Italy and Nazi Germany*, ed. R. Bessel, 1996, pp. 92–93

173

The female experience of the Fascist period was marked by its sheer diversity . . . When they tried to intervene most explicitly to mould gender roles, in their bid to stem or even reverse trends towards female emancipation through highly misogynous [anti-female] rhetoric and policy, they were far from successful. Although they preached, and wherever practical, legislated for female subordination, they were doomed ultimately to fail in their declared ambition to make women into 'angels of the hearth'. There were simply too many constraints on policy makers for legislation to have much impact, and despite the enormous amount of attention paid to gender roles in Fascist rhetoric, it seems that particular patterns of industrialisation, commercialisation, and urbanisation had more power to shape female experiences in this period than the crude tools of Fascist IDEOLOGY and policy.

Statistical and anecdotal evidence (from stories or by word of mouth) suggests the regime failed to implant its reactionary attitudes widely amongst women, partly as the growth of mass culture broadened attitudes and aspirations. Thus despite the chauvinist attitudes of Italy's leaders, and policies geared to restricting the role of women, many Italian women maintained their traditional role in the economy, and some even found their opportunities increased. At the most crucial level neither of the two key policies of the regime in relation to women – a great increase in the birth rate, and a reduction in paid employment – were achieved.

Key points from Chapter 9

1 Mussolini had traditional attitudes to the role of women, many of which he shared with the Church.
2 Broader social changes were challenging such ideas.
3 Mussolini believed women should stay at home and concentrate on child rearing.
4 The Fascists launched a Battle for Births, and encouraged women to have babies through pressure and incentives.
5 The birth rate continued to decline, and the regime failed to reach its target population figure of 60 million.
6 The Fascists discriminated against women in education and in 'unnatural' occupations.
7 The Fascists provided a range of welfare facilities for women.
8 Women were expected to maintain a traditional and unglamorous lifestyle, but the growth of mass culture broadened their horizons.
9 Although women were not given the vote, they were encouraged to join Fascist women's organisations.
10 Evidence suggests that the Fascists failed to implant their reactionary views in many women.

■ Activity

As a 'true believer', speak to the rest of the class
either
on your role as a woman in Fascist Italy,
or
as an emancipated woman criticise Fascist policies towards women.

Fascism and Catholicism: rivals or collaborators?

He is a man sent by providence. He has brought God back to Italy, and Italy back to God.

FOCUS ROUTE

As you read through Chapter 10, make notes under these headings:
a) Why did Mussolini want the support of the Catholic Church?
b) How did Mussolini win that support?
c) Evidence that the Concordat with the Catholic Church was a success for Mussolini.

What was the role of the Catholic Church in Italy?
Although the overwhelming majority of Italians claimed to be Catholic (over 90 per cent), their actual level of commitment varied. In the 1930s it is estimated that only five to ten per cent of Italians took communion regularly; another 20 per cent attended church at least every other Sunday; and a further 50 per cent considered themselves good Catholics! The Church was deeply involved in most aspects of Italian life, influencing everything from high culture to popular customs and morality. It controlled a strong network of educational, welfare and financial institutions. The Church was especially influential in the countryside, where peasant communities relied on their priests for news and views of outside events.

At first glance, the fulsome praise in Source 10.1 by the leader of the Catholic Church for Mussolini looks like a case of mistaken identity! For Mussolini was a former revolutionary socialist, who had described religion as a 'malaise of the brain', who remained an ATHEIST throughout his life, and led a movement which used violence to achieve and maintain power, and glorified war.

However, Pius XI knew what he was saying. Mussolini realised the importance of the Church, and was concerned to secure its support. So it was Mussolini who settled the Church–state quarrel that had plagued the kingdom of Italy since its creation. For many Italians, this was the greatest achievement of their DUCE. However, the compromise with the Church also served to limit Mussolini's attempt to create a new nation of committed Fascists.

CHART 10A   CHAPTER OVERVIEW

10 Fascism and Catholicism: rivals or collaborators?

A Why did Mussolini end the Church–state quarrel? (p. 174)

B How did relations develop after the Concordat? (pp. 175–77)

C Review: Fascism and Catholicism: rivals or collaborators? (pp. 178–79)

A Why did Mussolini end the Church–state quarrel?

At the beginning of his regime, Mussolini made conciliatory moves towards the Church (Chart 10B). This was part of his initial policy of favouring the social, economic and administrative ELITE to consolidate his regime. He was also continuing the improvement of relations between Church and state that had begun before the First World War.

A clear area of conflict, however, was Fascism's claim to be a TOTALITARIAN regime, which should not allow a powerful alternative set of beliefs. However, if he could win the support of the powerful Church, then the acceptance of a potentially rival doctrine was worth it. Mussolini also considered that the Roman Catholic Church encouraged people worldwide to look to Rome for leadership, which was a source of pride for Italians. Furthermore, an agreement with the Pope would certainly boost the Fascist regime's international image.

The Church worried about aspects of Fascism, although it was initially far more concerned about the danger of SOCIALISM. Mussolini seemed a far better bulwark than the previous Liberal state had been. Fascism and Catholicism shared other attitudes, such as the need for order, discipline and respect for hierarchy; the acceptance of an infallible leader and hostility to LIBERALISM and materialism. They also had a similar approach towards the family and the role of women. In addition, Corporativism seemed similar to Christianity's stress on social harmony. If the regime could provide a stable AUTHORITARIAN state, then there was reason to believe that Catholicism could flourish.

Early progress on reconciliation was slow, but after three years of negotiations a formal agreement was reached. This comprised a political treaty recognising the independence of the Vatican; a financial convention giving the Church compensation; and a Concordat* regulating Church–state relations.

■ **Activity**

Read Chart 10B and look at Sources 10.2–8.

Activity

Read Chart 10B and look at Sources 10.2–8.

1 What were the main reasons why Mussolini wanted an agreement with the Pope?
2 What do you think were the most important gains for him from the Concordat? What did the Pope gain?
3 How might the fact that the Church became such a major holder of state bonds affect its attitude to the state?

CHART 10B Mussolini and the Catholic Church

a) Early measures, 1923
  • Increased clerical* salaries
  • Religious Education reinstated in elementary schools
  • Crucifix restored in schoolrooms and courts

b) The Lateran* Pacts, 1929
  i) Lateran Treaty (a political treaty)
    • Vatican City*, 109 acres in Rome, made a SOVEREIGN state
    • The Pope recognised Rome as the Italian capital.
  ii) Financial Convention
    • Church given 750 million lire (about 30 million pounds) plus 1000 million lire in bonds as compensation for lands lost at unification
    • Church thus became largest holder of state bonds
  iii) Concordat (regulating Church–state relations)
    • Catholicism recognised as the sole religion of the state
    • State veto over major Church appointments
    • RE in secondary as well as elementary schools
    • Church marriages recognised by the state
    • Church control of divorce
    • The state accepted the existence of CATHOLIC ACTION.

c) Later relations
  • 1931 quarrel over Catholic Action. The Pope condemned some of Mussolini's statements as heretical.
  • 1931 Pope issued a critical ENCYCLICAL*, 'Non Abbiamo Bisogno' ('We have no need'). Compromise reached
  • 1938 Church critical of ANTI-SEMITISM

The basis of the Concordat was not challenged. The Church took part in the everyday life of Fascism. Priests participated in ONB activities. For example, at the 1938 Campo Dux meeting, the Mass began with the Fascist anthem *Giovinezza*, then a call for the divine being to aid Mussolini in his quest for EMPIRE. The PNF secretary served as the altar boy, and at the elevation of the host 15,000 youths drew their bayonets and pointed them to the sky. The ceremony ended with a prayer for the Duce.

Priests and party officials co-operated in campaigning against modern dancing, short skirts and decadent films. The slogan 'Per il papa e per il duce' (for Pope and Duce) stressed the unity of Church and state. A Catholic journal urged Catholics to 'go to the polls and give your vote for the government of the Hon. Mussolini'. Clergy gave Fascist salutes, and their pastoral letters praised the Duce. The Church hierarchy welcomed the 'crusades' against heathenism and BOLSHEVISM in Abyssinia and Spain. However, beneath the official reconciliation, there was some criticism on both sides. Some RADICAL Fascists considered the Concordat a betrayal of their aims. Some priests were concerned about their hierarchy's close identification with the Fascist state. When in 1930 the Archbishop of Milan openly praised Fascism, 300 of his priests circulated an open letter of protest saying good Catholics could not accept Fascism.

Furthermore, there were two major quarrels between the Church and the government in 1931 and 1937–38. The government considered Catholic Action was extending its role into areas claimed for the state, and closed down several of its branches. The Pope responded by publicly criticising the regime, in an encyclical printed in the papal newspaper *L'Osservatore Romano* and in foreign newspapers. A compromise was reached that Catholic Action would just run strictly religious, educational and recreational activities (though not sport), and would become more decentralised. The second quarrel, over anti-semitism (see page 182), developed into a broader challenge to the nature of Fascism. The Pope and priests publicly criticised the government for infringing Christianity by forbidding marriages between Jews (some of whom had converted to Catholicism) and Italians.

What was CATHOLIC ACTION? This was an international body set up by the Catholic Church in 1863 to organise Catholic laity* to defend Catholics and the Church. It had various sections, of which the most important was concerned with youth. With the end of Catholic unions, the Popolari and the Catholic Boy Scouts in the mid-1920s, Catholic Action became the only lay body supporting the interests of Catholics. Its position was formally recognised in the Concordat*, and it was declared apolitical (not involved in politics). However, its existence continued to cause considerable tension with the Fascist government, with its claims for totalitarian control. By the 1930s it had a membership of over one million, and remained an obstacle to full Fascist MOBILISATION of the Italians.

Church glossary

Here are explanations of some Church vocabulary used in the text and sources. Terms are marked with * in the text.

Cardinal	high-ranking Catholic priests (there were about 120 of them)
clerical	to do with the clergy/priests
concordat	an agreement
diocese	area presided over by a bishop
encyclical	letter from the Pope sent to all bishops
laity	non-priest members of the Church
Lateran	name of a palace in Rome where the Concordat and other agreements were signed
Monsignor	title given to priests
Pontiff	the Pope
Vatican City	the area around the Vatican Palace and St Peter's Church in Rome, controlled by the Pope

Although Mussolini benefited politically from the agreement, which helped establish the broad consensus of the early 1930s, the Church ultimately made more lasting gains. The Church continued its mission in its network of welfare, social and cultural institutions based on Christian rather than Fascist principles, which probably helped to undermine the impact of Fascist propaganda.

In the 1930s there was a considerable religious revival, with the numbers of church marriages, church schools and priests all increasing. The circulation of the Vatican newspaper *L'Osservatore Romano* and the activities of Catholic Action also grew. The careful Church leadership, with its 'don't rock the boat' approach, allowed the Church to weaken the totalitarian pretensions (claims) of the regime, and through Catholic Action it was able to provide an alternative environment for its one million members. Its students' federation, FUCI, helped the Church to emerge as a major political force with a new generation of leaders after the collapse of Fascism.

SOURCE 10.2 Extract from a 1928 official text on Fascist culture

As there is only one official state religion which is the Catholic faith so, too, there must be only one political faith ... [just as] religious dogmas are not to be discussed because they are the revealed truths of God, [so] Fascist principles are not to be discussed because they have come from the mind of a genius: BENITO MUSSOLINI.

SOURCE 10.3 Extract from *Fascism, Doctrine and Institutions*, 1934, by Mussolini

The Fascist State is not indifferent to religious phenomena in general, nor does it maintain an attitude of indifference to Roman Catholicism, the special positive religion of the Italians. The Fascist State sees in religion one of the deepest of spiritual manifestations [revelations], and for this reason it not only respects religion, but defends and protects it.

The Fascist State does not ... seek, as did Bolshevism, to efface [erase] God from the soul of man. Fascism respects the God of ascetics [monks], saints and heroes, and it also respects God as conceived by the ingenuous [innocent] and primitive heart of the people, the God to whom their prayers are raised.

SOURCE 10.4
A postcard celebrating the Concordat*, showing the King, the Pope and Mussolini

CHART 10C   Who gained what from the Concordat*?

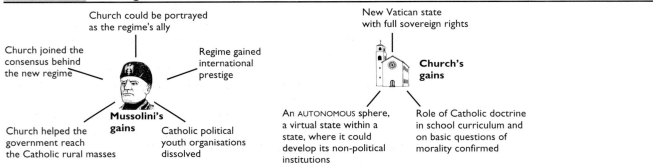

Church could be portrayed as the regime's ally

Church joined the consensus behind the new regime

Regime gained international prestige

Mussolini's gains

Church helped the government reach the Catholic rural masses

Catholic political youth organisations dissolved

New Vatican state with full sovereign rights

Church's gains

An AUTONOMOUS sphere, a virtual state within a state, where it could develop its non-political institutions

Role of Catholic doctrine in school curriculum and on basic questions of morality confirmed

SOURCE 10.5 The American magazine *Time* assesses the Concordat*, 1929

Mussolini ... watched Cardinals* and Monsignors* marching to the ballot box, attended by blaring brass bands and wildly cheering throngs ... Never before have Princes of the Church shepherded their clergy and people to vote in a parliamentary election ... Il Duce has restored a mite of earthly authority to Il Papa and last week cinema machines proved how mountainous is the Pontiff's* gratitude to the Dictator ... [Three Cardinals*] proceeded directly from the celebration of High Mass to vote at the head of their clergy. Pollsters estimated that His Holiness's influence had flung into the scale of Fascismo at least one million extra votes. Last week's election statistics prove that those Italians who went to the polls are 98.28 per cent pure endorsers of the Duce, a record eclipsed in the US only by Ivory Soap.

SOURCE 10.6 Borgese, a Professor of Literature who was exiled in 1931, assesses the Concordat*

There was no reason why Pope and Duce, whom a parallel destiny had brought in the same year to Rome, should not come together: no reason except in Christ; but Christianism was by no means the most decisive factor in Pope Ratti's mind. He was sure that he loved Italy; it is sure that he hated DEMOCRACY and Socialism ... the ruthless anti-Christianity of Fascism ... was nothing to him.

The Church became ancillary [an aid] to atheistic tyranny, and tyranny rewarded it by making it supreme in the elementary cell of society, the family. Marriage and divorce became a MONOPOLY of the Vatican, and the priest lent his hand to the squadrist in ... national violence and international anarchy ... Over her new black shirt Italy donned her old black gown [dress of the clergy].

SOURCE 10.7
A German cartoon from 1929. The title is 'King and Papal States' and the caption reads 'I beg you, great Mussolini, to give me too a corner of Italian territory where I can govern'

SOURCE 10.8 Extract from the encyclical* 'Non Abbiamo Bisogno', June 1931

A conception of the state which makes the rising generations belong to it entirely, without any exception, from the tenderest years up to adult life, cannot be reconciled by a Catholic either with Catholic doctrine or with the natural rights of the family. It is not possible for a Catholic to accept the claim that the Church and the Pope must limit themselves to the external practices of religion and that all the rest of education belongs to the state ...

[The Church has a] universal and divine mandate to educate children [and to stop the regime's effort] to monopolise the young ... for the sole and exclusive benefit of a party and of a regime based on an IDEOLOGY that clearly resolves itself into a veritable [truly] pagan worship of the state.

C Review: Fascism and Catholicism: rivals or collaborators?

In some respects, the Catholic Church collaborated with and buttressed Fascist rule. The Concordat* greatly boosted Mussolini's popularity. But though this helped Mussolini as leader, it hindered his attempt to forge a new Fascist nation. The strengthening of Catholicism in schools, and the continued growth of Catholic Action meant that many Italians encountered another perspective, which was sometimes similar to Fascism's, as over women, family and anti-Bolshevism, but sometimes different, as over respect for human life and militarism. At times this tension became public, as the Church criticised the regime and resisted its pressure. At other times, the Church hierarchy supported the regime. For many Italians, the varying responses of local priests was the greatest influence.

This complexity has led historians to develop different emphases on the extent of rivalry and collaboration. Some, like Pollard, stress the 'fundamental philosophical incompatibility between Catholicism and Fascism'; others, like Miccoli, stress how their alliance was not 'merely tactical' but reflected an 'essential consonance' (agreement).

Let us conclude by examining some historians' assessments of Church–state relations during the Fascist era.

SOURCE 10.9   Clark, pp. 155, 254 and 256

a) *The pacts were a triumph for the Duce. The cost was negligible, the benefits huge. Mussolini had solved the Roman question; he could count on worldwide prestige and a chorus of admiration.*

b) *The Catholic Church was the greatest obstacle to any 'totalitarian' regime in Italy. All the others, Parliament, press, opposition parties, unions, could be smashed or emasculated [weakened]; but not the Church.*

c) *Although the Church undoubtedly contributed to the Fascist consensus between 1926 and 1938, she was also a rival who was building up her strength.*

SOURCE 10.10   C. Duggan, *A Concise History of Italy*, 1994, pp. 226–27

The resolution of the Roman question was a great political coup for Mussolini. It increased his personal prestige, internationally as well as at home; and more importantly, it allowed Fascism to realise the dream long harboured by the Liberal state of using the Church as an instrument for securing mass political consent . . .

However, the reconciliation with the Church was bought at a high price. By conceding independence to Catholic Action, with its large network of parish-based organisations, Fascism surrendered any serious claim to a monopoly of ideology.

SOURCE 10.11   Koon, pp. 117, 142

The history of Church–state relations during the Fascist period is one of substantial collaboration, punctuated by periodic confrontation and almost continual tension.

The Church proved to be as tenacious a competitor as Mussolini had feared.

Both sides paid a price for the 1929 conciliation. Intransigent [obstinate] Fascist rhetoric notwithstanding, the regime had, however grudgingly, been forced to accept the Church's role in education and socialisation. The Lateran Accords guaranteed the presence of the Church in the Italian schools and in Fascist youth groups. The existence of Catholic youth groups over the years provided an alternative to Fascist conformity . . . The most serious dispute between the regime and the Church, in 1931, never led to an open break. The Pope charted a cautious course, willing to concede tactical victories in his overall strategy to preserve the gains of conciliation. Fascism never succeeded in totally co-opting the Church, but the Church, in the years after 1929, was never a rallying point of organised anti-Fascism.*

■ Activity

1 The papacy has been criticised for its approach to Fascism. From the historians' extracts (Sources 10.9–13), draw up two lists, one of evidence defending the Papacy, the other to criticise it.

2 Read the extracts from Ciano's diary (Source 16.2 on page 260). What do they reveal about Mussolini's attitude to Pius XI?

3 'Assessment of who gained most from the Concordat*, and of the relations between Church and state is a complex issue.' What evidence do the extracts from historians provide to support this view?

4 Organise a debate between two priests, one who favours collaboration with the Fascist government, and one who advocates trying to oppose it. (Decide on a particular date for your debate.)

SOURCE 10.12   J. Pollard, *The Vatican and Italian Fascism*, 1985

Given the 'ideological convergence' between the Vatican and Italian Fascism, it is perhaps not surprising that in the 1930s the Church ... was very active in its role as part of the 'bloc of consensus' underpinning the Fascist regime.

SOURCE 10.13   R. Grew, 'Catholicism in a Changing Italy', in Tannenbaum (ed.), *Modern Italy*, 1974, p. 268

To opponents of Fascism, the Church seemed ... inextricably implicated in Fascist policy, particularly during the Ethiopian War, for which bishops and clergy frequently expressed the most unrestrained support. Even the denunciations of particular Fascist policies were expressed in temperate [mild] tones that seemed a significant contrast with the fulminations [angry outbursts] against the Liberal MONARCHY.

Yet the Church ... did resist the persistent attacks on the remaining forms of Catholic Action and did formally denounce Mussolini's racial policy in late 1938. No opposition to a complete totalitarianism was more formidable.

FOCUS ROUTE

1   After studying Chapter 10, copy and complete the following assessment chart on the Concordat*.

	Mussolini	Church
Why did they make the agreement?		
What did they gain from it?		
What were its potential disadvantages?		

2   The Concordat* has been described as Mussolini's greatest, but least Fascist achievement. Do you agree? And if so, what does that tell us about the nature of Fascist Italy?
3   How did Church–state relations develop after 1929?

Key points from Chapter 10

1   There were fundamental differences between Catholicism and Fascism, but also grounds for co-operation.
2   The Catholic Church was a very powerful body in Italy, and from 1922 Mussolini tried to improve relations with it.
3   In 1929 a Concordat* and Lateran* Treaties were signed.
4   The Catholic Church gained formal recognition as Italy's state religion; freedom to operate as a religious body; agreement on the status of the Vatican City*; and compensation for lost territory.
5   Mussolini gained a veto on key Church appointments, and the support of the Church hierarchy.
6   The Concordat* greatly boosted Mussolini's popularity.
7   The survival of Catholic Action provided an alternative environment for many of those uncommitted to Fascism.
8   Relations later deteriorated, with tension over Catholic Action and anti-semitism.
9   The Church remained as a powerful influence, and survived to influence Italy's political development after 1943.
10 The Concordat* has been described as Mussolini's greatest but least Fascist achievement.

How effective was Mussolini's radicalisation of the regime in the late 1930s?

FOCUS ROUTE

As you work through Chapter 11, consider
a) why Mussolini tried to radicalise the regime in the late 1930s
b) what forms his policy took, and what its effects were.

For most of the time Mussolini was in power he generally co-operated with the ELITES, and disappointed some of the RADICALS in his own party who expected a Fascist revolution. However, in the late 1930s it appears that Mussolini tried to radicalise the regime. This chapter looks at why he did this and how successful he was.

CHART 11A   CHAPTER OVERVIEW

11 How effective was Mussolini's radicalisation of the regime in the late 1930s?

A The Reform of Customs: silly or significant?

SOURCE 11.1 Mussolini in conversation with Emil Ludwig, 1931

The whole country has to become a great school for perpetual political education which will make the Italians into complete Fascists, new men, changing their habits, their way of life, their mentality, their character and, finally, their physical makeup. It will no longer be a question of grumbling against the sceptical, mandolin-playing Italians, but rather of creating a new kind of man who is tough, strong-willed, a fighter, a latter-day legionary of Caesar for whom nothing is impossible.

In 1938 Mussolini tried to abolish the use of the friendly form of 'you', and the use of the handshake. This so-called 'Reform of Customs' can be seen as rather ridiculous, and such changes in themselves are of little significance. Certainly, they are often not given much stress in accounts of Fascist Italy, or are just used to poke fun at Mussolini's regime. However, it could be argued that they were illustrative of a much more fundamental shift of emphasis in the regime in the late 1930s. Greater radicalism became evident, something which can also be seen in educational and institutional changes, in foreign policy and in the introduction of ANTI-SEMITIC policies. What lay at the root of these changes?

From the beginning Mussolini had been trying to change the way Italians thought, to make them proud of being members of his new Fascist Italy. He hoped this would also influence their behaviour – that they would work harder, fight better, and have more children. However, by the mid-1930s Mussolini and some other Fascists like Starace and Bottai seem to have despaired of their countrymen. Most Italians had failed to take on board the Fascist spiritual revolution. Mussolini criticised what he called their 'BOURGEOIS mentality' – meaning that they were PACIFIST, complacent, and materialistic. They were too attracted to the Western DEMOCRACIES and they needed toughening up. As Mussolini said to Ciano in July 1938, 'Henceforth the revolution must impinge on the habits of Italians. They must learn to be less sympathetic in order to become hard, relentless and hateful – in other words masters.'

With the conquest of Abyssinia in 1936, and the growing likelihood of European war, it seems that Mussolini became more determined to try to forge a nation that could meet its IMPERIAL and aggressive destiny.

■ Activity

1 What measures did Mussolini take to try to create a new Fascist man?
2 In what ways can his campaign be seen as significant?

181

HOW EFFECTIVE WAS MUSSOLINI'S RADICALISATION OF THE REGIME IN THE LATE 1930S?

CHART 11B   The 'traditional' Italian (top) and the new Fascist man (bottom)

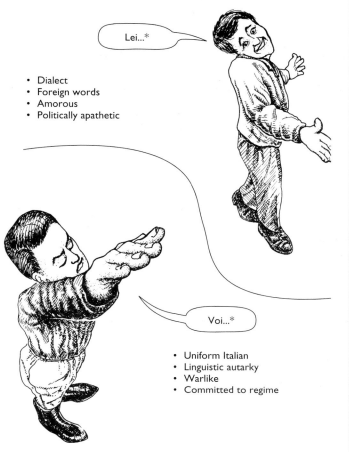

- Dialect
- Foreign words
- Amorous
- Politically apathetic

Lei...*

Voi...*

- Uniform Italian
- Linguistic autarky
- Warlike
- Committed to regime

*'You'

SOURCE 11.2   Mussolini demonstrating the 'passo romano', or goose-step

SOURCE 11.3   Fascist leaders showing how fit they were. All key party officials were ordered to learn how to ride horses and motorcycles. Party leaders had to do gymnastics – so pot-bellied, ageing Fascists could be seen in gym kit running, bouncing on trampolines, and even jumping through hoops of fire

SOURCE 11.4   Party leader Starace leaping through a hoop of fire

182

HOW EFFECTIVE WAS MUSSOLINI'S RADICALISATION OF THE REGIME IN THE LATE 1930S?

■ Talking point

In what circumstances can racism develop in a society? Does it normally originate from above, with government encouragement, or from popular feeling from below?

■ Activity

Look at the Sources 11.6–9 and Chart 11C. What do they tell you about:

a) Mussolini's attitude towards Italian Jews
b) the Church's attitude to Jews
c) Mussolini's policies on Italian Jews?

B Why did Mussolini adopt anti-semitism?

Another apparently more radical policy designed to harden up the Italian people was the adoption by the government of anti-semitism. Anti-semitism is one of the policies most closely associated with the Fascist regimes of the 1930s in the public mind. However, there were many differences between Italian Fascism and Nazism. This is clearly shown in their approach to Jews.

Initially there was very little anti-semitism in either Italy or the Fascist Party. Italian Jews made up under one per cent of the population. Most of them were deeply integrated into Italian life. There was no 'Jewish problem'. Italian Fascism was not anti-semitic; indeed a disproportionate number of Jews were members of the PNF. For sixteen years Jews received the same benefits and restrictions from the Fascist government as other Italians.

Yet in 1938 Mussolini introduced racist DECREES, discriminating against Jews (see Chart 11C). This change of policy is normally seen as a reflection of his subservience to Hitler, which in some ways it was, despite Mussolini's denials. It was not, however, imposed on Mussolini by Hitler. Mussolini chose to try and imitate Hitler. But anti-semitism was also a product of other trends, both international and domestic, and can be seen as part of the general radicalisation of the period. This has been well explained by the historian Bernardini.

SOURCE 11.5 The Italian historian Bernardini in an article 'The Origins and Development of Racial Anti-semitism in Fascist Italy', in *The Nazi Holocaust, The Final Solution outside Germany*, ed. M. Marrus, 1988, pp. 230, 238

His decision to formulate a policy which would weld together racism and anti-semitism was purely voluntary and flowed naturally from the confluence of Italy's imperial policies, the IDEOLOGICAL tenets of Fascism, and Italian national interests as enunciated [put forward] by Il DUCE . . .

The emergence of official anti-semitism . . . must be viewed not as a momentary aberration [mistake] on the part of Mussolini or the Grand Council, or as an attempt to honour the Nazis by copying the Nuremberg Laws. It was, rather, cut from the same cloth as the rest of Fascism's final costume and was an attempt, once and for all, to eradicate the vestiges [remains] of earlier values and mores [customs], to transform the Italian people from top to bottom, and to present the world with a truly new man, homo fascistus.

Both Mussolini and the Catholic Church made ambivalent statements about race and anti-semitism, as the following sources show.

SOURCE 11.6 Mussolini in conversation with the German writer Emil Ludwig in 1932

Of course there are no pure races left; not even the Jews have kept their blood unmingled. Successful crossings have often promoted the energy and beauty of a nation. Race! It is a feeling, not a reality; 95 per cent, at least, is a feeling. Nothing will ever make me believe that biologically pure races can be shown to exist today. Amusingly enough, not one of those who have proclaimed the 'nobility' of the Teutonic [German] race was himself a Teuton . . . Anti-semitism does not exist in Italy . . . National pride has no need of the delirium [madness] of race . . . Italians of Jewish birth have shown themselves good citizens, and they fought bravely in the war. Many of them occupy leading positions in the universities, in the army, in the banks.

SOURCE 11.7 Mussolini in *Il Giornale d'Italia*, September 1938

History teaches that while EMPIRES are conquered by force of arms, they are nevertheless maintained by prestige. And to have prestige it is necessary to develop a clear racial consciousness which establishes not only the sharpest differences between races, but also levels of superiority.

SOURCE 11.8 Mussolini commenting to friends in 1938

Race, it makes me laugh. But there are reasons of state which I must obey. In Italy racialism and anti-semitism are being made to appear as important politically as they are unimportant in real substance. The racial purity of this nation over which have passed so many invasions and which has attracted so many peoples . . . is clearly absurd.

SOURCE 11.9 The attitude of the Catholic Church

a) *L'Osservatore Romano*, 1924
   The Jew is the most tenacious enemy of Christianity.

b) **Pope Pius XI**, 1938
   Catholic means universal; it is not racist, NATIONALIST or separatist. Why, unfortunately, did Italy have to go and imitate Germany?

CHART IIC Jews in Fascist Italy

183

The position of Jews in the 1920s–mid-1930s

- About 50,000 Jews in Italy
- Hundreds of Jewish refugees moved to Italy.
- In 1938 10,000 were members of PNF.
- There were two Jewish government ministers: Finzi, Interior Undersecretary and Member of Fascist Grand Council 1922–24; and Jung, Finance Minister 1932–35.
- Mussolini had two Jewish mistresses.
- Mussolini criticised Hitler's anti-semitism.

However,

- Some Fascists, e.g. Farinacci, were anti-semitic.
- Mussolini occasionally made anti-semitic comments. These were 'ideological racism', i.e. criticising Jews for their beliefs or actions (e.g. that they were anti-nationalist) not 'biological racism', i.e. attacking Jews as inherently (biologically) inferior.

The position of Jews from 1935

- 1935 attack on Abyssinia and proclamation of the Empire encouraged development of racism to justify and buttress imperial control.
- 1936 decrees banning mixing of races in Abyssinia
- 1936 Axis alliance with Nazi Germany
- July 1938 Propaganda Ministry published MANIFESTO of Italian Racism.
- 1938 Racist decrees:
- – Jews banned from mixed marriages
- – No Jews in state service, e.g. civil service, schools, military (though exceptions were granted, mainly on grounds of previous war service)
- – No Jewish children in state schools
- – Jews not to have Aryan servants
- – Jews not allowed to own large firms
- – Foreign Jews expelled

Reasons for racist decrees

- Mussolini's desire to emulate (keep up with) Hitler; to strengthen the Axis
- Development of racist feelings during Abyssinian campaign
- Several Jews were prominent in the international campaign for sanctions against Italy over its attack on Abyssinia.
- Jews involved in some opposition groups, e.g. Rosselli brothers (see page 185)
- Implicit in Fascism as it developed in the 1930s and became more radical, with the Reform of Customs, were attacks on the bourgeoisie, a greater attempt to create a 'new Fascist man', and hostility to the BOLSHEVISM, INTERNATIONALISM and materialism associated with Jews.
- Internal pressure from Fascist radicals, e.g. Farinacci

Effects of anti-semitic measures

- Resented by many; unpopular; seen as Mussolini kowtowing to Hitler
- Along with Reform of Customs, turned many influential Italians against the regime
- Pope publicly critical; King privately
- One in twelve university teachers sacked
- Not properly enforced: Italian forces occupying captured territory, e.g. Nice, 1940, hindered Nazi attempts to deport Jews to extermination camps.
- German occupation in 1943 led to 9000 Jews being sent to extermination camps.

Significance of measures

- Show how Mussolini was coming under German influence
- Show harmful effects of Abyssinian campaign
- Show radicalisation of Fascist regime in the late 1930s
- Show limited impact of Fascism
- Contributed to declining support for Mussolini

SOURCE 11.10 A racist notice ('This shop is Aryan')

SOURCE 11.11 A cover of the newspaper *The Defence of the Race*

184

HOW EFFECTIVE WAS MUSSOLINI'S RADICALISATION OF THE REGIME IN THE LATE 1930S?

C Review: How effective was Mussolini's radicalisation of the regime in the late 1930s?

Other policies also reflected a greater attempt to fascistise the Italian people. A full Ministry of Popular Culture was created in 1937, and youth movements were placed under Fascist Party control with the creation of GIL. The Fascist School Charter of 1939, and the vast expansion of OND and the attempt of this and welfare and women's organisations to 'Go to the People' illustrated greater stress on creating a more committed nation of Fascists.

Mussolini began to talk more to his colleagues about replacing the MONARCHY, and became less concerned with appeasing the Church. In 1939 the new Chamber of Fasces and Corporations replaced the old Parliament. All this illustrates the shift of emphasis in the regime, from measures geared to reassure the elite to ones designed to strengthen contact with the masses.

However, this attempt at radicalisation was not accepted by the Italian people. The abolition of the handshake, the efforts to change the language and the introduction of goose-stepping were regarded with a mixture of hilarity and irritation by the greater part of the Italian population.

The anti-semitic decrees were also not popular, and were not properly enforced. It was only after Mussolini's overthrow in 1943, when the Germans took over northern Italy, that Italian Jews were sent to extermination camps.

Radicalisation did, however, along with the regime's growing links with Nazi Germany, serve to arouse concern amongst the elite about the direction of the regime. Doubts were raised as to whether Mussolini was the best protector of their interests. These concerns were to escalate during the Second World War.

Key points from Chapter 11

1 In the late 1930s Mussolini introduced the Reform of Customs to try to toughen up the Italian people.
2 He was also disillusioned with the way the bourgeoisie were not fully embracing Fascist ideals.
3 This was part of a broader radicalisation of the regime.
4 In practice the Reform of Customs brought only superficial changes to society.
5 Italy was not traditionally an anti-semitic country.
6 Racism began after the conquest of Abyssinia.
7 In 1938 it developed into anti-semitic legislation, which was partly imitation of Nazi Germany.
8 Anti-semitism only had a major impact when the Nazis occupied Italy from 1943.
9 The introduction of anti-semitic policies further alienated the elite from the regime, and was generally unpopular.
10 The Reform of Customs and anti–semitism illustrate how the regime was losing touch with the Italian people by the late 1930s.

How much opposition was there in Fascist Italy?

FOCUS ROUTE

Answer the following questions as you study Chapter 12:
1 List the various forms of opposition that occurred.
2 Which type of opposition do you think posed the greatest danger to the regime?
3 Why was opposition to Fascism in the end too weak to pose a major threat?

■ Activity

Make a preliminary list of the forms of opposition you might expect to find operating in Fascist Italy.

CHART 12A   CHAPTER OVERVIEW

12 How much opposition was there in Fascist Italy?

A What forms did opposition take? (pp. 185–87)

B Why was there so little effective opposition in Fascist Italy? (p. 188)

A   What forms did opposition take?

Opposition to Mussolini's regime showed itself in many different forms but this must not lead us to overestimate its effectiveness.

The stories of some of the people who opposed the regime illustrate the bravery but perhaps the futility of their attempts.

You have already studied what happened to Matteotti. His colleague Amendola also died as a result of being beaten by Fascist squads, as had about 2000 others in the struggles between SOCIALISTS and Fascists in the years 1919–22. There were other brave individuals, such as the two below.

The Rosselli brothers

Carlo (born 1899) and Nello Rosselli (born 1900) came from a wealthy Tuscan Jewish family. After a period in the army and university, both became lecturers. They became increasingly horrified by Fascist violence. Carlo was more RADICAL politically; he joined the PSI, and after 1922 participated in various anti-Fascist organisations, and spread anti-Fascist propaganda. He helped opponents escape to exile, but was arrested in December 1926. Sentenced to five years' imprisonment on Lipari island, he escaped in July 1929, and fled to Paris. Nello was also briefly arrested in 1927, and remained under police surveillance.

In Paris Carlo helped set up the radical anti-Fascist group Justice and Liberty (GL). This publicised conditions in Italy, smuggled propaganda leaflets into Italy, and helped secret activity there. When the Italian government sent troops to fight for Franco in the Spanish Civil War (see pages 222–23), he helped organise over 30,000 anti-Fascist Italians to join an anti-Fascist crusade in Spain. He made radio broadcasts to Italy about their struggle, claiming 'Today in Spain; tomorrow in Italy'. They helped inflict the defeat on Mussolini's troops at Guadalajara in March 1937. Rosselli publicised this humiliation, and helped provoke Mussolini's revenge. In June 1937 when Nello was visiting his brother they were both murdered by French Fascists, acting on Foreign Minister Ciano's orders.

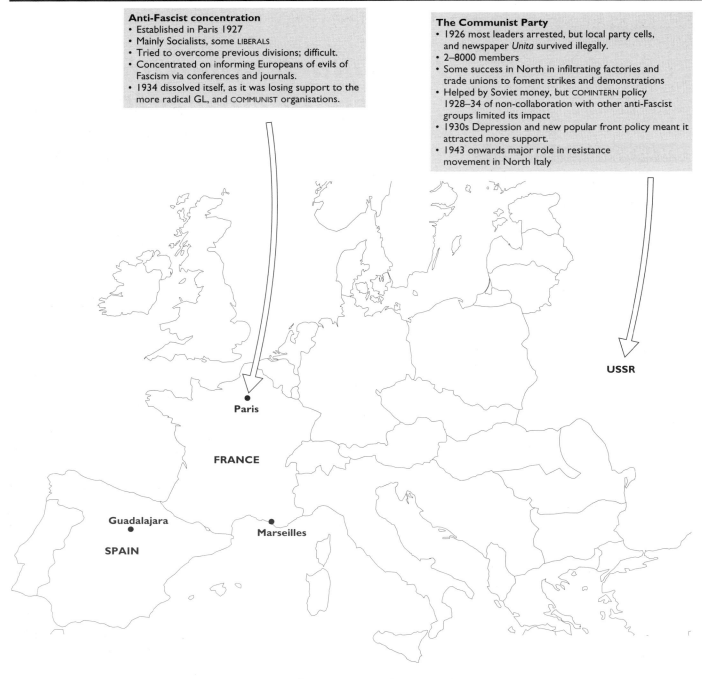

Anti-Fascist concentration
- Established in Paris 1927
- Mainly Socialists, some LIBERALS
- Tried to overcome previous divisions; difficult.
- Concentrated on informing Europeans of evils of Fascism via conferences and journals.
- 1934 dissolved itself, as it was losing support to the more radical GL, and COMMUNIST organisations.

The Communist Party
- 1926 most leaders arrested, but local party cells, and newspaper *Unita* survived illegally.
- 2–8000 members
- Some success in North in infiltrating factories and trade unions to foment strikes and demonstrations
- Helped by Soviet money, but COMINTERN policy 1928–34 of non-collaboration with other anti-Fascist groups limited its impact
- 1930s Depression and new popular front policy meant it attracted more support.
- 1943 onwards major role in resistance movement in North Italy

USSR

Paris

FRANCE

Guadalajara

Marseilles

SPAIN

Work in exile
- After 1924 many major politicians left Italy.
- Thousands of exiles (known as fuorusciti) publicised horrors of Fascism abroad, smuggled anti-Fascist literature into Italy, and planned for the overthrow of Fascism.
- From 1936 there were 3000 anti-Fascist volunteers fighting in Spain.
- Italian Garibaldi Legion defeated Italian Fascist troops at Guadalajara, March 1937.

■ **Talking point**

Is there ever justification for assassinating rulers? If so, under what circumstances?

The Church
- Despite the Concordat agreement, there was later criticism by the Catholic Church of Fascist pressure on Catholic Action (1931), and racist decrees (1938).
- Catholic Action organisations remained as potential rivals to Fascism.

The Fascist Party
- Fascism remained a diverse movement, and there was always simmering criticism from some, especially radicals, e.g. against the Concordat.
- 1943 majority of Grand Council voted to remove Mussolini from office.

The King
- Generally supportive; but privately expressed criticism of actions he saw as threatening his position, and various policies, e.g. racist decrees.
- July 1943 dismissed Mussolini.

Ethnic minorities
- Periodic protests, including bomb attacks and murders of policemen, at imposition of Italian language and culture on German and Slav minorities in Alto Adige and Venezia Giulia

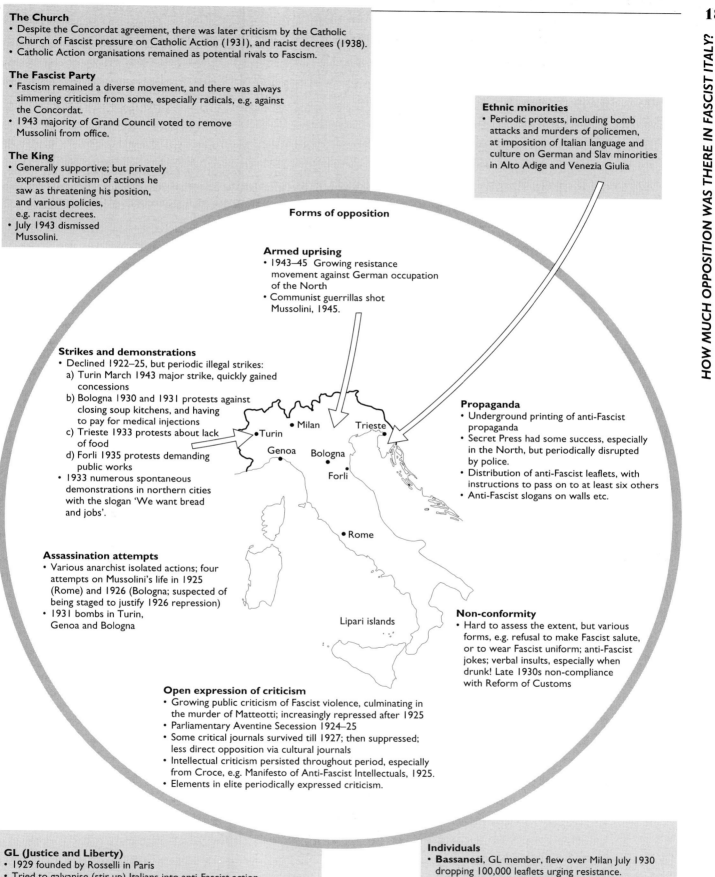

Forms of opposition

Armed uprising
- 1943–45 Growing resistance movement against German occupation of the North
- Communist guerrillas shot Mussolini, 1945.

Strikes and demonstrations
- Declined 1922–25, but periodic illegal strikes:
  a) Turin March 1943 major strike, quickly gained concessions
  b) Bologna 1930 and 1931 protests against closing soup kitchens, and having to pay for medical injections
  c) Trieste 1933 protests about lack of food
  d) Forli 1935 protests demanding public works
- 1933 numerous spontaneous demonstrations in northern cities with the slogan 'We want bread and jobs'.

Propaganda
- Underground printing of anti-Fascist propaganda
- Secret Press had some success, especially in the North, but periodically disrupted by police.
- Distribution of anti-Fascist leaflets, with instructions to pass on to at least six others
- Anti-Fascist slogans on walls etc.

Assassination attempts
- Various anarchist isolated actions; four attempts on Mussolini's life in 1925 (Rome) and 1926 (Bologna; suspected of being staged to justify 1926 repression)
- 1931 bombs in Turin, Genoa and Bologna

Non-conformity
- Hard to assess the extent, but various forms, e.g. refusal to make Fascist salute, or to wear Fascist uniform; anti-Fascist jokes; verbal insults, especially when drunk! Late 1930s non-compliance with Reform of Customs

Open expression of criticism
- Growing public criticism of Fascist violence, culminating in the murder of Matteotti; increasingly repressed after 1925
- Parliamentary Aventine Secession 1924–25
- Some critical journals survived till 1927; then suppressed; less direct opposition via cultural journals
- Intellectual criticism persisted throughout period, especially from Croce, e.g. Manifesto of Anti-Fascist Intellectuals, 1925.
- Elements in elite periodically expressed criticism.

GL (Justice and Liberty)
- 1929 founded by Rosselli in Paris
- Tried to galvanise (stir up) Italians into anti-Fascist action.
- Established underground network in Italy, but frequently smashed.
- After Rosselli brothers' murder, GL declined; then revived from 1943, during liberation struggle.

Individuals
- **Bassanesi**, GL member, flew over Milan July 1930 dropping 100,000 leaflets urging resistance. Major publicity coup for anti-Fascism.
- **De Bosis** taught himself to fly. On 3 October 1931 he dropped 400,000 leaflets over Rome telling people they should unite with the monarchy against Fascism.

B Why was there so little effective opposition in Fascist Italy?

SOURCE 12.1   Anti-Fascist Pento explained the problems he faced

I doubted that we could succeed. We were so few and the tyranny so strong and deeply rooted ... I did not know that there were many others ... who were struggling for the same idea.

Although there was a wide range of forms of opposition, and dissatisfaction increased in the late 1930s, they never posed a major threat to the regime. The regime was secure until its failures in the Second World War. The chief reasons for the comparative lack of opposition are well explained by the historians Clark and Thompson.

SOURCE 12.2   Thompson, p.32

In the absence of political and economic organisations which represented an alternative, opposing view of society to that imposed by Mussolini, the great majority of these individuals who were discontented found it expedient, indeed realistic, to adapt themselves to the changed circumstances of national life. Many simply withdrew into private life, compromising themselves minimally with the regime in carrying out the tasks required of them in their jobs or professions. They went through the necessary motions of acceptance in public but reverted to their habitual way of life behind closed doors or among friends.

SOURCE 12.3   Clark, pp. 252–53

Without institutions or organisations, the Italian anti-Fascists were ... sometimes infiltrated, usually persecuted, and always harmless ... Part of the explanation for the anti-Fascists' weakness lies in effective policing: Bocchini's [the chief of police's] informers were everywhere, and confino [imprisonment] or worse awaited dissidents. But perhaps the real reason for anti-Fascism's failure was that the Fascist regime seemed tolerable and was even popular, at least until 1937–38. It was careful not to alienate vested interests: even the workers had some safeguards, and journalists were flattered and bribed. Active resistance seemed pointless.

■ **Activity**

Study these three lists of problems facing potential opponents of a regime.

i) Strength of the government

- Strong repressive machinery
- Popular policies
- Propaganda
- Popularity of the leader

ii) Attitudes of ordinary people

- Mass apathy
- Careerism (concern to keep jobs)
- Reluctance to break the law
- Support for the government
- Fear of the government

iii) Practical problems

- Hard to organise meetings
- Hard to spread ideas

a) Referring back to work already covered, write a paragraph about how each of the points in list i) above helped reduce potential opposition.

b) It is harder to find firm evidence about the other points, but write a paragraph explaining why the points in lists ii) and iii) could also hinder opposition.

Key points from Chapter 12

1 Once Mussolini survived the Matteotti crisis, there was no major internal threat to the regime. The elite generally co-operated.

2 Fascist propaganda, Mussolini's popularity, policy successes and repression all served to reduce opposition.

3 Anti-Fascist groups in exile were relatively impotent. Mussolini survived a series of isolated assassination attempts.

4 Discontent with the regime grew in the late 1930s, but there was no major mass opposition until a series of strikes in 1943.

5 Mussolini was finally overthrown by the Fascist Grand Council and the King, not a mass movement.

The South and the Mafia: case studies in Fascist control

FOCUS ROUTE

As you read Chapter 13, consider the following questions:
1 Why did Fascism have a limited impact in the South?
2 How successful was Mussolini in breaking the power of the Mafia, and making all Italians identify with the Fascist state?

A Did Mussolini solve the Southern Problem?

Before we analyse Mussolini's success in creating a nation of Fascists let us challenge the DUCE head on, and see how successful he was in handling one of the most difficult obstacles to creating a fully unified Italy: the so-called Southern Problem.

To create a truly united nation of Fascists Mussolini would have to tackle the Southern Problem. Liberal Italy had failed to modernise this backward area which retained its own social structure and lifestyles. Any significant advances in the South would be regarded as a triumph for Fascism.

Fascism as a movement had never been strong in the South and in 1922 was virtually unknown in many areas. However, when the Fascists came to power they quickly attracted support from the southern ELITE, eager to maintain their local dominance. So they adapted to the new government (in a new version of TRASFORMISMO) and just put on blackshirts.

Some new policies filtered down to the South, but generally the impact of Fascism was very limited there. The South remained physically remote with poor communications and a lack of resources. Traditional rivalries and practices continued, with a Fascist veneer in the local administration.

Government policies had some impact, particularly on infrastructure, e.g. roads and harbours, but protection for grain production served to buttress the position of the LATIFONDISTI. Fascist institutions like ONB and OND were established in the region, but poor attendance at schools limited the regime's ability to MOBILISE children, and membership of OND was far lower in the South than elsewhere. Indeed, there was a sense of the regime washing its hands of the South as it actually banned discussion of the 'Southern Problem' and forbade damaging references in the press to poverty or crime.

What Fascism meant in the South can be well assessed from the eyewitness commentary, and the two historians' perspectives which follow.

■ **Activity**

1 Read Source 13.1. According to Levi, how did
   a) the gentry
   b) the peasants
   view the state?
2 Referring to the source's origin, content and tone, how reliable do you think it is as evidence of Italians' reactions?

SOURCE 13.1   An account of life in the South of Italy in the 1930s. Carlo Levi (writer, artist and anti-Fascist, who in 1943 became a COMMUNIST Senator) was sent to Lucania in 1933–35, and wrote of his experiences in *Christ Stopped at Eboli* (1944)

The gentry [lesser nobility] were all party members, even the few, like Dr Milillo, who were dissenters. The party stood for power, as vested in the government and the state, and they felt entitled to a share of it. For exactly the opposite reasons none of the peasants were members; indeed it was unlikely that they should belong to any political party whatever, should, by chance, another exist. They were not Fascists, just as they would never have been Conservatives or SOCIALISTS or anything else. Such matters had nothing to do with them; they belonged to another world and they saw no sense in them. What had the peasants to do with power, government and the state? The state, whatever form it might take, meant 'the fellows in Rome'. 'Everyone knows', they said, 'that the fellows in Rome don't want us to live like human beings. There are hailstorms, landslides, droughts, malaria and . . . the state. These are inescapable evils; such there always have been and there always will be. They make us kill our goats, they carry away our furniture, and now they are going to send us away to wars. Such is life!'

SOURCE 13.2   Tannenbaum, p. 203

The schools were most ineffective in the South and in Sicily and Sardinia, which remained the semi-colonial ghettos of the northern half of the country . . . The economic and cultural gap between these regions and the north was wider than ever.

SOURCE 13.3   J. Steinberg, 'Fascism in the South: The case of Calabria' in Forgacs (ed.), pp. 85, 105

Fascism failed, as had the movement to unify Italy before it and postwar DEMOCRACY after it, to change the way the region was governed . . .
  Fascism was imposed on the region, like the unification of Italy and like democracy after 1943, as something alien to be suffered passively.
  The great mass of the peasantry remained beyond the reach of Fascism. Speaking dialect, still largely illiterate, unable to understand the regime's sonorous [loud] slogans but certain they meant nothing but trouble, the peasants continued to exist as they had for centuries.

SOURCE 13.4   Poor southern farmers in the early part of the century

■ **Activity**

1 There is a Sicilian proverb, 'The husband is like the government at Rome, all pomp; the wife is like the Mafia, all power.' What does this suggest about Sicily?

2 What broader points about the nature of the regime emerge from this account of Fascism and the Mafia?

■ **Talking points**

1 Why do you think the Mafia has remained so powerful a force in southern Italian society?

2 Can you think of any other examples of top people getting away with activities while subordinates have been prosecuted?

SOURCE 13.5 Reported crime in Palermo province

	1922	1928
Homicides	223	25
Robberies	246	14
Extortions	53	16

B What happened to the Mafia?

In 1925 Mussolini sent the energetic PREFECT Mori to Sicily to smash the Mafia. Being informed that many ambushes occurred from behind high walls, he ordered all walls should be lowered to one metre within 24 hours! A further decree allowed the authorities to detain those with a questionable past. Mori rounded up hundreds of suspects, and laid siege to whole villages to catch fugitives. By 1928 the impact of this 'Battle against the Mafia' appeared impressive, as shown in the reported crime figures (see Source 13.5).

However, when Mori directed his inquiries towards some of the local pillars of the community who were involved in the Mafia, he was dismissed for fear of upsetting relations between the regime and Sicilian leaders. The government shied away from attacking the Mafia's top leaders; instead it concentrated on reducing the actions of its rank and file. After Mori's dismissal a less vigorous approach was pursued.

Mussolini had had to take on the Mafia because he could not tolerate competition for the control of violence, and the state had to maintain a reputation of strength by guaranteeing order. Overall, however, the Fascist regime largely attacked the outward manifestations (signs) of the Mafia, whilst leaving intact the basic network and social problems on which it thrived. Many Mafiosi just went underground. They re-emerged in 1943 and co-operated with the invading American forces, and were able quickly to resume their former influence.

What exactly is the Mafia?
The term 'mafia' is used worldwide for powerful criminal groups, but it originates in Italy. The term (meaning 'swank') was probably first used in Sicily in the 1840s for a number of rural bands successfully opposing the encroaching authority of the Naples government. It developed into a network of local bosses who used threats, violence, favours and political influence to dominate their local communities. Its fluid and unstructured composition enabled it to change its form and thereby survive the many threats it encountered, whereas a more rigid and unified organisation would have failed. It was based upon the strong family and clan links in the South. Mafiosi indulged in criminal activities, and used extortion, protection and ransom. The Mafia was protected by a code of silence reinforced by reprisals. It established close links with the local elite, and was used by the great landowners of Sicily to manage their estates.

A report in 1875 concluded that 'it is the development and perfection of strong-arm tactics aimed at all evil purposes; it is the instinctive, brutal, self-serving solidarity that brings together at the expense of the state, the laws and lawful organisations, all the individuals and social strata that prefer to derive their existence and their well-being not from work but from violence, deceit and intimidation'.

This hostile view underplays the social community aspect of the Mafia, which helps explain its strength. It acted in support of its members, and to establish its own view of 'justice' through direct action. Raimondo Catanzaro, the author of a major study of the Mafia, called his book *Men of Respect*.

When thousands of southern Italians emigrated to the USA, Mafia groups (also known as the Cosa Nostra – Our Affair) became established there.

The Mafia remains a major problem for Italian governments seeking to reform the South.

Key points from Chapter 13

1 Mussolini, just like other rulers, failed to tackle the major social problems of the South.

2 The regime made little impact on the lives of the southern peasantry.

3 The southern elite quickly adapted to the Fascist regime.

4 Mussolini proclaimed the battle against the Mafia.

5 Mafia activities were restricted but it survived underground and re-emerged as a powerful force in 1943.

Sections 2 and 3 Review: How successful was Mussolini in creating a nation of Fascists?

Now that you have studied how Mussolini secured his position and tried to create a nation of Fascists, you need to pull all this material together to assess the overall domestic impact of the regime. This review looks at how Italians responded to the Fascist regime, its impact on the class structure, the question of how far Fascism modernised Italy, and how TOTALITARIAN the regime was. You conclude your study with an essay on overall achievement.

SOURCE 1 A joke told in the early 1940s

Mussolini asked a friend, 'Tell me sincerely, what do the Milanese think? Don't hide anything.'

The friend answered: 'I'll be sincere: three-quarters are still SOCIALIST . . . of the other quarter, a good part are COMMUNISTS. The rest are Catholic.'

Mussolini slammed his hand on the table: 'By God, and the Fascists?'

'Oh, they are all Fascists.'

A How did Italians respond to the Fascist regime?

In many ways this joke (Source 1) provides some important clues about the extent to which Mussolini had managed to create a nation of Fascists. However, it is impossible to answer the question conclusively. There are always major problems when assessing popular reactions, and this is even more so in Fascist Italy. It was a DICTATORSHIP, so expression of opinion, certainly in public, was limited. The over 40 million Italians were divided by regional, class and gender differences, and experienced the regime in different ways. The experience of a schoolteacher in Milan would be very different to that of a peasant in Sicily. People also had different experiences at different times.

However, the historian's task (and yours!) is to try to put together a general picture, so to conclude this section we have reproduced some assessments from contemporaries.

■ Activity

1 Make and complete a chart like the one below about Italians' reactions to the regime.

   a) Row A lists their possible reactions. Row B requires you to fill in possible reasons for these reactions from the list below.

   - Not concerned with politics
   - Believed in the DUCE and Fascism
   - Wanted to keep their jobs and other benefits
   - Prepared to take risks to work for an alternative, better society
   - Critical of regime but realised it was difficult to do much.

   b) Then read the sources about Italians' reactions, and write the source number in the appropriate section of row C. (A single source may provide evidence of more than one reaction.)

A Reaction	Active commitment	Passive consent	Apathy	Passive opposition	Active opposition
B Reason					
C Source					

2 List the various reasons which emerge as to why the Fascist regime gained support.
3 How much active opposition do the sources suggest there was? Does this prove little *existed*?

193

HOW SUCCESSFUL WAS MUSSOLINI IN CREATING A NATION OF FASCISTS?

SOURCE 2 Statistical evidence

a) Results of PLEBISCITE on government list of candidates
1929 90% yes
1934 97% yes
The turn-out was 90%. Voters had to ask for a different-coloured ballot paper, depending on whether they were going to vote yes or no.

b) Membership of PNF
1933 1.4 million
1939 2.6 million
1943 4.8 million

c) Estimated number of political prisoners
About 5000 at any one time

d) Government expenditure on the police, including OVRA
1924–26 7.5% of state expenditure
1926–36 6.1%
1936–40 4.6%

◼ Talking point

In a regime that claims to be totalitarian, should non-involvement be acceptable?

SOURCE 5   A 1931 account from the British commentator B. King, *Fascism in Italy*

The crowds which cheered Mussolini's speeches in Tuscany and Lombardy last summer are quoted as evidence of his popularity among the masses; the reports did not mention that fifteen trainloads of Blackshirts followed him to swell and overawe the crowd, that workshops were closed and the men driven to meetings under pain of dismissal, that his arrival at each town was preluded by the arrests of suspects by the hundred.

SOURCE 7   A 1935 cartoon showing the French ELITE moving their gold (presumably to avoid taxation), while Italian women donate theirs to their country

SOURCE 3   Ordinary Italians recount their experiences

a) *Notwithstanding all the big talk about 'faith' in Fascist Italy, in the IMPERIAL destiny of the nation and in the 'Duce', what I saw every day was the wretched spectacle of a bunch of humble people who liked the quiet life adapting themselves to living from day to day without 'making waves'. They did this by donning the Fascist boots and uniform with no other preoccupation than keeping their position or acquiring some privilege that would allow them to live in a less sordid way and to be able to 'lord it' over people worse off than they were.*

b) *With the coming of Fascism my village was split in two. Fascism divided people; it ruined friendships. On one side there were the real Fascists and on the other there were those who were forced to be Fascists, the 'meal ticket' ones. Here in Barolo we were no longer free to say what we wanted. At the local [inn] we were always on our guard, we always looked round before we said anything; after all, it only needed a word out of place and you were in trouble.*

c) *Until my last year in high school ... I cannot say that Fascism was for me much more than a word. I lacked any sense of its opposite, the experience of a different reality.*

d) *We had to make Italy a great country. Get rid of the rich, do away ... with the cowards ... go to the people ... What youth with blood in his veins does not love to see justice where there is injustice, who does not feel love for his country, who does not feel himself shiver with pride if he is called to make history? These great, immense words – history, fatherland, justice – they filled us with enthusiasm.*

e) *Socialist mother of son joining the Balilla*
What can you do? His teacher is sold on Fascism. There's no way out. Better than having him fail a whole year.

f) *My wife's family were never really Fascist, but they accepted material help like coal, food and clothing from the Fascist social services.*

g) *What the Duce did wrong was the war – apart from that the government was all right, it was him that brought in the pension.*

SOURCE 4   Police reports

a) *Everyone belongs. Few, however, are really enthusiastic.*

b) *Until now Fascist penetration has been relatively ineffectual. On the other hand, we have only thirteen subversives on file, and they are constantly under surveillance.*

SOURCE 6   Mussolini saluting the crowds in Novara, Piedmont in May 1939

194

HOW SUCCESSFUL WAS MUSSOLINI IN CREATING A NATION OF FASCISTS?

■ **Activity**

Read the following historians' interpretations (Sources 8–12). What does each of them show about:

a) the degree of support for the regime and the reasons for it

b) the degree of criticism/discontent and the reasons for it

c) trends in support and reasons for this?

 ## How have historians judged Mussolini's success?

Responses to Mussolini's regime varied between Italians, and between different periods of the regime. Many historians, led by de Felice (see page 255), have argued that for the first half of the 1930s the Fascist regime was supported by a broad consensus, helped by the Concordat and success in Abyssinia. From 1936, closer links with Nazi Germany and more RADICAL domestic policies alienated not just many in the elite, but ordinary Italians. There is also considerable evidence that Fascism failed to win the commitment of the young, and failed to train a new elite to replace the ageing leadership. Many Italians, even PNF members, complained about corruption and the lack of a bold spirit in Fascist leaders.

One must also try to distinguish between Mussolini's popularity, broad support for the regime and commitment to Fascism. There is plenty of evidence that for much of the time Mussolini enjoyed great popularity, and that most Italians who had a view on politics supported the regime. Many took pride in Italy's foreign policy and sporting successes, and welcomed some of the services the state provided. However, as the poor response to the radical domestic and foreign measures of the late 1930s showed, they had not been transformed into the new Fascists that Mussolini had tried to create. For a time Mussolini had turned many Italians into a nation, but not a nation of Fascists.

SOURCE 8   C. Leeds, *Italy under Mussolini*, 1972, p. 95

During the late 1920s Fascism was widely accepted by the people who were pleased that it provided ordered rule and an end to class conflict. Many joined the party realising it offered special advantages ... The numerous colourful street parades and anniversaries gave many people opportunities to enter national self-admiration.

Industrialists enjoyed preferential treatment ... many workers and peasants were never reconciled to Fascism but because they were ill-prepared for a life in exile, they bided their time.

During the late 1930s open criticism of the Fascist regime became evident. People resented the increased interference in private life. They also resented the ANTI-SEMITIC laws and the close ties which Mussolini insisted on having with Hitler. The wealthy and industrial classes became irritated by the extravagance and bureaucracy of Fascism. Formerly it had been welcomed for its efficiency and ability to deal with strikes, but now it seemed corrupt and inefficient.

By 1939 most Italians were fed up with Mussolini and Fascism, although unable to find any way of overthrowing the government.

SOURCE 9   Tannenbaum, pp. 152, 167

Society [was] dominated by Fascist slogans if not by Fascist ideals ...

A large proportion of Italians of all ages were simply unable to grasp such abstract notions as the nation, the state, Fascism and the EMPIRE.

SOURCE 10   Clark, p. 247

Did all this Fascist effort at 'social control' work? The judicious historian gives a prosaic [dull] answer: yes and no. Yes, in the sense that until 1936 most people swallowed most of the propaganda most of the time, at a fairly superficial level. Italy was stable, the Duce was popular, open dissenters were rare. It made sense to go along with the regime, and patriotism is a natural feeling even in Italy. But there was little enthusiasm for Fascism – as opposed to patriotism or to Mussolinism – and the regime's claims to 'totalitarianism' were laughable. Religion, family sentiment, individual ambition and cunning, the parish pump [local concerns], the art of arrangiarsi [local fiddles or arrangements], all these traditional institutions and values survived and flourished. The Fascists totally failed to arouse warlike zeal among the general population, a failure which became very evident by the late 1930s. In short, there was acceptance but not devotion, consensus but not commitment, let alone 'hegemony'. Still, even the Fascist consensus was a great deal more than most Italian regimes had achieved. On balance the IDEOLOGICAL efforts paid off. It took years for most people to see through Fascism.

195

HOW SUCCESSFUL WAS MUSSOLINI IN CREATING A NATION OF FASCISTS?

SOURCE 11 Payne, p. 243

[By the late 1930s] public opinion and political support no longer had the same importance in Mussolini's thinking as they did during the first decade of the regime. He seems to have failed to notice the lack of response to more militant Fascist propaganda ... Younger Fascists grew more restive with anti-semitism and pseudo-Nazification. The increasing military activism was disconcerting and indeed frightening to millions of Italians, while conservatives had become increasingly sceptical ... There was no particular increase in political opposition ... What was developing was a growing uneasiness and a kind of internal psychological distancing from the radicalisation of Fascism. If the regime were to enjoy continued success in foreign and military affairs, and in economic growth, this psychological malaise might well be overcome; if not, it would continue to grow.

SOURCE 12 C. Ipsen, *Dictating Demography*, 1996, pp. 9–10, 12

Fascism did at times enjoy broad support among the Italian population, particularly at the moment of its greatest successes in foreign policy ... This consensus was pursued by propaganda, policy and new and old institutions intended to organise Italian society under Fascist authority ... When it came to test the depth of this consensus in opposing both the internal enemy, by means of racial policy, and the external one, the Italian population showed itself insufficiently committed to the Fascist vision and the fragility of the Fascist consensus became all too apparent ...

Ultimately the Italian Fascist revolution failed. Mussolini neither achieved a profound consensus, nor created a new civilisation, nor erected a totalitarian regime, [which shows] his failure to fascistise Italian society.

Perhaps we should leave the last words to Mussolini himself, by quoting comments he made during the Second World War.

SOURCE 13 Mussolini

a) *This war is not for the Italian people. They do not have the maturity or consistency for a test so grave and decisive. This war is for the Germans and the Japanese, not for us.*

b) *A people who for sixteen centuries have been an anvil cannot become a hammer within years.*

c) *A tenacious therapy of twenty years has succeeded in modifying only superficially the Italian character.*

d) *I must ... recognise that the Italians of 1914 were better than these. It is not flattering for the regime, but that's the way it is.*

FOCUS ROUTE

1 Make notes on the range of reactions to the Fascist regime.
2 What do they reveal about the extent to which Italians committed themselves to Fascism?
3 Essay: 'How successful was Mussolini in creating a nation of Fascists?'

196

HOW SUCCESSFUL WAS MUSSOLINI IN CREATING A NATION OF FASCISTS?

C What impact did Fascism have on the class structure?

For all its radical rhetoric, Fascism tended to reinforce the existing class structure rather than change it. There were two main reasons for this. Firstly, Mussolini realised his power rested on the support of the traditional elites, so he did not wish to threaten their position.

However, this needs to be modified for the later 1930s where a strong case can be argued that Mussolini then shifted his emphasis away from securing the interests of the elites, to trying to win the support of the masses. In many ways Mussolini was more naturally a man of the people than of the elites – so when he felt secure, by the 1930s, he became less influenced by the needs of the elites. Thus in the 1930s Mussolini embarked on policies which worried some powerful groups. However, such policies, whilst disturbing his former supporters, did not succeed in inspiring commitment from the masses.

The second reason for Fascism's limited impact on the class structure was Mussolini's priorities. As with his fellow dictator Hitler, Mussolini was more concerned with people's attitudes and behaviour than their social position. Fascism claimed to transcend class interests; it reconciled all Italians in one united nation. Class divisions were unimportant, so the existing class structure, now linked together in the Corporative State, would not be an obstacle to creating a united nation of Fascists.

D How far did Mussolini modernise Italy?

There has developed a lively debate amongst historians about the extent to which Fascism had a modernising impact on Italy. The American historian A. J. Gregor (in *Italian Fascism and Developmental Dictatorship*, 1979) argued that Fascism played a major role in modernising Italy. He cites the development of a mixed economy with the intervention of the IRI alongside private companies, land reclamation, the overall rate of economic growth, particularly in the electrical and chemical industries, and improvements in both agricultural and industrial productivity. Further evidence of modernisation is the 'nationalisation of the masses', helped by improved communications and new propaganda techniques, and the development of a system of state welfare and mass leisure. The advance of literacy and the growth of female employment have also been cited.

There were, however, clearly many features that were more conservative than modernising, such as the increased role of the Church, Fascist policies towards women, and the regime's pro-ruralism. Mussolini's initial compromise with the conservative elite who had helped him into power restricted the extent of institutional and social change. The limited impact of indoctrination, especially the failure of Fascism to penetrate the still numerically dominant peasantry, suggests limited modernisation. Gregor's optimistic assessment of the economy has also been challenged by evidence from a series of specialised studies. Fascist policies were essentially improvised, in a similar way to those of Liberal Italy, and not part of a clear modernisation programme. It has also been argued that many of the modernising trends had little to do with Fascism per se, and would have occurred anyway during such a long period.

FOCUS ROUTE

1 Draw up and complete a chart like the one below. Try to make some generalisations about which areas underwent most change, and which least.
2 The chart is necessarily a simplification, and highlights the contrast between pre-Fascist and late Fascist Italy. Were there periods of greater and lesser change between 1922 and 1940?
3 Use your change/continuity chart and other material to debate the proposition that 'Fascism had a major modernising effect on Italy'.

Change and continuity within Italy 1919–40

Area	Position in c1920	Position in c1940	Degree of change 1920–40
MONARCHY			
Parliament/elections			
Government			
Administrative structures			
Individual and group liberties			
Industry			
Agriculture			
Communications			
The South			
Position of women			
Living standards			
Education			
Church			
Sense of NATIONALISM/Fascism			
Others			

You might want to complete this comparative assessment by including military might, international prestige, extent of territory, etc. These are not particularly relevant for assessing domestic impact, but you might later like to round off your assessment of the degree of change during the period. This will require you to look at Chapters 14 and 15.

What was the totalitarian temptation?

Most of us nowadays react in horror against so-called totalitarian regimes, and assume that they must have been imposed on a frightened population. But Mussolini was proud of his totalitarian regime. Many people in the interwar period, suffering economic hardship and general disillusionment, were attracted to what has been called the 'totalitarian temptation'. This attractiveness but ultimate horror of totalitarianism has been well described by the Czech writer Milan Kundera (Source 14).

■ **Talking point**

To what extent does Fascist Italy illustrate the wisdom of Kundera's comment (Source 14)?

E How totalitarian was Fascist Italy?

Mussolini made great claims for the dramatic changes that had taken place. He claimed to have replaced a failed system with a new, vigorous Italy, organised in a totalitarian state. This implies that Fascism had a great impact. Your examination of Fascist Italy might suggest this was not the case.

So let us now examine how totalitarian Fascist Italy was. First we need to be clear about what this term means. Mussolini was the first major politician to use the term. In 1925 he spoke of Italy as 'everything within the state, nothing outside the state; everything for the state'. And in 1941 he defined it thus: 'The Fascist conception of the state is all-embracing; outside it no human or spiritual values may exist, much less have any value. Thus understood Fascism is totalitarian.'

Total state control of all aspects of a country is perhaps impossible to achieve. But historians have drawn up various criteria to help assess the extent to which a state is totalitarian (see Chart A).

This has become a very politicised issue. The term became widely used in the 1950s as a term of criticism of DICTATORIAL governments of both Right (Fascist Italy, Nazi Germany) and Left (the Soviet Union). In its classic 1950s formulation it was used to reinforce the view that the Soviet Union was as evil a regime as the recently defeated Nazi one. The use of the term in the context of the Cold War does not, however, invalidate it. It certainly can be of use in helping assess the nature of the Italian regime.

SOURCE 14   The writer Milan Kundera

Totalitarianism is not only hell, but also the dream of paradise – the age-old dream of a world where everybody would live in harmony, united by a single common will and faith . . .

If totalitarianism did not exploit these archetypes [standard feelings] which are deep inside us all . . . it could never attract so many people, especially during the early phases of its existence. Once the dream of paradise starts to turn into reality, however, here and there people begin to crop up who stand in its way, and so rulers of paradise must build a little gulag [prison camp] on the side of Eden [paradise]. In the course of time this gulag grows ever bigger and more perfect, while the adjoining paradise gets ever smaller and poorer.

■ **Activity**

Complete an assessment grid like the one below. In column 1, fill in the areas of totalitarianism as shown in Chart A. In the final column, give each aspect a mark out of five, five meaning strong evidence of totalitarianism, and 0 meaning strong evidence to the contrary.

Of course when considering this issue, you will need to take account of changes in the role of the state during the long Fascist era 1922–43. Did Fascist Italy become more or less totalitarian as it developed?

Refer back to material earlier in the book. You may also wish to complete the exercise on historians' views on totalitarianism (see below) before completing this exercise.

How totalitarian was Fascist Italy?

Area	Evidence that it was totalitarian	Evidence that it was *not* totalitarian	Overall assessment 5–0

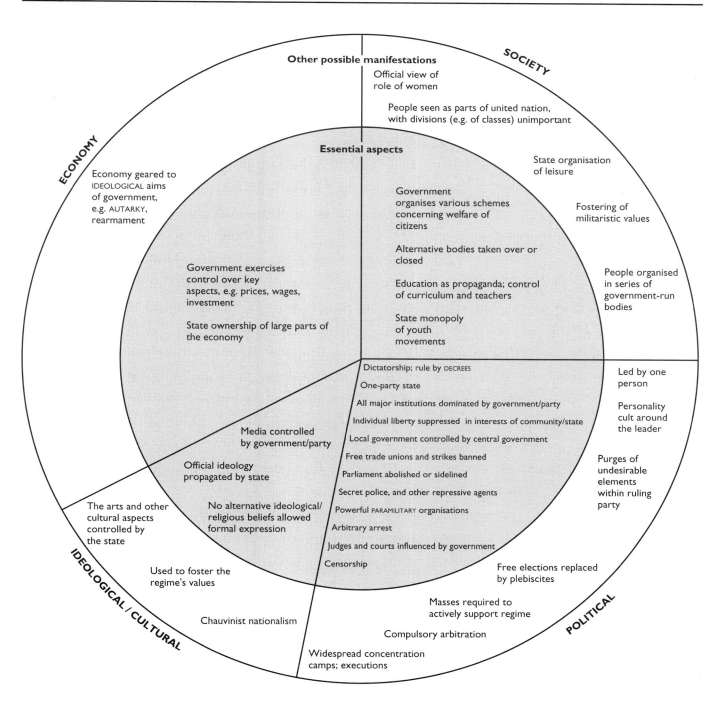

Other possible manifestations

SOCIETY

ECONOMY

Official view of
role of women

People seen as parts of united nation,
with divisions (e.g. of classes) unimportant

Essential aspects

State organisation
of leisure

Economy geared to
IDEOLOGICAL aims
of government,
e.g. AUTARKY,
rearmament

Government
organises various schemes
concerning welfare of
citizens

Fostering of
militaristic values

Government exercises
control over key
aspects, e.g. prices, wages,
investment

Alternative bodies taken over or
closed

People organised
in series of
government-run
bodies

Education as propaganda; control
of curriculum and teachers

State ownership of large parts of
the economy

State monopoly
of youth
movements

Dictatorship; rule by DECREES

Led by one
person

One-party state

All major institutions dominated by government/party

Personality
cult around
the leader

Media controlled
by government/party

Individual liberty suppressed in interests of community/state

Local government controlled by central government

Official ideology
propagated by state

Free trade unions and strikes banned

Purges of
undesirable
elements
within ruling
party

Parliament abolished or sidelined

The arts and other
cultural aspects
controlled by
the state

No alternative ideological/
religious beliefs allowed
formal expression

Secret police, and other repressive agents

Powerful PARAMILITARY organisations

Arbitrary arrest

Judges and courts influenced by government

Used to foster the
regime's values

Censorship

Free elections replaced
by plebiscites

IDEOLOGICAL / CULTURAL

Chauvinist nationalism

Masses required to
actively support regime

POLITICAL

Compulsory arbitration

Widespread concentration
camps; executions

Some points to consider in relation to Fascist Italy:
- Is a fully totalitarian regime possible?
- Is Mussolini's claim that Fascist Italy was a totalitarian state important
  in assessing the regime?
- Were there trends over time? Did the regime become more totalitarian?
- What happened to the position of the Church, monarchy, and the military
  and economic elites?
- Did the regime exercise the same degree of control
  over all groups/classes?

- Did the regime try to obliterate class differences, or just class
  consciousness?
- Was the old elite replaced by the Fascist regime or did it just adapt to it?
- Was Italy an AUTHORITARIAN rather than a totalitarian state?
- Was foreign policy used to enhance the power of the state?

200

HOW SUCCESSFUL WAS MUSSOLINI IN CREATING A NATION OF FASCISTS?

■ **Talking point**

The historians Griffin and Mack Smith have suggested that Fascist Italy was less totalitarian than Nazi Germany, partly due to character differences between Italians and Germans. Would you accept this view? Explain your answer.

How have historians judged the extent to which Fascist Italy was a totalitarian regime? Read the following historians' assessments of how totalitarian Fascist Italy was. In Source 17 the paragraphs are numbered for reference.

SOURCE 15   Leeds, p. 93

Fascism never did penetrate to the roots of Italian society. It was tolerable because it tended to be more satisfied by appearances than reality. Although the state was proclaimed 'totalitarian' it did not, in fact, achieve its aim of controlling all aspects of public and private life, and most people still kept considerable independence. It had to compromise with traditional forces. Various groups were neutralised, never destroyed or absorbed. They included the monarchy ... the military, the landowners, the industrialists and the Vatican.

SOURCE 16   Blinkhorn, p. 45

Fascism obtained power not through revolution but as the result of Mussolini's compromise with conservative and ostensibly [apparently] LIBERAL interests. Many of Fascism's activists achieved office, status and a measure of power within the regime which subsequently emerged, but the total revolution of which some dreamed never materialised. Instead, the regime evolved into one strongly Fascist in external appearances, limited in its supposed totalitarianism by the survival of AUTONOMOUS, mainly conservative forces, and distinguished by the personal power of its Duce. If Mussolini's regime may be said to have served the interests of his conservative allies in certain respects, this was neither deliberately and consistently intended nor necessarily bound to prove permanent. By the 1930s the decisions most liable to affect Italy's future lay in the realm of foreign policy and rested not in the hands of CAPITALISTS or militant Fascists but in those of Mussolini himself. It was those decisions, taken independently and increasingly against the wishes of his conservative fellow-travellers, that led to Mussolini's downfall and the collapse of Fascism.

SOURCE 17   Cassels, pp. 73–76

[1]   *Mussolini often used the word totalitarian, but it should be borne in mind that he normally did so in a limited sense. Thereby he meant no more than the supremacy of Fascist party organs in all walks of national life, especially economics. Up to a point, this goal was attained in Mussolini's one-party state. But to the social scientists who, in the aftermath of the Second World War, forged the theoretical construct of totalitarianism, mere ubiquitous party influence [reaching everywhere] was not enough. They postulated [put forward] other and more exacting criteria. By these standards it is generally conceded that the Italian Fascist state in several regards fell short of totalitarianism – certainly as it was conceived and practised contemporaneously in Hitler's Germany and Stalin's Russia.*

[2]   *The* Enciclopedia Italiana *itself, again under the heading of Fascism, offers a further test of totalitarianism: 'No individuals or groups (political parties, cultural associations, economic unions, social classes) outside the state.' But in fact, groups, classes, and institutions did maintain their identity in Fascist Italy. The most obvious were the Church and the monarchy. The most authoritative work on Italian Fascist totalitarianism, Alberto Aquarone's* L'organizzazione dello stato totalitario *(1965), states flatly: 'The Fascist state proclaimed itself constantly and with great vocal exuberance a totalitarian state; but it remained until the end a dynastic [monarchical] and Catholic state, and therefore not totalitarian.' In addition, behind the corporative facade the CONFINDUSTRIA and the LATIFONDISTI perpetuated their OLIGARCHY. The armed forces, too, especially the navy, kept a good measure of autonomy under Mussolini. (The civilian bureaucracy, on the contrary, fell pretty heavily under Fascist control.) The phenomenon of independent subgroups was illustrated in microcosm [on a small scale] in Sicily where the Fascists launched a drive against the local power structure, the Mafia. During the Fascist era, the Mafia was almost completely quiescent, and many Mafiosi enlisted in the Fascist Party. None the less, in July 1943 when the Allies landed in Sicily, the Mafia reemerged*

201

HOW SUCCESSFUL WAS MUSSOLINI IN CREATING A NATION OF FASCISTS?

■ End of Section test

(Marks are given in brackets.)
How totalitarian was Fascist Italy?

Read Source 15.
1 What important contrast in Fascist Italy does Leeds identify? [2]
2 Identify three words (two nouns, one verb) which illustrate the limited degree of control the state had. [3]
3 Which institutions illustrate this? [3]

Read Source 16.
4 Choose the one sentence which makes Blinkhorn's key point on the nature of the regime. [2]
5 How does he explain why this occurred? [2]
6 What is his explanation for the collapse of the regime? [3]

Read Source 17.
7 Paragraph 1. In what different ways has the word totalitarianism been used? [3]
8 Paragraph 2. Which groups/institutions does Cassels identify that illustrate limited totalitarianism? [3]
9 Paragraph 4. What else, besides control of groups/institutions, does Cassels argue totalitarianism requires? [3]
10 Did Mussolini succeed in this respect? [4]
11 Paragraph 5. What else, required for totalitarianism, was lacking in Fascist Italy? [3]
12 Paragraph 7. Why did Mussolini seek a totalitarian regime? [3]

Summary
13 Write down three key points arguing Fascist Italy was not fully totalitarian, and three that could be used as evidence of a considerable degree of totalitarianism. [6]

[Total: 40 marks]

into the open. In the western part of the island, it was influential enough to persuade most of the Italian troops to defy orders from Rome, and to lay down their arms to save the local villages from destruction.

[3] *Mussolini came to terms with these groups from the monarchy to the Mafia. But at most he neutralised them; he neither annihilated nor absorbed them. They outlived his regime, and their existence undercut the Fascist claim to totalitarianism.*

[4] *A totalitarian state cannot be content with outward conformity. If it were, it would be no more than a traditional caesarian dictatorship [like that of strong Roman rulers]. A totalitarian state requires the mental, not merely the physical, allegiance of its subjects. The dearth [lack] of popular enthusiasm behind Fascism's rise to power could be explained away; it was the function of an elite to appreciate the general will sooner than the multitude. But a totalitarian elite, once in power, had to convert the masses to its view of the general will. This was the purpose of all the indoctrination. Yet the Fascists failed to overcome the national trait of scepticism which had frustrated their* LIBERAL *forerunners; Mussolini himself sorrowfully admitted that a whole generation would have to pass before the 'new man' of Fascism could be manufactured in quantity. At the close of the Second World War, Germany endured the trauma [shock] of the Nuremberg Trials and denazification while Italy underwent only a mild dose of defascistizzazione. Many factors contributed to this distinction, but among them certainly was a tacit [silent] recognition that social conditioning in Fascist Italy, compared to that in Nazi Germany, had been a shallow and deficient process.*

[5] *The nature of the Fascist Italian consensus precluded [ruled out] totalitarianism in another respect. Dependence on a series of compromises with interest groups and fiancheggiatori (flankers), rather than on mass* MOBILISATION *and grass-roots enthusiasm, bred what one writer has called 'hyphenated Fascism,' a hybrid [cross-bred] phenomenon necessarily devoid of [lacking] a clear-cut ideology. A genuine totalitarian movement requires some quintessential [central] set of ideas to guide and justify all its actions, and it is difficult to isolate any such driving faith at the core of Italian Fascism …*

[6] *It may be appropriate to quote Hannah Arendt's verdict on Fascist Italy (1951): 'Not totalitarian, but just an ordinary nationalist dictatorship.'*

[7] *Indeed, since 1915, by far the most consistent thread running through Mussolini's career had been his attachment to the nationalist cause. One wonders, therefore, whether, for the Duce, totalitarianism was not so much an end in itself as an instrument in the service of Italian nationalism. Totalitarian unity at home was required because it was anticipated that the pursuit of a nationalist foreign policy would sooner or later involve Italy in war. Ironically, when that happened in 1940, the Second World War brutally exposed the shortcomings of Italian Fascist totalitarianism.*

202

HOW SUCCESSFUL WAS MUSSOLINI IN CREATING A NATION OF FASCISTS?

■ Activity

1 'Just 30 Seconds'
Do you know the popular radio game 'Just a Minute'? You're going to play that with Fascist Italy's domestic policy as your subject. We'll be kind and reduce your time to 30 seconds. You have to speak without hesitation, repetition or deviation on one of the following:

- The Concordat
- The PNF
- The Matteotti crisis
- Mussolini's domestic battles
- Autarky
- The Corporative State
- The Balilla
- The DOPOLAVORO
- Italian ANTI-SEMITISM.

2 Look at Chart B. Identify which features of Fascist Italy are shown.

FOCUS ROUTE

Concluding essay: 'The domestic achievements of Fascism in Italy were remarkably limited.' Discuss.

 # What was the overall impact of the Fascist regime?

In Section 2 you examined the impact the regime made on the political and economic structure.

In Chapters 4–6 you looked at the development of the political structure in Fascist Italy. Key points with which you should by now be familiar are:

- The important role of Mussolini himself
- The limited role of the Fascist Party
- The continuation of much of the traditional administrative structure
- The role of propaganda in sustaining the regime.

In Chapter 7 you looked at economic and social policy. Key points there were:

- General economic growth during the Fascist period, interrupted by the Great Depression
- The move towards autarky
- Increased government intervention in the economy
- The great claims but limited impact of the Corporative State
- The lack of major improvements in Italians' living standards.

In Section 3 (Chapters 8–13) you assessed the extent to which Mussolini succeeded in creating a nation of Fascists:

- How he used schools and youth movements to try, with limited effect, to create a new generation of Fascists
- The limited impact of Fascism's traditionalist policies on women
- The compromise the regime made with the Catholic Church
- How the state tried, with limited success, to change the behaviour of Italians
- The limited extent of opposition.

The Focus Route asks you to write an essay on domestic achievements. Before you can write your essay you must understand the title. In this particular example, there should be no words that cause problems. However, it is useful to try and paraphrase the question, to put it in your own words. It is clearly about what Mussolini did at home, and says his policies were not very successful. Obvious key words are domestic achievements and Fascism, but certain other words, which you might well skim over, are also important, e.g. 'remarkably' and 'limited'.

Thus the essay requires you to consider the following:

- What did Mussolini (and the Fascists; note the distinction) want to achieve?
- How did they try to achieve it? (The means employed often influence the result.)
- What did they achieve in the key areas (see above)? This should lead to consideration of how limited these achievements were.
- Were the limitations of their achievements remarkable? In other words, why might one have expected them to have achieved more (e.g. the length of their time in power)? Why, though, might one not be so surprised (e.g. size of inherited problems, the heterogeneous nature of Fascism, the degree to which the regime was a compromise with existing powers, etc.)?

Section

How significant was Mussolini's foreign policy?

SOURCE I Mussolini, December 1925

I consider the ... nation to be in a permanent state of war.

One of Mussolini's major priorities was to make Italy ready for war. His Fascist IDEOLOGY, in as much as it had any clear content, praised war as an ennobling activity. War would help strengthen the character of the Italian people. It would forge a strong nation, turn Italy into a major power and recreate the glories of the Roman EMPIRE.

Although Mussolini began his foreign policy in a generally cautious and traditional fashion, he made no secret of his grander aims. In this section we examine how, after much initial success, he led the Italian people into an increasing number of wars which culminated in his downfall.

As you study this section, bear in mind the central question:

- **How significant was Italian foreign policy? This will involve considering the effect it had on:**
  a) **the domestic strength of the regime**
  b) **Italy's world status and general international relations.**

Other important issues to consider are:

- **What were Mussolini's aims and methods?**
- **What role did Mussolini play in foreign policy?**
- **How far did Mussolini's foreign policy differ from earlier Italian policy?**
- **How far did**
  a) **Italy's resources and**
  b) **the international context**
  influence Italian foreign policy?

CHART A SECTION OVERVIEW

Section 4 How significant was Mussolini's foreign policy?

14 How successful was Mussolini's foreign policy 1922–39? (pp. 208–37)

15 Why did Mussolini's regime lose the war and collapse? (pp. 238–51)

Review: How significant was Mussolini's foreign policy? (pp. 252–53)

■ Activity

Study Sources 1–10 to establish some key features of Mussolini's policies.

1 What evidence is there of the following aspects?
   a) The importance Mussolini placed on foreign policy
   b) Mussolini's desire to live up to the glories of the Roman Empire
   c) His aim to assert Italy's role in the world
   d) An ideological element in Mussolini's foreign policy
   e) Mussolini's link with Hitler, and how this developed
   f) The different methods he used
   g) The overambitious nature of Mussolini's foreign policy

2 Using the symbols in Chart C to guide you, identify how Mussolini's methods in foreign policy appear to change over time.

SOURCE 2 Mussolini announcing victory in the Abyssinian War, May 1936

SOURCE 3 Mussolini speaking about foreign policy

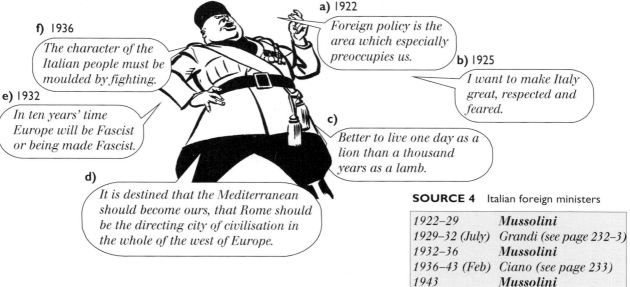

f) 1936
The character of the Italian people must be moulded by fighting.

e) 1932
In ten years' time Europe will be Fascist or being made Fascist.

d)
It is destined that the Mediterranean should become ours, that Rome should be the directing city of civilisation in the whole of the west of Europe.

a) 1922
Foreign policy is the area which especially preoccupies us.

b) 1925
I want to make Italy great, respected and feared.

c)
Better to live one day as a lion than a thousand years as a lamb.

SOURCE 4 Italian foreign ministers

1922–29	**Mussolini**
1929–32 (July)	Grandi (see page 232–3)
1932–36	**Mussolini**
1936–43 (Feb)	Ciano (see page 233)
1943	**Mussolini**

SOURCE 5 A photomontage of Italian troops marching past a statue of the Roman emperor Augustus

SOURCE 6 A 1936 cartoon showing Mussolini as a wolf. The other figures are (left to right) the rulers of Germany (Hitler), Turkey (Atatürk), Greece (Metaxas), Spain (Franco), and the British Fascist Oswald Mosley

SOURCE 7   A 1938 Italian postcard celebrating the alliance between Hitler and Mussolini

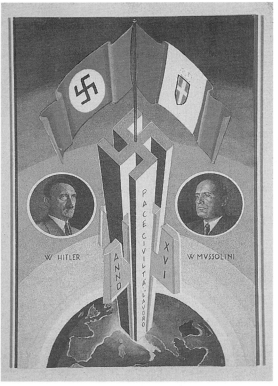

SOURCE 9   A 1936 Russian cartoon of Hitler and Mussolini

SOURCE 8   A June 1940 cartoon by David Low entitled 'The Dream and the Nightmare'

SOURCE 10   Mussolini and Hitler at the Munich Peace Conference, 1938. The other figures (left to right) are British and French Prime Ministers Chamberlain and Daladier, and Ciano

CHART B   Mussolini's foreign policy: the main places

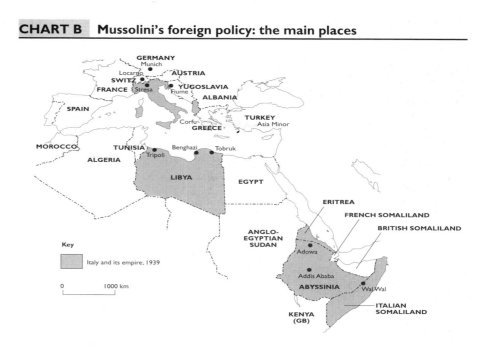

Key

▨ Italy and its empire, 1939

0 ____ 1000 km

CHART C   Timeline 1922–45

Oct 1922	Mussolini becomes Prime Minister
Aug 1923	Italy bombards the Greek island of Corfu 👤👤
Jan 1924	Italy gains the disputed port of Fiume 🐟
Oct 1925	Italy signs the Locarno Treaties, guaranteeing Germany's western borders 🐟
1926	Italy brings Albania under Italian control as a protectorate 👤
1927	Mussolini encourages Croatian separatists who want to break away from the new Yugoslav state ⁄
1928	Mussolini encourages Arab nationalists challenging the British and French Empires ⁄
1929	Mussolini encourages Macedonian separatists in Yugoslavia ⁄
1932	Italian colony of Libya is finally subdued after a thirteen-year campaign 👤👤
Jan 1933	Hitler becomes Chancellor of Germany
July 1933	Mussolini proposes Four-Power Pact 🐟
July 1934	Italy sends troops to protect Austria from the threat of Nazi takeover 👤
Apr 1935	Italy attends Stresa Conference to discuss measures against Germany's rearmament 🐟
Oct 1935	Italy invades Abyssinia 👤👤👤
May 1936	Italy conquers Abyssinia 👤👤👤
July 1936	Italy intervenes, alongside Germany, to help the conservative General Franco against the Left in the Spanish Civil War. The war goes on till 1939 👤👤👤
Oct 1936	Italy joins the Axis agreement with Germany 🐟
Nov 1937	Italy joins the Anti-Comintern Pact with Germany and Japan, directed at the USSR 🐟

Dec 1937	Italy withdraws from the League of Nations 🐟
Sept 1938	Mussolini attends the Munich Conference which prevents war over Nazi claims on Czechoslovakia 🐟
Apr 1939	Italy invades Albania 👤👤👤
May 1939	Italy and Germany sign the Pact of Steel military alliance 🐟
Sept 1939	Italy stays out of the Second World War
June 1940	Italy declares war on France and Britain 👤👤👤
Sept-Oct 1940	Italy invades Egypt and Greece 👤👤👤
June 1941	Italy declares war on the USSR 👤👤👤
Dec 1941	Italy declares war on the USA 👤👤👤
1942	Italy suffers major losses in Africa 👤👤👤
July 1943	Southern Italy is invaded by the Allies 👤👤👤
	Mussolini is overthrown
	Germans take control of North Italy
	Mussolini becomes the puppet leader of the German satellite Salo Republic in North Italy
Apr 1945	Mussolini is killed by Italian Communist guerrillas

Key

👤 Deployment of troops, but no actual fighting

👤👤 Use of troops; some violence

👤👤👤 War

🐟 Diplomacy, supporting the status quo

🐟 Diplomacy, to change the status quo (revisionist)

⁄ Attempt to undermine a foreign regime

How successful was Mussolini's foreign policy 1922–39?

CHART 14A   CHAPTER OVERVIEW

14 How successful was Mussolini's foreign policy 1922–1939?

A The nature of Mussolini's foreign policy 1922–39 (pp. 208–11)

B Key events in Italy's foreign policy (pp. 212–13)

C What were the effects of the Abyssinian War? (pp. 214–20)

D Was Mussolini's intervention in the Spanish Civil War a success? (pp. 221–23)

E 'The fatal friendship'. Why, and with what effects, did Mussolini ally with Hitler? (pp. 224–33)

F Why didn't Italy enter the Second World War in 1939? (pp. 234–35)

G Review: How successful was Mussolini's foreign policy 1922–39? (pp. 236–37)

A   The nature of Mussolini's foreign policy 1922–39

Mussolini's foreign policy aims sounded grand and far-reaching but most of them were not totally new. Furthermore, like all leaders he had to work in the environment in which he found himself. Initially, he relied on the foreign office staff he inherited (Contarini as Foreign Ministry Secretary-General, for example). They shared his belief in Italy's right to gain territory and spheres of influence in the Eastern Mediterranean and in Africa. Mussolini's style might be different, but the actual substance would be along familiar lines. By the 1930s, however, Mussolini became less restrained, and pursued a more assertive policy. He was convinced the future lay with 'young', virile states like Italy and Germany, and not 'decadent' ones like Britain and France. From the mid-1930s he took what he saw as good opportunities at last to establish Italy as a major power.

Study Charts 14B and 14C to discover what else, besides the leader's aims, would determine the nature of Italy's foreign policy.

■ Activity

1 Below are six objectives for Mussolini's foreign policy. Discuss which you think would be easiest, and which hardest to achieve.
   a) Building national prestige
   b) Increasing domestic support for the regime
   c) Gaining dominance over the Balkans
   d) Achieving dominance in the Mediterranean
   e) Establishing an EMPIRE
   f) Spreading Fascism abroad
2 How different do these seem compared to the foreign policy aims of Liberal Italy? (Refer back to page 15.)

I

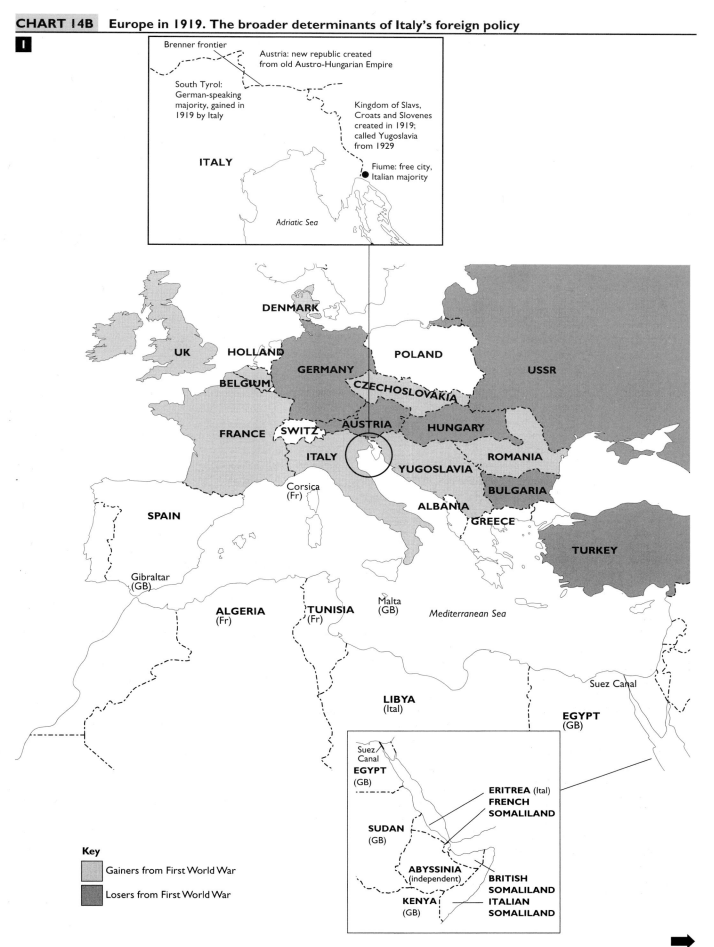

Brenner frontier

Austria: new republic created
from old Austro-Hungarian Empire

South Tyrol:
German-speaking
majority, gained in
1919 by Italy

Kingdom of Slavs,
Croats and Slovenes
created in 1919;
called Yugoslavia
from 1929

ITALY

Fiume: free city,
Italian majority

Adriatic Sea

DENMARK

UK

HOLLAND

POLAND

USSR

GERMANY

BELGIUM

CZECHOSLOVAKIA

FRANCE

SWITZ

AUSTRIA

HUNGARY

ITALY

YUGOSLAVIA

ROMANIA

Corsica
(Fr)

BULGARIA

ALBANIA

SPAIN

GREECE

TURKEY

Gibraltar
(GB)

ALGERIA
(Fr)

TUNISIA
(Fr)

Malta
(GB)

Mediterranean Sea

LIBYA
(Ital)

Suez Canal

EGYPT
(GB)

Suez
Canal

EGYPT
(GB)

ERITREA (Ital)
**FRENCH
SOMALILAND**

SUDAN
(GB)

ABYSSINIA
(independent)

**BRITISH
SOMALILAND**

KENYA
(GB)

**ITALIAN
SOMALILAND**

Key

Gainers from First World War

Losers from First World War

HOW SUCCESSFUL WAS MUSSOLINI'S FOREIGN POLICY 1922–39?

2

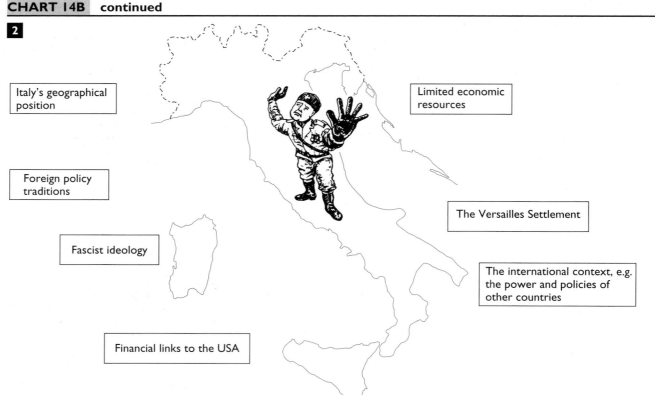

Italy's geographical position

Limited economic resources

Foreign policy traditions

The Versailles Settlement

Fascist ideology

The international context, e.g. the power and policies of other countries

Financial links to the USA

■ Activity

1 Identify:
   a) countries which gained from the peace treaties
   b) countries which lost territories from them.
2 List what Italy gained from the settlement, and what it claimed and failed to get. (Refer back to page 26.)
3 Some countries' attitudes towards the Versailles Settlement are described as 'conservative', and some as 'REVISIONIST'. What do you think is meant by these terms?
4 Which term, if any, would best suit Italy's attitude? Why?
5 Study the map in Chart 14B. Why might Italy be particularly interested in the following areas?

   a) Austria
   b) The Balkans
   c) The countries around the Mediterranean Sea
   d) Abyssinia
6 How would you expect Mussolini to react to the following situations:
   a) The murder of Italians working in a foreign country
   b) An attempt by Germany to incorporate Austria
   c) Condemnation of Italy for aggression by the League of Nations
   d) A RIGHT-WING revolt against a SOCIALIST government in a country bordering the Mediterranean?

■ Activity

1 Explain Graham's view of Mussolini's probable foreign policy.
2 How useful is such a source to the historian?

■ Talking point

Do you think a country's foreign policy should just be based on 'sacred egoism' (self-interest)?

SOURCE 14.1   Sir Ronald Graham, British ambassador in Rome, in dispatches to the British government

a) January 1923

To understand the situation here one must remember that omnipotent [all-powerful] as [he] is, his position is full of difficulty and some striking success in foreign policy is of vital importance to him . . . He is having serious trouble with sections of his own followers . . . In any case his foreign policy will be pure OPPORTUNISM, and Italian friendship is on offer to the highest bidder. My impression is that he would prefer to work with Great Britain, at a price . . . It is a policy of sacred egoism carried to extremes. Possible economic necessities of Italy and those of his own political position afford some extenuating [justifying] circumstances.

b) June 1923

It must be remembered that Italian foreign policy is not based upon principles similar to those which actuate His Majesty's Government. It is frankly opportunistic and egotistic . . . Signor Mussolini . . . has proclaimed from the first, and has since emphasised it, that his foreign policy will be in the sole interests of Italy and one of 'nothing for nothing'.

■ **Talking point**

What do you understand by the term 'balance of power'?

Italy's 'makeweight' policy
Ever since Italy was unified, it had tried to establish its status as a great power. Its limited economic and military resources made this difficult. Many Italian statesmen realised Italy's best strategy for making territorial gains was to exploit the rivalry of the major powers and their alliances. Italy could offer to join one side or the other in return for concessions. This required a rough balance of power between rival blocs in which Italy's intervention could determine the outcome. This policy, classically favoured by Mussolini's most able diplomat Grandi, was known as the 'determining weight' or 'makeweight' policy.

■ **Activity**

Study Chart 14C. In which situation, 1 or 2, might Italy be able to assert more influence? Explain your answer.

The chart below tries to represent the relative position of the major powers in Europe, first in the 1920s, then in the mid-1930s.

CHART 14C   Europe in the mid-1920s (1) and the mid-1930s (2)

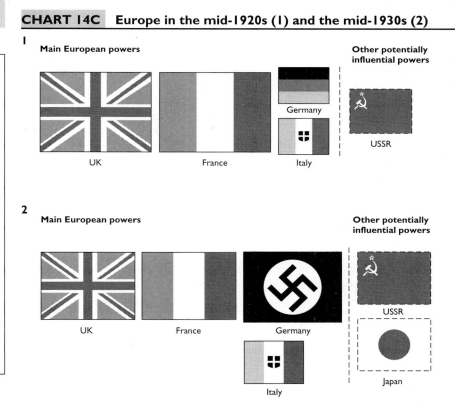

Explanation

1 1920s
   a) Germany was potentially powerful, but was hemmed in by the newly imposed Versailles Settlement.
   b) The USSR was initially involved in civil war, and was then trying to recover.

2 1930s

   a) Britain was weaker because it was overstretched. France was politically weak, with unstable governments and political divisions.

   b) Germany had been rearming despite Versailles; and was now led by a determined NATIONALIST, Hitler, who aimed to reassert German might.

   c) Italian rhetoric suggested it was a great power; but reality showed otherwise.

   d) France and Britain were becoming more concerned about the growing might of the USSR, and of the threat to their empires in the East from militaristic Japan.

B Key events in Italy's foreign policy

Mussolini's war with Abyssinia in 1935 is often regarded as the pivotal point in his foreign policy. We will study this event in detail, but meanwhile it will be helpful to gain an overview of Mussolini's foreign policy up to 1939. We have divided the period in two, separated by the crucial Abyssinian War.

■ Activity

1 These two pages explain the key events in Italian foreign policy 1922–39. You will find an imaginary Italian headline for each event.
   Write a hostile headline to counter each Fascist one.
2 Use as many historians' accounts as possible to do detailed research on one of the events in foreign policy 1922–39. Make notes as described below. Be prepared to report your findings to the rest of the class.
   Events 8, 9 and 10 are studied in depth later in this chapter.

Making notes
As you look at each event, examine the following key areas for historical enquiry:
- **What** happened?
- **Why?**
- **How** successful was it for Italy?

These will all help you to assess its historical **significance**.

1922–35 Most of the events in this period can be seen as relatively minor affairs, which were presented by the regime's propaganda as great successes. Undoubtedly, however, they helped to consolidate Mussolini's domestic position and created an image, more myth than reality, of a new Italy as a rising great power.

1
Mussolini shows you don't mess with Italy
Corfu 1923 – Mussolini forces compensation payment from Greece
An Italian official was killed whilst trying to resolve a Greek–Albanian border dispute. Mussolini demanded that Greece should apologise, and pay 50 million lire [around £25 million today] in compensation. Greece was conciliatory but Italy invaded Greek Corfu. The League of Nations condemned Italy and demanded its withdrawal. Britain threatened naval intervention, and Mussolini withdrew after Greece paid the 50 million lire. Italian propaganda proclaimed the incident a great success!

2
At last, Italy gains its beloved port
Mussolini gains Fiume, 1924
Mussolini sent an Italian military commander to rule the disputed territory of Fiume. In January 1924 Yugoslavia agreed to give Fiume to Italy. This was portrayed as another great Italian success, but Fiume's importance as a port gradually declined as Yugoslavia developed a rival port, Split.

3
Mussolini resolves European frontiers
The Locarno Pacts, 1925; Mussolini guarantees Germany's western borders
Mussolini was persuaded to attend the Locarno meeting and join Britain in guaranteeing the Locarno Pacts whereby Germany, France and Belgium accept their existing boundaries. Mussolini's attempt to get Italy's Brenner border with Austria included in the guarantee failed.

4
Italy gains client state
Albania becomes an Italian protectorate, 1926
Mussolini extended Italian influence and declared Albania an Italian PROTECTORATE.

5
Mussolini brings all major powers together
Four-Power Pact, 1933
The leaders of Germany, Britain, France and Italy met in Rome. Mussolini hoped to build a rival to the League of Nations to sort out European affairs. Four-power co-operation and spheres of influence, with agreed revisions, were discussed. This was portrayed by the Italian press as displaying Italy at the centre of European diplomacy, but nothing concrete came of the meeting.

6
Mussolini saves Austria
Mussolini warns Hitler to stay out of Austria, 1934
Austrian Nazis, wanting union (Anschluss) with Germany, assassinated Austrian Chancellor Dolfuss. Mussolini MOBILISED his troops on Italy's Austrian border and claimed that this deterred Anschluss. Hitler was probably not intending to take over Austria then anyway.

7
Mussolini, Guarantor of European Order
Stresa Front, 1935. Mussolini is offered a free hand in Africa in return for support against the growing menace of Hitler
Britain, France and Italy protested against Hitler's rearmament, which violates the Versailles Settlement. They agreed to prevent any future changes in Europe. Mussolini believes he has French and British consent for expansion into Abyssinia.

1935–39 In this period Italy was at war virtually all the time. This ironically contributed to Mussolini's reluctant decision not to join Germany in war in 1939

213

HOW SUCCESSFUL WAS MUSSOLINI'S FOREIGN POLICY 1922–39?

8

Italian Empire established
October 1935–April 1936, Mussolini conquers Abyssinia
After a border clash with Abyssinia, Mussolini sent in troops. The League of Nations imposed some sanctions. These led to a growth of nationalist support for the war in Italy.
Britain and France failed to arrange a compromise. In May 1936 Italy defeated Abyssinia. King Victor Emmanuel was crowned Emperor of Abyssinia.

9

Mussolini leads anti-Bolshevik Crusade
Mussolini intervenes in the Spanish Civil War, July 1936
Mussolini sent planes and troops to help the nationalist General Franco's revolt against Spain's Socialist government. He expected a short war, but it lasted three years. Italian troops were defeated at Guadalajara, but eventually Franco won.

10

Italy and Germany unite to control the future
The Rome–Berlin Axis. Mussolini joins Hitler, 1936
Mussolini announced a 'Rome–Berlin Axis'. This was a vague alliance with no formal commitment. In November 1937 Italy joined Germany and Japan in the Anti-COMINTERN Pact, directed against the USSR.

11

A common border with our ally Germany
Mussolini accepts Hitler's invasion of Austria
In March 1938 Hitler gave Mussolini twelve hours' notice of his invasion of Austria. Mussolini accepted Anschluss. This was unpopular in Italy.

12

Mussolini, Arbiter of the World
Mussolini hailed as European peacemaker, Munich, September 1938
Mussolini took a high profile at the conference giving the Czech Sudetenland to Germany and averting the threat of European war, but really did little.

13

Major territorial gain in key area
Mussolini invades Albania, March 1939
Mussolini imitated Hitler's seizure of Czechoslovakia by invading Albania, which he already virtually controlled. King Zog fled, and there was little resistance.

14

Firm Treaty. Nothing can stop us now
Pact of Steel, May 1939. Two great countries joined together
Mussolini proposed a pact with Germany. They agreed to co-operate fully in the event of war. Italy said it would not be ready to fight until 1943, but this was not written into the agreement.

15

Italy awaits the right moment
September 1939. Italy declares herself non-BELLIGERENT
Mussolini accepted that Italy was not ready for war and stayed out of the Second World War.

FOCUS ROUTE

1 Having looked at the events of Mussolini's foreign policy in chronological order we will now reorganise our thoughts to assess them thematically. On your own copy of the table below, place the events in the correct place in the blank column. (Some events may appear more than once.)
   Events
   Fiume   Corfu   Austria 1934   Stresa   Abyssinia   Axis   Spain   Anti-Comintern Pact   Austria 1938
   Munich   Pact of Steel

Mussolini's foreign policy		Examples
Aims	• Search for empire	
	• Distraction from domestic problems	
	• Revising Versailles	
	• Revenge for earlier defeat	
	• Trying to match Hitler's success	
	• To put on a show	
	• Ideological	
Methods	• Use of troops	
	• Diplomacy	
Effects, Significance	• Increased domestic prestige	
	• Sacrificing Italy's real interests	
	• Waste of Italian resources	

2 'From Corfu to Stresa Mussolini's foreign policy was remarkably successful.' Explain with supporting evidence whether you agree with this comment on Italian foreign policy 1922–35.
3 Mussolini has been called a bully. What evidence is there for this?

As you study pages 214–20 make notes on the Abyssinian War focusing on:
a) why it happened
b) what Mussolini gained from the war
c) actual and potential problems resulting from the war.

C What were the effects of the Abyssinian War?

You have probably never been involved in a war. Nor have we. It was very different for Mussolini. War played a major part in his career. He had leapt to dominance in the Italian Socialist Party through his emotive opposition to the Libyan War. He then split with that party when he supported the First World War. He fought in that war, and founded the Fascist movement largely from rebellious fellow ex-combatants. Mussolini exploited the expectations, fears and turmoil caused by the First World War to gain power.

Given all this, it is perhaps surprising that Fascist Italy did not embark on a war until 1935. Most historians locate the reasons in the international context. But from then on, Italy was engaged in wars until 1945, with a brief interlude from July 1939 till June 1940. We will now explore two of Mussolini's wars which illustrate the benefits and the problems that war caused for the regime.

CHART 14D Timeline of the Abyssinian War

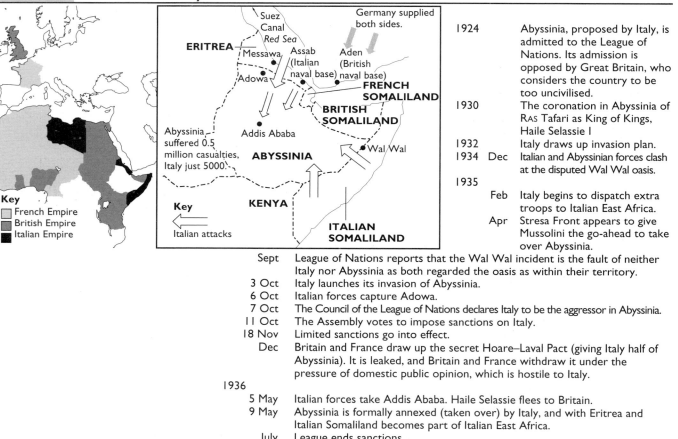

1924		Abyssinia, proposed by Italy, is admitted to the League of Nations. Its admission is opposed by Great Britain, who considers the country to be too uncivilised.
1930		The coronation in Abyssinia of RAS Tafari as King of Kings, Haile Selassie I
1932		Italy draws up invasion plan.
1934	Dec	Italian and Abyssinian forces clash at the disputed Wal Wal oasis.
1935		
	Feb	Italy begins to dispatch extra troops to Italian East Africa.
	Apr	Stresa Front appears to give Mussolini the go-ahead to take over Abyssinia.
	Sept	League of Nations reports that the Wal Wal incident is the fault of neither Italy nor Abyssinia as both regarded the oasis as within their territory.
	3 Oct	Italy launches its invasion of Abyssinia.
	6 Oct	Italian forces capture Adowa.
	7 Oct	The Council of the League of Nations declares Italy to be the aggressor in Abyssinia.
	11 Oct	The Assembly votes to impose sanctions on Italy.
	18 Nov	Limited sanctions go into effect.
	Dec	Britain and France draw up the secret Hoare–Laval Pact (giving Italy half of Abyssinia). It is leaked, and Britain and France withdraw it under the pressure of domestic public opinion, which is hostile to Italy.
1936		
	5 May	Italian forces take Addis Ababa. Haile Selassie flees to Britain.
	9 May	Abyssinia is formally annexed (taken over) by Italy, and with Eritrea and Italian Somaliland becomes part of Italian East Africa.
	July	League ends sanctions.

SOURCE 14.2 Memorandum from Marshal Badoglio, Chief of General Staff to Mussolini, December 1934

The problem of Italian–Abyssinian relations has very recently shifted from a diplomatic plane to one which can be solved by force only ...

The object ... is nothing more or less than the complete destruction of the Abyssinian army and the total conquest of Abyssinia. In no other way can we build the Empire ...

The speedier our action the less likely will be the danger of diplomatic complications. In the Japanese fashion there will be no need whatever officially for a declaration of war and in any case we must always emphasise the purely defensive character of operations. No one in Europe would raise any difficulties provided the prosecution of operations resulted rapidly in an accomplished fact. It would suffice to declare to England and France that their interests would be recognised.

Activity

Read Sources 14.2 and 14.3. Explain the different views as to whether Italy should conquer Abyssinia and the possible effects of its action.

Why are Rastafarians so called?

You might be surprised to see such a question raised in a book on Fascist Italy, but there is a link. You have already come across the word 'ras' to mean an Ethiopian leader. Haile Selassie's original name was Tafari, hence he was Ras Tafari.

When some American blacks in the early twentieth century were seeking to establish their cultural identity, they looked back to their African origins, and were attracted by Ethiopia, then one of only two African states that were independent. Rastafarians have developed a distinct culture, including wearing dreadlocks. They look upon Haile Selassie as a Messiah figure, and expect one day to return to their promised land in Africa.

Abyssinia/Ethiopia

Both names were used at the time for the country we now call Ethiopia. We have used the first term as it was more generally called Abyssinia at the time.

The Italian Empire

This had developed in East Africa from the 1880s. Italy's control was limited. Attempts to encourage thousands of Italians to settle as colonists failed. In 1935 there were only 250 Italian settlers in Somaliland; by 1937 only 1300 families had emigrated to Libya.

SOURCE 14.3 Margherita Sarfatti to Mussolini, 1935

You have enough already to colonise in Apulia, in Sicily and in Calabria. There's positive work to do here. If you go into Ethiopia you will fall into the hands of the Germans and then you will be lost. If we have to pay for the Empire with the ruin of Europe we will pay too high a price.

Why did Mussolini attack Abyssinia?

General long-term reasons

a) International
- A long-held Italian NATIONALIST dream
- To avenge the 1896 Adowa defeat
- To consolidate Italy's position in East Africa
- To show Italy as an IMPERIAL power like Britain and France
- To increase Italian prestige

b) Political
- To develop the cult of the DUCE
- The desire to act, to keep Fascism on the boil
- To have a war to foster excitement; Fascism favoured war
- To rally support at home

c) Economic
- To develop emigration and export markets
- To find oil

Why at that time?
- To divert attention from the failings of the Corporative State, and the Depression
- To exploit the favourable international situation
- To show Hitler Italy's power, and to get war over before Germany got too strong
- At Stresa and on other occasions Mussolini gained the impression that the British and French would have no objection to Italy making gains in Abyssinia.

What did Italy gain?
- A great victory, avenging Adowa
- Consolidated its territory in 'Italian East Africa'
- Sanctions rallied the nation; the Queen Mother led the campaign to give gold rings to finance the war effort.
- The Church praised the civilising mission.
- Mussolini's finest hour? Mussolini at the peak of his popularity?

But:
- Bred complacency in Mussolini; boosted his already inflated ego
- Drain on economic and military resources
- Budget deficit rose from 2.5 billion to 16 billion lire.
- Settlement of 130,000 Italians in Abyssinia was costly
- Needed 250,000 occupying troops, dependent on supplies 2000 miles away
- In October 1936 the lira was devalued by 40 per cent.
- By 1939 only two per cent of Italian trade was with its colonies.
- Italian rule was repressive and corrupt.
- Italy only fully controlled a few areas.
- Italy had to fight a guerrilla war until Abyssinia was lost to the British in 1941.
- Fascist Italy gained a reputation for brutality.
- Upset Britain and France
- Sanctions forced trade shift to Germany.
- Showed weakness of the League of Nations, which encouraged Hitler's ambitions
- Allowed Hitler to remilitarise without foreign intervention, thus increasing German influence

What was the war actually like?

War gave Mussolini the opportunity to indulge in propaganda glorifying Italy's military prowess, which masked the death and destruction caused by a brutal conflict between a modern industrial state and a near-feudal African kingdom.

The language of justification began on 4 September when Italy alleged that Abyssinia was a barbarous and uncivilised state which 'by its conduct openly placed itself outside the Covenant of the League [the statement of principles accepted by all members in 1919]'. A month later the world was told that Abyssinia's 'warlike, aggressive spirit' had 'imposed' war on Italy. Four hundred thousand Fascist fighters were mobilised. 'These happy Italian troops' who were observed by the *Times* correspondent 'singing joyously' as they embarked for Abyssinia from Naples were made the unlikely promise that the 'modern methods' of warfare to be employed (tanks, aircraft and gas) would 'guarantee a war without tears'.

In reality, the Italians' use of mustard gas and vast numbers of aircraft made for a brutal subjugation of the African troops. The Abyssinians were ill-equipped and psychologically ill-prepared for the sort of war with which they were faced. Haile Selassie's ragged army, with its spears and 1874 vintage rifles never really had any hope of stemming the advance of the Blackshirt militia and regular Italian troops with their Fiat machine guns and overwhelming preponderance of modern weapons. Mussolini's son Vittorio was exhilarated by the war. In his snappily titled book *Flying over Ethiopian Mountain Ranges* he described the war as a period of 'magnificent sport . . . one group of horsemen gave me the impression of a budding rose unfolding as the bombs fell in their midst, and blew them up. It was exceptionally good fun.'

The war should have been over in a matter of weeks. Yet it took seven months for the two Italian armies to meet their objectives. Although Italian troops were used extensively, it was the Eritreans from Italy's first colony who bore the brunt of the fighting against the Abyssinians. Mussolini's critics observed that the Italians had built the roads, and the natives had done the fighting.

Yet by May 1936 Mussolini had generated great popular support in Italy, and had perhaps reached the zenith (high point) of his career. While he gloried in his victory, the Abyssinians reeled from the Italian conquerors' brutal pacification tactics. Orders were given for ten Abyssinians to be killed for every Italian casualty. Some villages were gassed, and all the male inhabitants killed in others. Adowa was avenged!

■ Source activity

1 What do Sources 14.5 and 14.7 predict will be the effect of Mussolini attacking Abyssinia?

2 **a)** How far does Source 14.6 support the view of Source 14.7?
  b) How might this be explained?

3 Look at Source 14.4. What might be the reaction of Mussolini, an avid reader of the foreign press, to such cartoons?

4 Explain the contrasting views of the effects of the Abyssinian War in Sources 14.8–10.

5 What are the advantages and disadvantages of cartoons like these as historical sources?

SOURCE 14.4 A cartoon by David Low

THE LEAGUE? PAH!
THE LEAGUE IS CONTEMPTIBLE!
THE LEAGUE CAN DO NOTHING!

SOURCE 14.5 A cartoon by the British cartoonist David Low, May 1935. The figures on the right are Goebbels, Hitler, and Goering

TO THE ABYSSINIAN GAMBLE

THE GIRLS HE LEFT BEHIND HIM.

SOURCE 14.6   A cartoon from *Punch*, 14 August 1935

THE AWFUL WARNING.

FRANCE AND ENGLAND *(together?)*.

"WE DON'T WANT YOU TO FIGHT,
BUT, BY JINGO, IF YOU DO,
WE SHALL PROBABLY ISSUE A JOINT MEMORANDUM
SUGGESTING A MILD DISAPPROVAL OF YOU."

SOURCE 14.7   A cartoon from *Punch*, August 1935

"BY THAT SIN FELL THE ANGELS."

THE EXILE OF DOORN. "THINK TWICE BEFORE YOU DEFY WORLD-OPINION. I TRIED
IT ONCE, AND FOUND IT DIDN'T PAY."

SOURCE 14.8   An Italian army poster, showing the freeing of Abyssinians

SOURCE 14.9   A cartoon by Low entitled 'The Man who took the Lid Off', October 1935

THE MAN WHO TOOK THE LID OFF.

SOURCE 14.10   A British cartoon entitled 'Barbarism. Civilisation.'

How popular was the Abyssinian War?

SOURCE 14.11   Mussolini's speech launching the war, October 1935

Blackshirts of the Revolution, men and women of all Italy, Italians scattered throughout the world, across the mountains and across the oceans, listen!

A solemn hour is about to strike in the history of the fatherland. Twenty million men are at this moment gathered in the piazzas throughout the whole of Italy. Never in the history of mankind has there been seen a more gigantic demonstration. Twenty million men: a single heart, a single will, a single decision. This demonstration is meant to show and it does show to the world that the identity between Italy and Fascism is perfect, absolute, and unchangeable . . .

For many months the wheel of destiny, under the impulse of our calm determination, has been moving toward the goal. In these last hours the rhythm has become faster and cannot be halted. Not only is an army marching towards its objectives, but 44,000,000 Italians are marching in unison with this army, because there is an attempt to commit against them the blackest of all injustices, to rob them of their place in the sun.

When in 1915 Italy united its lot with those of the Allies, how many shouts of admiration and how many promises! But after the common victory, to which Italy had brought the supreme contribution of 670,000 dead, 400,000 disabled, and 1,000,000 wounded, when it came to sitting around the table of the stingy peace, to us were left only the crumbs from the sumptuous colonial booty of others. For thirteen years we have been patient while a ring was being tightened ever more rigidly about us to suffocate our overflowing vitality. With Ethiopia we have been patient for forty years. Now, that's enough!

At the League of Nations, instead of recognising the just rights of Italy, they talk of sanctions . . . I refuse to believe that the true people of Britain want to spill blood and push Europe on the road to catastrophe in order to defend an African country universally stamped as a barbarous country and unworthy of taking its place with civilised peoples . . .

Let nobody delude himself that he can deflect us without first having to defeat us. A people which is proud of its name and its future cannot adopt a different attitude . . .

Never more than in this historic epoch has the Italian people revealed the force of its spirit and the power of its character. And it is against this people to which humanity owes the greatest of its conquests, it is against this people of heroes, poets, artists, navigators and administrators that they dare to speak of sanctions.

PROLETARIAN and Fascist Italy, Italy of Vittorio Veneto and of the Revolution! To your feet! Let the cry of your decision fill the heavens and be a comfort to the soldiers who are about to fight in Africa, and let it be a spur to our friends, and a warning to our enemies in all parts of the world, a cry of justice and a cry of victory!

SOURCE 14.12   'For the Sanctity of the Cause': a poster showing women giving up wedding rings to support the war effort

SOURCE 14.13   Mussolini announcing the Empire, May 1936

SOURCE 14.14   An Italian Senator to a British diplomat

You have achieved the miracle of uniting the whole of Italy behind Mussolini.

SOURCE 14.15   British Foreign Minister Hoare

No one doubts that Italy is behind Signor Mussolini.

SOURCE 14.16   Barzini, an Italian journalist in the 1930s, describes the effect of the war

[Mussolini's] pictures were cut out of newspapers and magazines and pasted on the walls of the poor peasant cottages, at the side of the Madonna and Saint Joseph. Schoolgirls fell in love with him as a film star. His more memorable words were written on village houses for all to read. One of his collaborators exclaimed, after listening to him announce from the balcony that Abyssinia had been conquered and that Rome had again become the capital of an Empire, 'Is he like a god?' 'No,' said another, 'He is God.'

SOURCE 14.17   Peasant reaction to the Abyssinian War, as recounted in *Christ Stopped at Eboli* by Carlo Levi, a writer banished to the South. The book was written in 1944

The peasants were not interested in war ... War they considered just another inevitable misfortune, like the tax on goats. They were not afraid to go; 'To live like dogs here or to die like dogs there is just the same,' they said. But no one except Donna Caterina's husband enlisted. It soon became clear that not only the purpose of the war, but the way it was being conducted as well, was the business of that other Italy beyond the mountains, and had little to do with the peasants. Only a few men were called up, two or three in the whole village, besides those who had reached the age for military service ... 'The war is for the benefit of those in the north. We're to stay at home until we starve. And now there's no chance of going to America.'

3 October, which marked the official opening of the war, was a miserable sort of day. Twenty or twenty-five peasants, roped in by the CARABINIERI and the Fascist scouts, stood woodenly in the square to listen to the historical pronouncements that came over the radio. Don Luigi [the Fascist schoolmaster] had ordered flags to be displayed over the town hall, the school, the houses of the well-to-do; their bright colours waving in the breeze made a strong contrast to the black death-pennants on the doors of the peasants' huts ...

The war so light-heartedly set in motion in Rome was greeted in Caglioni with stony indifference. Don Luigi spoke from the balcony of the town hall. He enlarged upon the eternal grandeur of Rome, the seven hills, the wolf that suckled Romulus and Remus, Caesar's legions, Roman civilisation, and the Roman Empire that was about to be revived. He said that the world hated us for our greatness, but that the enemies of Rome would bite the dust ... because Rome was everlasting and invincible. In his falsetto voice he said a great many more things about Rome which I no longer remember, then he opened his mouth and started to sing Giovinezza [the Fascist anthem], motioning imperiously with his hands to the schoolchildren in the square below to accompany him in the chorus. Around him on the balcony were the sergeant and everyone of importance; all of them sang (except one) ... Huddled against the wall below, the peasants listened in silence, shielding their eyes with their hands from the sun and looking, in their black suits, as dark and gloomy as bats.

SOURCE 14.18   Fascist journalist Pini in 1937

Having made the Empire, we must make imperialists.

■ **Source activity**

(Marks are given in brackets.)

Source 14.11

1 Explain the references to 'Vittorio Veneto' and 'Revolution'.   [2]

2 How does Mussolini try to boost a sense of nationalism?   [2]

3 How does he justify Italy's cause?   [3]

4 What impression of the popularity of the war is given?   [3]

Sources 14.17 and 14.18

5 What evidence is there even now of the gap between 'real' and 'legal' Italy that had existed in Liberal Italy?   [3]

6 Does this seem apparent in Source 14.11? How can you explain the difference?   [3]

7 What is the peasants' attitude to the war?   [3]

8 What do you think Pini meant in Source 14.18?   [2]

Overall

9 What do each of Sources 14.12–16 show about the popularity of the Abyssinian War?   [3]

10 Referring to the provenance, dates and contents of at least three of the sources, explain the different impressions that emerge of Italians' reactions to the war.   [6]

11 Using these sources and your own knowledge, assess how the Abyssinian War affected Mussolini's popularity.   [10]

(Total: 40 marks)

■ **Activity**

1 Read Sources 14.19–22. Draw up two lists; one of the beneficial effects for Mussolini of the Abyssinian War, and one of the harmful effects.
2 For Mussolini what do you consider were the most significant
   a) gains of the war
   b) lessons for the future
   c) shifts in his European relations?
3 Structured essay.
   a) Explain why Mussolini invaded Abyssinia.
   b) What were the consequences of the Abyssinian War for Italy?

■ **Talking point**

Can you think of other examples of wars which have helped win support for the victorious government?

Historians' assessments of the effects of the Abyssinian War

SOURCE 14.19   Carocci, p. 103

In response to League of Nations' sanctions for a few months the identification of 'Italian' with 'Fascist', which had been proclaimed for about the last ten years, seemed a true one.

SOURCE 14.20   Clark, p. 282

It was his finest hour. Mussolini had triumphed contra mundum [against the world]. The Empire was popular, so was the Duce ... But in every other respect the conquest of Ethiopia was a disaster. The economic cost was huge; militarily the victory led to complacency. Diplomatically, Italy was left isolated in a hostile world ... the British, Italy's traditional ally, never forgave Mussolini.

SOURCE 14.21   P. Bell, *Origins of the Second World War*, 1986, pp. 63–64

The immediate effects of victory were exhilarating. Mussolini had succeeded where the old Italy had failed. He had defeated not only the Abyssinians but the League of Nations. He abandoned his former cautious approach to foreign affairs and looked for new worlds to conquer.

SOURCE 14.22   Whittam, pp. 110–15

The colonial war in Ethiopia proved to be the crucial turning point in the history of the Fascist regime and in the diplomatic history of inter-war Europe ... In the short term it mobilised the Italian nation, enhanced [increased] the prestige of the regime and raised the cult of the Duce to dizzying heights. Yet in less than ten years his corpse was hanging upside down ... reviled [scorned] by the mob ...

This war was the most popular war in the history of modern Italy ... The Italians had defied the world. Their leader had confirmed the truth of the writing on the wall proclaiming 'Mussolini is always right'. Despite Badoglio, the King, and the diplomats Mussolini had pressed ahead with his campaign and proved them all wrong. In another sense, however, the writing was on the wall.

The euphoria [great happiness] of 1935–36, partly manufactured and partly genuine, was short-lived. The problem with euphoria is that it is hard to sustain and once dissipated [disappeared] leaves behind a sense of disillusionment and anticlimax ... Mussolini and Ciano believed that a dynamic foreign policy would maintain the momentum. These efforts proved to be counterproductive. The increased emphasis on racism was a product of the Ethiopian war ... Mussolini became over-confident, scornful of the advice proffered by professional soldiers and diplomats, and too prone to believe his own propaganda. The war had been very expensive and there had been high wastage ... of weapons and transport ... There was almost continuous guerrilla warfare until the British liberated the country in 1941, and this was a heavy burden for a faltering economy and overstretched military establishment ... Mussolini's African adventure also led to grandiose [over-ambitious] schemes for marching to the oceans. This concentration on breaking out of the Mediterranean not only meant confrontation with the western DEMOCRACIES but also abandonment of other spheres of influence ... Mussolini realised he could no longer act as the protector of Austria ...

In 1936 Mussolini had basically three choices: he could try to act as mediator between Germany and the western democracies, he could rejoin the British and French in a revived Stresa Front, or he could align himself with the Third Reich. The impact of the Ethiopian war made the last alternative seem the most attractive.

Was Mussolini's intervention in the Spanish Civil War a success?

CHART 14E   The sides in the Spanish Civil War

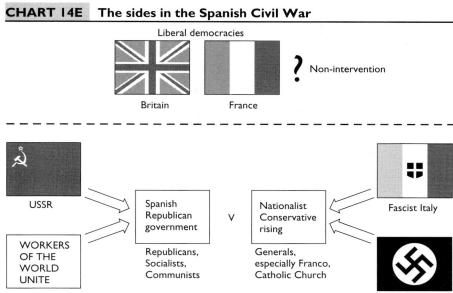

Liberal democracies

Britain   France

? Non-intervention

USSR

WORKERS OF THE WORLD UNITE

International

Spanish Republican government

Republicans, Socialists, Communists

V

Nationalist Conservative rising

Generals, especially Franco, Catholic Church

Fascist Italy

Nazi Germany

In July 1936 Mussolini responded to a request from RIGHT-WING rebels fighting the Spanish Republican government. He sent twelve planes which together with 30 German planes were crucial in allowing General Franco to transport his Army of Morocco to Spain. This helped sustain a revolt which otherwise might have collapsed. Spain was split in two, in an increasingly bitter war which was to last three years. By its end Mussolini's initially small assistance had turned into a major deployment of resources.

SOURCE 14.23   Italian prisoners of war. Far from being volunteers, many of these soldiers had been pressured into going to Spain by their officers

Reasons why Mussolini intervened

International
- To stop French, LEFT-WING influence in Spain
- To cultivate an ally in a strategic area
- To establish greater Italian influence in the Mediterranean
- To demonstrate Italy's might

Ideological
- To fight against decadent democracy and SOCIALISM
- To help spread Fascism

Domestic
- To maintain the momentum for fascistisation at home

General
- To stay in the limelight
- To have another war
- He had become overambitious after the Abyssinian victory.

Mussolini considered the conflict would be over quickly. The decision to get involved was very much his own; few others favoured it, given the potential costs and little anticipated gain.

What effect did Italy's intervention have on the country?

a) Economic
- Disrupted Italian trade and reinforced the trend of increasing trade with Germany
- 'Bled Italy white', as Mussolini said. It cost fourteen billion lire (half a year's tax revenue), and required special levies.
- The lira was devalued.
- Italy lost half its foreign currency reserves.

b) Political
- Made the government unpopular, apart from with the Church

c) Military
- Italy was on the winning side, and claimed a great victory.
- Prevented Italy consolidating its strength after the Abyssinian conflict
- Used up much needed weapons and ammunition
- Italy's military strength was less in 1939 than in 1936; it was unprepared for a major war in 1939.
- Humiliated at Guadalajara; Italian weaknesses were exposed.

d) International
- Italy gained a potential supporter in a strategic position, facing France and Britain.
- Helped establish another Fascist regime
- Italy gained little of real value; just Spanish neutrality.
- Diverted Italian attention from the German threat to Austria
- Increased Italy's links with Nazi Germany
- It reinforced Italy's quarrel with Britain and France (but they still wanted Italian friendship).

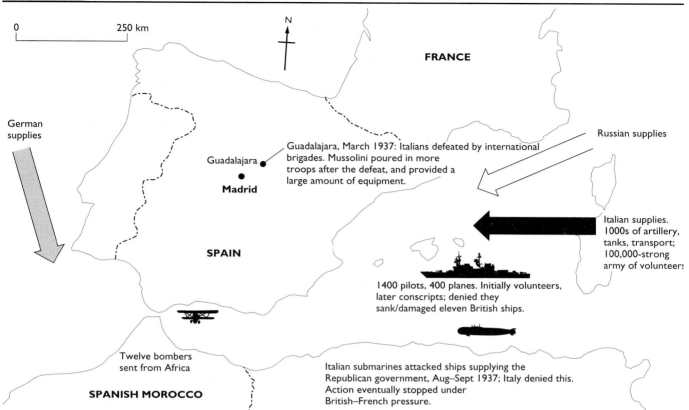

0   250 km

N

FRANCE

German supplies

Russian supplies

Guadalajara, March 1937: Italians defeated by international brigades. Mussolini poured in more troops after the defeat, and provided a large amount of equipment.

Guadalajara

Madrid

Italian supplies. 1000s of artillery, tanks, transport; 100,000-strong army of volunteers

SPAIN

1400 pilots, 400 planes. Initially volunteers, later conscripts; denied they sank/damaged eleven British ships.

Twelve bombers sent from Africa

Italian submarines attacked ships supplying the Republican government, Aug–Sept 1937; Italy denied this. Action eventually stopped under British–French pressure.

SPANISH MOROCCO

■ Activity

1   What does von Hassell (Source 14.25) consider the effect of the Spanish War could be?
2   How valuable is this source as evidence of the effects of Italy's foreign policy?

SOURCE 14.24   One of the 'Garibaldi brigades', who fought for the Republic

SOURCE 14.25   A report to Berlin by the German Ambassador in Rome, Ulrich von Hassell, 18 December 1936

Germany has in my opinion every reason for being gratified if Italy continues to interest herself deeply in the Spanish affair. The role played by the Spanish conflict as regards Italy's relations with France and England could be similar to the Abyssinian conflict, bringing out clearly the actual, opposing interests of the powers and thus preventing Italy from being drawn into the net of the Western powers and used for their machinations [intrigues]. The struggle for dominant political influence in Spain lays bare the natural opposition between Italy and France: at the same time the position of Italy as a power in the Western Mediterranean comes into competition with that of Britain. All the more clearly will Italy recognise the advisability of confronting the Western powers shoulder to shoulder with Germany.

'The fatal friendship'. Why, and with what effects, did Mussolini ally with Hitler?

When Mussolini invaded Abyssinia he believed that he had at least the tacit (silent) support of the Western democracies. In April 1935 at the so-called Stresa Front Italy had aligned itself with Britain and France against German expansionism in Europe. Britain and France made no comment about Italian expansionism in Africa. However, relations had soured during the Abyssinian War, not least because of sanctions, and Italy had moved closer to Germany. Mussolini's intervention in Spain from July 1936 was to reinforce this trend.

However, there were still possibilities for Fascist Italy to exploit the growing tension between Britain/France and Nazi Germany to make gains. Italy could try to indulge in 'makeweight diplomacy'. Other factors pointed to Italy's reinforcing its links with the West to counter the growing power of Germany. Alternatively, Mussolini could associate Italy with the growing might of Germany. He had to consider which would be the best way to advance further his ambition of making Italy a great power. Should Mussolini have allied with Germany or the Western democracies?

FOCUS ROUTE

As you work through pages 224–233
Either:
Note down the key factors in favour and those against Mussolini making an alliance with Hitler.
Or:
Write a government memo advising Mussolini on the best future course in foreign policy. Either explain why you recommend strengthening Italian ties with Britain and France, or why you favour a link with Nazi Germany.

■ Activity

Should Mussolini ally with Germany or the Western democracies?
Study Chart 14G which looks at:

- aspects of Italian affairs in 1936
- issues relevant to relations with Britain and France
- issues relevant to relations with Nazi Germany.

1 Divide into groups. Look at the various issues, and decide whether each issue favours a German alliance, a Western alliance, or could operate either way. You might use a chart like the one below, or work on a copy of Chart 14G.

Issue	Favours German alliance	Favours British/French alliance	Not clear-cut case for either side

2 Some groups should now prepare for a debate arguing the case for closer ties with Nazi Germany. Others should do the same for a Western alliance.
3 Debate the issue.
4 Did you agree with the decision Mussolini made?
5 Why do you think he made this decision?
6 What alternative was there to Italy committing itself to either side? What might be the advantages and disadvantages of this?

SOURCE 14.26 Mussolini and Neville Chamberlain at the Munich Conference, 1938

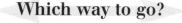
Which way to go?

SOURCE 14.27 Hitler greeting Mussolini at the Brenner Pass, 1940

CHART 14G **Italy: which way to go? Key issues**

225

Britain and France
- Democratic states
- Mussolini considered them declining states
- Sections in their elites admired Mussolini for his actions against the threat of Communism
- Supported status quo; major powers in League of Nations
- Favoured a peaceful Europe
- Closely linked to powerful USA
- Imposed sanctions (but omitting coal, oil and steel) over Abyssinia
- Dominated Mediterranean
- Had the largest number of African colonies
- Had blocked previous Italian colonial expansion
- Wanted support against Hitler
- Britain had the world's largest fleet
- France was Italy's neighbour
- France protected anti-Fascist exiles

Italy
- Traditional Italian hostility to 'uncivilised' Germans
- King and elite traditionally friendly with Britain
- German alliance unlikely to be popular
- Little evidence that Fascist propaganda had created a warlike nation
- Economy not yet self-sufficient
- Vulnerable to naval attack
- Resources had been used up in Abyssinia, and now in Spain
- Military power more impressive on paper than in reality
- Mussolini wanted to keep fascistisation momentum going following war with Abyssinia
- Mussolini wanted to dominate Mediterranean

Spanish Civil War
1936–39

Nazi Germany
- Fellow Fascist state
- Dynamic, vigorous state
- Accepted Mediterranean as Mussolini's sphere of influence
- Like Italy, Germany had visions of living space (Lebensraum/spazio vitale)
- Hitler favoured Italian alliance in *Mein Kampf*
- Favoured war
- Hitler wanted to unite with Austria

- Italy contained a quarter of a million German speakers in South Tyrol, but Hitler had made no claims on this territory
- Had left League of Nations in 1933
- Hitler refused to apply sanctions against Italy during the Abyssinian crisis
- Became a major supplier of materials and energy crucial to Italy
- Had supplied both sides with arms during the Abyssinian War
- Was helping Franco in the Spanish Civil War

How did the Axis develop?

CHART 14H   The development of the Axis

Key

➡️ Moving closer to Nazi Germany

⬅️ Moving towards Britain/France

1923	Hitler imitates Mussolini's March on Rome; fails	
1933	Hitler comes to power in Germany	
	Germany withdraws from League of Nations	
1934	Mussolini moves troops to stop possible Anschluss	
June	Hitler meets Mussolini in Venice	
1935	Italy joins Stresa Front v Germany	
	Abyssinian War; big shift	
1936	**July** Both Germany and Italy independently give help to Franco in Spanish Civil War. This continues until 1939	
	Oct Mussolini talks of an Axis after agreements with Hitler. Italian initiative.	
1937	Gentleman's Agreement with Britain accepting Mediterranean status quo	
	Sept Mussolini visits Germany; impressed	
	Nov Italy joins Anti-Comintern Pact with Germany and Japan	
	Dec Italy withdraws from League of Nations	
1938	**April** British agreement with Italy; recognises Italian Abyssinia	
	May Hitler visits Italy; Italy rejects military alliance	
	Mussolini accepts Anschluss	
	Anti-semitic decrees in Italy	
	Munich conference; Mussolini plays an apparently prominent role. He is impressed by the power of Germany, contrasted to the feebleness of the West.	
	Mussolini is seen by the West as helping to restrain Germany and keep the peace	
1939	**Feb** Mussolini announces his long-term programme	
	March Hitler breaks Munich agreement and seizes Bohemia without consulting Mussolini	
	Mussolini briefly toys with idea of a new Stresa Front to resist German domination	
	April Italy invades Albania to show its power	
	May Mussolini sends Ciano to negotiate military alliance; terms left to Germany; Pact of Steel signed	
	Aug Germany signs Nazi-Soviet Pact, breaking the Anti-Comintern Pact	
	Aug Mussolini wavers continually between joining Germany if war breaks out in the hope of gains, and declaring Italy neutral	
	1 Sept Germany attacks Poland; Mussolini declares Italy non-belligerent	
	3 Sept Britain and France declare war on Germany	
	3 Sept Mussolini tries to arrange another Munich-style conference to avoid war	
1940	**June** Italy declares war on France and Britain	

■ Activity

1 Compare Mussolini's view of Germany in 1934 and 1937. How can the differences be explained?
2 What occurred between the Axis agreement and the signing of the Pact of Steel to confirm Mussolini in his alliance with Germany?
3 How does Mussolini's aim, as shown in Source 14.30, help explain why he decided to ally with Germany?
4 What evidence is there, however, that Mussolini had not committed himself to full support for Nazi Germany before 1940?

■ Talking point

Can you think of any other international agreements which are based on the shared political beliefs of the participants?

June 1934 Venice First meeting
Tense. Hitler not wearing uniform; felt inferior to uniformed Mussolini.

Mussolini insisted on using his poor German. Dismissed Hitler as 'just a garrulous [talkative] monk' and a 'silly little clown'.

SOURCE 14.28 Hitler and Mussolini meeting in 1934

SOURCE 14.29 Mussolini speaking in September 1934

Thirty centuries of history allow us to regard with supreme indulgence certain doctrines taught beyond the Alps by the descendants of people who were wholly illiterate in the days when Caesar, Virgil and Augustus flourished in Rome.

In **September 1937** Mussolini visited Germany and was very impressed. In Berlin he spoke to a crowd of 900,000. He was deeply moved by what he described as 'the most powerful nation in modern Europe rising magnificently to greatness'.

In **1938** Hitler said he would 'never forget' what Mussolini had done by allowing Anschluss.

SOURCE 14.30 Mussolini announcing his long-term programme to the Fascist Grand Council, 4 February 1939

Those states which do not have free access or are trapped inside inland seas are semi-independent ... Italy is in an inland sea which is linked to the oceans by the Suez Canal ... and by the Straits of Gibraltar, dominated by the guns of Great Britain. Italy therefore does not have free access to the oceans; Italy therefore is truly a prisoner in the Mediterranean (Corsica, Tunisia, Malta, Cyprus, Greece, Turkey, Egypt encircle Italy). We must draw the following conclusions:

1. It is the aim of Italian policy, which cannot have and does not have territorial ambitions in continental Europe, except for Albania, to begin by breaking the bars of the prison.

2. Having broken the bars, Italian policy has just one basic aim: to march towards the ocean. Which ocean? The Indian Ocean through linking up the Sudan, Libya and Ethiopia or the Atlantic Ocean through French North Africa.

In either case we find ourselves confronted by the French and the British. To attempt to solve such a problem without securing our rear in the continent would be stupid. The policy of the Rome–Berlin Axis is therefore the answer to this fundamentally important historical problem.

Pact of Steel: a major blunder?

- Mussolini initially wanted a defensive alliance.
- He allowed Germany to draw up the terms.
- Each side committed itself to support the other.
- It tied Italy to German decisions; assumed a four-year breathing space before war.
- Ciano told Germany Italy would not be ready for war until 1943, but this was not written into the terms. The Germans implied acceptance of this delay, but were secretly planning to attack Poland. The day after the Pact was ratified (given formal approval), Hitler told his generals, 'Secrecy is an essential condition of success. Italy and Japan will not be told of our plans.'
- Mussolini should have been more aware of German dynamism; the Axis partners were moving at different speeds.
- The Italian press proclaimed that the Pact was popular as it would enable Italy to realise its great dreams; none of this was correct.

In August 1939 Ribbentrop (the German foreign minister) and Hitler told Ciano they were planning to attack Poland, and negotiating for an alliance with the USSR; they insisted it would be a localised war and accepted Italy was free to stay out. Ciano was horrified, and felt Italy had been duped. Ciano commented in his diary, 'I return to Rome completely disgusted with the Germans, with their leader, and their way of doing things. They have betrayed us and lied to us.'

Contemporary comments on the Axis

SOURCE 14.31 Mussolini's announcement of the Rome–Berlin Axis, Milan, 1 November 1936

This vertical line between Rome and Berlin is ... an axis around which all the European states animated [inspired] by the will to collaboration and peace can collaborate. It is not a matter for surprise that today we hoist the flag of anti-BOLSHEVISM ...

We have in common many elements of our Weltanschauung [way of looking at the world]. Not only have National Socialism and Fascism everywhere the same enemies, in the service of the same master, the Third INTERNATIONAL, but they have many conceptions of life and history in common. Both believe in will as the determining power in the life of nations and the driving force of their history ... Both are based on young people, whom we train in discipline, courage, resistance, love of the fatherland, and contempt for easy living ... Germany and Italy follow the same goal in the sphere of economic AUTARKY. Without economic independence the political independence of a nation is doubtful.

SOURCE 14.32 Italy joins with Germany and Japan in the Anti-Comintern Pact; part of the protocol (agreement) signed in 1937

Considering that the Communist International continues constantly to endanger the civilised world in the West and East, and disturbs and destroys peace and order ... Considering that, Italy, which since the beginning of the Fascist government has combated this danger with inflexible determination ... has decided to take its place against the common enemy side by side with Germany and Japan.

SOURCE 14.33 Extracts from Mussolini's directive to Ciano, passed on to Ribbentrop 4 May 1939, and then to Hitler

It is my definite opinion that the two European Axis powers need a period of peace of not less than three years.

It is only from 1943 that a warlike effort can have the greatest chance of success. A period of peace is necessary for Italy for the following reasons:

a) *To settle Libya and Albania militarily and to pacify Ethiopia, where an army of half a million men must be recruited*

b) *To finish the building or reconstruction of the six battleships now proceeding*

c) *For the renewal of all our heavy and medium-calibre artillery*

d) *To carry out autarkic plans calculated to avert all attempts at a blockade by the wealthy democracies*

e) *To hold the Exposition scheduled for 1942 [see page 116], which, besides presenting a record of what Italy has achieved in the last twenty years, may secure for us a reserve of foreign currency*

h) *To strengthen ever more firmly the bonds, not only between the Axis goverments, but also between the various peoples.*

For all these reasons Fascist Italy does not desire a premature war of a European character, although convinced that it is inevitable. It may also be possible that within three years Japan will have brought the war in China to an end.

SOURCE 14.34 The Pact of Steel, May 1939

Firmly united by inner affinity [similarity] between their ideologies and the comprehensive solidarity of their interests, the German and Italian nations are resolved in future to act side by side with united forces to secure their living space and to maintain peace.
Article 1: The contracting parties will remain in standing contact with each other in order to come to an understanding on all questions touching common interests of the European situation as a whole ...
Article 3: If, contrary to the wishes and hopes of the High Contracting Parties, it should happen that one of them became involved in warlike complications with another Power or Powers, the other High Contracting Party would immediately come to its assistance as an ally and support it with all its military forces on land, at sea and in the air.

■ Talking point

What are the possible dangers of two countries making a commitment to support each other if one becomes involved in war?

■ Activity

(Marks are given in brackets.)

1 Explain the reference in Source 14.34 to
   a) 'High Contracting Parties'
   b) 'another Power or Powers'. [2]

2 What, according to Sources 14.31, 14.32 and 14.33, do Italy and Germany have in common? [5]

3 What weight would you put on their reference to peace? [2]

4 What differences do Sources 14.31 and 14.34 show between the terms of the Axis and the Pact? [4]

5 What can be deduced from Source 14.33 about the limited success of some Fascist policies? [6]

6 Referring to Sources 14.33 and 14.34, and your own knowledge of discussions between the Italians and Germans at the time, explain how wise you consider it to have been for Mussolini to sign the Pact. [6]

(Total: 25 marks)

SOURCE 14.35 A 1938 Italian cartoon. *Asse* is 'axis'. The characters in the foreground are labelled Masonry, Communism, PLUTOCRACY, Anarchy, CAPITALISM and MARXISM

SOURCE 14.36 A 1938 Italian drawing entitled 'The Founding of Europe'

SOURCE 14.37 An Italian cartoon. The caption was 'It's no good – we can't cut through it!'

SOURCE 14.38 A 1938 Italian underground cartoon entitled 'Roman Welcomes'

SOURCE 14.39 A 1937 British cartoon

SOURCE 14.40 A 1940 Russian cartoon

■ **Source activity**

1 Explain as fully as possible, referring to both text and image, the message of each of Sources 14.35–40.

2 What perspectives on the Axis emerge from these sources?

What were the effects of the Axis?

Austria: the first victim of the Axis?

Mussolini's decision to link himself with the growing might of Germany entailed a major shift in his attitude to Austria. Let us compare Mussolini's actions in 1934 and 1938.

CHART 14I   Mussolini and Austria

Austria 1934

(after the murder by Austrian Nazis of the Austrian Chancellor Dollfuss)

- Mussolini sent troops to Italy's Brenner frontier. This may have stopped Hitler taking over Austria.
- Mussolini earned prestige at home and abroad for standing up to Germany.

CONSULTING THE ORACLE.
(As recorded by Mr. Punch's magic microphone.)

HERR HITLER. "WHAT IS YOUR MESSAGE FOR GERMANY!"
SIGNOR MUSSOLINI. "TELL HER SHE MUST BE CAREFUL TO KEEP ON THE RIGHT SIDE OF ITALY."
HERR HITLER. "AND HOW CAN SHE MAKE SURE OF DOING THAT?"
SIGNOR MUSSOLINI. "BY KEEPING ON THE OTHER SIDE OF AUSTRIA."

SOURCE 14.41
A *Punch* cartoon, 20 June 1934

Austria 1938

- In June 1936 Mussolini had told Austria to deal directly with Germany, implying that he was not prepared to defend Austria. He was thus giving up one of Italy's most important strategic gains from the First World War.
- In March 1938 Hitler told Mussolini he was invading Austria; Mussolini accepted this.
- Hitler promised not to forget this support.
- There was considerable (private) concern amongst some Italian ministers.
- Many saw this as a humiliation for Italy; Mussolini's policy was unpopular with Italians.

SOURCE 14.42   A *Punch* cartoon, 23 February 1938

Whatever the international effects of the Axis, it would be hard to argue against the view that domestically it weakened the regime. Italy's growing dependence on Germany was viewed uneasily by many Italians. The historian Carocci (p. 134) argues: 'There was no liking between the two peoples, only fear and constraint on the one hand, contempt on the other.' The 'loss' of Austria was resented by many educated Italians, and the apparent domestic effects of the Axis alienated more. We have already seen the negative domestic response when Mussolini sought to implement Nazi ideas in the Reform of Customs and in the introduction of anti-semitic policies (see pages 183–84).

Did the Axis commit Mussolini to Germany, and cut Italy off from the West?

Mussolini's decision in 1936 to link Fascist Italy with Nazi Germany in the Axis has been seen as his greatest mistake, and the cause of his ultimate downfall. Some historians argue that for both IDEOLOGICAL and GEOPOLITICAL reasons such a step was virtually inevitable, and that once the Axis agreement was signed, Mussolini's fate was sealed.

Others argue that even after the signing of the agreement in 1936 there were alternative courses open to Mussolini. There was pro-Western sympathy amongst many of the Italian elite. In 1937 the King put gentle pressure on Mussolini to modify his enthusiasm for Germany; and stressed the traditional Italian friendliness towards Britain. Contacts were maintained with the West. Mussolini might still be following a policy of equidistance, and certainly the diplomatic situation from 1936 to 1940 was very fluid. Italian historian de Felice argues that right up to 1940 Mussolini seriously considered the option of joining Britain and France against Germany. It was only in 1940 when Hitler had shown his great might by conquering much of Europe that Mussolini finally decided to commit himself to the Nazi side. The conservative Italian

■ Activity

1. What relationship between Mussolini and Hitler is portrayed in Source 14.41?
2. How is the relationship portrayed in Source 14.42?
3. What difference in Mussolini's attitude to Austria is conveyed?
4. Was Mussolini's lack of action over the Anschluss in Italy's best interests?
5. Do Hitler's actions in Austria in 1938 support Ciano's comment on the Axis (see page 260)?

historian Quartararo, and the British historian Lamb in a recent study *Mussolini and the British* argue that it was only Britain's arrogant attitude to the Italians that prevented Mussolini from joining them in an alliance.

However, most historians would agree with Morgan, who believes that 'in both timing and content, the Axis of 1936 indicated that Mussolini had made a choice. It was a statement of perceived division in Europe between the DICTATORSHIPS and the democracies, which was accentuated [strengthened] by Mussolini's actions in both foreign and internal policy thereafter.'

Historians on the nature of the Axis

SOURCE 14.43 Wiskemann, p. 65

From 1936 until the end nothing can be discerned that deserves the name of Italian foreign policy . . . nothing but a surrender to the pressure from Hitler with no regard for Italy's interest or capacity.

SOURCE 14.44 Cassels, p. 91

Mussolini . . . contrived a special relationship with Germany of his own free will. At the outset, the Rome–Berlin Axis was in no sense a concrete political arrangement . . . In Mussolini's eyes, it was vague enough to be jettisoned if need be. But within 18 months, the Axis became for Fascist Italy an obligation dictated by harsh necessity, from which there was no exit . . . The beginning of the end of Fascist Italy can be dated from the Anschluss of March 1938 . . . Fascist Italy became, in fact, a satellite of Nazi Germany.

SOURCE 14.45 Blinkhorn, p. 48

The Axis of October 1936, a loose association initiated and named by Mussolini, marked the first step in what was to prove a fatal relationship: the die was cast in 1938 with Mussolini's adoption of a neutral stance over Germany's absorption of Austria . . . Henceforth the relative positions of the two dictators were reversed. Mussolini, bedazzled by German military strength during a visit in September 1937, was becoming indisputedly the lesser figure and Italy the junior partner in the new relationship. Subsequent events re-emphasised Italy's subordinate status.

SOURCE 14. 46 Clark, p. 283

In 1938–39 Mussolini was still playing along with Hitler, in order to wring concessions from France and Britain, and to extend the new empire. It was a dangerous game.

SOURCE 14.47 R. Overy and A. Wheatcroft, *The Road to War*, 1989, p. 169

During 1936, as a direct result of Ethiopia and Spain, Italy moved out of the Western camp and closer to Hitler's Germany. This was a product of necessity rather than intention . . . As one German diplomat put it: 'The new German–Italian friendship was created not by the spontaneous inner urge of two countries which are similar in nature . . . but ad hoc [bit by bit, with no plan], on rational grounds as the result of necessities confronting both of them.' What they both had in common was the fact that 'they were have-nots in contrast to the powers which were satiated [satisfied] by the peace treaties . . . Mussolini could never reconcile himself fully to the fact that although he was demonstrably the senior Fascist in Europe, Hitler had greater national power behind him . . . The fact that they were both Fascist powers gave the relationship a gloss of ideological brotherhood and dictatorial solidarity, but co-operation between them was always more cautious and formal. Italy was useful to Hitler as a Fascist outpost in the Mediterranean keeping Britain and France away from Central Europe. Germany was useful to Mussolini as a source of economic assistance for rearmament, and as a power to divert the attention of Britain and France from Italian adventures in the Mediterranean. Each saw the other as an instrument in his own power game; manipulation rather than friendship bound them together.

Activity

1 Study Sources 14.43–45. What does each historian see as the determining moment in Mussolini's relationship with Hitler?
2 To what extent does Source 14.46 differ from the earlier three sources?
3 What does Overy in Source 14.47 see as the main reasons for the close relationship of Italy and Germany?
4 To what extent do Overy and Bell (Source 14.48) agree on the importance of ideological factors in the Axis?
5 What different emphasis does Lamb provide (Source 14.49)?

SOURCE 14.48 Bell, p. 67

Ideology was called in at a late date to consolidate an alliance which began with political and economic matters: German support for Italy during the Abyssinian conflict; the supply of German coal, on which Italy became increasingly dependent; and co-operation in the Spanish Civil War. Above all, the objectives which Mussolini set for his foreign policy, amounting to Italian domination in the Mediterranean, could only be attained in opposition to France and Britain, and therefore only in alliance with Germany.

FOCUS ROUTE

Structured essay.

a) Why and how did Mussolini move closer to Hitler between 1936 and 1939?

b) What were the effects of this on Italy?

To tackle the first part, you could examine events (mainly from the Abyssinian War to the outbreak of the Second World War in 1939), to analyse the trend. Consider the role various factors played in the developing relationship, e.g:

- ideological
- economic
- geopolitical/strategic
- personal (i.e. how the leaders viewed and treated each other; were they drawn to each other more by mutual attraction or common interests?).

To tackle the second part, you should concentrate on the effect it had on Italy's foreign policy, in particular:

- policy towards Austria
- relations with the West
- Italy's determining weight strategy.

You could then consider domestic effects, and assess the overall impact on Mussolini's position.

SOURCE 14.49 R. Lamb, *Mussolini and the British*, 1997, pp. 7, 14–15

There is strong evidence to suggest that with co-operation from Eden [Britain's Foreign Secretary] Mussolini could have been kept out of Hitler's camp and the balance of power in Europe preserved.

The evidence is conclusive that once he had conquered Abyssinia, Mussolini wanted to renew friendship with Britain. He both feared and disliked Hitler, and was intent on preserving Austria from the Nazis. The British policy of appeasing Hitler and opposing Mussolini was disastrous. Abyssinia and the Spanish Civil War were mere side-shows compared with Hitler's fanatical determination to use his enormously powerful armies for aggression. Unfortunately, Eden could never see this.

Mussolini would have been a slippery and treacherous ally, but in the face of the Nazi menace his goodwill was essential for peace in Europe. Like all dictators, he was temperamental. His obsession with DE JURE *recognition by Britain of the Italian conquest of Abyssinia may have been unreasonable, but the British Ambassador in Rome made it clear what a priority it was in Mussolini's mind – yet, because of public opinion at home, the Baldwin and Chamberlain governments delayed from Spring 1936 until Autumn 1938 before giving in. There can, surely, be little doubt that if this recognition had been granted in 1936, Mussolini would have stayed out of Hitler's arms. On such small things great events depend.*

Who controlled Italy's foreign policy?

Right from the beginning Mussolini was determined to exercise overall control of foreign policy, whether he was Foreign Minister himself or not. In the 1920s he was ably assisted by Grandi, and then, as Mussolini desired a more assertive policy, he appointed his ambitious son-in-law Ciano as Foreign Minister. Ciano favoured closer links with Germany, but soon became disillusioned with Hitler's treatment of Italy. In 1943 Grandi and Ciano combined to try and rescue Italy from the German alliance by supporting the COUP against Mussolini.

Dino Grandi (born 1895, died 1988)

Grandi was one of the ablest Fascists and played a particularly significant role in foreign policy.

An ex-Socialist, he joined the Fascists in September 1920, and his rise was extremely rapid. Although he disagreed with some of Mussolini's policies, he realised that the Duce was indispensable for the movement. He was a key leader in the March on Rome.

As undersecretary in the Foreign Ministry from 1925, Grandi had a major influence on Mussolini's involvement in the Locarno Pacts, and in 1929 was appointed Minister of Foreign Affairs. He gave foreign policy a unity and consistency of goals that it had previously lacked. His two basic goals were to challenge French dominance and to create a vast colonial empire in Africa. Grandi felt this had to be done without a European war, which Italy could not survive. He favoured working through the League of Nations, and acting as a 'determining weight' between France and Germany.

In the early 1930s Mussolini favoured a more dynamic foreign policy, and he himself took control in July 1932. Grandi was sent as ambassador to London 1932–39. There he was very helpful to the Italian cause, and had a great deal to do with League of Nations sanctions not being extended to oil during the Abyssinian War. He developed some independence from instructions from Rome, but was also a skilful presenter of Italy's policy. He helped persuade Chamberlain to ask Mussolini to arrange the Munich conference in 1938.

Although he became more critical of Mussolini's foreign policy, he considered his rule necessary, and maintained his post by flattering Mussolini.

Grandi was convinced that in the event of a European war Italy's place should be on the Anglo-French side. Even after the Pact of Steel, he thought Italy could switch sides as in 1915. He was recalled from London in July 1939, when Mussolini had to show the Germans his good faith, and became Minister of Justice. He tried to prevent Italy's entry into the war until France's impending military collapse made it inevitable.

After experiencing military disaster in Greece, he decided the King must reassert his position and take Italy out of the war. His opportunity came after the Allied landing in Sicily, when he persuaded Mussolini to call the Fascist Grand Council. He presented a motion which implied Mussolini should be replaced, and it was passed by nineteen votes to seven. He then tried to organise an armistice. The Americans insisted that he should not be included in the new Italian government. Grandi was condemned to death in his absence by the Salo Republic for organising the anti-Mussolini coup. In 1947 he was tried and acquitted by the High Commission for the Expurgation (Destruction) of Fascism.

Count Galeazzo Ciano (born 1903, died 1944)

Son of an aristocrat, he trained as a lawyer, and briefly became a journalist. He entered the foreign service in 1925. After marrying Mussolini's daughter Edda in 1930, his career took off, much to the disgust of others who saw him as a man of indiscretion and ambition. In 1933 he became Chief of Mussolini's Press Office and in 1936 Minister for Press and Propaganda. He then fought in the Abyssinian War as a bomber pilot. In 1936 he was named Minister for Foreign Affairs at the age of 33. Ciano centralised the foreign office and pursued a personal style of diplomacy based on his own friendships and dislikes. He certainly lacked Grandi's perceptiveness, and is generally characterised as a shallow character.

His early policies were similar to Mussolini's: penetration into the Balkans, intervention in the Spanish Civil War, and friendly relations with Nazi Germany.

However, he began to differ with Mussolini on his policy towards Hitler, becoming more critical of the German alliance. He opposed the Pact of Steel, and wanted a barrier in the Balkans against the Germans – and so was a major advocate of the invasion of Albania. He helped keep Italy out of the war in 1939. He went out of favour in 1940 because of his anti-German stance at a time when Germany was doing so well. Eventually he accepted the logic of joining Germany at war, and was involved in the disastrous Greek campaign. He kept his post but not his power until he was dismissed in February 1943.

He voted with Grandi in the Fascist Grand Council meeting which overthrew Mussolini in July 1943. He was imprisoned by the new government, but escaped to Germany. He was then sent to the Salo Republic, and was tried and shot as a traitor, despite the pleas of his wife. Ciano's diaries have been a major source for historians since (see pages 260–61).

He lacked Grandi's wisdom, and was resented for his success. Muggeridge, who edited his diaries, has said of him, 'The focus of his life and thought was power. Mussolini represented power, and therefore he attached himself to Mussolini.'

■ Activity

1 Note down the major contributions of Grandi and Ciano.
2 How far did their policies differ from the Duce's?
3 What do their careers show about the nature of the Fascist regime?
4 If they had had more power how might events have taken a different course?

FOCUS ROUTE

1 List reasons in Sources 14.50–56 explaining why Italy did not join the war.
2 List reasons why it might have done.
3 Do you consider Mussolini's decision was wise? What do the extracts generally suggest about Mussolini's qualities as a ruler by 1939?
4 What does Mussolini's decision not to join the war suggest about the impact of his policies?

F Why didn't Italy enter the Second World War in 1939?

'The Italians are behaving exactly as they did in 1914.' So remarked Hitler on 25 August 1939 when told that Italy would not join in the approaching war. Much to Mussolini's disappointment, Fascist Italy repeated Liberal Italy's policy – to stay out of a major war. When war broke out in September 1939 over Hitler's invasion of Poland, Mussolini reluctantly declared Italy 'non-belligerent'. At first sight this looks a real puzzle:

- One of Mussolini's major aims was to build up the military strength of Italy, and develop a warlike people.
- He believed that war helped forge a strong nation.
- By 1939 Mussolini had had seventeen years of power to prepare Italy for war.
- He was bound by the Pact of Steel to join Hitler in any war.

Read the following sources explaining Italy's non-belligerence in 1939.

SOURCE 14.50 A German interpreter describing Ciano's explanation on 11 August to German Foreign Minister Ribbentrop as to why Italy could not join a war in 1939

It was impossible materially and politically, militarily and psychologically for Italy to participate in a war at this early stage. She had in effect been waging war for years on end. What with intervention in the Spanish Civil War and the conquest of the Abyssinian Empire, the Italian people had been pushed into one armed conflict after another, and the result was a pronounced degree of war weariness. In addition these years had virtually exhausted Italy's scant stock of materials.

SOURCE 14.51 Extracts from Ciano's diary, August–September 1939. Ciano argued strongly for Italy to stay out of the war in 1939

a) Recounting a conversation with the King, 24 August
In his judgement we are absolutely in no condition to wage war. The Army is in a 'pitiful' state ... The officers of the Italian Army are not qualified for the job and our equipment is old and obsolete. To this must be added the state of mind of the Italians, which is distinctly anti-German.

b) Ciano asked Party Secretary Starace
... not to keep from Il Duce the country's true state of mind, which is clearly anti-German ... The Italian people do not want to fight alongside Germany in order so to enhance German strength that one day will menace us.

c) Police chief Bocchini told Ciano
If there should be demonstrations in favour of neutrality, the CARABINIERI and the regular police would make common cause with the people.

d) Mussolini's feelings

13 August *At first he agreed with me. Then he said that honour required him to march with Germany. Finally he said he wanted his share of the loot in Croatia and Dalmatia.*

15 August *[Mussolini said] it would not be good to irritate the Germans, because we ought to get our share of the spoils too.*

16 August *[Mussolini said that] this time it was war, and we could not take part in it because we were in no position to do so.*

26 August *The Duce was really out of his wits. His military instinct and his sense of honour were leading him to war. Reason has now stopped him. But this hurts him very much. In the military field he was badly served by his advisers who, under the illusion of eternal peace, have fostered dangerous illusions in him. Now he has had to confront the hard truth. This, for the Duce, is a great blow.*

SOURCE 14.52   Mussolini to Hitler, 25 August

Given the state of military preparations in Italy, I cannot take the initiative in any warlike operations. The war was planned for 1942 and at that date I should have been ready.

SOURCE 14.53   A letter sent on 26 August by Mussolini with a list of immediate needs from Germany – including 1.75 million tons of petrol, coal, and steel. (Seventeen thousand freight train journeys would have been required to transport all of this.)

Führer, I would not have sent you this list if I had had the time (on which we had agreed) to accumulate a stockpile and to accelerate the growth of self-sufficiency.

SOURCE 14.54   A telegram from Hitler to Mussolini, read out on Italian radio

Duce, I offer my heartiest thanks for the diplomatic and political assistance that you have recently given to Germany and to her just cause . . . I do not expect to need Italy's military aid. I thank you also, Duce, for everything that you will be able to do in the future for the common cause of Fascism and National Socialism.

SOURCE 14.55   The text on posters which appeared briefly in several Italian cities in September 1939

Italian workers will never fight alongside the butchers of their Polish brothers.

SOURCE 14.56   The historian Gallo, p. 303, comments on Mussolini's behaviour in late August 1939

. . . a man rocked between one decision and another by events that he had not anticipated, a man whose mind could be changed by whoever talked to him cleverly enough, a nervous man who had no plan and who with every day lost more of his grasp on reality.

It was a reality that he refused even to see. The facade was cracking in every direction: the military position was disastrous and the myth of the 'Fascist grand army' was evaporating . . .

After seventeen years of Fascism the situation was in every respect worse than in 1915: though 42 divisions had been mobilised, in actuality there were only 37, or the equivalent; on paper there was a figure of 73, but in order to make 37 it had been necessary to reduce the number of regiments in each. In the air force, which was the best branch of the Fascist armed services, there were 700 modern planes, but not all were in flying condition, and, besides, no one knew where they were based.

The industrial backing for this army was laughably understocked: on 1 September 1939 there was enough steel for two weeks, iron ore for six months, nickel for twenty days. Furthermore, the equipment produced by Italian industry was indescribably inefficient: the grenades did not explode, the nails fell out of the shoes, and the soles wore through within miles.

■ **Talking point**

How valid is it to talk of 'the Italians' reaction' to an event?

The fact that neither the Italian economy nor armed forces were ready for war can be seen as indicating the failure of much of Mussolini's domestic policy. He had also failed to produce a nation of warlike subjects as suggested by the Italians' positive reaction to the peace at Munich and to non-intervention in 1939. However, for all the criticism that can be made of Mussolini, it is hard to deny that in 1939 he made the correct choice. Whether his change of policy in 1940 was equally wise remains to be seen.

G Review: How successful was Mussolini's foreign policy 1922–39?

SOURCE 14.57 An American cartoon, 13 March 1938

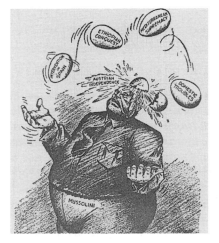

SOURCE 14.58 A cartoon from a RADICAL German magazine, November 1922. The caption read: 'Just blow hard – Italy has to get bigger!'

Consider the following evidence about Mussolini's foreign policy.

SOURCE 14.59 Mack Smith in *Mussolini's Roman Empire*, 1977, pp. vi, viii

By his own standards he was certainly successful in much of what he tried to do. In so far as he aimed to make Italy feared and hated in the world, he achieved his purpose, even though he also provoked the additional and unexpected reaction of scorn and contempt. He used to say that he wanted to test the mettle [courage] of Italy in war, and here too he succeeded. He meant to assert Italy's 'rights' to territorial expansion ... He was as good as his word ... he prided himself on being a realist who saw life as struggle and perpetual combat. The fact that he incidentally brought economic ruin and civil war to Italy ... was unintended.

Any history of Mussolini's foreign policy has to be also, or even mainly, a history of propaganda. By persuading foreign governments that he was the strong leader of a strong country, he made it possible to pursue a belligerent foreign policy without having to waste scarce money on providing the material sinews [resources] of war.

SOURCE 14.60 Italian historian L. Villari, *Foreign Policy under Mussolini*, 1956, p. 374

Mussolini's conduct of Italy's foreign relations conferred on the country a position of prestige such as it had never enjoyed before. No Italian Minister of Foreign Affairs since Cavour had achieved such success, and never before had Italy been so greatly respected abroad. Not only did its diplomats realise this, but even its humblest emigrants felt at last that they could hold up their heads and say, 'Civis Italicus sum' [I am an Italian citizen].

In 1939 Italy had a brief respite from war. Most Italians were probably relieved. They had been concerned about the German alliance, but at least their ruler had not joined Hitler in war. In some respects, if you were to judge his foreign policy from the position in 1939, Mussolini had been quite successful, with the Abyssinian adventure the highlight of his regime to date. When you examine what Italy actually gained from his policies you might be more critical. Furthermore, there was growing evidence that his economic and military resources were not as powerful as his future ambitions were to require. Mussolini could not resist further aggression, and the next four years were to see a virtually continuous series of setbacks, which partly stemmed from his policies in the late 1930s.

You should now be able to assess the success of Mussolini's foreign policy to date. You could do this by assessing either his major actions, or the extent to which he fulfilled his aims.

■ **Activity**

1 What criticism of Mussolini's approach to foreign policy is made in Source 14.57?
2 What common theme do Sources 14.58 and 14.59 highlight?
3 To what extent does Villari agree with Mack Smith's view?

■ **Activity**

1 Make a judgement on how well Mussolini had met each of his foreign policy objectives by 1939. Fill in a table like the one below.

Objective	Possible example of achievement	Degree of success
Building national prestige		
Increasing domestic support		
Gaining dominance over the Balkans		
Achieving dominance in the Mediterranean		
Establishing an empire		
Spreading Fascism		

2 Now consider the strength of Italy's international position in 1939. What has happened in Italy's relations with
  a) France/Britain
  b) Germany
  c) its ability to act as a makeweight?

3 How did both domestic factors and the international context encourage Mussolini to adopt a more assertive foreign policy in the 1930s than in his first decade in power?

4 To what extent is it appropriate to describe Italian foreign policy 1922–39 as 'Mussolini's foreign policy'? To answer this question you will need to consider both the extent to which Mussolini's aims reflected his personal rather than broader Italian objectives, and the extent to which Mussolini was involved in foreign policy. (Look at his official position; the roles of his foreign ministers, and their comparative role in key decisions.) Is there any major decision which was not made by Mussolini?

FOCUS ROUTE

Concluding essay: 'How successful was Mussolini's foreign policy between 1922 and 1939?'

For this essay you will need to identify what Mussolini's aims were, and the degree to which he achieved them. You could also comment on whether you think his aims were in Italy's interests, as it could be that he was successful in achieving some aims which were not in Italy's best interests.

Although the main focus of the essay will be foreign policy, you will also need to consider the domestic effects of foreign policy, for example:

• Did foreign policy help to consolidate Mussolini's position at home?
• Did the costs of wars harm his domestic policy?

Key points from Chapter 14

1 Mussolini's ambitions in foreign policy were to reinforce domestic support, gain international prestige, and build an empire.
2 Mussolini himself increasingly controlled the regime's foreign policy.
3 For over ten years Mussolini acted fairly cautiously, aware of Italy's limited opportunities.
4 In the mid-1930s Mussolini was able to exploit Italy's position as a 'determining weight' in Europe.
5 The conquest of Abyssinia established him at the height of his power.
6 Involvement in the Spanish Civil War was a great drain on the nation's resources with little obvious gain.
7 The Rome–Berlin Axis brought Mussolini into Nazi Germany's orbit and began a process of subservience to Hitler, shown in his acceptance of Anschluss.
8 The Nazi alliance influenced his domestic policy and started to alienate the Italian elite on whom he had so long depended.
9 Mussolini was unable to enter the war in 1939, and reluctantly declared Italy non-belligerent.
10 By 1939 Mussolini's foreign policy looked fairly successful, but in reality he had wasted Italy's resources for little real gain. Failure lay ahead.

A look ahead

You will need to consider the events of 1940–43 in Chapter 15 before making a final decision on the success of Mussolini's foreign policy. Some of the themes which contributed to his downfall will be further developed there:

• The unpopularity of the German alliance
• The alienation of conservative groups in Italy
• The pressure on resources caused by his ambitions
• Increasingly desperate decision making without proper evaluation of the likely consequences.

Why did Mussolini's regime lose the war and collapse?

'Created by war, destroyed by war.' Why did a state, whose raison d'être was to wage war, do so badly when it did eventually join the Second World War? This chapter looks at the course of the war and assesses why the Fascist armed forces performed so poorly.

The close link between the defeat in war and Mussolini's own dismissal is the second theme of this chapter.

A Why did Mussolini declare war in 1940?

Mussolini had told Germany at the time of the Pact of Steel that he would be ready for war in 1943. So when Hitler was unable to meet Italy's requests for economic assistance in 1939, Mussolini did not join in the war. What then precipitated Italy's entry into the war less than a year later?

FOCUS ROUTE

1 Below is a list of reasons why Mussolini entered the Second World War. What evidence can you find in the sources and text opposite to support each reason? Make and complete your own copy of the chart.
2 Mussolini's decision to enter the war is often seen by historians as another example of blundering. From the perspective of June 1940 can the decision be viewed in a different light?

Reasons for entering the war	Evidence
State of the war	
Economic	
Prestige	
Domestic	
Personal	
IDEOLOGICAL	

CHART 15B	A timeline showing the speed of German successes
1939 Sept	Poland defeated
1940 April	Denmark occupied
	Norway occupied
May	Belgium and Holland occupied
	British forces evacuated from Dunkirk
Early June	German troops move rapidly through France
22 June	France surrenders

Germany had turned Italy into a virtual economic colony, purchasing its food and textiles. By August 1939 Germany owed Italy 40 million dollars. In return, Italy was increasingly dependent on German, not British coal. It had to get seven million tons per year, two-thirds of this from Germany by sea. In March 1940 the British navy blockaded all German coal ports. Italy had to rely on 5000 trains a day carrying German coal across the Alps. Furthermore, much of Italy's Mediterranean trade was disrupted.

SOURCE 15.1 R. N. L. Absalom, *Italy since 1800: A Nation in the Balance*, 1995, p. 141

Boxed in by his structural compromises at home, he backed his instinct for joining the winning side in the struggle between two world systems.

SOURCE 15.2 Clark, p. 285

Fear mingled with greed in Mussolini's frenetic [frantic] mind. Important, too, were his sense of honour, his urge to transform his sheeplike people into wolves, and above all his need to be doing something. Mussolini was a bellicose [warlike] NATIONALIST. *He could not sit around in Rome, while the map of Europe was redrawn. His whole past, his whole propaganda, his whole regime had glorified war. Now there was one, and he had to join it.*

SOURCE 15.3 Gallo, p. 310

*Non-*BELLIGERENCE *meant the defeat not only of Mussolini but also of the party and the system, and, the longer inaction continued, the greater was the repudiation of eighteen years of warlike oratory and of all those who had engaged in it . . . Neutrality could lead only to crisis for Il* DUCE, *the party, and the government. Intervention on Germany's side, on the other hand, offered the chance of winning the gamble of war and hence of saving Il Duce, the party, and the system . . . Either way, the fate of Fascism was at stake, whether Italy entered the war or stayed out.*

Taking into account all the circumstances, Mussolini's decision was almost inevitable. It was not easy for a regime which had vilified (scorned) LIBERAL Italy's neutrality and which was held together by an IMPERIALIST and aggressive rhetoric to stand idly by while great victories were being won by its ally. Mussolini was strongly aware that his regime would be at the mercy of whoever won, and many in Italy saw that there could be strong benefits in joining the winning side as the war seemed to be drawing to a close.

Although Churchill blamed Italy's entry into the war on 'one man, and one man alone', in fact by June 1940 even Grandi and Ciano accepted that joining was sensible.

SOURCE 15.4 Mussolini speaking before Italy's entry into the war

e) April 1940

To make a people great it must be sent into battle even if it has to be kicked in the ass.

a)

Italy cannot remain neutral for the entire duration of the war without resigning her role, without reducing herself to the level of a Switzerland multiplied by ten.

d) Mussolini's reply to Badoglio's comment that the army did not have enough shirts

I know, but I need only a few thousand dead, so that I shall be able to sit at the peace table with the victor.

b) Mussolini to Ciano, March 1940

Neutrality would take Italy out of the class of the great powers for a century, and discredit her for all eternity as a Fascist regime; Italy would become a grade B country.
When a people is dominated by the instincts of the vegetative life, there is only one way to save it; by the use of force. Even those whom it strikes down will be grateful for it . . . The Italian race is a race of sheep, and eighteen years are not enough to change it.

c) Mussolini to Roosevelt, May 1940

Italy cannot remain absent at a moment in which the fate of Europe is at stake.

B How did Italians react to Italy entering the war?

Mussolini had finally got the great war his nation had been preparing for. In a speech from the balcony of the Palazzo Venezia, he called the people of Italy to rush to arms:

SOURCE 15.5 An extract from Mussolini's speech declaring war, June 1940

An hour that has been marked out by destiny is sounding in the sky above our fatherland! (Lively acclaim) *The hour of irrevocable [irreversible] decisions! The declaration of war has already been handed* (acclamations, loud shouts of 'War! War!') *to the ambassadors of Great Britain and France. We are going onto the battlefield against the* PLUTOCRATIC *and* REACTIONARY DEMOCRACIES *of the West who at every stage have hindered the march and have often threatened the very existence of the Italian people.*

If today we have decided to face the risks and sacrifices of a war, it is because honour, our interests, and our future firmly demand it, since a great people is truly such only if it holds sacred its obligations and does not evade the supreme tests that determine the course of history.

After having solved the problem of our land frontiers, we are taking up arms in order to establish our maritime frontiers. We want to break the territorial and military chains that are strangling us in our own sea. A nation of 45 million souls is not truly free unless it has free access to the ocean.

This gigantic struggle is only one phase of the logical development of our revolution; it is the struggle of peoples who though poor are rich in workers versus exploiters who cling fiercely to their MONOPOLY *of all the world's wealth and gold; it is the struggle of young and fertile peoples against sterile ones who stand on the verge of decline; it is the struggle between two centuries and two ideas.*

Italians! In a memorable meeting that took place in Berlin, I said that according to the laws of Fascist morality, whenever one has a friend, he stands by him to the end. We have done that, and we shall do it with Germany, with her people, and with her marvellous armed forces . . .

If his TOTALITARIAN regime had been working, the response in Italy should have been joyous, but considerable evidence suggests this was not the case.

SOURCE 15.6 The historian Max Gallo, who remembers Fascist Italy from his childhood, describes the reaction to the declaration of war

Mussolini was speaking from the balcony of the Palazzo Venezia. There was no emotion in the crowd, and only little knots of uniformed Fascists raised the cry of Guerra! Guerra! [War! War!] There was nothing of the vibrant enthusiasm that had filled the square after the Ethiopian war. Party officials had jostled the crowd into ranks, from which there came shouts of Crepa! Crepa! [Drop dead! Drop dead!], but the words were drowned in the deafening blare of trumpets and bands.

SOURCE 15.7 Herbert Matthews, head of the *New York Times* Rome Bureau 1939–42, describes Mussolini's declaration of war, 1940. Originally a supporter of Fascism, he turned against it because of Italian aggression

There was an immense demonstration in front of the Piazza Venezia for the Duce, but it was entirely organised. The local fasci had their orders to collect members, meet at a certain time and proceed to the square.

Fascists went round telling shopkeepers that they had to close at 5 o'clock. There was not the slightest spontaneous feeling, and the only cheering came from those, especially the students, who had been brought to the centre of the mob, under the balcony. Outside of that relatively tiny group of organised applauders, there was a light-hearted indifference which was really appalling, considering what was happening.

■ **Activity**

Contrast Mussolini's reaction to the prospect of war with that documented in Sources 15.6 and 15.7. How might the differences be explained?

FOCUS ROUTE

1 Outline the main details of the Italian war record.

2 What is a parallel war? How realistic a concept was it for Hitler and Mussolini?

3 **Either:**

Explain from material in this chapter and your wider knowledge of Fascist Italy why the following occurred:

- The armed forces were ill-prepared and unsuccessful.
- The economy was too weak to support a war effort.
- The regime lost the support of the ELITE.
- The regime became unpopular amongst the mass of Italians.
- Mussolini's leadership declined.

Or:

Essay: 'Why was Fascist Italy unable to meet the challenges of the Second World War?'

C How did Italy perform in the war?

Entry into the war ought to have been the crowning moment for a Fascist state since Mussolini had built his nation on preparation for war. As it was, the war revealed the inefficiencies in the state and hastened the dissolution of the broad coalition of interests which had sustained the Fascists since the 1920s. Now study Chart 15C on page 242 to gain an overview of the main Italian campaigns.

Parallel war

To take account of their varied interests and priorities the Axis partners decided to fight two separate campaigns of equal importance, a 'parallel' war for the same broad objectives. Italy and Germany would fight the same opponents, but in different theatres and for specifically national aims – Italy for its spazio vitale, Germany for its Lebensraum (see Source 15.8).

SOURCE 15.8   Map showing spazio vitale and Lebensraum, 1940

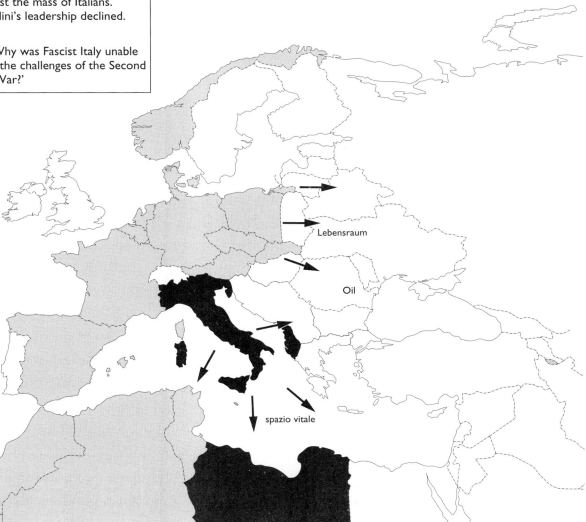

Key

Germany, satellite states and friendly states

Italian EMPIRE

■ Activity

1 Explain which area had the greatest potential for causing tension between Italy and Germany.

2 It has been argued that it was not the parallel war strategy which was at fault but Italy's military weakness compared to that of Germany. Do you agree?

Italy at war

CHART 15C   Italian foreign policy 1939–43

1 September 1939. Italy stays out of the war.
25 August Hitler tells Mussolini of his plan to invade Poland. Mussolini says Italy isn't ready to join, and needs massive resources from Germany. Hitler accepts this is impossible, and Mussolini declares Italy a 'non-belligerent'.

2 June 1940. Italy at war.
With France on the verge of surrender, Italy declares war in the hope of picking up some of the spoils of victory. It makes little impact; 32 Italian divisions are repulsed by 5 French ones. Mussolini fails to gain any colonies. Another mutilated victory?

3 September 1940. Italy launches an attack on British Egypt.
Italian troops in Libya attack Egypt.
After initial successes, the Italians are driven back.
The Germans have to divert resources to reinforce the Italians.
(British forces conquer all Italian land in East Africa by May 1941.)

4 October 1940. Italy invades Greece.
To match Hitler's occupation of Romania, Mussolini launches an attack on Greece from Albania, just after his attack on Egypt.
After a series of setbacks, the Germans are forced to intervene to sort out the muddle.
The parallel war seems to be dead.
Major blow to Fascist myth of power.

5 June 1941. Mussolini joins the war v USSR.
Unasked by Hitler, Mussolini sends 227,000 troops, needed in North Africa, to Hitler's attack on Russia. They make very little contribution, and are eventually defeated.

6 December 1941. Italy declares war on USA.
Mussolini follows Hitler in declaring war on the USA after the Japanese attack on Pearl Harbor.

7 1941–43.
After Italy's initial advance into Egypt, its troops are forced back into Libya. In 1941 the arrival of the German Afrika Korps under Rommel leads to new Axis advances, but after mixed fortunes by October 1942 the Axis powers are in retreat. In May 1943 the Axis North African army surrenders to British and American troops.

8 July–October 1943. Allies invade Sicily, and cross to mainland.
The Allied invasion precipitates the overthrow of Mussolini.
The new Italian government, controlling Central and Southern Italy, joins the Allies and fights against the German-controlled North.

9 September 1943. Mussolini becomes puppet ruler of new Salo REPUBLIC.
The Germans rescue Mussolini and install him as a puppet ruler in North Italy. A two-year campaign against Allied troops and Italian guerrillas ends in Mussolini's defeat and execution.

Military strategy
- No clear overall plan; Mussolini thought all his campaigns would be quickly won.
- Oct 1940 ordered demobilisation; then a week later decided to attack Greece.
- The three services were fighting virtually separate wars. Mussolini had kept the traditional structures of the armed services, each branch of which was jealous of the others.
- Lack of co-operation with German allies
- Mussolini failed to prioritise; wasted resources in Russia, and on Italy's northern border facing Germany.

Military resources
- Failed to build up modern resources
- Rifles from 1891 were the only arms for 35 of the army's 80 divisions
- Only five months' supply of fuel in 1939
- Only 1500 tanks, mainly light
- Large airforce, but mostly outdated
- Virtually no anti-aircraft guns
- No aircraft carriers (as the airforce was hostile to navy control)
- Naval resources concentrated on eight prestige battleships (only two saw major conflict), rather than a wider range of ships
- Large submarine fleet, but low quality; one-tenth lost in first three weeks of war
- Military production increased during the war, but up to one-third of equipment was lost in transit across the Mediterranean.

When Chief of Army Staff Graziani complained in May 1940 that there were only 1.3 million rifles, many without bayonets, despite the boast of 8 million bayonets, Mussolini told him not to worry as the army was intended for show not action.

Economy
- Italy lacked basic raw materials, and its poor trading record meant it lacked the currency reserves to build up resources through imports. Once war broke out, importing became even more difficult. Germany was unable to fill the gaps.
- Germans took more resources (e.g. labour – 350,000 in 1942, and food) than it supplied (coal, iron).
- Growing shortages of oil and coal crippled industry.
- Industrial production fell by 25 per cent 1940–43.
- Agricultural production also fell by 25 per cent, as there were shortages of labour and fertiliser.
- Taxes went up (taking one-quarter of the national income, but only covering one-third of government expenditure).

Society
- Average calorie consumption was one-fifth of pre-war levels.
- Food rationing was at the same levels as in Nazi-occupied Poland.
- Signs of disillusionment with war, especially after the 1942 Allied bombing raids in North increased grumbling rather than uniting the people.
- Police reported growing disillusionment.
- Growing social unrest, especially strikes. Major wave in North, March 1943. 100,000 involved; first major strikes for twenty years. Leaflets called for 'Bread, Peace and Freedom'. Graffiti: 'Fascism is Hunger', 'Death to the Duce', 'Stalin is coming'.

■ Activity

1. Study Chart 15C. List the evidence of Italy's military failures.
2. Research exercise. In groups, allocate each one of the major events in Chart 15C to one student to research more detail about it. Make notes to report back your findings.
3. The following have all been identified as Mussolini's poorest decision. Explain which one you favour.
   - a) Declaring war on France and Britain in June 1940
   - b) Attacking both Egypt and Greece in Autumn 1940
   - c) Declaring war on and sending troops to fight the USSR in June 1941
   - d) Declaring war on the USA in December 1941

Political
- Fascist administration was inefficient and corrupt.
- The state depended upon the co-operation of the elite whom Mussolini had to keep in place and placate (keep happy): they acted as a brake on the full fascistisation of the state which might otherwise have allowed the effective utilisation of resources.
- The elite became increasingly disillusioned with Mussolini, as he embarked on domestic radicalisation, and as Italy suffered defeats.
- The Party was unable to cope with its assigned roles, e.g. organising civil defence, welfare, price controls, stockpiles, and keeping up morale. 'The Party is absent and impotent,' lamented Farinacci in 1943.
- Mussolini speaking to the PNF: 'There are four million members of the fasci, eight million in GIL ... The regime controls something like 25 million individuals ... Well, what are all these people doing? I ask myself what are they doing?'
- Elements in the Fascist Party, army, Vatican and royal household began considering alternatives, culminating in the July 1943 coup.

Mussolini
- He took all the top positions, e.g. Commander in Chief on all fronts; War Minister; Minister for all three services.
- He took all the decisions, but failed to co-ordinate strategy.
- No proper discussions; Mussolini relied on his intuition.
- As police chief Bocchini said, 'By trying to control everything he was deceived and disobeyed by almost everyone.'
- Failing health. From February 1940 he had a serious stomach ulcer, was physically unfit, and was ageing rapidly.
- Increasingly out of touch. He became a victim of his own propaganda (especially after the death of his brother Arnaldo in 1931, one of the few people who had dared to tell Mussolini the truth).

SOURCE 15.9   An Allied cartoon with the caption 'Buck Benito rides again'

SOURCE 15.10   Clark, p. 292

[By 1943] the whole Fascist regime was crumbling. Reality had caught up with it. The facades of bellicose activism, of controlling the economy, of Youth and Patriotism, all were collapsing in the harsh glare of war.

SOURCE 15.11   Absalom, p. 157

The Fascist regime was already in 1940 fundamentally unsound. It was incapable of developing a coherent diplomacy or military strategy, and was politically so fragile that after twenty years of undisputed power its leadership was unable to MOBILISE *its economic and* DEMOGRAPHIC *resources to wage effective war.*

SOURCE 15.12   Mack Smith, *Mussolini*, 1981, p. 298

In war, as in peace, [Mussolini] made the mistake of sacrificing substance for effect, preoccupied above all with demonstrating that he alone was in command.

SOURCE 15.13   A joke told by de Bono to Italian senators

Hitler and Mussolini met at the Brenner Pass, and after talking for a while, Hitler excused himself. The Duce reached over for a bottle of champagne, but as he opened it the cork flew out and gave him a black eye. When the Führer returned, he took one look at Mussolini, shook his head sadly and said, 'Duce, Duce, if I leave you alone for a moment, you get beaten up.'

Mack Smith makes the following points about Mussolini's failure:

SOURCE 15.14   Mack Smith, 1981, pp. 15, 16

Mussolini made a conscious choice that bread and circuses should be a top priority in the budget. Although he also wanted an expansionist foreign policy, it was his hope that a mere facade might be the most effective as well as the cheapest component of such a policy, on the assumption that one could probably fool nearly all the people for nearly all the time.

But above all the explanation of Italy's weakness must be sought in his great sense of showmanship and in the propaganda-consciousness which allowed him to seize on the dangerous half-truth that it was less important to do things in politics than to seem to do things; and in the process he without doubt, often and demonstrably, confused the two.

■ Activity

Clark writes (p. 287), 'Most infantrymen were peasants, as in 1915–18. They were fighting, and dying, far from home for a cause which few of them understood. They fought, for the most part, with discipline and courage.' Does this opinion confirm the stereotype?

■ Talking point

If you had been a Sicilian peasant CONSCRIPTED into the army and sent to fight in the USSR, how enthusiastic do you think you would have been?

■ Learning trouble spot

'A shambles': Why was Fascist Italy unable to cope with the Second World War?

Many students find it hard to understand why Fascist Italy performed so badly in the Second World War. After all, Mussolini had been in power for nearly twenty years by 1940. He had stressed the importance of preparing Italy for war, and believed war both desirable and inevitable.

Various explanations can be put forward. One point is that between 1935 and 1939 Italy had already been involved in two wars which had reduced its military capacity. When Mussolini signed the Pact of Steel he warned Hitler that Italy would not be ready for a major war until 1943. This explains why he stayed out of the war in 1939. As we have seen, he only joined in 1940 when he considered the war was nearly over. So far, so good. But then why, once France was knocked out, did he widen the war in 1940 by invading both Greece and Egypt in the same period; and then even more amazingly, declare war on the USSR and the USA in 1941?

It seems that he considered these campaigns would be easy victories. Greece was a minor power; the British Empire was weak, so Egypt, trapped between Libya and Italian East Africa, would fall. The USSR had been desperate to avoid war as it was so weak, and the all-conquering Hitler would easily knock it out in 1941 (as indeed he nearly did). America was seen as another feeble democracy that was good at jazz but not fighting.

Further explanation can come from the importance Mussolini placed on propaganda. He realised that if he could make Italy appear as a great power, he might be able to get his way by bullying and making even major powers see the need to appease him. Thus he did not really need to increase massively Italy's military might, but just convince other powers of it. Hence his great boasts about his airforce that would 'blot out the sun', and that he had 'eight million bayonets'. He could get gains for Italy through bluff, and through short campaigns against weak opponents.

However, it has been argued that Mussolini became a victim of his own propaganda. He had spent so long telling the world what a great power Italy was, that he began to believe it. Thus Mussolini, the skilled realist of the 1920s, became the deluded buffoon of the late 1930s.

Another element in the explanation could be that Mussolini became entrapped by Hitler. He was so impressed by Germany's might he believed that with his ally he could achieve his grand ambitions. He combined this with some resentment of Hitler's power, which he had dreams of matching.

Another factor could relate to the spirit of Fascism. Mussolini stressed the importance of 'will' in history; that if the spirit was strong, then assertive peoples could achieve their aims. This was evident in his economic policies, such as AUTARKY, and can explain how he took Italy into situations beyond its objective ability to tackle. However, although Mussolini's will may have been strong, that of the Italian people certainly wasn't.

Thus Italy's failure at war can also be taken as evidence of the limited impact of fascistisation. Mussolini had failed, as he later admitted, to create that nation of warlike Italians to which he aspired. Furthermore, his tactical reliance on the traditional elite meant the regime could not withstand the loss of that support which military failure caused. Hence his overthrow.

More traditionally, one can stress Italy's lack of economic and military resources. As we have seen, Italy did not have the military hardware to win major wars. This was partly due to its comparative lack of vital economic resources, such as coal, iron and oil. However, this problem was increased by Mussolini's failure to use the resources available effectively, and to give military production sufficiently high priority. This is partly explained by his belief that his campaigns would be short, and he would not need to use great resources. Mussolini failed to acknowledge the extent of administrative inefficiency and corruption which further sapped all Italy's war effort.

D How was Mussolini overthrown?

CHART 15E   The slide to the end

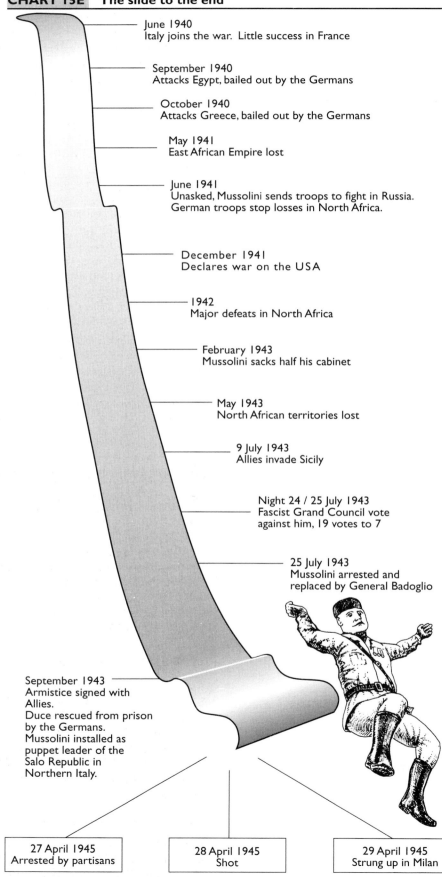

June 1940
Italy joins the war. Little success in France

September 1940
Attacks Egypt, bailed out by the Germans

October 1940
Attacks Greece, bailed out by the Germans

May 1941
East African Empire lost

June 1941
Unasked, Mussolini sends troops to fight in Russia.
German troops stop losses in North Africa.

December 1941
Declares war on the USA

1942
Major defeats in North Africa

February 1943
Mussolini sacks half his cabinet

May 1943
North African territories lost

9 July 1943
Allies invade Sicily

Night 24 / 25 July 1943
Fascist Grand Council vote
against him, 19 votes to 7

25 July 1943
Mussolini arrested and
replaced by General Badoglio

September 1943
Armistice signed with
Allies.
Duce rescued from prison
by the Germans.
Mussolini installed as
puppet leader of the
Salo Republic in
Northern Italy.

| 27 April 1945 Arrested by partisans | 28 April 1945 Shot | 29 April 1945 Strung up in Milan |

Hitler was defeated by the greatest coalition of forces the world had ever seen. Stalin was defeated only by age. Mussolini was overthrown by his own people. That contrast in itself is significant.

The Second World War destroyed Mussolini and, as you have seen, Fascist Italy proved itself incapable of fighting a major war.

Mussolini, as he later came to regret, had never been strong enough to remove all alternative power structures in Italy. He had co-operated with the MONARCHY for 21 years, despite mutual dislike. Although ultimately it was the King who dismissed Mussolini, the initiative in his overthrow was taken by key colleagues at the top of the Fascist Party itself.

By 1943 Italy was facing military defeat. The Allies had invaded Italy, and it was suffering heavy bombing. Discontent and unrest were growing. During the war Mussolini had toyed with various options, such as peace with the USSR, but he never really considered the one move which might have saved him, a break with Hitler. In February 1943 Mussolini sacked half his Cabinet. This increased the discontent within the party. Others amongst the political, industrial and ecclesiastical elites were exploring various options. The crisis broke in July 1943 when the Fascist Grand Council met for the first time since 1939. This meeting was engineered by various Fascist leaders; some, like Farinacci, wanted to cement further the alliance with Germany; others, like Grandi and Bottai, were secretly looking for the Duce's dismissal. Mussolini was persuaded to agree to the meeting.

A move to end the DICTATORSHIP, but to maintain a Fascist government, was debated for nine hours, and finally passed by nineteen votes to seven. Next day Mussolini went to the King who ordered his arrest. Thousands of Italians rejoiced on hearing of Mussolini's dismissal. It was not just the end of Mussolini, but also, contrary to many plotters' wishes, of Fascism. Fascism could not survive without its leader. Hitler was bemused by that 'Fascism which melts like snow in the sun'.

A new government was formed under Marshal Badoglio. It banned all Fascist organisations, withdrew from the war, and soon switched sides by joining the Allies. Mussolini was imprisoned.

FOCUS ROUTE

1 Each of Sources 15.15–20 has a view on the failed dictatorship in Italy. What are the main reasons given for Mussolini's downfall?
2 Read Source 15.17. Why did members of the Fascist Grand Council take the initiative to remove Mussolini?
3 Read Source 15.20. How valid do you consider Hitler's views of the role of Italy?
4 Imagine you were at the 1943 Grand Council debate which deposed Mussolini, and write the speech of either
  a) Grandi calling for Mussolini's dismissal; or
  b) Mussolini defending his position.
  In groups or pairs listen to each speech and debate the issues.

SOURCE 15.15 Federzoni describes the aim of the Grand Council meeting

... to secure as quickly as possible Italy's release from the German alliance and from the war. By then we knew that Mussolini was incapable of doing this; it was therefore necessary to force him to leave so that the country would not suffer a complete disaster ... It was up to us to act. It was clear that the King himself needed some formal motive, some CONSTITUTIONAL excuse; and, most important of all, only the Grand Council, because it was a Fascist institution, would be able to neutralise, as in fact it did, any possible revolt by the party and the militia in support of Mussolini.

SOURCE 15.16 Grandi in the Grand Council, 24 July 1943

The real enemy of Fascism is dictatorship. From the day when the old motto 'Liberty and Fatherland' inscribed on the action squads was replaced by the other 'Believe, Obey, Fight', Fascism was finished. The narrow, absurd formula of the

Fascist war has brought the nation to ruin. The responsibility for this disaster lies not with Fascism but with the dictatorship. It is the latter which has lost the war...

You believe you have the support of the Italian people. You lost it the day you tied Italy to Germany.

SOURCE 15.17   Extract from Federzoni's summary of Grandi's speech

The Head of Government has spoken of the unpardonable errors committed by military leaders and by the armed forces that he himself personally commands. But Mussolini, Head of Government and the minister in charge of all the armed services, has had seventeen years to create, organise, prepare and to select the officer corps, the troops and the equipment ... Military preparedness was ... the major task for the man who had the honour of guiding the destiny of the nation ...

The Grand Council must decide to restore all the authority and responsibility of state institutions which the dictatorship has absorbed and return to the crown, the Grand Council, the Parliament and the corporations all the tasks assigned to them by our constitutional laws.

SOURCE 15.18   Victor Emmanuel to Mussolini, 25 July 1943

My dear Duce, it's no longer any good. Italy has gone to bits. Army morale is at rock bottom. The soldiers don't want to fight any more ... You can certainly be under no illusion as to Italy's feelings with regard to yourself. At this moment you are the most hated man in Italy.
[Mussolini replied] I realise the people's hatred.

SOURCE 15.19   Report by the office of the German foreign ministry

The crisis of July 25th undoubtedly has its origins in happenings of the already distant past. Grave signs of internal decay, especially corruption, the lack of a clear lead and above all the presence of totally unqualified persons in leading positions, had already long discredited the edifice of the Fascist regime in the eyes of the entire nation.

SOURCE 15.20   Extract from the *Political Testament* of Hitler, May 1945

Judging events coldly, leaving aside all sentimentality, I have to admit that having unyielding friendship for Italy, and for the Duce, could be added to the list of my mistakes. It is visible that the Italian alliance rendered more service to the enemy than to ourselves. The intervention of Italy will have only brought us an infinitesimal aid in comparison with the numerous difficulties which it has created for us. It will have contributed, if we do not win in spite of everything, to making us lose the war. The greatest service which Italy could have done to us was to have kept out of the conflict ...

Our Italian ally has embarrassed us everywhere ... Italy's entry into the war at once gave our adversaries [opponents] their first victories ... Although incapable of holding out in Abyssinia and Libya, the Italians had the nerve, without asking our advice and even without warning us, to launch into an absolutely useless campaign in Greece. Their dishonourable setbacks aroused the ill humour of certain Balkan states with regard to us ... This led us, contrary to all plans, to intervene in the Balkans, whence the catastrophic delay in unleashing the war against Russia ... If the war had remained one conducted by Germany, and not by the Axis, we would have been able to attack Russia as from May 15th, 1941 ...

My attachment to the person of the Duce has not changed ... but I regret not having listened to reason which imposed on me a brutal friendship with regard to Italy ...

■ **Talking point**

After the defeat of Germany and Japan, some of their leaders were tried and executed as war criminals. There were no international trials of Italian Fascists. Why do you think this was?

FOCUS ROUTE

1 What was the Salo Republic?
2 What does the Salo Republic reveal about the nature of Mussolini and Fascism?

After his arrest Mussolini was moved to various secure places. Eventually he ended up at a winter sports hotel on the slopes of the highest mountain of the Apennines, Gran Sasso. Hitler decided to rescue him. A cleverly conceived land and air scheme was devised, including the landing of gliders on the only flat land near the mountain hotel. The operation was successfully carried out on 12 September 1943 and Mussolini was flown to Germany to meet the Führer.

'I have come to receive my orders.' Thus Mussolini greeted Hitler, after his rescue. It was a pathetic position, and finally revealed the increasing imbalance in the Axis. Hitler wanted Mussolini to re-establish a Fascist state in northern Italy. The Duce hesitated before eventually agreeing. Observing this, one German observer noted, 'He is not a revolutionary like the Führer or Stalin'.

Mussolini's new puppet regime called itself the Italian Social Republic. It was derisively (scornfully) known as the Salo Republic after the name of the city where its ministry of propaganda was based. Many books make a brief mention of the Salo Republic, almost as an afterthought. However, is there a case for interpreting this as the route Fascism might have followed after 1922? Does it reinforce the view that we came across in the Reform of Customs, that Mussolini was trying to reorientate Fascism away from the conservative regime it had become?

Certainly it spoke loudly about workers' rights and the collective interest. In September 1943 Mussolini announced the formation of the new republic and its principles (see Source 15.22). He later claimed, in his last public speech, that the programme of Republican Fascism 'is but the logical continuation of the programme of 1919'. The Fascist revolution had been prevented by the compromises he had made with the elite; now he was free to embark on true Fascism. But this was another, his last, pathetic illusion. The Germans exercised real power in Salo, and they wanted to exploit Italian resources, not to indulge in social experiments.

Thus the presence of the Germans, the overall weakness of the Salo regime and the continuing civil war meant that in practice little actually happened.

SOURCE 15.21   B. Sullivan in Cannistraro (ed.), p. 287

The RSI [Repubblica Sociale Italiana] has been damned as camouflage for brutal German occupation and praised as the pure expression of Fascist idealism. In fact, the RSI reflected many of the contradictory strains within Fascism (which Mussolini's earlier regime had suppressed) as well as Mussolini's attempt to vindicate his reputation. Its ultimate reality, however, was German control.

SOURCE 15.22   Extract from a radio broadcast by Mussolini from Munich, 18 September 1943, declaring the principles of his new Italian Social Republic

After a long silence my voice reaches you again ... The State which we wish to set up will be national and social ... that is, it will be Fascist, thus going back to our origins. While waiting for the movement to develop until it becomes irresistible, our fundamental approach will be the following: to take up arms alongside Germany, Japan ... ; to set about reorganising our armed forces around the militia formations ... ; to eliminate the traitors ... who ... had been active ... in the ranks of the Party and who had gone over to the ranks of the enemy; to annihilate the parasite plutocracies and at last to make labour the theme of our economy and the indestructible basis of the State.

SOURCE 15.23 A cartoon showing Mussolini in Hitler's pocket

SOURCE 15.24 Mussolini as leader of the Salo Republic

As Mack Smith writes (p. 185), 'The Republic could decide on anything and enact little or nothing.' All government actions had to be approved by the German ambassador Rahn, and SS General Wolff. Northern Italy was to be exploited for the final fling of the German war effort. The Germans saw socialisation as sabotage and did not enact it. A worn-out Mussolini became wrapped up in bureaucracy; he only attended one public rally.

In Italy itself the Germans and Salo Italians had to fight both against the slowly advancing Allies, and the rapidly growing resistance movement, led by a coalition of COMMUNISTS and Catholics. This war of liberation has been called the second Italian RISORGIMENTO, and it later took on even greater importance than it did at the time.

By the Spring of 1945 everything was over. Mussolini, trying to escape with the Germans over the border, was recognised by Communist guerrillas, and shot. His body was later publicly displayed. The Italians who for twenty years had cheered his voice now desecrated his body.

■ Talking point

Why do you think Italians pay a lot more attention to the war of liberation than do foreign writers?

■ Activity

1 Study the chart below. Look at the policies of the Salo Republic and Source 15.22 and compare them with what Mussolini did between 1922 and 1943. What are the main differences between the two regimes? How might you explain this?
2 Does this support the view that the Salo Republic was an attempt to return to original Fascism?
3 The Salo Republic can be viewed as a useful insight into true Fascism now that Mussolini owed nothing to his conservative supporters, or as a mere sad postscript to his career. What is your view?

Features of early Fascism	Fascist Italy until 1943	The Salo Republic 1943–45
Republicanism	Monarchy retained	Republican
National SYNDICALISM, with powerful Fascist SYNDICATES	Workers' rights submerged within the Corporative State which favoured employers	State to regulate industry in the interest of employees and employers. Firms to be run by boards with 50% workers. Plans for single national union
Squadrismo	Squads merged into state militia	Squads re-formed in new Black Brigades
Duce as dominant leader	Duce dominated the government and mass rallies, but King remained	Mussolini was officially head of state, but largely a recluse; his decisions had to pass through German hands
National greatness	Conquered Abyssinia and Albania	Germany annexed some Italian gains from First World War in South Tyrol. State controlled less than half of Italy

F Review: Why did Mussolini's regime lose the war and collapse?

FOCUS ROUTE

What does the period 1940–45 reveal about the nature of Mussolini's regime?
Refer to:

- Italy's military performance
- the quality of Mussolini's decision making
- how Mussolini was overthrown
- the lack of resistance to his overthrow
- the nature of the Salo Republic.

■ **Activity**

Do you tend to favour Taylor or Morgan's view?

This chapter has investigated the disastrous conduct of the Second World War and linked the defeat with Mussolini's dismissal.

A.J.P. Taylor has argued that if Mussolini had not joined in the Second World War he would have remained in power, and probably emerged as a founding father of NATO. The experience of Franco (who stayed in power in Spain until 1975) adds some plausibility to this argument.

On the other hand, the initial premise of this view is open to challenge. Was Mussolini's decision to declare war on Germany's side just a particular decision that could have gone the other way, or did it reflect the very nature of Mussolini and his Fascist regime? Indeed, are Fascism and war inseparable? Recently the British historian Morgan has argued:

SOURCE 15.25 Morgan, pp. 187–88

It is futile to argue retrospectively that Fascism would have survived but for the external factor of the Second World War. It might have done, but it would not have been Fascism. War was essential not incidental to Fascism ... War was means and end, the way of subverting both the existing internal and international order, effecting both conquest and 'fascistisation' ... War was meant to accelerate things, but it destroyed any basis of rapport and support the regime had achieved.

Key points from Chapter 15

1. Italy entered the war in June 1940 believing it was about to finish and that it could share the spoils.
2. Mussolini agreed to fight a parallel war with Germany, each pursuing national objectives in different spheres.
3. Economically, militarily and psychologically the Italians were unprepared for war.
4. The Italian army was defeated in all its theatres of war.
5. Hitler increasingly became involved in Italian areas as he bailed out Mussolini.
6. Defeats in war encouraged elements in the elite to consider replacing Mussolini.
7. The Fascist Grand Council voted to reduce his powers. The King dismissed and imprisoned him.
8. Rescued by Hitler, Mussolini reluctantly set up a Republican Fascist state in northern Italy to resist the Allied advance.
9. Little more than a German puppet state, it failed to establish itself and had to fight a guerrilla war against partisans.
10. In April 1945 Mussolini was captured and shot.

Section 4 Review: How significant was Mussolini's foreign policy?

We began this section by asking about the significance of Fascist foreign policy within the context of the whole Fascist experiment. Let us now try to summarise the effect Mussolini's foreign policy had on his regime, and on international relations. Did Mussolini's foreign policy strengthen or weaken the regime? You may want to answer this question in two stages, considering the following issues:

a) 1922–36
   Success and prestige in the early period
   Popularity over Abyssinia
b) 1936–43
   Involvement in wars 1936–39, 1940–43
   Domestic effects of the Nazi alliance.

Did Mussolini succeed in raising Italy's international status?

Mussolini stressed how he wanted to make Italy a respected power. Judgement on how far he succeeded would partly depend on the period concerned. Certainly in the 1920s he won much international acclaim for his domestic achievements, but his foreign policy was less successful, and his eventual decision to join the Second World War in 1940 finally ruined his reputation in the West, without impressing Hitler.

Look at these historians' assessments.

SOURCE I   Overy, p. 181

Mussolini certainly raised Italy's international status, and provided hard-won achievements in Africa and Spain. But in the process he succeeded in persuading much stronger powers, France and Britain, that Fascist Italy was a dangerous, REVISIONIST state. In challenging their power, Mussolini overstretched Italian resources and ran much greater risks, which finally exposed Italian weakness ... [Italy became tied to Germany who saw through him.] German armies were needed to save Italy from disaster in Greece and North Africa. This has always been the paradox of Italy's position: only German help could bring about the revision Italy wanted, but German help would cost Italy the international independence of action revision was supposed to achieve.

What impact did Fascist Italy have on general international relations?

Traditionally Fascist Italy is seen as the poor relation to Nazi Germany when it comes to assessing the development of international relations, especially the causes of the Second World War. It is hard to disagree with this judgement, yet as Lee argues (Source 2), Mussolini perhaps had a greater impact than the might of Italy warranted.

Another interesting angle on this is the effect of Mussolini's actions on Hitler, and vice versa.

■ Activity

1 Consider the following issues:
• Did Mussolini's action in Abyssinia weaken the League of Nations?
• Did his challenge to the European order encourage Hitler to be more aggressive?
• How significant was his impact on the Spanish Civil War?
• How important was Mussolini's role at the Munich conference?
• Referring to the previous issues, did Mussolini contribute to the origins of the Second World War?
2 Read Sources 1 and 2. Do you agree with these assessments? Give your reasons.

SOURCE 2   Lee, 'Mussolini's Foreign Policy in Perspective' in *History Review 20*, 1994, pp. 33–35

[By the 1930s] Italy now acquired an influence out of all proportion to her real power, moving from a peripheral [on the edges] to a pivotal position in European affairs. The results were unexpected and devastating as Mussolini became, between 1935 and 1938, the main catalyst [agent] in the transformation of the international scene ...

The fact that Mussolini's policies failed should not detract from his real importance as one of the most important catalysts for change in the inter-war period.

The fatal friendship. Mussolini and Hitler: who killed whom?

Although Mussolini himself did not blame Hitler for his downfall, many historians argue that Mussolini's decision to tie himself to Nazi Germany was fatal for his regime. Hitler in 1945 blamed Mussolini for his defeat (see Chart A).

■ Activity

Study Chart A. Then organise a debate in 1944 between an Italian Fascist blaming Hitler for Italy's problems, and a German Nazi blaming Mussolini for harming Germany's war effort.

CHART A   Italy and Germany: their effect on each other

Effect of Italy on Germany

a) 1933–35: restraining

1934   Over Austria, then at Stresa, 1935, Italy acted as a deterrent on Hitler, so he was cautious.

b) 1935–39: helpful

1935   Abyssinia: distracted Britain and France from Germany, encouraged Hitler to take over Rhineland.

1936   Spanish Civil War: showed Western weakness, further encouraging Hitler to break Versailles Settlement.

c) 1940 onwards: harmful

1940–41 Mussolini's failings in Greece led to Hitler intervening in the Balkans, crucially delaying his attack on the Soviet Union.
Italian failure in North Africa diverted Hitler from Europe, and weakened his Russian campaign.

1943   Mussolini's overthrow forced the Germans to occupy north Italy.

Effect of Germany on Italy

a) 1933–35: helpful

West's fear of revived Germany gave Mussolini opportunities to exploit situation to make Italian gains.

b) 1936 onwards: unachievable role model

Mussolini, increasingly impressed by Germany, allied himself to Germany. Adopted racist policy at home. Both moves were unpopular.

1939   Mussolini invaded Albania and in 1940 declared war to try to gain victory spoils.

c) 1941 onwards: harmful

Mussolini joined Hitler in declaring war on USSR and USA, which weakened further the Italian war effort in North Africa.

d) 1943–45: exploitative

1943 Military defeat led to Mussolini's overthrow.
Germany rescued Mussolini, and used him as a puppet.

Interpretations of Fascist Italy

 ## How have historians interpreted Fascist Italy?

'One doesn't read history; one reads historians.' This view reminds us that the history that we read is produced by historians. These historians all have their own political and historical perspectives. They study and write in particular contexts, and examine only some of the records of the past. They try to create as accurate an interpretation as possible of the aspects of the past they consider important. Although there have not developed major 'schools', such as the intentionalist versus structuralist debate over the importance of Hitler's own aims and broader factors in Nazi foreign policy, there are considerable differences in historians' assessments of Mussolini and Fascist Italy.

Hostile contemporary views

The first interpretation of Italian Fascism, still widely held, was made by its opponents whilst Mussolini was still in power. Fascism was seen, both in Italy and more generally, as the political expression of discontented lower-middle-class groups, reacting in the turbulent period after the First World War to worsening economic conditions and political instability. The upper classes reluctantly used Fascism to restore their traditional dominance of the state which was threatened by the growing power of the masses, especially the SOCIALISTS. The writings of exiles like Salvemini stressed the repressive nature of Fascism, and its disastrous impact on Italy. In the late 1920s the official COMMUNIST view of Fascism saw it as a reflection of the terminal condition of CAPITALISM, and a last desperate attempt by capitalists to hold on to power.

Post Second World War Italian views

Mussolini's dismissal in 1943, and the Italian government's change of sides in the Second World War, encouraged the view that Fascism could be largely blamed on one man, Mussolini. He had held the Italian people in his sway, partly by propaganda, partly through repression, but they had eventually seen the true nature of the man and his regime. The resistance movement in occupied northern Italy 1943–45, in which both Catholics and Communists participated, was seen as representing the true beliefs of the Italian people.

Thus from 1943 onwards Fascism had to be condemned; only a small minority on the Right argued for any benefits. Debate, however, did soon surface; firstly over the reasons why Italy fell into Fascism.

Debate over the origins of Fascism

a) Fascism as a diversion

In the 1940s a major debate developed over the place of Fascism in Italian history. The philosopher-historian Croce argued that Fascism was a 'parenthesis' (a temporary digression) in Italian history, a form of disease which suddenly afflicted Italy, but from which it recovered. This somewhat reassuring view was attacked as disguising the mistakes that the ELITE (like Croce himself!) had made in collaborating with Fascism. It was also seen as neglecting the deeper roots of Fascism, and elements of continuity with LIBERAL Italy.

b) Fascism as 'revelation'

An alternative view, that of Fascism as 'revelation', stressed what Fascism revealed about the nature of Italian history, emphasising continuity in Italian history since unification. In this view Fascism was a logical consequence of the way Italy was unified, and its resultant weaknesses. Italy had been made by an elite distrustful of the masses; Liberal Italy reflected this in the gap between real and legal Italy. In the post First World War crisis, the conservative ruling elite turned to Fascism as a logical move to consolidate its power. Aside from this debate, there was still a broad consensus on the PETTY BOURGEOIS origins of the movement, the conservative function of the regime, and criticism of the effects of Fascism.

De Felice and revisionism

In the 1960s access to state archives was considerably improved, and a mass of primary source material became available. The passage of time suggested it might be possible for Italians to examine Fascism more objectively. By far the most important of the historians who now plunged into a detailed examination of the new sources was Renzo de Felice (see pages 256–57). His most controversial argument was his reassessment of Mussolini's achievements by the mid-1930s in a more positive light, and his view that the regime was genuinely popular. The orthodox view that Italians had been forced to submit to a hated tyrant with a farcical IDEOLOGY could not be sustained. De Felice's view of the era challenged the anti-Fascist political consensus on the nature of Fascism which had helped sustain the Italian REPUBLIC since its creation in 1946.

Recent greater diversity

Despite the uproar de Felice caused, especially in Italy, for saying the unthinkable, he inspired a variety of new interpretations as old assumptions were challenged. New techniques and perspectives encouraged a wider variety of approaches to historical study, and attempts were made to portray the day-to-day lives of Italians under Fascism, instead of relying on official documents. Development of new sociological perspectives, the use of oral history by Passerini and others, a host of local studies, and examination of the mass organisations OND and ONB, as well as specialist studies of women, have helped produce a more complex picture of the Fascist state. Parallel study of Nazi Germany – which has deepened understanding of the pressures for conformity – and a more sophisticated understanding of the limitations of TOTALITARIAN regimes have all helped create greater diversity of interpretation.

In many ways the history of the history of Italian Fascism has been a modified version of the great debates which have served both to distort and illuminate our understanding of Nazi Germany and the Soviet Union. The influence of political factors, the bias against a discredited regime and the resulting attempt to blame others, the impact of new historical approaches and the examination of new sources, and the limitations of the totalitarian model are all shown in Italian HISTORIOGRAPHY.

■ Activity

1 Identify examples and explain how the following have influenced historians' views of Fascism:
   a) The political viewpoint of historians
   b) The dominance of a political consensus
   c) The availability of sources
   d) New research methods
   e) Study of other countries.

2 Explain this comment, made by the British historian Pollard in a 1980 article 'Changing Interpretations of Fascism': 'Given prevailing attitudes towards Italy's past, no matter what the weight of supporting evidence, it is inconceivable and unacceptable that an historian should present Fascism as anything but wicked and disastrous, or Mussolini as anything except a fraud and a failure.'

Renzo de Felice

His work

De Felice was an Italian Jew who survived the Holocaust. He originally was attracted to Communism and was in the PCI until 1956, but he gradually grew more conservative. His first historical works were on the Italian Jacobins, Jews under Fascism, and d'Annunzio, but he made his name with his massive biography of Mussolini. The first volume, *Mussolini the Revolutionary*, was published in 1965, with the last volume coming in the 1990s, shortly before his death.

The titles of the volumes are a useful indication of his views.

1 Mussolini the Revolutionary, 1883–1920
2 Mussolini the Fascist
   a) Conquest of Power, 1921–25
   b) Organisation of the Fascist State, 1925–29
3 Mussolini, Il DUCE
   a) Years of Consensus, 1929–36
   b) Totalitarian State 1936–40
4 Mussolini the Ally 1940–45 (unfinished)
   a) Italy at War 1940–43
   b) Crisis and Agony of the Regime

De Felice argued that Fascism was a movement of a rising middle class, especially civil servants and peasants. They had an optimistic, creative spirit, seen in Fascist ideas of PRODUCTIVISM and corporativism. They formed a truly progressive and revolutionary movement, wanting to MOBILISE the masses to transform Italy, and take power from the traditional elite; hence Mussolini 'the Revolutionary'. De Felice stresses the distinction between Fascism as a movement (before it gained power), inherently dynamic, and Fascism as a regime (when in power), where compromises with the elite were necessary. But the movement retained its vitality, expressing itself in the Abyssinian War, ANTI-SEMITISM, and finally in the Salo Republic.

His major stress is on the degree of support the regime had achieved by the mid-1930s, a view partly deriving from his more positive assessment of Mussolini's policies, and a preparedness to stress the genuine expression of support in the PLEBISCITES, where other historians stress pressure on voting. Not surprisingly, he was accused of sympathising with Fascism, a charge he rejected.

He emphasised the differences from Nazism, and argued that the Nazi alliance was the crucial policy which led to a weakening of the consensus, though he maintained there was support until well into the war. According to de Felice, the resistance was a small minority.

His methods

De Felice was criticised not just for his analysis but for his methods. He greatly relied on the records of the Fascist Party and government in the central state archives in Rome, supplemented by private papers of some leading Fascists. To some extent he became a victim of such an impressive wealth of new material; he was criticised for putting too much stress on it, as well as for his impressionistic use of the material. He naturally rejected such charges, and maintained his conclusions were tentative, and that he was prepared to modify them in his genuine attempt to discover the truth. Indeed, not surprisingly, his views do vary across the volumes.

Unfortunately, and interestingly, his massive biography of Mussolini has not been translated into English. However, he did contribute a long entry on Mussolini in Cannistraro's invaluable *Historical Dictionary of Fascist Italy*, 1982. The following extract from that entry gives a clear survey of his overall view.

In 1929, with the Lateran Pacts and a national plebiscite that sought to demonstrate popular consensus for Fascism, the regime was solidly established. From that moment Mussolini's actions assumed new, wider dimensions, extending from the domestic politics that had previously preoccupied him, to other areas: the ideological elaboration of Fascism (his 'Dottrina del Fascismo' was published in 1932): the cautious development of the corporative state; the formation of a new Fascist ruling class; and with increasing emphasis, the formulation of a foreign policy that sought to exploit Italy's 'decisive weight' in the European balance and the possibility that it offered for Italy to manoeuver between the Anglo-French and the Germans – all in order to give Italy a 'true' colonial EMPIRE and Mediterranean hegemony [dominance] . . .

Out of this policy there emerged the conquest of Ethiopia in 1935–36, unquestionably one of Mussolini's great successes despite the negative consequences it was to bear. In one sense the war began to reduce the flexibility of his foreign policy and signalled the progressive movement toward Nazi Germany; the Italian intervention in the Spanish Civil War, pushed by Foreign Minister Galeazzo Ciano even more than by Mussolini, had a significant influence on the growing association with Germany. In another sense, the war transformed the basic insecurity of the Duce into an excessive belief in his own political abilities at the very moment when the first symptoms of his physical decline had begun to manifest themselves. To all this must be added that after the Ethiopian War Mussolini underwent a decisive phase of ideological evolution . . . This process led him to believe that Europe and the world were undergoing a profound 'crisis of civilisation' from which would emerge a 'new civilisation' characterised by the rapid decline of countries like France and England and the rise of Germany, Japan, Russia, and Italy. In this view, Fascist Italy had to fulfil its own special 'mission' by exercising its 'moral primacy' over other nations, in addition to realising its Mediterranean hegemony. In order to achieve this aim it was necessary, according to Mussolini, for the Italian people to free themselves from the negative constraints of 'BOURGEOIS mentality' and the Catholic Church and profoundly feel Italy's 'historic mission'. Hence Musssolini's attempts between 1937 and 1939 to produce a Fascist 'cultural revolution' that would transform the Italians and especially the young generations – and his recurrent proposals to eliminate the MONARCHY. Absorbed fully by these problems and certain that the regime faced no internal dangers, after the second half of 1936 Mussolini increasingly entrusted the supervision of domestic policies . . . to Ciano . . . and Starace . . .

Despite his obvious political abilities, Mussolini found himself faced with numerous difficulties after mid-1936. On the international level he sought to control a situation determined increasingly by Hitler. He was torn on the one hand by his innate [inborn] political realism, which made him fear both international isolation and the Germans, and on the other hand by his conviction that Italy had to participate in the great historic struggle that would usher in the 'new civilisation', and that only he could lead Italy through it successfully. He therefore tried in vain to delay his entry into World War II until after 1942–43, hoping thereby to prepare Italy more fully and to be in a position – rather than Hitler – to determine the political strategy, the timing, and the priorities of the war (he intended, for example, that France alone would be the enemy, leaving action against England for a later moment).

On the domestic level, the greatest problems for Mussolini stemmed from the opposition and hostility that his foreign policy and his efforts to create a 'cultural revolution' encountered on all levels. These were not problems of decisive importance, for critics and opponents never succeeded in forming any credible alternative, and the consensus on which the regime was based, although weakening, was never in crisis. Unquestionably, however, they did lead him to impose on the regime and on Italian society a form of totalitarianism which he believed essential for the future of Fascism, for the creation of the Fascist 'new man', and for the achievement of Italy's 'historic mission' in the context of Europe's 'new order' and 'new civilisation'.

Activity

1 Summarise de Felice's main interpretation of Mussolini and Fascism, referring in particular to:
   a) the effects of the conquest of Abyssinia
   b) domestic radicalisation in the late 1930s
   c) his growing problems.
2 De Felice has been accused of being too sympathetic to Mussolini. Is there any evidence in this extract to substantiate this?

CHART 16B   Views of Fascism

This chart is an attempt to present the main interpretations of Fascism. We have simplified them into six particular views, even though there is some common ground between them.

1   Fascism as a general product of mass society

This view stresses how the masses were disorientated by industrialisation and war. They lost their sense of identity, and became attracted to CHARISMATIC speakers offering simple programmes. Fascism appealed emotionally with its attempts to restore dislocated people's sense of identity and community, hence its appeal in 1920s Italy and 1930s Germany.

2   Fascism as totalitarianism

This view, initially a product of the Cold War, sees Fascism, like Nazism and Communism, as a version of a totalitarian regime, with an all-powerful government holding sway over the people through terror. Its main focus was always Nazi Germany and the Soviet Union, with the latter linked to Nazism to justify Cold War hostilities; but Italian Fascism is seen in the same light, even if generally acknowledged to be the least totalitarian regime of the three. The similarities between Nazism and Fascism are stressed.

3   Fascism as an agent of capitalism

The MARXIST view sees Fascism as a last-ditch attempt by capitalism in crisis to preserve itself; Italy was the first example of this trend, seen later in Germany.

4   Fascism as an agent of modernisation

A more recent view, most notably propounded by Gregor, sees Fascism as a relatively successful response to Italian backwardness. The stress on productivism, control of labour, state assistance to heavy industry, advances in a welfare state, and the 'nationalisation' of the people through new mass organisations are all taken as evidence of a modernising DICTATORSHIP.

5 Fascism as the creation of one man, Mussolini

In this view Fascism is seen primarily as the vehicle for the ambitious Mussolini to gain and keep power. He hoodwinked and intimidated the Italians to conform, and indulged his ambitions for 21 years until overthrown. Italian history was diverted by the antics of one person.

6 Fascism as the product of deep trends in Italian history

In this view, importance is placed on earlier developments. The united Italian state suffered from major weaknesses, particularly the failure to gain the commitment of the masses. This made it vulnerable to the populist appeal of Fascism.

■ Activity

Each of the views in Chart 16B has been criticised. Match up the criticisms below with the views in Chart 16B:

a) Fascism as a movement was far more than the mere creation of Mussolini. It satisfied deep needs, and had wider roots than the ambitions of Mussolini.

b) Mussolini's economic and welfare policies were improvised, with only gradual, piecemeal state intervention. Mass organisations failed to reach most of the rural population. Italy's economic development in the twenty years of Fascism was very modest.

c) Although Mussolini frequently used the word 'totalitarian', the degree of control he exercised over the Italian state machine, let alone over the people, was too limited for his claims to be taken as reality.

d) The stress on mass psychological unease underplays the extent to which Fascism gained support through its practical policies, appealing to rational self-interest.

e) Fascism was not inevitable. Particular decisions by the Italian elite, and Mussolini's OPPORTUNISM helped him gain office, but Italy could have developed in a different way.

f) This view of Fascism has been challenged both as underplaying the mass base of Fascism, and exaggerating the extent it was supported by, and served the interests of, the elite.

■ **Activity**

1 Explain what light the extracts in Source 16.2 shed on relations between:
   a) Mussolini and the King
   b) Mussolini and the Pope
   c) Fascist Italy and Nazi Germany.
2 How does Ciano view Mussolini by 1943? Why?
3 How useful is Ciano's final comment in helping us assess the contents of his diary?
4 How valuable to a historian can the diaries of politicians be?

B Ciano's diaries

Ciano kept a diary from 1936 till his death in 1944. In it he recorded daily the major events in which he was involved. Although his account of his meetings, and what people said, form the bulk of the diary, he also made some direct reflections on events. It gives a particularly close insight into Mussolini, whom Ciano admired both genuinely and for career purposes, though he eventually realised his failings.

American special representative Sumner Wells, who had several discussions with Ciano and wrote the preface to Muggeridge's edition, described the diary

SOURCE 16.2   Extracts on particular issues
a) The King and Mussolini

23 March 1939   *Inauguration of the new corporative Parliament. The wording of the oath has been changed; we no longer swear allegiance to the 'Royal House'. There is a great deal of talk about this, and those who are most outspoken are, as usual, Balbo and de Bono, who use it in order to further their petty anti-Fascist intrigues. However, I do not know whether the innovation is appropriate at this time. I knew nothing about it. If I had been forewarned I should have been strongly against it.*

24 March   *It seems that His Majesty would like to show some appreciation of the Duce the day after tomorrow; but what? A title of nobility would not be welcome . . . the King's gesture is significant just at this moment, when certain people are attempting to create the impression that there is dissension between the regime and the dynasty.*

27 March   *The Duce was very angry with the King this morning, when the King found an opportunity of telling him three distasteful things: (1) he was not in agreement with the policy on Albania since he did not see the point of risking such a venture in order to 'grab four rocks'; (2) that the offer made by Acquarone [Minister of the Royal Household] to give the Duce some honorary title on the tenth anniversary of Fascism was decided upon in order to 'forestall any repetition by the Fascists of the "humiliation" inflicted upon the King when, without his knowledge, the Duce was given the title of Marshal of the Empire – a humiliation which the King still resents'; (3) that Conrad of Bavaria had told him that in certain quarters of Munich Mussolini is called 'The Gauleiter [local Nazi party leader] of Italy'. The Duce commented bitterly on the King's words. He said: 'If Hitler had had to deal with a nincompoop of a King he would never have been able to take Austria and Czechoslovakia', and he went on declaiming [saying strongly] that the monarchy does not like Fascism because Fascism is a unifying force, 'and the monarchy desires that the country be divided into two or three factions, which could be played one against the other in such a way as to permit the monarchy to control everybody without compromising itself'.*

25 May   *The Duce attacks the monarchy and says: 'I envy Hitler, who need not drag along with him so many empty baggage cars.'*

3 June   *The Duce declares that . . . the King is a 'small grumpy man, untrustworthy . . . I am now considering whether we ought*

to finish the House of Savoy [the royal family].'

b) The Pope and Mussolini

2 January 1939   *A conversation with the Duce and Pignatti [the Ambassador to the Vatican]. The Duce told the Ambassador to tell the Vatican that he is dissatisfied with the policy of the Holy See, especially with reference to the CATHOLIC ACTION Movement. He also spoke of the opposition of the clergy to the policy of the Axis, as well as to racial legislation. Let them not be under any illusion as to the possibility of keeping Italy under the tutelage [guardianship] of the Church. The power of the clergy is imposing, but more imposing is the power of the state, especially a Fascist state. We do not want a conflict, but we are ready to support the policy of the state, and in such a case we shall arouse all the dormant ANTI-CLERICAL rancour [bitterness]; let the Pope remember that Italy is Ghibelline. [The Ghibellines were medieval opponents of the Papacy.] Pignatti spoke in a satisfactory manner. He said that the Vatican had made many mistakes, but that the Pope is a man of good faith, and that, more than any other prelate [priest], he thinks as an Italian. I have given him instructions to act tactfully. With all due respect to Starace, I should like to avoid a clash with the Vatican, which I should consider very harmful.*

9 February   *During the meeting of the Supreme Defence Council I showed the Duce the typewritten record of Pignatti's telephone call concerning the Pope's heart attack, and he only shrugged his shoulders with open indifference. Strange. For some time now Mussolini has shown an increasingly obvious indifference to anything related to the Church. Once it was not so.*

c) The Axis

14 March 1939   *The Axis functions only in favour of one of its parts, which tends to preponderate, and acts entirely on its own initiative with little regard for us. I expressed my point of view to the Duce. He was cautious in his reaction and did not seem to attach great importance to the event [German plans to absorb all Czechoslovakia].*

15 March   *Events are precipitated during the night. After a meeting between Hitler, Hacha [the Czech President] and Chwalkowsky [the Polish ambassador in Berlin], German troops began their occupation of Bohemia. The thing is serious, especially since Hitler had assured everyone that he did not*

as 'one of the most valuable historical documents of our time'. Study these extracts from 1939 and 1943 to see if you agree on its value.

Ciano's diary consisted of well over 1000 pages, covering 1936–43. Most historians, let alone students, do not have the time to study the full version. How can one effectively use such a large source? We have just used the volume for 1939–43, concentrating on 1939.

want to annex [take over] one single Czech. This German action does not destroy the Czechoslovakia of Versailles, but the one that was constructed at Munich and at Vienna. What weight can be given in the future to those declarations and promises which concern us more directly?

It is useless to deny that all this worries and humiliates the Italian people. It is necessary to give them satisfaction and compensation: Albania. I spoke about it to the Duce, to whom I also expressed my conviction that at this time we shall find neither local obstacles nor serious international complications in the way of our advance. He authorised me to telegraph to Jacomoni [Ciano's agent in Albania, later made its governor], asking him to prepare local revolts, and he personally ordered the Navy to hold the second squadron ready at Taranto . . .

Jacomoni foresees handing this ultimatum to the King [of Albania]: either he accepts the arrival of the Italian troops and asks for a PROTECTORATE, or the troops will arrive anyway. I conferred again with the Duce, and he seemed to me to be less cool about the operation.

In the meantime Hesse [German special envoy] arrived with the usual message. This time it is a verbal message, and not very satisfactory. The Führer sends word that he acted because the Czechs would not demobilise their military forces; because they were continuing to keep their contacts with Russia, and because they mistreated Germans. Such pretexts [excuses] may be good for Goebbels' propaganda, but they should not use them when talking with us, whose only fault is that we deal too loyally with the Germans . . .

I returned to the Duce after Hesse left. I found him unhappy and depressed over the message. He did not wish to give Hesse's news to the press ('The Italians would laugh at me; every time Hitler occupies a country he sends me a message') . . .

I had another meeting with the Duce. He now believes that Prussian [German] hegemony in Europe is established. In his opinion a coalition of all other powers, including ourselves, could check German expansion, but could not undo it. He did not count too much on the military help which the small powers could give. I asked whether, as things stand, it would be more desirable for us to bind ourselves in an alliance rather than to maintain our full freedom to orient [direct] ourselves in the future according to our best interests. The Duce declared himself decidedly in favour of the alliance. I expressed my misgivings, because the alliance will not be popular in Italy, and also because I fear that Germany might take advantage of it to push ahead its policy of political expansion in Central Europe.

19 March   The events of the last few days have reversed my opinion of the Führer and of Germany: he, too, is unfaithful and treacherous and we cannot collaborate with him. I have also worked today with the Duce for an understanding with the Western Powers. But will they have at least a minimum of good sense in Paris, or will attempts to reach an understanding be once more frustrated by unwillingness to make any concession? The Duce thinks that British irritation runs very deep at this time.

13 August   I return to Rome completely disgusted with the Germans, with their leader, with their way of doing things. They have betrayed us and lied to us. Now they are dragging us into an adventure which we do not want and which may compromise the regime and the country as a whole. The Italian people will boil over with horror when they know about the aggression against Poland and will most probably want to fight the Germans.

SOURCE 16.3   Some later comments on Mussolini from the diary

January 1943   He continues to lull himself with many dangerous illusions, which distort his clear vision of reality, a reality which is now apparent to everybody.

December 1943   From Salzburg on . . . the policy of Berlin towards Italy was nothing but a network of lies, intrigue and deceit. We were never treated like partners, but always as slaves. Every move took place without our knowledge; even the most fundamental decisions were communicated to us after they had been put into execution. Only the base cowardice of Mussolini could tolerate this without protest, and pretend not to see it.

SOURCE 16.4   Ciano's last words in his diary

23 December 1943   In this state of mind which excludes any falsehood I declare that not a single word of what I have written in my diary is false or exaggerated or dictated by selfish resentment. It is all just what I have seen and heard. And if, when making ready to take leave of life, I consider allowing the publication of my hurried notes, it is not because I expect posthumous revaluation or vindication [being seen more positively after my death], but because I believe that an honest testimonial of the truth in this sad world may still be useful in bringing relief to the innocent and striking at those who are responsible.

C Did domestic or foreign policy predominate in the regime's thinking?

This book has looked at domestic and then foreign policy, but on several occasions full understanding of the former required knowledge about the latter, and vice versa. Now that you have covered both aspects, we can also address important issues about the causal links between them. Chart 16C examines this issue.

■ **Talking point**

Do you think it more likely that a DEMOCRATIC or totalitarian regime would be more influenced in its foreign policy by domestic considerations?

■ **Activity**

1 Study Chart 16C.
   Find examples of domestic and foreign policy actions that illustrate the trends identified.

2 Look back at the timeline in the introduction to Section 2 (pages 68–69). There we identified four broad periods during the regime. Now that you have studied events thoroughly, write a brief assessment of how valid you think that periodisation was.

CHART 16C **Overview of the Fascist regime's domestic and foreign policy**

	1922	1924	1926	1928	1930	1932	1934	1936	1938	1940	1942	1943	1945
DOMESTIC POLICY	Consolidation of policies favouring elite		Creation of personal dictatorship		Greater attempt to broaden support by going 'to the people'		Years of consensus		Radicalisation or Mussolini's degenerating pragmatism	Elite moving away from regime		Salo Republic: reversion to earlier radicalism	
FOREIGN POLICY	A few dramatic gestures							Increasing involvement in wars	Mussolini comes under Hitler's influence				
INTERNATIONAL CONTEXT	Dominance of Britain/France so limited opportunities for Italy							Rise of Nazi Germany initially gives Italy opportunities to exploit as Britain and France need its support.	Germany increasingly dominant		Hitler declines 1943 onwards		

Three views of the relationship between domestic and foreign policy have been put forward.

View 1: The primacy of domestic policy

Mussolini's greater aggression from 1935 was a reflection of his domestic failures. The Depression was still hitting Italians and the much vaunted Corporative State had lost its gloss. Mussolini invaded Abyssinia to divert attention from domestic failures.

In a rather different version, Mussolini wanted to radicalise Italian society and saw war as a means to achieve this.

View 2: The primacy of foreign policy

Mussolini's main concern was foreign policy, with the requirements of war dictating domestic policy. In the 1920s Mussolini began preparing his country for expansion, and after 1935 the international context gave him opportunities. The need to mobilise the nation for war required more RADICAL domestic policies.

View 3: The complementarity of domestic and foreign policy

Mussolini's foreign and domestic policies, at least in the 1930s, are best seen as too interlinked for either one to be given primacy. Mussolini wanted to change both Italy's domestic and international position. He wanted to fascistise Italy both for domestic purposes, and to help Italy be victorious abroad.

■ **Activity**

The chart below summarises the broad historical assessments of the relationship between domestic and foreign policy.

View	Main purpose/ends	Means
1 D, i.e. domestic dominant	Win support at home and strengthen Fascism	Aggressive foreign policy
2 F, i.e. foreign policy dominant	Make Italy great abroad	Reorganise Italy domestically
3 M, i.e. both aspects mixed together, as part of Fascist dynamism	Reorganise Italy's situation at home and abroad	Reorganise political–social structure, and fight wars

Read the historians' assessments below, and decide to which of the categories in the chart (D, F or M) each one belongs.

■ **Activity**

Which of these views do you consider more convincing?
a) Fascist foreign policy was going to be aggressive anyway; in the 1920s it was less so as external circumstances did not allow it to be, but in the 1930s circumstances were more favourable for aggression.
b) Fascism just became aggressive in the 1930s to solve domestic problems.

SOURCE 16.5 Wiskemann, p. 74

The completion of the Fascist AUTHORITARIAN state required an aggressive foreign policy with the risk of war.

SOURCE 16.6 Cassels, p. 75

The entire Fascist experiment became geared to break through Italy's old diplomatic limitations. The drive for a totalitarian society, AUTARKIC and martial, was nothing more or less than an endeavour to escape dependence on foreign powers.

SOURCE 16.7 G. Procacci, *History of the Italian People*, 1973 p. 431

The economic crisis had also shaken the regime's political prestige . . . So the regime was faced with an uphill climb . . . in terms of its own popularity and public support.

The classic means was to seek for an assertion of prestige on the level of foreign policy; besides, war supplies would, and in fact did, help some sectors of industry to escape finally from the crisis. The chosen object was Ethiopia.

SOURCE 16.8 Carocci, pp. 65, 104

It was said that Fascism subordinated internal policy to foreign policy. The opposite was also true: in his foreign policy Mussolini sought for successes and diversions to emphasise or consolidate the prestige of Fascism at home . . . The decision to solve . . . the Ethiopian Problem was taken by Mussolini after consideration not only of foreign policy but of domestic affairs as well. The situation at home was worse than at any time since 1927. People all over the country felt indifferent to the regime, detached from it. In order to overcome these feelings, in order to galvanise the masses and try and break the vicious circle of economic crisis, more drastic and more attractive measures were needed than public works, and social and corporative propaganda.

SOURCE 16.9 Mack Smith, 1981, p. 101

Some of his immediate subordinates were sure he acted in foreign affairs with an eye on domestic policy. Either he was trying to distract attention from internal problems or he wanted to impress Italians with successes abroad, even if these successes were ephemeral [short-lived] or illusory and won him few foreign friends. What he seemed to be searching for was the grand gesture.

SOURCE 16.10 M. Knox, in *Journal of Modern History* 56, 1984, p. 57

Foreign policy was internal policy and vice versa; internal consolidation was a PRECONDITION for foreign conquest, and foreign conquest was the decisive prerequisite for a revolution at home that would sweep away inherited institutions and values . . . Mussolini and Hitler simultaneously sought to overthrow their societies and their neighbours.

SOURCE 16.11 Morgan, pp. 131, 137, 142, 144, 188

From its inception, Fascism was IMPERIALIST. Mussolini took the notion of the struggle between rival imperialisms as an inescapable fact of international relations, and of war as the inevitable and even desirable test of a nation's will to power and expansion . . . Only a new internal political and social order, unifying and concentrating resources through totalitarian controls, could enable the country to fight and win its battles in the international arena . . . The purpose of the totalitarian state was to equip Italy and Italians for war . . . In foreign affairs . . . Mussolini could act with more freedom than seemed possible domestically, and a dramatic and successful foreign policy COUP could unblock the road to further 'fascistisation' of Italian society . . . The period after 1936 was perhaps the real totalitarian phase of Fascism, marked by the almost total complementarity of foreign and domestic policy . . . War was means and end, the way of subverting both the existing internal and international order, effecting both conquest and 'fascistisation'.

D What are we to make of Mussolini?

Was Mussolini a genuine Fascist?

Early on you examined Mussolini's role in Fascist Italy because an understanding of this extraordinary man is central to any study of Fascist Italy. Now that you have studied both his domestic and foreign policies, you can develop your final analysis of Mussolini. He might be seen from two points of view.

View 1: The degenerating pragmatist, victim of his own propaganda

Mussolini was primarily motivated by a desire for power. He created his own movement – Fascism – and moved it from left to right to gain power. Once in power his actions were largely pragmatic; he did what he considered necessary to gain and keep power. His actions were not greatly influenced by clear ideological aims. This is clearly demonstrated by events between 1919 and 1935.

But what about such seemingly ideologically driven mistakes as the Axis, intervention in Spain, and domestic radicalisation? These were due to Mussolini becoming a victim of his propaganda. He lost his sense of pragmatism, and believed the picture his propaganda portrayed of Italy as the great nation. His success in Abyssinia went to his head and distorted his grasp of reality.

View 2: The genuine Fascist

Mussolini had radical ideals, which he held fairly consistently from the beginning. All along he wanted to create a great nation of virile Italians through transforming the nature of the state. Initially he was forced to compromise with the elite that had helped him into power, but once he felt secure he could enact more of his Fascist programme. This required war and conquest, which itself required domestic transformation. In the late 1930s he aimed to reduce his dependence on the elites, and broaden the basis of the regime, by winning over the masses to achieve his new Fascist state. Hence the 'to the people' movement of the mid- and late 1930s, and the increased stress on propaganda. In order to prepare Italy for war, the traditional conservative forces – monarchy, Church, and the economic elites – had to be weakened, and the Italian people had to be galvanised (stirred up) by the party to become committed to Mussolini's vision of a powerful empire. In this view, Mussolini's overthrow was a product of his post-Abyssinian activism, both at home and abroad, which alienated the key elites who had initially appointed him, and maintained him in office. Once free from these elites in the Salo Republic, he revived a radical Fascism.

CHART 16D   Why did Mussolini stay in power so long?

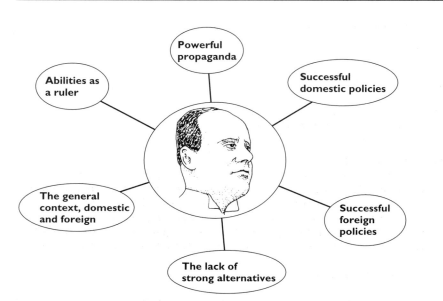

Why did he last so long?

Mussolini is often seen as a talented propagandist but little else. This raises the interesting question of why he was able to stay in power for longer than most of his contemporary European leaders. Chart 16D seeks to explain this, and Chart 16E examines why he was overthrown.

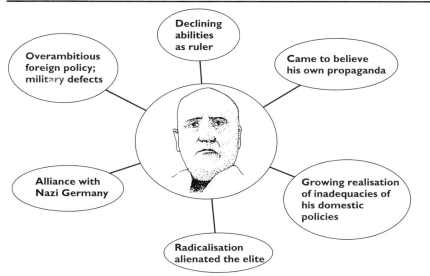

Overambitious foreign policy; military defects

Declining abilities as ruler

Came to believe his own propaganda

Alliance with Nazi Germany

Growing realisation of inadequacies of his domestic policies

Radicalisation alienated the elite

■ **Activity**

1 Note down five pieces of evidence to support view 1, and five to support view 2. On balance, which do you consider the more convincing view?

2 Hold a major debate on Mussolini. Debate the following viewpoints: 'a remarkably gifted leader' or 'a blustering incompetent'?
   a) Choose from the points below and others most relevant for your argument.
   b) Find evidence to support these points.
   c) Debate the issue.
   Possible points from which to select:

   • Stayed in power for 21 years
   • Realised value of propaganda in a modern state
   • Skilfully played off potential opponents
   • Healed Italy's wounds
   • Presided over a chaotic government
   • MONOPOLISED key positions
   • Failed to tackle corruption and inefficiency
   • Skilfully used bluff to get his way
   • Deluded by success
   • Managed to reassure elites yet benefit masses
   • Became victim of own propaganda

   • Man of the people who lost touch with the people
   • Understood needs of masses
   • One of the few European rulers remaining in power during the Depression
   • Major policy successes
   • Major policy failures
   • Adopted policies way beyond Italy's means
   • Made the best use of Italy's limited resources
   • Whole policy geared to war, yet when it came Italy was totally unprepared
   • Misjudged strength of his opponents in war

3 What was Mussolini's worst mistake?
   In groups make a list of what you consider Mussolini's three biggest mistakes; then try to rank them in order of importance. Argue your case to the rest of the group.

4 Match up the myth and the reality in the following list. Find evidence to support each 'reality' point.
   Myth
   a) Revolution of youth
   b) Continuing revolution
   c) Social justice
   d) Infallible Duce
   e) Military might
   f) Unique Italian spirit
   g) National greatness

   Reality
   i)   Failure in war
   ii)   Increasingly subordinate to Nazi Germany
   iii) Incompetent leader
   iv)   Ageing leadership
   v)   Bureaucratic Corporative State exploiting workers
   vi)   Compromises with privileged classes
   vii) Imitation of Germany

5 'A fitting end'? Discuss this question. Did Mussolini deserve his fate?
   In April 1945 Mussolini was shot by partisans, and his body hung upside down for public vilification (abuse). Shortly beforehand he had commented: 'Everyone dies the death which befits his character.' Do you think this was true of Mussolini?

6 It seems likely that if Mussolini had not been shot by the partisans, he might have been put on trial by the new Italian government. Interestingly, in 1943 a book called *The Trial of Mussolini* was printed in England, describing an imaginary trial.
   Devise your own trial of Mussolini, in 1943 or 1945. As a whole group, agree on three or four separate charges. Split into two groups, one prosecution, one defence. (Either your teacher, or a small number of jurors can stay neutral and decide the verdict.)
   Each group should draw up a list of witnesses, and prepare evidence for your case.
   Act out the trial.

E **What was Fascism's legacy?**

An interesting insight into the legacy of Fascism can be gleaned from these recent English newspaper headlines.

A

Mafioso claims Garibaldi built modern Italy on a bribe

SICILY MOBS ANDREOTTI AS TRIAL OPENS

[October 1995. Former Prime Minister accused of having colluded with the Mafia.]

The Imposters paid go-betweens up to £8000 for cushy government posts

Clean hands, dirty business

As a result of investigations over the past three years, some of Italy's most prominent politicians have been accused of corruption, involvement with organised crime and even murder. In the aftermath of the so-called Clean Hands investigations, Italy's political system is in turmoil.

B

Italian President names new Prime Minister

Shadowy 'fixer' takes top job

RIGHT WING PROLONGS ITALY'S AGONY

Breakthrough to power at last for Italy's Left

Victorious Left promises era of co-operation

C

La Mussolini loses her lethal magic

POST-FASCIST LEADER DETERMINED TO LIFT DUCE'S SHADOW

Savoys await call to return

Italy's showman threatens to bring the house down

Bossi rallies Greenshirts to take up arms against Rome

Call by Bossi for breakaway state challenges Italy

Blackshirts clash with police in protest against 'Padania'

BOSSI'S SECESSIONISTS GIVE ROME ULTIMATUM

D

Transformed but not reformed

While Italy's political system has been weak for decades, its economy is one of Europe's strongest

Activity

1 Study the newspaper headlines on page 266.
   a) Give an appropriate heading to each of groups A, B, C and D.
   b) What evidence is there on pages 266–67 of:
      i) aspects of Fascist Italy remaining
      ii) reaction to Fascism
      iii) similarities with Liberal Italy and thus perhaps the limited impact of Fascist Italy
      iv) Italy's continuing problems
      v) Italian success?
2 Make two lists, one covering harmful legacies of Fascism, one beneficial ones.

Talking point

How fair is it to make judgements on foreign countries on the basis of newspaper headlines?

SOURCE 16.12 W. Salomone, *Italy from the Risorgimento to Fascism*, 1971, p. 25

In the general ruin of the years 1943 to 1946, Italians of all political faiths were obliged to recognize the unpalatable [unwelcome] truth that neither Giolitti nor Mussolini, neither parliamentarism nor Fascism, had done very much to alter the basic character of Italian society – to close the tragic gap between North and South, rich and poor, peasant and city dweller.

SOURCE 16.13 Mack Smith, 1981, Preface

His influence has been durable and not only inside Italy. Most people, but not all, would call his legacy disastrous. Though the Fascist regime may be credited with some positive achievements especially in its early years, its crude belief in political violence and authoritarian repression had negative effects that lasted long after 1945, and its praise of war as something inherently beautiful and beneficial was a cruel absurdity that did untold harm and ultimately turned any positive achievements to dust and ashes.

In July 1943, after Mussolini was overthrown and Fascism collapsed, the Germans had taken control of North Italy. For two years they ruled northern Italy, before being defeated by a combination of Allied and Italian guerrilla troops. This resistance movement was important as it was used by Italians to illustrate their resistance to Fascism. In 1945, in an attempt to save the monarchy, Victor Emmanuel III abdicated in favour of his son. In 1946 a referendum was held on the future of the monarchy. The North voted overwhelmingly for a republic, the South to maintain the monarchy; overall the republicans narrowly won. There was only a half-hearted purge of Fascists, with most officials remaining in place, just as they had in 1922. The developing Cold War favoured drawing a line after 1943, and establishing a united front against Communism.

A new system of PROPORTIONAL REPRESENTATION was introduced to contrast with Fascist dictatorship, but its failure to produce effective government has led to periodic calls for stronger government. In various forms Italy has been governed by right-of-centre governments, led by the Christian Democrats. The Communists have regularly gained about one-third of the votes in national elections, and ruled certain municipalities, but until 1996 were kept out of national government. Italy had over 50 different governments between 1946 and 1995, in what has been described as a modern version of TRASFORMISMO. In 1996, for the first time ever, the Italians narrowly elected a LEFT-WING government, though yet another coalition.

Although Italy's post-war democratic political system has been described as the antithesis (opposite) of Fascism, much of the administrative work of the Fascist regime was left largely intact. Thus Rocco's legal code, the Concordat, the IRI, and the idea of OND survived. The structure of the Corporative State was not kept, but the stress on collaboration and regulation has been kept, though in a more balanced way. Public works schemes have been maintained. The Fascist legacy can also be seen visually in a partially destroyed Roman forum, and in pretentious monumental architecture.

The Fascist Party was banned in post-war Italy, but the neo-Fascists, MSI (now renamed the National Alliance), have averaged about five per cent of the vote, though in 1994 they gained thirteen per cent, mainly in the South (as a protest vote). They briefly entered a coalition government. Their leader Fini has described the movement as 'post-Fascist'. He has generally tried to distance the movement from Fascism, whilst arguing that until 1938 Mussolini had a positive impact. His claim that Mussolini was the greatest statesman of the twentieth century created a storm.

In the 1990s, in protest against the continuing burden of backward southern Italy on the more advanced North, a new political force, the Northern Leagues, attracted a lot of support and some started to question the continuation of a nation state, instead favouring FEDERALISM. In 1996 their leader Bossi declared independence for the new state of 'Padania', but this extreme move gained little support.

By the mid-1990s Italy's standard of living had overtaken that of Britain, and Italy had the sixth-largest industrial economy in the world, though the South remained poor. Italy was plagued with corruption and scandals, and the Mafia survived various government assaults.

In the 1995 celebrations to mark the fiftieth anniversary of the end of the Second World War, some Italians laid flowers at memorials to Italians killed by the Allies; some at those to the victims of Fascists. Italians are still divided over their past as well as their future.

SOURCE 16.14 Cassels, p. 118

Fascism's legacy has . . . proved meagre for Mussolini's regime specialised in gestures but was always short on performance.

Glossary

agrari   large landowners

anti-clericalism   hostility towards the Church

anti-semitism   hatred of Jews

Arditi   Italian shock troops

atheist   someone who does not believe in God

authoritarianism   belief in strong, non-democratic government

autarky   national economic self-sufficiency

autonomy   self-rule

belligerent   warlike

blacklegs   people who continue to work during a strike

Bolshevik   Russian Communist

bourgeois   middle class

capitalism   economic system based on private enterprise

carabinieri   military police

cartel   group of businesses linked together to control the market

Catholic Action   Catholic lay organisation

CGL   Confederazione Generale del Lavoro; Socialist-controlled General Confederation of Trade Unions

CIL   Confederazione Italiana del Lavoro; Catholic-controlled trade union organisation

charismatic   inspiring

collectivisation   Communist policy of combining small farms into publicly owned large ones

Communism   belief in a society where all are equal and there is no private property

Comintern   see (Communist) International

Confindustria   employers' organisation

conscription   government forcing people to join the army

constitution   written document laying down the basic political structure

coup d'état   sudden seizure of power

Covenant of the League   statement of principles accepted by all members of League of Nations

decree   like a law, but not usually passed by Parliament. In Fascist Italy decrees were issued by the King as head of state, and later by Mussolini who in January 1926 was given the authority to issue decrees

de jure   in law

deflation   decline in the economy and prices

demagogue   leader stirring up popular passions

democracy   government run by the people

demography   to do with population

determinism   belief that the course of events is fixed

dictatorship   rule by one all-powerful person or body

Dopolavoro   see OND

Duce   leader

elite   powerful groups at top of society, e.g. industrialists, aristocrats, Church leaders

empire   state that rules over other countries

EOA   Agency for Welfare Activities

encyclical   letter from Pope to all his bishops

ERR   rural radio agency

EUR   Universal Exhibition of Rome, a model city planned by Mussolini for 1942

federal   state that is split up into smaller units that have a lot of power to run themselves

Federterra   Organisation of agricultural unions

Fourteen Points   Principles stated by American President Wilson in January 1918, based on ideas of national self-determination and peace

FUCI   Catholic federation of university students

futurists   modern painters and poets glorifying violence and speed

geopolitical   to do with the influence of geography on a country's policies

GIL   Gioventù Italiana del Littorio; body controlling all youth organisations from 1937

GL   Giustizia e Libertà (Justice and Liberty)

gold standard   currencies that can be converted to gold

GUF   Gruppi Universitari Fascisti; Fascist student body

historiography   the history of history; historical methodology

ideology   set of beliefs or principles

IMI   organisation to support Italian banks

imperialism   belief in one country taking over another

indemnity   compensation, financial payments

(Communist) International   international organisation of communists, based on Moscow; see also Comintern

internationalism   belief in different countries working together

interventionism   favouring joining the war

IRI   Istituto per la Ricostruzione Industriale (Institute for Industrial Reconstruction); government body to take over failing industries

laissez faire   let things be; belief that governments should not intervene in the economy

latifondisti   owners of vast estates in the South

left-wing   wanting major changes; often socialist

liberalism   belief in representative government and individual liberty

lockout   where employers close a factory to prevent workers entering, to put pressure on them to agree to terms

LUCE   L'Unione Cinematografica Educativa; government-controlled film agency

Magna Carta   document signed by King John in 1215 granting basic rights to barons, hence statement of key rights

manifesto   written statement of a party's principles and policies

martial law   emergency powers given to government to use army to re-establish order

Marxism   communist ideas put forward by Karl Marx

mobilisation   to get ready, especially for the army to prepare for war

monarchy   king or queen ruling a country

monopoly   something with sole power; totally dominant

MSI   Italian neo-Fascist party

municipal   to do with a town

MVSN   Milizia Volontaria per la Sicurezza Nazionale; Fascist militia

nationalism   belief that a nation should rule itself

nationalisation   the process of putting industries under government control and ownership

oligarchy   government by a few

ONMI   Opera Nazionale di Maternita e d'Infanzia; government body supervising mothers' and children's welfare

ONB   Opera Nazionale Balilla; Fascist Youth organisation

OND   Opera Nazionale Dopolavoro; Fascist leisure organisation

opportunism   tactic of seizing opportunities, often in contradiction to one's beliefs

OVRA   Volunteer organisation for the repression of anti-Fascism; secret police

pacifism   rejection of war

paramilitary   semi-military; private army

PCI   Partito Communista Italiano; Italian Communist Party

petty bourgeoisie   lower middle class, especially shopkeepers, artisans, moderately successful peasants, teachers, etc

plebiscite   referendum

plutocracy   government by the rich

PNF   Partito Nazionale Fascista; Fascist Party

podesta   new powerful appointed local official replacing elected mayors

PPI   Partito Popolare Italiano (Popolari); party representing Catholics

preconditions   situation necessary before something is to happen

prefects   powerful local agent of central government

productivism   belief in the importance of maximising production

proletariat   industrial working class; word often used by Marxists

proportional representation   electoral system where a party gains deputies in direct proportion to its votes

protectorate   country which is protected/dominated by a more powerful one, but not fully taken over

PSI   Partito Socialista Italiano; Italian Socialist Party

quadrumvirs   four leaders who led March on Rome, October 1922

radical   extreme; could be right- or normally left-wing

ras   Ethiopian leader; also a local Fascist leader

reactionary   someone wanting to reverse change; extreme conservative wanting to turn the clock back

rentier   someone living off savings

republic   country without a monarch; usually headed by a president instead

revisionist   trying to change what had previously been agreed

right-wing   conservative

Risorgimento   the unification of Italy

RSI   Repubblica Sociale Italiana; Italian Social Republic

sharecroppers   tenants who give part of their crop to the landowner as rent

socialism   belief in country where the good of the people as a whole is stressed over individual rights; in some forms a step on the way to communism

SOLD   Section for Factory and Home Workers; Fascist body to help women

sovereign   ruler; or full power

statuto   statute; usually refers to the constitution granted to Piedmont in 1848 which became base of united Italy's constitution

status quo   the existing situation

suffrage   the right to vote

syndicalism   radical form of trade unionism; belief in unions becoming the key body in a new society

syndicate   trade union

tariffs   taxes placed on goods

temporal   to do with this world, not the spirit

totalitarian   government having full control of all aspects of a country

trasformismo   system of changing government by winning support from former opponents

Absalom R. N. L., *Mussolini and the Rise of Italian Fascism*, Methuen 1969

Absalom R. N. L., *Italy since 1800: A Nation in the Balance?*, Longman 1995

Becker L. and Caiger-Smith M., *Art and Power: Images of the 1930s*, Hayward Gallery 1995

Bell P., *Origins of the Second World War*, Longman 1986

Benton T., Hobsbawn E. and Fraquelli S., *Art and Power. Europe under the Dictators 1930–45*, Hayward Gallery Catalogue 1995

Bessel R., *Fascist Italy and Nazi Germany*, Cambridge University Press 1996

Blinkhorn M., *Mussolini and Fascist Italy* (Lancaster Pamphlets), Methuen 1984

Bosworth R., *Italy and the Wider World 1860–1960*, Routledge 1996

Cannistraro P. (ed.), *Historical Dictionary of Fascist Italy*, Greenwood 1982

Carocci G., *Italian Fascism*, Penguin 1974

Cassels A., *Fascist Italy*, Routledge and Kegan Paul 1969

Catanzaro R., *Men of Respect: A Social History of the Sicilian Mafia*, The Free Press 1988

Clark M., *Modern Italy 1871–1982*, Longman 1984

De Grand A., *Italian Fascism, its Origins and Development*, University of Nebraska Press 1982

De Grand A., *Fascist Italy and Nazi Germany*, Routledge 1995

Delzell C., *Mediterranean Fascism, Selected Documents*, Macmillan 1970

De Felice R., *Mussolini*, 1965–90

Di Scalia S., *Italy, From Revolution to Republic*, Westview Press 1995

Duggan C., *A Concise History of Italy*, Cambridge University Press 1994

Eatwell R., *Fascism, a History*, Chatto & Windus, London 1995

Forgacs D. (ed.), *Rethinking Italian Fascism*, Lawrence & Wishart 1986

Finney P. (ed.), *The Origins of the Second World War*, Arnold 1997

Gallo M., *Mussolini's Italy*, Macmillan 1974

Golomstock I., *Totalitarian Art*, HarperCollins 1990

Gregor A. J., *Italian Fascism and Developmental Dictatorship*, Princeton University Press 1979

Griffin R., *The Nature of Fascism*, Routledge 1991

Hibbert C., *Benito Mussolini*, Penguin 1965

Ipsen C., *Dictating Demography*, 1996

Kedward H., *Fascism in Western Europe*, Blackie 1969

Knox M., *Mussolini Unleashed 1939–41*, Cambridge University Press 1982

Koon T., *Believe, Obey, Fight. Socialisation of Youth in Fascist Italy*, University of North Carolina, 1985

Lamb R., *Mussolini and the British*, John Murray, 1997

Leeds C., *Italy under Mussolini*, Wayland 1972

Lyttleton A., *The Seizure of Power. Fascism in Italy 1919–29*, Weidenfeld & Nicholson 1987

Mack Smith D., *Italy, A Modern History*, University of Michigan, 1969

Mack Smith D., *Mussolini*, Weidenfeld & Nicholson, 1981

Mack Smith D., *Italy and its Monarchy*, Yale University Press, 1989

Mack Smith D., *Mussolini's Roman Empire*, Penguin 1977

Maier C., *In Search of Stability*, Cambridge University Press 1987

Marrus M. (ed.), *The Nazi Holocaust, the Final Solution outside Germany*, University of Toronto 1988

Morgan P., *Italian Fascism 1919–45 (The Making of the 20th Century)*, Macmillan 1995

Mussolini B., *My Autobiography*, Paternoster Library, The Mayflower Press 1928

Mussolini B., *Fascism: Doctrine and Institution*, Ardita 1935

Overy R. and Wheatcroft A., *The Road to War*, Macmillan 1989

Payne S., *History of Fascism 1914–45*, UCL Press 1995

Pollard J., *The Vatican and Italian Fascism*, Cambridge University Press 1985

Procacci G., *History of the Italian People*, Pelican 1973

Ridley J., *Mussolini*, Constable 1997

Roberts D., *The Syndicalist Tradition in Italian Fascism*, Manchester University Press 1979

Robson M., *Italy: Liberalism and Fascism*, 1992

Salomone A. W., *Italy from the Risorgimento to Fascism*, David & Charles 1971

Seton-Watson C., *Italy from Liberalism to Fascism 1870–1925*, Methuen 1967

Tannenbaum E., *Fascism in Italy*, Allen Lane 1973

Tannenbaum E. (ed.), *Modern Italy: A Topical History since 1861*, New York University Press 1974

Thompson D., *State Control in Fascist Italy*, Manchester University Press 1991

Vajda M., *The Rise of Fascism in Italy and Germany*, 1972

Whittam J., *Fascist Italy* (New Frontiers in History), Manchester University Press 1995

Williamson D., *Mussolini, from Socialist to Fascist*, Hodder & Stoughton 1997

Wiskemann E., *Fascism in Italy: Its Development and Influence* (The Making of the 20th Century), Macmillan 1969

Zamagni V., *Economic History of Italy 1860–1990*, Oxford University Press 1993